ICTS 110 Elementary-Middle Grades

Teacher Certification Exam

By: Sharon Wynne, M.S.
Southern Connecticut State University

"And, while there's no reason yet to panic, I think it's only prudent that we make preparations to panic."

MANKOFF

XAMonline, Inc.

Boston

Library of Congress Cataloging-in-Publication Data

Wynne, Sharon A.
    Elementary-Middle Grades 110: Teacher Certification / Sharon A. Wynne. -2nd ed.
    ISBN 978-1-58197-996-1
    1. Elementary-Middle Grades 110. 2. Study Guides.   3. ICTS
    4. Teachers' Certification & Licensure.   5. Careers

Disclaimer:
The opinions expressed in this publication are the sole works of XAMonline and were created independently from the National Education Association, Educational Testing Service, or any State Department of Education, National Evaluation Systems or other testing affiliates.

Between the time of publication and printing, state-specific standards as well as testing formats and website information may change that are not included in part or in whole within this product. Sample test questions are developed by XAMonline and reflect similar content as on real tests; however, they are not formal tests. XAMonline assembles content that aligns with state standards but makes no claims nor guarantees teacher candidates a passing score. Numerical scores are determined by testing companies such as NES or ETS and then are compared with individual state standards. A passing score varies from state to state.

Printed in the United States of America   œ-1

ICTS: Elementary-Middle Grades 110
ISBN: 978-1-58197-996-1

Table of Contents

DOMAIN V.   THE ARTS, HEALTH, AND PHYSICAL EDUCATION

COMPETENCY 19.0 UNDERSTAND HISTORICAL, CULTURAL, AND SOCIETAL CONTEXTS FOR THE ARTS AND THE INTERRELATIONSHIPS AMONG THE ARTS

COMPETENCY 20.0 UNDERSTAND CONCEPTS, TECHNIQUES, AND MATERIALS RELATED TO VISUAL ART, MUSIC, AND DRAMATIC ACTIVITIES AND HOW TO PROVIDE STUDENTS WITH LEARNING OPPORTUNITIES THAT ENCOURAGE THEM TO EXPRESS THEMSELVES THROUGH THE ARTS

COMPETENCY 22.0 UNDERSTAND PRINCIPLES AND PRACTICES RELATED TO PERSONAL, FAMILY, AND COMMUNITY HEALTH AND SAFETY AND WAYS TO PROVIDE STUDENTS WITH KNOWLEDGE AND SKILLS THAT WILL HELP THEM MAKE SOUND HEALTH-RELATED DECISIONS

Great Study and Testing Tips!

What to study in order to prepare for the subject assessments is the focus of this study guide but equally important is *how* you study.

You can increase your chances of truly mastering the information by taking some simple, but effective steps.

Study Tips:

1. Some foods aid the learning process. Foods such as milk, nuts, seeds, rice, and oats help your study efforts by releasing natural memory enhancers called CCKs (*cholecystokinin*) composed of *tryptophan, choline*, and *phenylalanine*. All of these chemicals enhance the neurotransmitters associated with memory. Before studying, try a light, protein-rich meal of eggs, turkey, and fish. All of these foods release the memory-enhancing chemicals. The better the connections, the more you comprehend.

Likewise, before you take a test, stick to a light snack of energy boosting and relaxing foods. A glass of milk, a piece of fruit, or some peanuts all release various memory-boosting chemicals and help you to relax and focus on the subject at hand.

2. Learn to take great notes. A by-product of our modern culture is that we have grown accustomed to getting our information in short doses (i.e. TV news sound bites or *USA Today*-style newspaper articles.)

Consequently, we've subconsciously trained ourselves to assimilate information better in neat little packages. If your notes are scrawled all over the paper, it fragments the flow of the information. Strive for clarity. Newspapers use a standard format to achieve clarity. Your notes can be much clearer through use of proper formatting. A very effective format is called the *"Cornell Method."*

> Take a sheet of loose-leaf lined notebook paper and draw a line all the way down the paper about 1-2" from the left-hand edge.
>
> Draw another line across the width of the paper about 1-2" up from the bottom. Repeat this process on the reverse side of the page.

Look at the highly effective result. You have ample room for notes, a left-hand margin for special emphasis items or inserting supplementary data from the textbook, a large area at the bottom for a brief summary, and a little rectangular space for just about anything you want.

3. <u>Get the concept then the details</u>. Too often we focus on the details and don't gather an understanding of the concept. However, if you simply memorize only dates, places, or names, you may well miss the whole point of the subject.

A key way to understand things is to put them in your own words. If you are working from a textbook, automatically summarize each paragraph in your mind. If you are outlining text, don't simply copy the author's words.

Rephrase them in your own words. You remember your own thoughts and words much better than someone else's, and subconsciously tend to associate the important details to the core concepts.

4. <u>Ask Why?</u> Pull apart written material paragraph by paragraph and don't forget the captions under the illustrations.

Example: If the heading is "Stream Erosion," flip it around to read "Why do streams erode?" Then answer the questions.

If you train your mind to think in a series of questions and answers, not only will you learn more, but it also helps to lessen the test anxiety because you are used to answering questions.

5. <u>Read for reinforcement and future needs</u>. Even if you only have ten minutes, put your notes or a book in your hand. Your mind is similar to a computer; you have to input data in order to have it processed. *By reading, you are creating the neural connections for future retrieval.* The more times you read something, the more you reinforce the learning of ideas.

Even if you don't fully understand something on the first pass, *your mind stores much of the material for later recall.*

6. <u>Relax to learn so go into exile</u>. Our bodies respond to an inner clock called biorhythms. Burning the midnight oil works well for some people, but not everyone.

If possible, set aside a particular place to study that is free of distractions. Shut off the television, cell phone, and pager and exile your friends and family during your study period.

If you really are bothered by silence, try background music. Light classical music at a low volume has been shown to aid in concentration over other types. Music that evokes pleasant emotions without lyrics is highly suggested. Try just about anything by Mozart. It relaxes you.

7. <u>Use arrows not highlighters</u>. At best, it's difficult to read a page full of yellow, pink, blue, and green streaks. Try staring at a neon sign for a while and you'll soon see that the horde of colors obscure the message.

A quick note, a brief dash of color, an underline, and an arrow pointing to a particular passage is much clearer than a horde of highlighted words.

8. <u>Budget your study time</u>. Although you shouldn't ignore any of the material, *allocate your available study time in the same ratio that topics may appear on the test.*

Testing Tips:

1. Get smart, play dumb. Don't read anything into the question. Don't make an assumption that the test writer is looking for something else than what is asked. Stick to the question as written and don't read extra things into it.

2. Read the question and all the choices *twice* before answering the question. You may miss something by not carefully reading, and then re-reading both the question and the answers.

If you really don't have a clue as to the right answer, leave it blank on the first time through. Go on to the other questions, as they may provide a clue as to how to answer the skipped questions.

If later on, you still can't answer the skipped ones . . . *Guess.* The only penalty for guessing is that you *might* get it wrong. Only one thing is certain; if you don't put anything down, you will get it wrong!

3. Turn the question into a statement. Look at the way the questions are worded. The syntax of the question usually provides a clue. Does it seem more familiar as a statement rather than as a question? Does it sound strange?

By turning a question into a statement, you may be able to spot if an answer sounds right, and it may also trigger memories of material you have read.

4. Look for hidden clues. It's actually very difficult to compose multiple-foil (choice) questions without giving away part of the answer in the options presented.

In most multiple-choice questions you can often readily eliminate one or two of the potential answers. This leaves you with only two real possibilities and automatically your odds go to fifty-fifty for very little work.

5. Trust your instincts. For every fact that you have read, you subconsciously retain something of that knowledge. On questions that you aren't really certain about, go with your basic instincts. **Your first impression on how to answer a question is usually correct.**

6. Mark your answers directly on the test booklet. Don't bother trying to fill in the optical scan sheet on the first pass through the test.

Just be very careful not to miss-mark your answers when you eventually transcribe them to the scan sheet.

7. Watch the clock! You have a set amount of time to answer the questions. Don't get bogged down trying to answer a single question at the expense of ten questions you can more readily answer.

DOMAIN I.   **LANGUAGE ARTS AND LITERACY**

COMPETENCY 1.0   **UNDERSTAND WORD ANALYSIS STRATEGIES AND VOCABULARY DEVELOPMENT AND HOW TO USE EFFECTIVE, DEVELOPMENTALLY APPROPRIATE APPROACHES TO PROMOTE STUDENTS' WORD ANALYSIS AND VOCABULARY SKILLS**

Skill 1.1   **Demonstrate knowledge of phonics and its role in decoding; of ways to assess students' phonic skills; and of effective instructional strategies, activities, and materials for promoting students' phonetic analysis skills**

Phonological Awareness

Phonological awareness means the ability of the reader to recognize the sound of spoken language. This recognition includes how these sounds can be blended together, segmented (divided up), and manipulated (switched around). This awareness then leads to phonics, a method for teaching children to read. It helps them "sound out words."

Development of phonological skills may begin during pre-K years. Indeed by the age of five, a child who has been exposed to rhyme can recognize a rhyme. Such a child can demonstrate phonological awareness by filling in the missing rhyming word in a familiar rhyme or rhymed picture book. I surprised my mother by filling in missing rhymes in a familiar nursery rhyme book at the age of four. She was trying to rush ahead to complete the book, but I wouldn't be cheated of even one rhyme!! Little did I know that I was phonologically aware at four!!

You teach children phonological awareness when you teach them the sounds made by the letters, the sounds made by various combinations of letters, and to recognize individual sounds in words.

Phonological Awareness Skills include:

1. Rhyming and syllabification
2. Blending sounds into words—such as pic-tur-bo-k
3. Identifying the beginning or starting sounds of words and the ending or closing sounds of words
4. Breaking words down into sounds—also called "segmenting" words
5. Recognizing other smaller words in the big word by removing starting sounds, such as "hear" to ear

Phonemic Awareness

Phonemic awareness is the idea that words are comprised of sounds. To be phonemically aware means that the reader and listener can recognize and manipulate specific sounds in spoken words.

Phonemic awareness deals with sounds in words that are spoken. The majority of phonemic awareness tasks, activities, and exercises are ORAL.

Theorist Marilyn Jager Adams, who researches early reading, has outlined five basic types of phonemic awareness tasks.

Task 1 - Ability to hear rhymes and alliteration

For example, the children would listen to a poem, rhyming picture book, or song and identify the rhyming words heard which the teacher might then record or list on an experiential chart.

Task 2 - Ability to do oddity tasks (recognize the member of a set that is different (odd) among the group

For example, the children would look at the pictures of a blade of grass, a garden, and a rose—which starts with a different sound?

Task 3 – The ability to orally blend words and split syllables

For example, the children can say the first sound of a word and then the rest of the word and put it together as a single word.

Task 4 – The ability to orally segment words

For example, the ability to count sounds. The children would be asked as a group to count the sounds in "hamburger."

Task 5 - The ability to do phonics manipulation tasks

For example, replace the "r" sound in rose with a "p" sound.

Since the ability to distinguish between individual sounds, or phonemes, within words is a prerequisite to association of sounds with letters and manipulating sounds to blend words, a fancy way of saying "reading," the teaching of phonemic awareness is crucial to emergent literacy (early childhood K-2 reading instruction). Children need a strong background in phonemic awareness in order for phonics instruction (sound to spelling and relationship to printed materials) to be effective. Instructional methods that may be effective for teaching phonemic awareness can include:

- Clapping syllables in words
- Distinguishing between a word and a sound
- Using visual cues and movements to help children understand when the speaker goes from one sound to another
- Incorporating oral segmentation activities which focus on easily distinguished syllables rather than sounds
- Singing familiar songs (e.g., Happy Birthday, Knick Knack Paddy Wack) and replacing key words in it with words with a different ending or middle sound (oral segmentation)

- Dealing children a deck of picture cards and having them sound out the words for the pictures on their cards or calling for a picture by asking for its first and second sound

Skill 1.2 **Demonstrate knowledge of word analysis strategies, including syllabication, morphology (e.g., use of affixes and roots), and context clues; of ways to assess students' use of word analysis strategies; and of effective instructional strategies, activities, and materials for promoting students' word analysis and contextual analysis skills**

The Structure of Language
Morphology is the study of word structure. When readers develop morphemic skills, they are developing an understanding of patterns they see in words. For example, English speakers realize that cat, cats, and caterpillar share some similarities in structure. This understanding helps readers to recognize words at a faster and easier rate, since each word doesn't need individual decoding.

Syntax refers to the rules or patterned relationships that correctly create phrases and sentences from words. When readers develop an understanding of syntax, they begin to understand the structure of how sentences are built, and eventually the beginning of grammar.

Example:
"I am going to the movies."
This statement is syntactically and grammatically correct.

Example:
"They am going to the movies."
This statement is syntactically correct since all the words are in their correct place, but it is grammatically incorrect with the use of the word "they" rather than "I."

Semantics refers to the meaning expressed when words are arranged in a specific way. This is where connotation and denotation of words eventually will have a role with readers.

All of these skill sets are important to eventually developing effective word recognition skills, which help emerging readers develop fluency.

Phonics
As opposed to phonemic awareness, the study of phonics must be done with the eyes open. It is the connection between the sounds and letters on a page. In other words, students learning phonics might see the word "bad" and sound each letter out slowly until they recognize that they just said the word.

Phonological awareness means the ability of the reader to recognize the sound of spoken language. This recognition includes how these sounds can be blended together, segmented (divided up), and manipulated (switched around). This awareness then leads to phonics, a method for teaching children to read. It helps them "sound out words."

Development of phonological skills may begin during pre-K years. Indeed by the age of five, a child who has been exposed to rhyme can recognize a rhyme. Such a child can demonstrate phonological awareness by filling in the missing rhyming word in a familiar rhyme or rhymed picture book. I surprised my mother by filling in missing rhymes in a familiar nursery rhyme book at the age of four. She was trying to rush ahead to complete the book, but I wouldn't be cheated of even one rhyme!! Little did I know that I was phonologically aware at four!!

You teach children phonological awareness when you teach them the sounds made by the letters, the sounds made by various combinations of letters, and to recognize individual sounds in words.

Phonological Awareness Skills include:

6. Rhyming and syllabification
7. Blending sounds into words—such as pic-tur-bo-k
8. Identifying the beginning or starting sounds of words and the ending or closing sounds of words
9. Breaking words down into sounds—also called "segmenting" words
10. Recognizing other smaller words in the big word by removing starting sounds, such as "hear" to ear

Decoding, Word Recognition, and Spelling
Word analysis (a.k.a., phonics or decoding) is the process readers use to figure out unfamiliar words based on written patterns. Word recognition is the process of automatically determining the pronunciation and some degree of the meaning of an unknown word. In other words, fluent readers recognize most written words easily and correctly without consciously decoding or breaking them down. The following elements of literacy, decoding and spelling, are skills readers need for word recognition.

To decode means to change communication signals into messages. Reading comprehension requires that the reader learn the code within which a message is written and be able to decode it to get the message. Encoding involves changing a message into symbols. For example, one can encode oral language into writing (spelling), encode an idea into words, or encode a mathematical or physical idea into appropriate mathematical symbols.

Although effective reading comprehension requires identifying words automatically (Adams, 1990; Perfetti, 1985), children do not have to be able to identify every single word or know the exact meaning of every word in a text to understand it. Indeed, Nagy (1988) says that children can read a work with a high level of comprehension even if they do not fully know as many as fifteen percent of the words within a given text. Children develop the ability to decode and recognize words automatically. They then can extend their ability to decode to multisyllabic words.

Spelling instruction should include spelling words misspelled in daily writing, generalizing spelling knowledge, and mastering objectives in progressive phases of development. Developmental stages of spelling include the following:

1) *Pre-phonemic spelling*—Children know that letters stand for a message, but they do not know the relationship between spelling and pronunciation.
2) *Early phonemic spelling*—Children are beginning to understand spelling. They usually write the beginning letter correctly, with the rest consonants or long vowels.
3) *Letter-name spelling*—Some words are consistently spelled correctly. The student is developing a sight vocabulary and a stable understanding of letters as representing sounds. Long vowels are usually used accurately, but silent vowels are omitted. Unknown words are spelled by the child attempting to match the name of the letter to the sound.
4) *Transitional spelling*—This phase is typically entered in late elementary school. Short vowel sounds are mastered and some spelling rules are known. Children are developing a sense of which spellings are correct and which are not.

Derivational spelling—This is usually reached from high school to adulthood. This is the stage where spelling rules are being mastered.

How Words Are Built
Knowledge of how words are built can help students with basic and more advanced decoding. A *root word* is the primary base of a word. A *prefix* is the affix (a morpheme that attaches to a base word) that is placed at the start of a root word, but can't make a word on its own. Examples of prefixes include re-, pre-, and un-. A *suffix* follows the root word to which it attaches and appears at the end of the word. Examples of suffixes include –s, -es, -ed, -ly, and –tion. In the word unlikely, "un" is a prefix, "like" is the root word, and "ly" is a suffix.

Skill 1.3   Demonstrate knowledge of the role of vocabulary development in reading; of ways to assess students' vocabulary development; and of effective instructional strategies, activities, and materials for promoting students' vocabulary development

If there were two words which could be synonymous with reading comprehension as far as the balanced literacy approach is concerned, they would be "Constructing Meaning."

Cooper, Taberski, Strickland, and other key theorists and classroom teachers conceptualize the reader as designating a specific meaning to the text using both clues in the text and his/her own prior knowledge. Comprehension for the balanced literacy theorists is a strategic process.

The reader interacts with the text and brings his/her prior knowledge and experience to it or LACK of prior knowledge and experience to it. Writing is interlaced with reading and is a mutually integrative and supportive parallel process. Hence the division of literacy learning by the balanced literacy folks into reading workshop and writing workshop, with the same anchor readings or books being used for both.

Consider the sentence, "The test booklet was white with black print, but very scary looking."

According to the idea of constructing meaning as the reader reads this sentence, the schemata (generic information stored in the mind) of tests that he or she has personally is activated by the author's ideas that tests are scary. Therefore the ultimate meaning that the reader derives from the page is from the reader's own responses and experiences with the ideas the author presents. The reader constructs a meaning that reflects the author's intent and also the reader's response to that intent.

It is also to be remembered that generally readings are fairly lengthy passages, comprised of paragraphs which in turn are comprised of more than one sentence. With each successive sentence, and in every new paragraph, the reader refocuses. The schemata are reconsidered, and a new meaning is constructed.

The purpose of reading is to convert visual images (the letters and words) into a message. Pronouncing the words is not enough; the reader must be able to extract the meaning of the text. When people read, they utilize four sources of background information to comprehend the meaning behind the literal text (Reid, pp.166-171).

1. *Word Knowledge:* Information about words and letters. One's knowledge about word meanings is lexical knowledge—a sort of dictionary. Knowledge about spelling patterns and pronunciations is orthographic knowledge. Poor readers do not develop the level of automaticity in using orthographic knowledge to identify words and decode unfamiliar words.

2. *Syntax and Contextual Information:* When children encounter unknown words in a sentence, they rely on their background knowledge to choose a word that makes sense. Errors of younger children therefore are often substitutions of words in the same syntactic class. Poor readers often fail to make use of contextual clues to help them identify words or activate the background knowledge that would help them with comprehension. Poor readers also process sentences word by word, instead of "chunking" phrases and clauses, resulting in a slow pace that focuses on the decoding rather than comprehension. They also have problems answering wh- (who, what, where, when, why) questions as a result of these problems with syntax.

3. *Semantic Knowledge:* This includes the reader's background knowledge about a topic, which is combined with the text information as the reader tries to comprehend the material. New information is compared to the background information and incorporated into the reader's schema. Poor readers have problems with using their background knowledge, especially with passages that require inference or cause-and-effect.

4. *Text Organization:* Good readers are able to differentiate types of text structure, e.g., story narrative, exposition, compare-contrast, or time sequence. They use knowledge of text to build expectations and construct a framework of ideas on which to build meaning. Poor readers may not be able to differentiate types of text and miss important ideas. They may also miss important ideas and details by concentrating on lesser or irrelevant details.

Research on reading development has yielded information on the behaviors and habits of good readers vs. poor readers. Some of the characteristics of good readers are:

- They think about the information that they will read in the text, formulate questions that they predict will be answered in the text, and confirm those predictions from the information in the text.

- When faced with unfamiliar words, they attempt to pronounce them using analogies to familiar words.

- Before reading, good readers establish a purpose for reading, select possible text structure, choose a reading strategy, and make predictions about what will be in the reading.

- As they read, good readers continually test and confirm their predictions, go back when something does not make sense, and make new predictions.

COMPETENCY 2.0 UNDERSTAND STRATEGIES FOR READING FOR DIFFERENT PURPOSES AND CONSTRUCTING MEANING FROM A VARIETY OF READING MATERIALS

Skill 2.1 Demonstrate knowledge of various reading comprehension strategies and study skills (e.g., previewing, rereading) for different purposes (e.g., to review facts for a test, to analyze literature, to conduct research, to respond to social or business correspondence)

The point of comprehension instruction is not necessarily to focus just on the text(s) students are using at the very moment of instruction, but rather to help them learn the strategies that they can use independently with any other text.

Some of the most common methods of teaching instruction are as follows:

- Summarization: This is where, either in writing or verbally, students go over the main point of the text, along with strategically chosen details that highlight the main point. This is not the same as paraphrasing, which is saying the same thing in different words. Teaching students how to summarize is very important, as it will help them look for the most critical areas in a text and in nonfiction. For example, it will help them distinguish between main arguments and examples. In fiction, it helps students to learn how to focus on the main characters and events and distinguish those from the lesser characters and events.

- Question answering: While this tends to be over-used in many classrooms, it is still a valid method of teaching students to comprehend. As the name implies, students answer questions regarding a text, either out loud, in small groups, or individually on paper. The best questions are those that cause students to have to think about the text (rather than just finding an answer within the text).

- Question generating: This is the opposite of question answering, although students can then be asked to answer their own questions or the questions of peer students. In general, we want students to constantly question texts as they read. This is important because it causes students to become more critical readers. To teach students to generate questions helps them to learn the types of questions they can ask, and it gets them thinking about how best to be critical of texts.

- Graphic organizers: Graphic organizers are graphical representations of content within a text. For example, Venn diagrams can be used to highlight the difference between two characters in a novel or two similar political concepts in a social studies textbook. Or, a teacher can use flow-charts with students to talk about the steps in a process (for example, the steps of setting up a science experiment or the chronological events of a story). Semantic organizers are similar in that they graphically display information. The difference, usually, is that semantic organizers focus on words or concepts. For example, a word web can help students make sense of a word by mapping from the central word all the similar and related concepts to that word.

- Text structure: Often in nonfiction, particularly in textbooks and sometimes in fiction, text structures will give important clues to readers about what to look for. Often, students do not know how to make sense of all the types of headings in a textbook and do not realize that, for example, the side-bar story about a character in history is not the main text on a particular page in the history textbook. Teaching students how to interpret text structures gives them tools in which to tackle other similar texts.

- Monitoring comprehension: Students need to be aware of their comprehension, or lack of it, in particular texts. So, it is important to teach students what to do when text suddenly stops making sense. For example, students can go back and re-read the description of a character. Or, they can go back to the table of contents or the first paragraph of a chapter to see where they are headed.

- Textual marking: This is where students interact with the text as they read. For example, armed with Post-it notes, students can insert questions or comments regarding specific sentences or paragraphs within the text. This helps students focus on the importance of the small things, particularly when they are reading larger works (such as novels in high school). It also gives students a reference point on which to go back into the text when they need to review something.

- Discussion: Small group or whole-class discussion stimulates thoughts about texts and gives students a larger picture of the impact of those texts. For example, teachers can strategically encourage students to discuss concepts related to the text. This helps students learn to consider texts within larger societal and social concepts, or teachers can encourage students to provide personal opinions in discussion. By listening to various students' opinions, this will help all students in a class to see the wide range of possible interpretations and thoughts regarding one text.

Many people mistakenly believe that the terms "research-based" or "research-validated" or "evidence-based" relate mainly to specific programs, such as early reading textbook programs. While research does validate that some of these programs are effective, much research has been conducted regarding the effectiveness of particular instructional strategies. In reading, many of these strategies have been documented in the report from the National Reading Panel (2000).

However, just because a strategy has not been validated as effective by research does not necessarily mean that it is not effective with certain students in certain situations. The number of strategies out there far outweighs researchers' ability to test their effectiveness. Some of the strategies listed above have been validated by rigorous research, while others have been shown consistently to help improve students' reading abilities in localized situations. There simply is not enough space to list all the strategies out there that have been proven effective; just know that the above strategies are very commonly cited ones that work in a variety of situations.

Skill 2.2 **Apply knowledge of strategies for promoting the reading comprehension skills of students who are at different stages of reading and for facilitating comprehension before, during, and after reading (e.g., prompting students to make predictions)**

Making Predictions
One theory or approach to the teaching of reading that gained currency in the late sixties and the early seventies was the importance of asking inferential and critical thinking questions of the reader, which would challenge the children and engage them in the text. This approach to reading went beyond the literal level of what was stated in the text to an inferential level of using text clues to make predictions and to a critical level of involving the child in evaluating the text. While asking engaging and thought-provoking questions is still viewed as part of the teaching of reading, it is only viewed currently as a component of the teaching of reading.

Prior Knowledge
Prior knowledge can be defined as all of an individual's prior experiences, learning, and development which precede his/her entering a specific learning situation or attempting to comprehend a specific text. Sometimes prior knowledge can be erroneous or incomplete. Obviously, if there are misconceptions in a child's prior knowledge, these must be corrected so that the child's overall comprehension skills can continue to progress. Prior knowledge of even kindergarteners includes their accumulated positive and negative experiences both in and out of school.

These might range from wonderful family travels, watching television, visiting museums and libraries, to visiting hospitals, prisons, and surviving poverty. Whatever the prior knowledge that the child brings to the school setting, the independent reading and writing the child does in school immeasurably expands his/her prior knowledge and hence broadens his/her reading comprehension capabilities.

Literary response skills are dependent on prior knowledge, schemata, and background. Schemata (the plural of schema) are those structures which represent generic concepts stored in our memory. Effective comprehenders of text, whether they are adults or children, use both their schemata and prior knowledge PLUS the ideas from the printed text for reading comprehension, and graphic organizers help organize this information.

Graphic Organizers

Graphic organizers solidify in a chart format a visual relationship among various reading and writing ideas: sequence, timelines, character traits, fact and opinion, main idea and details, and differences and likenesses (generally done using a VENN DIAGRAM of interlocking circles, KWL Chart, etc). These charts and formats are essential for providing scaffolding for instruction through activating pertinent prior knowledge.

KWL charts are exceptionally useful for reading comprehension by outlining what students KNOW, what they WANT to know, and what they've LEARNED after reading. Students are asked to activate prior knowledge about a topic and further develop their knowledge about a topic using this organizer. Teachers often opt to display and maintain KWL charts throughout a text to continually record pertinent information about students' reading.

When the teacher first introduces the K-W-L strategy, the children should be allowed sufficient time to brainstorm in response to the first question to find out what all of them in the class or small group actually know about the topic. The children should have a three-columned K-W-L worksheet template for their journals, and there should be a chart to record the responses from class or group discussion. The children can write under each column in their own journal, and should also help the teacher with notations on the chart. This strategy involves the children actually gaining experience in note taking and having a concrete record of new data and information they have gleaned from the passage about the topic.

Depending on the grade level of the participating children, the teacher may also want to channel them into considering categories of information they hope to find out from the expository passage. For instance, they may be reading a book on animals to find out more about the animals' habitats during the winter or about the animals' mating habits.

When children are working on the middle, "What I want to know," section of their K-W-L strategy sheet, the teacher may want to give them a chance to share what they would like to learn further about the topic and help them to express it in question format.

K-W-L is useful and can even be introduced as early as grade two with extensive teacher discussion support. It not only serves to support the child's comprehension of a particular expository text, but also models for children a format for note taking. Beyond note taking, when the teacher wants to introduce report writing, the K-W-L format provides excellent outlines and question introductions for at least three paragraphs of a report.

Cooper (2004) recommends this strategy for use with thematic units and with reading chapters in required science, social studies, or health textbooks. In addition to its usefulness with thematic unit study, K-W-L is wonderful for providing the teacher with a concrete format to assess how well children have absorbed pertinent new knowledge within the passage (by looking at the third L section). Ultimately it is hoped that students will learn to use this strategy, not only under explicit teacher direction with templates of K-W-L sheets, but also on their own by informally writing questions they want to find out about in their journals and then going back to their own questions and answering them after the reading.

Note Taking
Older children take notes in their reading journals, while younger children and those more in need of explicit teacher support contribute their ideas and responses as part of the discussion in class. Their responses are recorded on the experiential chart.

Connecting Texts
The concept of readiness is generally regarded as a developmentally based phenomenon. Various abilities, whether cognitive, affective, or psychomotor, are perceived to be dependent upon the mastery or development of certain prerequisite skills or abilities. Readiness, then, implies that the necessary prior knowledge, experience, and readiness prerequisites have been obtained. Students should not engage in the new task until first acquiring the necessary readiness foundation.

Readiness for subject area learning is dependent not only on prior knowledge, but also on affective factors such as interest, motivation, and attitude. These factors are often more influential on student learning than the pre-existing cognitive base.

When texts relate to a student's life or other reading materials or areas of study, they become more meaningful and relevant to students' learning. Students enjoy seeing reading material connect to their life, other subject areas, and other reading material.

Discussing the Text

Discussion is an activity in which the children (and this activity works well from grades 3 to 6 and beyond) conclude a particular text. Among the prompts, the teacher-coach might suggest that the children focus on words of interest they encountered in the text. These can also be words that they heard if the text was read aloud. Children can be asked to share something funny or upsetting or unusual about the words they have read. Through this focus on children's response to words as the center of the discussion circle, peers become more interested in word study.

Furthermore, in the current teaching of literacy, reading, writing, thinking, listening, viewing, and discussing are not viewed as separate activities or components of instruction, but rather as developing and being nurtured simultaneously and interactively.

Skill 2.3   Demonstrate knowledge of literal comprehension skills (e.g., recognizing facts and opinions, sequence of events, main ideas, or supporting details in a text)

Main Idea

A **topic** of a paragraph or story is what the paragraph or story is about.

The **main idea** of a paragraph or story states the important idea(s) that the author wants the reader to know about a topic.

The topic and main idea of a paragraph or story are sometimes directly stated.

There are times; however, that the topic and main idea are not directly stated, but simply implied.

Look at this sample paragraph:

> Henry Ford was an inventor who developed the first affordable automobile. The cars that were being built before Mr. Ford created his Model T were very expensive. Only rich people could afford to have cars.

The topic of this paragraph is Henry Ford. The main idea is that Henry Ford built the first affordable automobile.

The **topic sentence** indicates what the passage is about. It is the subject of that portion of the narrative. The ability to identify the topic sentence in a passage will enable the student to focus on the concept being discussed and better comprehend the information provided.

You can find the main ideas by looking at the way in which paragraphs are written. A paragraph is a group of sentences about one main idea. Paragraphs usually have two types of sentences: a topic sentence, which contains the main idea, and two or more detail sentences which support, prove, provide more information, explain, or give examples.

You can only tell if you have a detail or topic sentence by comparing the sentences with each other.

Look at this sample paragraph:
Fall is the best of the four seasons. The leaves change colors to create a beautiful display of golds, reds, and oranges. The air turns crisp and windy. The scent of pumpkin muffins and apple pies fill the air. Finally, Halloween marks the start of the holiday season. Fall is my favorite time of year!

Breakdown of sentences:
Fall is the best of the four seasons. (TOPIC SENTENCE)
The leaves change colors to create a beautiful display of golds, reds, and oranges. (DETAIL)
The air turns crisp and windy. (DETAIL)
The scent of pumpkin muffins and apple pies fill the air. (DETAIL)
Finally, Halloween marks the start of the holiday season. (DETAIL)
Fall is my favorite time of year! (CLOSING SENTENCE – Often a restatement of the topic sentence)

The first sentence introduces the main idea and the other sentences support and give the many uses for the product.

Tips for Finding the Topic Sentence

- The topic sentence is usually first, but could be in any position in the paragraph.

- A topic is usually more "general" than the other sentences, that is, it talks about many things and looks at the big picture. Sometimes it refers to more than one thing. Plurals and the words "many," "numerous," or "several" often signal a topic sentence.

- Detail sentences are usually more "specific" than the topic, that is, they usually talk about one single or small part or side of an idea. Also, the words "for example," "i.e.," "that is," "first," "second," "third," etc., and "finally" often signal a detail.

- Most of the detail sentences support, give examples, prove, talk about, or point toward the topic in some way.

How can you be sure that you have a topic sentence? Try this trick: switch the sentence you think is the topic sentence into a question. If the other sentences seem to "answer" the question, then you've got it.

For example:
Reword the topic sentence "Fall is the best of the four seasons" in one of the following ways:

"Why is fall the best of the four seasons?"
"Which season is the best season?"
"Is fall the best season of the year?"

Then, as you read the remaining sentences (the ones you didn't pick), you will find that they answer (support) your question.

If you attempt this with a sentence other than the topic sentence, it won't work.

For example:
Suppose you select "Halloween marks the start of the holiday season," and you reword it in the following way:

"Which holiday is the start of the holiday season?"

You will find that the other sentences fail to help you answer (support) your question.

Supporting Details
The **supporting details** are sentences that give more information about the topic and the main idea.

The supporting details in the aforementioned paragraph about Henry Ford would be that he was an inventor and that before he created his Model T, only rich people could afford cars because they were too expensive.

Skill 2.4	Demonstrate knowledge of inferential comprehension skills (e.g., summarizing, drawing conclusions, or making generalizations from given information; drawing inferences about character, setting, or cause and effect relationships in an excerpt)

o   See Skill 2.1 and 2.2

Inferences and Conclusions
In order to draw **inferences** and make **conclusions**, a reader must use prior knowledge and apply it to the current situation. A conclusion or inference is never stated. You must rely on your common sense.

Read the following passage.

The Smith family waited patiently around carousel number seven for their luggage to arrive. They were exhausted after their five hour trip and were anxious to get to their hotel. After about an hour, they realized that they no longer recognized any of the other passengers' faces. Mrs. Smith asked the person who appeared to be in charge if they were at the right carousel. The man replied, "Yes, this is it, but we finished unloading that baggage almost half an hour ago."

From the man's response we can infer that:

        (A) The Smiths were ready to go to their hotel.
        (B) The Smiths' luggage was lost.
        (C) The man had their luggage.
        (D) They were at the wrong carousel.

Since the Smiths were still waiting for their luggage, we know that they were not yet ready to go to their hotel. From the man's response, we know that they were not at the wrong carousel and that he did not have their luggage. Therefore, though not directly stated, it appears that their luggage was lost. Choice (B) is the correct answer.

Conclusions are drawn as a result of a line of reasoning. Inductive reasoning begins with particulars and reasons to a generality. For example: "When I was a child, I bit into a green apple from my grandfather's orchard, and it was sour" (specific fact #1). "I once bought green apples from a roadside vendor, and when I bit into one, it was sour" (specific fact #2). "My grocery store had a sale on green Granny Smith apples last week, and I bought several only to find that they were sour when I bit into one" (specific fact #3). Conclusion: All green apples are sour. While this is an example of inductive reasoning, it is also an example of the weakness of such reasoning. The speaker has not tasted all the green apples in the world, and there very well may be some apples that are green that are not sour.

Deductive reasoning begins with the generalization: "Green apples are sour" and supports that generalization with the specifics.

An inference is drawn from an inductive line of reasoning. The most famous one is "all men are mortal," which is drawn from the observation that everyone a person knows has died or will die and that everyone else concurs in that judgment. It is assumed to be true and for that reason can be used as proof of another conclusion: "Socrates is a man; therefore, he will die."

Sometimes the inference is assumed to be proven when it is not reliably true in all cases, such as "aging brings physical and mental infirmity." Reasoning from that *inference*, many companies will not hire anyone above a certain age. Actually, being old does not necessarily imply physical and/or mental impairment. There are many instances where elderly people have made important contributions that require exceptional ability.

Cause and Effect

Linking cause to effect seems to be ingrained in human thinking. We get chilled and then the next day come down with a cold; therefore, we think getting chilled caused the cold even though medical experts tell us that the virus that causes colds must be communicated by another human being. Socrates and the other Greek orators did a lot of thinking about this kind of thinking and developed a whole system for analyzing the links between causes and their effects and when they are valid—that is, when such and such a cause did, in fact, bring about a particular effect—and spelled out ways to determine whether or not the reasoning is reliable or whether it is not reliable, in which case it is called a fallacy.

A common fallacy in reasoning is the *post hoc ergo propter hoc* ("after this, therefore because of this"), or the false-cause fallacy. These occur in cause/effect reasoning, which may either go from cause to effect or effect to cause. They happen when an inadequate cause is offered for a particular effect; when the possibility of more than one cause is ignored; and when a connection between a particular cause and a particular effect is not made.

An example of a *post hoc*: "Our sales shot up thirty-five percent after we ran that television campaign; therefore the campaign caused the increase in sales." It might have been a cause, of course, but more evidence is needed to prove it.

An example of an inadequate cause for a particular effect: "An Iraqi truck driver reported that Saddam Hussein had nuclear weapons; therefore, Saddam Hussein is a threat to world security." More causes were needed to prove the conclusion.

An example of failing to make a connection between a particular cause and an effect assigned to it: "Anna fell into a putrid pond on Saturday; on Monday she came down with polio; therefore, the polio was caused by the water in the pond." This, of course, is not acceptable unless the polio virus is found in a sample of water from the pond. A connection must be proven.

Skill 2.5 **Demonstrate understanding of interpretive and evaluative comprehension skills (e.g., analyzing an author's purpose or point of view; evaluating the use of language or illustration to portray characters, develop plot, or create an emotional impact)**

In both fiction and nonfiction, authors portray ideas in very subtle ways through their skillful use of language. Style, tone, and point of view are the most basic of ways in which authors do this.

Style is the artful adaptation of language to meet various purposes. For example, authors can modify their word choice, sentence structure, and organization in order to convey certain ideas. For example, an author may write on a topic (the environment, for example) in many different styles. In an academic style, the author would use long, complex sentences, advanced vocabulary, and very structured paragraphing. However, in an informal explanation in a popular magazine, the author may use a conversational tone utilizing simple words and sentence structures.

Author's Purpose
An author may have more than one purpose in writing. An **author's purpose** may be to entertain, to persuade, to inform, to describe, or to narrate.

There are no tricks or rules to follow in attempting to determine an author's purpose. It is up to the reader to use his or her judgment.

Read the following paragraph.

> Charles Lindbergh had no intention of becoming a pilot. He was enrolled in the University of Wisconsin until a flying lesson changed the entire course of his life. He began his career as a pilot by performing daredevil stunts at fairs.

The author wrote this paragraph primarily to:

(A) Describe
(B) Inform
(C) Entertain
(D) Narrate

Since the author is simply telling us or informing us about the life of Charles Lindbergh, the correct answer here is (B).

Author's Tone and Point of View

Tone is the attitude an author takes toward his or her subject. That tone is exemplified in the language of the text. For example, consider the environment once again. One author may dismiss the idea of global warming; his tone may be one of derision against environmentalists. A reader might notice this through the style (word choice, for example), the details the author decides to present, and the order in which details are presented. Another author may be angry about global warming and therefore might use harsh words and other tones that indicate anger. Finally, yet another author may not care one bit about the issue of the environment, either way. Let's say this author is a comedian who likes to poke fun at political activists. Her tone is humorous; therefore, she will adjust her language accordingly, as well. All types of tones are about the same subject—they simply reveal, through language, different opinions and attitudes about the subject.

The **author's tone** is his or her attitude as reflected in the statement or passage. His or her choice of words will help the reader determine the overall tone of a statement or passage.

Read the following paragraph.

> I was shocked by your article, which said that sitting down to breakfast was a thing of the past. Many families consider breakfast time, family time. Children need to realize the importance of having a good breakfast. It is imperative that they be taught this at a young age. I cannot believe that a writer with your reputation has difficulty comprehending this.

The author's tone in this passage is one of

(A) Concern
(B) Anger
(C) Excitement
(D) Disbelief

Since the author directly states that he "cannot believe" that the writer feels this way, the answer is (D) disbelief.

Finally, point of view is perspective. While most of us think of point of view in terms of first or third person (or even the points of view of various characters in stories), point of view also helps explain a lot of language and presentation of ideas in nonfiction and fiction texts. The above environmentalism example proves this. Three points of view are represented, and each creates a different style of language.

Students need to learn that language and text are changed dramatically by tone, style, and point of view. They can practice these concepts by exploring these elements in everything they read. It takes little time for each nonfiction or fiction text they have to read in class, but it goes a long way in helping them comprehend text at a more advanced level.

Skill 2.6   Demonstrate knowledge of the diverse body of works, authors, and movements of U.S. and world literature, children's and young adult literature, and other resources that promote students' literary response and analysis skills (e.g., promoting cultural awareness or addressing student issues with young adult literature)

The social changes of post—World War II significantly affected adolescent literature. The Civil Rights movement, feminism, the protest of the Vietnam conflict, and issues surrounding homelessness, neglect, teen pregnancy, drugs, and violence have bred a new vein of contemporary fiction that helps adolescents understand and cope with the world they live in.

Popular books for preadolescents deal more with establishing relationships with members of the opposite sex (Sweet Valley High series) and learning to cope with their changing bodies, personalities, or life situations, as in Judy Blume's *Are You There, God? It's Me, Margaret*. Adolescents are still interested in the fantasy and science fiction genres as well as popular juvenile fiction. Middle school students still read the Little House on the Prairie series and the mysteries of the Hardy boys and Nancy Drew. Teens value the works of Emily and Charlotte Bronte, Willa Cather, Jack London, William Shakespeare, and Mark Twain as much as those of Piers Anthony, S.E. Hinton, Madeleine L'Engle, Stephen King, and J.R.R. Tolkein, because all of these works are fun to read, whatever their underlying worth may be.

Older adolescents enjoy the writers in these genres:

1.   Fantasy: Piers Anthony, Ursula LeGuin, Ann McCaffrey

2.   Horror: V.C. Andrews, Stephen King

3.   Juvenile fiction: Judy Blume, Robert Cormier, Rosa Guy, Virginia Hamilton, S.E. Hinton, M.E. Kerr, Harry Mazer, Norma Fox Mazer, Richard Newton Peck, Cynthia Voight, and Paul Zindel

4.   Science fiction: Isaac Asimov, Ray Bradbury, Arthur C. Clarke, Frank Herbert, Larry Niven, H.G. Wells

These classic and contemporary works combine the characteristics of multiple theories. Functioning at the concrete operations stage (Piaget), being of the "good person," orientation (Kohlberg), still highly dependent on external rewards (Bandura), and exhibiting all five needs previously discussed from Maslow's hierarchy, these eleven- to twelve-year-olds should appreciate the following titles, grouped by reading level. These titles are also cited for interest at that grade level and do not reflect high-interest titles for older readers who do not read at grade level. Some high-interest titles will be cited later.

Reading level 6.0 to 6.9

- Barrett, William. *Lilies of the Field*
- Cormier, Robert. *Other Bells for Us to Ring*
- Dahl, Roald. *Danny, Champion of the World; Charlie and the Chocolate Factory*
- Lindgren, Astrid. *Pippi Longstocking*
- Lindbergh, Anne. *Three Lives to Live*
- Lowry, Lois. *Rabble Starkey*
- Naylor, Phyllis. *The Year of the Gopher; Reluctantly Alice*
- Peck, Robert Newton. *Arly*
- Speare, Elizabeth. *The Witch of Blackbird Pond*
- Sleator, William. *The Boy Who Reversed Himself*

For seventh and eighth grades
Most seventh and eighth grade students, according to learning theory, are still functioning cognitively, psychologically, and morally as sixth graders. As these are not inflexible standards, there are some twelve- and thirteen-year-olds who are much more mature socially, intellectually, and physically than the younger children who share the same school. They are becoming concerned with establishing individual and peer group identities, which presents conflicts with breaking from authority and the rigidity of rules. Some at this age are still tied firmly to the family and its expectations, while others identify more with those their own age or older. Enrichment reading for this group must help them cope with life's rapid changes or provide escape, and thus must be either realistic or fantastic depending on the child's needs. Adventures and mysteries (the Hardy Boys and Nancy Drew series) are still popular today. These preteens also become more interested in biographies of contemporary figures rather than legendary figures of the past.

Reading level 7.0 to 7.9

- Armstrong, William. *Sounder*
- Bagnold, Enid. *National Velvet*
- Barrie, James. *Peter Pan*
- London, Jack. *White Fang; Call of the Wild*
- Lowry, Lois. *Taking Care of Terrific*

- McCaffrey, Anne. *The Dragonsinger series*
- Montgomery, L. M. *Anne of Green Gables* and sequels
- Steinbeck, John. *The Pearl*
- Tolkien, J. R. R. *The Hobbit*
- Zindel, Paul. *The Pigman*

Reading level 8.0 to 8.9

- Cormier, Robert. *I Am the Cheese*
- McCullers, Carson. *The Member of the Wedding*
- North, Sterling. *Rascal*
- Twain, Mark. *The Adventures of Tom Sawyer*
- Zindel, Paul. *My Darling , My Hamburger*

Development theories and existing social conditions influence the literature created and selected for and by child/adolescent readers.

* meant to teach

Child/adolescent literature has always been to some degree didactic, whether nonfiction or fiction. Until the twentieth century, "kiddie" lit was also morally prescriptive. Written by adults who determined either what they believed children needed or liked or what they should need or like, most books, stories, poems, and essays dealt with experiences or issues that would make children into better adults. The fables, fairy tales, and epics of old set the moral/social standards of their times while entertaining the child in every reader/listener. These tales are still popular because they have a universal appeal. Except for the rare exceptions discussed earlier in this section, most books were written for literate adults.

Educated children found their pleasure in the literature that was available. Because of the rapid social changes, topics that once did not interest young people until they reached their teens—suicide, gangs, homosexuality—are now subjects of books for even younger readers. The plethora of high-interest books reveals how desperately schools have failed to produce on-level readers and how the market has adapted to that need. ** an oversupply or excess.*

However, these high-interest books are now readable for younger children whose reading levels are at or above normal. No matter how tastefully written, some contents are inappropriate for younger readers. The problem becomes not so much steering them toward books that they have the reading ability to handle but encouraging them toward books whose content is appropriate to their levels of cognitive and social development. A fifth grader may be able to read V.C. Andrews' book *Flowers in the Attic* but not possess the social/moral development to handle the deviant behavior of the characters.

At the same time, because of the complex changes affecting adolescents, the teacher must be well versed in learning theory and child development as well as competent to teach the subject matter of language and literature.

Skill 2.7 **Analyze major characteristics of classic and contemporary literature from the United States and throughout the world, key features of various literary genres (e.g., folk tale, myth, poetry, fiction), and the use of literary elements (e.g., figurative language, dialogue, setting, mood) in various texts**

The major literary genres include allegory, ballad, drama, epic, epistle, essay, fable, novel, poem, romance, and the short story.

Allegory: A story in verse or prose with characters representing virtues and vices. There are two meanings, symbolic and literal. John Bunyan's *The Pilgrim's Progress* is the most renowned of this genre.

Ballad: An *in medias res* story told or sung, usually in verse and accompanied by music. Literary devices found in ballads include the refrain, or repeated section; and incremental repetition, or anaphora, for effect. Earliest forms were anonymous folk ballads. Later forms include Coleridge's Romantic masterpiece, "The Rime of the Ancient Mariner."

Drama: Plays – comedy, modern, or tragedy - typically in five acts. Traditionalists and neoclassicists adhere to Aristotle's unities of time, place, and action. Plot development is advanced via dialogue. Literary devices include asides, soliloquies, and the chorus representing public opinion. The greatest of all dramatists/playwrights is William Shakespeare. Other dramaturges include Ibsen, Williams, Miller, Shaw, Stoppard, Racine, Moliére, Sophocles, Aeschylus, Euripides, and Aristophanes.

Epic: Long poem usually of book length reflecting values inherent in the generative society. Epic devices include an invocation to a muse for inspiration, purpose for writing, universal setting, protagonist and antagonist who possess supernatural strength and acumen, and interventions of a God or the gods. Understandably, there are very few epics: Homer's *Iliad* and *Odyssey*, Virgil's *Aeneid*, Milton's *Paradise Lost*, Spenser's *The Fairie Queene*, Barrett Browning's *Aurora Leigh*, and Pope's mock epic, *The Rape of the Lock*.

Epistle: A letter that is not always originally intended for public distribution, but due to the fame of the sender and/or recipient, becomes public domain. Paul wrote epistles that were later placed in the Bible.

Essay: Typically a limited-length prose work focusing on a topic and propounding a definite point of view and authoritative tone. Great essayists include Carlyle, Lamb, DeQuincy, Emerson, and Montaigne, who is credited with defining this genre.

Fable: A terse tale offering up a moral or exemplum. Chaucer's "The Nun's Priest's Tale" is a fine example of a *bete fabliau,* or beast fable, in which animals speak and act characteristically human, illustrating human foibles.

Legend: A traditional narrative or collection of related narratives, popularly regarded as historically factual but actually a mixture of fact and fiction.

Myth: Stories that are more or less universally shared within a culture to explain its history and traditions.

Novel: The longest form of fictional prose containing a variety of characterizations, settings, local color, and regionalism. Most have complex plots, expanded description, and attention to detail. Some of the great novelists include Austin, the Brontes, Twain, Tolstoy, Hugo, Hardy, Dickens, Hawthorne, Forster, and Flaubert.

Poem: The only requirement is rhythm. Sub-genres include fixed types of literature, such as the sonnet, elegy, ode, pastoral, and villanelle. Unfixed types of literature include blank verse and dramatic monologue.

Romance: A highly imaginative tale set in a fantastical realm dealing with the conflicts between heroes, villains, and/or monsters. "The Knight's Tale" from Chaucer's *Canterbury Tales*, *Sir Gawain and the Green Knight,* and Keats's "The Eve of St. Agnes" are prime representatives.

Short Story: Typically a terse narrative, with less developmental background about characters. May include description, author's point of view, and tone. Poe emphasized that a successful short story should create one focused impact. Considered to be great short story writers are Hemingway, Faulkner, Twain, Joyce, Shirley Jackson, Flannery O'Connor, de Maupassant, Saki, Edgar Allen Poe, and Pushkin.

Children's Literature is a genre of its own and emerged as a distinct and independent form in the second half of the 18th century. *The Visible World in Pictures* by John Amos Comenius, a Czech educator, was one of the first printed works and the first picture book. For the first time, educators acknowledged that children are different from adults in many respects. Modern educators acknowledge that introducing elementary students to a wide range of reading experiences plays an important role in their mental/social/psychological development. Some of the most common forms of literature specifically for children follow:

Traditional Literature: Traditional literature opens up a world where right wins out over wrong, where hard work and perseverance are rewarded, and where helpless victims find vindication—all worthwhile values that children identify with even as early as kindergarten. In traditional literature, children will be introduced to fanciful beings, humans with exaggerated powers, talking animals, and heroes that will inspire them. For younger elementary children, these stories in Big Book format are ideal for providing predictable and repetitive elements that can be grasped by these children.

Folktales/Fairy Tales: Some examples: *The Three Bears*, *Little Red Riding Hood*, *Snow White*, *Sleeping Beauty*, *Puss in Boots*, *Rapunzel* and *Rumpelstiltskin*. Adventures of animals or humans and the supernatural characterize these stories. The hero is usually on a quest and is aided by other-worldly helpers. More often than not, the story focuses on good and evil and reward and punishment.

Fables: Animals that act like humans are featured in these stories and usually reveal human foibles or sometimes teach a lesson. Example: *Aesop's Fables.*

Myths: These stories about events from the earliest times, such as the origin of the world, are considered true in their own societies.

Legends: These are similar to myths except that they tend to deal with events that happened more recently. Example: Arthurian legends.

Tall tales: Examples: Paul Bunyan, John Henry, and Pecos Bill. These are purposely exaggerated accounts of individuals with superhuman strength.

Modern Fantasy: Many of the themes found in these stories are similar to those in traditional literature. The stories start out based in reality, which makes it easier for the reader to suspend disbelief and enter worlds of unreality. Little people live in the walls in *The Borrowers* and time travel is possible in *The Trolley to Yesterday*. Including some fantasy tales in the curriculum helps elementary-grade children develop their senses of imagination. These often appeal to ideals of justice and issues having to do with good and evil; and because children tend to identify with the characters, the message is more likely to be retained.

Science Fiction: Robots, spacecraft, mystery, and civilizations from other ages often appear in these stories. Most presume advances in science on other planets or in a future time. Most children like these stories because of their interest in space and the "what if" aspect of the stories. Examples: *Outer Space and All That Junk* and *A Wrinkle in Time*.

Modern Realistic Fiction: These stories are about real problems that real children face. By finding that their hopes and fears are shared by others, young children can find insight into their own problems. Young readers also tend to experience a broadening of interests as the result of this kind of reading. It's good for them to know that a child can be brave and intelligent and can solve difficult problems.

Historical Fiction: *Rifles for Watie* is an example of this kind of story. Presented in a historically accurate setting, it's about a young boy (sixteen years) who serves in the Union army. He experiences great hardship but discovers that his enemy is an admirable human being. It provides a good opportunity to introduce younger children to history in a beneficial way.

Biography: Reading about inventors, explorers, scientists, political and religious leaders, social reformers, artists, sports figures, doctors, teachers, writers, and war heroes helps children to see that one person can make a difference. They also open new vistas for children to think about when they choose an occupation to fantasize about.

Informational Books: These are ways to learn more about something you are interested in or something that you know nothing about. Encyclopedias are good resources, of course, but a book like *Polar Wildlife* by Kamini Khanduri shows pictures and facts that will capture the imaginations of young children.

Mood

The mood of a story is the atmosphere or attitude the writer conveys through descriptive language. Often, mood fits in nicely with theme and setting. For example, in Edgar Allen Poe's stories, we often find a mood of horror and darkness. We get that from the descriptions of characters and the setting, as well as from specific plot elements. Mood simply helps us better understand the writer's theme and intentions through descriptive, stylistic language.

Nonfiction vs. Fiction

Students often misrepresent the differences between fiction and nonfiction. They mistakenly believe that stories are always examples of fiction. The simple truth is that stories are both fiction and nonfiction. The primary difference is that fiction is made up by the author, whereas nonfiction is generally true (or an opinion). It is harder for students to understand that nonfiction entails an enormous range of material, from textbooks to true stories to newspaper articles to speeches. Fiction, on the other hand, is fairly simple—made-up stories, novels, etc. But it is also important for students to understand that most of fiction throughout history has been based on true events. In other words, authors use their own life experiences to help them create works of fiction.

Important in understanding fiction, apart from nonfiction, is the artistry in telling a story to convey a point. When students see that an author's choice in a work of fiction is for the sole purpose of conveying a viewpoint, they can make better sense of the specific details in the work of fiction.

Important in understanding nonfiction, apart from fiction, is realizing what is truth and what is perspective. Often, a nonfiction writer will present an opinion, and that opinion is very different from a truth. Knowing the difference between the two is very crucial.

In comparing fiction to nonfiction, students need to learn about the conventions of each. In fiction, students can generally expect to see a plot, characters, setting, and themes. In nonfiction, students may see a plot, characters, settings, and themes, but they will also experience interpretations, opinions, theories, research, and other elements.

Overall, students can begin to see patterns that identify fiction apart from nonfiction. Often, the more fanciful or unrealistic a text or story is, the more likely it is fiction.

Story Elements

Most works of fiction contain a common set of elements that make them come alive to readers. In a way, even though writers do not consciously think about each of these elements as story elements when they sit down to write, all stories essentially contain these "markers" that make them the stories that they are. But, even though all stories have these elements, they are a lot like fingerprints: Each story's story elements are just a bit different.

Let's look at a few of the most commonly discussed elements. The most commonly discussed story element in fiction is plot. Plot is the series of events in a story. Typically, but not always, plot moves in a predictable fashion:

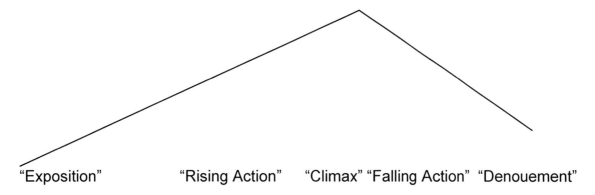

"Exposition"   "Rising Action"   "Climax" "Falling Action" "Denouement"

Exposition is where characters and their situations are introduced. *Rising action* is the point at which conflict starts to occur. *Climax* is the highest point of conflict, often a turning point. *Falling action* is the result of the climax. *Denouement* is the final resolution of the plot.

Character is another commonly studied story element. We will often find in stories heroes, villains, comedic characters, dark characters, etc. When we examine the characters of a story, we look to see who they are and how their traits contribute to the story. Often, because of their characteristics, plot elements become more interesting. For example, authors will pair unlikely characters together, and somehow that, in turn, creates specific conflict.

The setting of a story is the place or location where it occurs. Often, the specific place is not as important as some of the specifics about the setting. For example, the setting of *The Great Gatsby*, New York, is not as significant as the fact that it takes place amongst incredible wealth. Conversely, *The Grapes of Wrath*, although taking place in Oklahoma and California, has a more significant setting of poverty. In fact, as the story takes place *around* other migrant workers, the setting is even more significant. In a way, the setting serves as a reason for various conflicts to occur.

Themes of stories are the underlying messages, above and beyond all plot elements, that writers want to convey. Very rarely will one find that good literature is without a theme—or a lesson, message, or ideal. The best writers in the English language all seem to want to convey something about human nature or the world, and they turn to literature in order to do that. Common themes in literature are jealousy, money, love, human against corporation or government, etc. These themes are never explicitly stated; rather, they are the result of the portrayal of characters, settings, and plots. Readers get the message even if the theme is not directly mentioned.

Finally, the mood of a story is the atmosphere or attitude the writer conveys through descriptive language. Often, mood fits in nicely with theme and setting. For example, in Edgar Allen Poe's stories, we often find a mood of horror and darkness. We get that from the descriptions of characters and the setting, as well as from specific plot elements. Mood simply helps us better understand the writer's theme and intentions through descriptive, stylistic language.

Figurative Language

Figurative language is present in both fiction and nonfiction. Figurative language is language, usually in fiction or nonfiction prose, that utilizes creative or poetic methods to convey points. Figurative language is used for effect, as well as to make a point stand out. The most common examples of figurative language include hyperbole, metaphor, personification, simile, and idiom. Each is explained in the following:

Hyperbole: The term, hyperbole, is the literary version of exaggeration. When authors exaggerate in their text, they are using hyperbole. Often, hyperbole is used as irony, often to overemphasize a point.

Metaphor: A metaphor is any time one thing is used in place of something else in text, signifying some sort of resemblance. For example, we might say that "it is raining cats and dogs." Hopefully, this is not literally true--ever! Instead, we use this to signify heavy rain. Authors use metaphor for emphasis, creativity, and often clarity. Sometimes, metaphors provide a better picture than accurate language.

Personification: Whenever an author gives life to an inanimate item, personification is used. For example, we might say that the wind is whistling. Authors use personification to provide a more poetic look at common events.

Simile: Similes are comparisons between two objects (or between a person and an object, for example). Similes are like metaphors; however, they typically use "like" or "as" to identify the similarities. For example, "love is like a rose."

Idiom: Idioms are locally-flavored phrases or words. For example, a common American idiom, found anywhere in the country, is "break a leg," which is a wish for good luck. However, each region of the country has its own, distinctive idioms as well. Idioms are used in writing generally to spice the language with local flavor. Often, idioms are used to make characters seem more real--or even to indicate where in the country the action is taking place.

COMPETENCY 3.0 UNDERSTAND THE PROCESS OF WRITING AND WRITING STRATEGIES FOR A VARIETY OF PURPOSES AND AUDIENCES

Skill 3.1 Recognize characteristics of children's development of writing skills, factors that influence development of writing skills, signs that a student may be experiencing difficulties in written language, and strategies for addressing written language needs

Children develop writing skills through a series of steps. The steps and their characteristics are:

Role-Play Writing

In this stage, the child writes in scribbles and assigns a message to the symbols. Even though an adult would not be able to read the writing, the child can read what is written, although it may not be the same each time the child reads it. He/She will be able to read back the writing because of prior knowledge that print carries a meaning. The child will also dictate to adults, who can write a message or story.

Experimental Writing

In this stage the child writes in simple forms of language. Children usually write with letters according to the way the letters sound, such as the word "are" written as "r". However, the child does display a sense of sentence formation and writes in groups of words with a period at the end. He/She is aware of a correspondence between written words and oral language.

Early Writing

Children start to use a small range of familiar text forms and sight words in their writing. The topics they choose for writing are ones that have some importance for them, such as their family, friends, or pets. Because they are used to hearing stories, they do have a sense of how a story sounds and begin to write simple narratives. They learn that they do have to correct their writing so that others can easily read it.

Conventional Writing

By the time students reach this stage of writing, they have a sense of audience and purpose for writing. They are able to proofread their writing and edit it for mistakes. They have gained the ability to transfer between reading and writing so that they can get ideas for writing from what they read. By this time students also have a sense of what correct spelling and grammar look like, and they can change the order of events in the writing so that it makes sense for the reader.

Proficient Writing

This is the final stage of writing, in which the students have developed through the stages of the writing process and can easily work through the drafting, revising, and editing stages. They are able to look for precise words to express meaning and use a variety of sentence structures. They are able to adopt different points of view and are able to fully develop a topic.

Students do need to have all the writing strategies modeled for them. Along with direct instruction, modeling is the greatest influential factor in developing students' writing abilities. Children whose parents write at home come to school with the knowledge that writing has meaning and try to simulate putting their thoughts on paper. When students are read to on a daily basis, they realize that writing can be a fun activity as one makes up stories. A classroom designed to inspire writers should be one that is rich in print. Along with books, magazines, and posters, there should be a bulletin board where the students' writings are displayed for all to see.

Some of the signs that may tell teachers that a student is experiencing difficulties with writing include:

- a lack of knowledge about the stages of prewriting, even though the student has had explicit instruction in planning and organizing ideas
- difficulty coming up with ideas for writing or selecting a topic to write on
- difficulty expressing ideas or telling about experiences
- constant desire to know how much to write
- slow handwriting skills or takes a lot of time to get ideas down on paper
- illegible printing or handwriting

It is important for teachers to teach students how to access their background knowledge when searching for writing ideas. A suggested activity is brainstorming a list of ideas, in which the teacher accepts all ideas and even helps students to expand on them. This will give them ideas for extending the information they want to present. Students also need graphic organizers to help them with writing, such as the use of a brainstorm sheet or a story map.

When editing and revising, a checklist is helpful for all students to keep them on track. Do not expect the students to edit everything in one piece of writing. Allow them to look for one type of mistake, such as capitalization in one piece of writing. In another piece of writing, the teacher can expand the list to include capitalization and punctuation.

Students need to write every day, and the teacher should read to them on a daily basis. For students that have difficulty with the actual handwriting, allow them to use a word processor.

Skill 3.2   Demonstrate knowledge of factors to consider when conducting research and writing for various audiences and purposes (e.g., expressive, informative, persuasive)

In the past teachers have assigned reports, paragraphs, and essays that focused on the teacher as the audience with the purpose of explaining information. However, for students to be meaningfully engaged in their writing, they must write for a variety of reasons. Writing for different audiences and aims allows students to be more involved in their writing. If they write for the same audience and purpose, they will continue to see writing as just another assignment. Listed below are suggestions that give students an opportunity to write in more creative and critical ways.

- Write letters to the editor, to a college, to a friend, or to another student that would be sent to the intended audience.
- Write stories that would be read aloud to a group (the class, another group of students, a group of elementary school students) or published in a literary magazine or class anthology.
- Write plays that would be performed.
- Have students discuss the parallels between the different speech styles we use and writing styles for different readers or audiences.
- Allow students to write a particular piece for different audiences.
- Expose students to writing that is on the same topic but with a different audience and have them identify the variations in sentence structure and style.
- As part of the prewriting have students identify the audience. Make sure students consider the following when analyzing the needs of their audience:

-
     1. Why is the audience reading my writing? Do they expect to be informed, amused, or persuaded?
     2. What does my audience already know about my topic?
     3. What does the audience want or need to know? What will interest them?
     4. What type of language suits my readers?

Remind your students that it is not necessary to identify all the specifics of the audience in the initial stage of the writing process but that at some point they must make some determinations about audience.

Writing about literature is a very tough task. It demands that students have fully comprehended the text. It demands that they understand unstated elements of the text, such as character motives. It demands that they dig deeply into their personal experiences to help make connections to the author's intentions. Finally, it also demands that they consider other works of literature to help explain literary conventions, issues, and other complex components of literature.

Of course, when you incorporate writing into the mix just presented above, you make the task even more difficult! Imagine just for a moment that you, the teacher, have given students the assignment of writing about a novel or story they have just read. Your students must face a blank piece of paper and make sense of a complex piece of literature. They must explain literary conventions, characters, settings, and plot. Most will sit and stare at the blank piece of paper, nervous about how to even begin.

What are some ways to help students get beyond that fear of writing about literature? First, utilizing graphic organizers helps students make visual sense of various literary elements. This often helps them organize their writing. Sometimes, outlining major points is also helpful.

Even more helpful is to give students a more authentic task than simply writing about literature in an abstract sense. Although writing about literature analytically may be the end goal in mind, teachers can help students get there by giving them very specific writing tasks. For example, teachers can ask students to write a newspaper story explaining an event in the story. Or they can have students write a letter from one character to another. Once students feel comfortable with these tasks, teachers can move them beyond this stage by having them incorporate knowledge of more than one book, or they can have them involve their own personal experiences in writing about literature. Eventually, with enough practice, students will be facile enough with writing about literature that an analysis writing task will not be so strenuous. The key, though, is building students up to the task by first having them experiment with writing about the literature in fun, authentic, and natural ways.

Skill 3.3 **Apply knowledge of techniques for generating topics and developing ideas (e.g., brainstorming, outlining, semantic mapping); methods of organizing written presentations; and strategies for drafting, revising, editing, proofreading, and publishing materials (e.g., peer conferences)**

Students gather ideas before writing. Prewriting may include clustering, listing, brainstorming, mapping, free writing, and charting. Providing many ways for a student to develop ideas on a topic will increase his/her chances for success.

Remind students that as they prewrite, they need to consider their audience. Prewriting strategies assist students in a variety of ways. Listed below are the most common prewriting strategies students can use to explore, plan, and write on a topic. It is important to remember when teaching these strategies that not all prewriting must eventually produce a finished piece of writing. In fact, in the initial lesson of teaching prewriting strategies, it might be more effective to have students practice prewriting strategies without the pressure of having to write a finished product.

- Keep an idea book so that they can jot down ideas that come to mind
- Write in a daily journal.
- Write down whatever comes to mind; this is called free writing. Students do not stop to make corrections or interrupt the flow of ideas.

A variation of this technique is focused free writing—writing on a specific topic—to prepare for an essay.

- Make a list of all ideas connected with their topic; this is called brainstorming.
- Make sure students know that this technique works best when they let their mind work freely. After completing the list, students should analyze the list to see if they can find a pattern or way to group the ideas.
- Ask the questions Who? What? When? Where? and How? Help the writer approach a topic from several perspectives.
- Create a visual map on paper to gather ideas. Cluster circles and lines to show connections between ideas. Students should try to identify the relationship that exists between their ideas. If they cannot see the relationships, have them pair up, exchange papers, and have their partners look for some related ideas.
- Observe details of sight, hearing, taste, touch, and sound.
- Visualize by making mental images of something and write down the details in a list.

After they have practiced with each of these prewriting strategies, ask them to pick out the ones they prefer and ask them to discuss how they might use the techniques to help them with future writing assignments. It is important to remember that they can use more than one prewriting strategy at a time. Also they may find that different writing situations may suggest certain techniques.

Most libraries will only allow the downloading and printing of seventy-five pages of information during any given month. The point is to provide the user with a hard copy of specific information in a limited and environmentally friendly manner. Libraries limit the number of pages that could be wasted during a singular download, which limits the number of trees needed to conduct Internet research and subsequent printing. Once the information is collected and categorized according to the research design and outline, the user can begin to take notes on the gathered information to create a cut and paste format for the final report.

Being effective note takers requires consistent technique, whether the mode of note taking is on five-by-seven inch note cards; lined notebook; or on a computer. Organizing all collected information according to a research outline will allow the user to take notes on each section and begin the writing process. If the computer is used, then the actual format of the report can be word processed and information put in to speed up the writing process of the final research report. Creating a title page and the bibliography page will allow each downloaded report to have its resources cited immediately in that section.

Note taking involves identification of specific resources that include the author's or organization's name, year of publication, title, publisher location, and publisher. When taking notes, whether on the computer or using note cards, use the author's last name and page number on cited information. In citing information for major categories and subcategories on the computer, create a file for notes that includes summaries of information and direct quotes. When direct quotes are put into a word file, the cut and paste process for incorporation into the report is quick and easy.

In outline information, it is crucial to identify the headings and subheadings for the topic being researched. When researching information, it is easier to cut and paste information under the indicated headings in creating a visual flow of information for the report. In the actual drafting of the report, the writer is able to lift direct quotations and citations from the posted information to incorporate into the writing.

Students may have their work displayed on a bulletin board, read aloud in class, or printed in a literary magazine or school anthology. It is important to realize that the writing steps are recursive; as a student engages in each aspect of the writing process, he or she may begin with prewriting and then write, revise, write, revise, edit, and publish. They do not engage in this process in a lockstep manner; it is more circular.

There are many uses of technology for each of the steps of the writing process. When students write in school, they do not get the opportunity to fully express their sense of creativity and talent by simply turning in text for the teacher to read. That is why students gain so much from presenting their writing to other students as well as mixing multimedia elements into their writing. For example, a report on history comes alive when students can develop a multimedia presentation that involves photographs, short video, music, poetry, and narration. Such activity definitely requires good technology, however. When it is available, teachers find that it dramatically enhances students' enjoyment and learning.

Skill 3.4   Analyze and revise written work in relation to English grammar and mechanics (i.e., usage, sentence structure, punctuation, capitalization, spelling)

Revise misplaced or dangling modifiers
Particular phrases that are not placed near the one word they modify often result in misplaced modifiers. Particular phrases that do not relate to the subject being modified result in dangling modifiers.

> Error: Weighing the options carefully, a decision was made regarding the punishment of the convicted murderer.

> Problem: Who is weighing the options? No one capable of weighing is named in the sentence; thus, the participle phrase "weighing the options carefully" dangles. This problem can be corrected by adding a subject of the sentence capable of doing the action.

> Correction: Weighing the options carefully, the judge made a decision regarding the punishment of the convicted murderer.

Sentence completeness
Avoid fragments and run-on sentences. Recognition of sentence elements necessary to make a complete thought, proper use of independent and dependent clauses, and proper punctuation will correct such errors.

Recognize simple, compound, complex, and compound-complex sentences. Use dependent (subordinate) and independent clauses correctly to create these sentence structures.

Simple	Joyce wrote a letter.
Compound	Joyce wrote a letter, and Dot drew a picture.
Complex	While Joyce wrote a letter, Dot drew a picture.
Compound-Complex	When Mother asked the girls to demonstrate their new-found skills, Joyce wrote a letter, and Dot drew a picture.

Note: Do **not** confuse compound sentence elements with compound sentences.

Simple sentence with compound subject → *two different people (subject) referring to the same thing*
    <u>Joyce</u> and <u>Dot</u> wrote letters.
    The <u>girl</u> in row three and the <u>boy</u> next to her were passing notes across the aisle. *(pronoun)*

Simple sentence with compound predicate → *is when you have 1 subject including two different things*
    Joyce <u>wrote letters</u> and <u>drew pictures</u>.

    The captain of the high school debate team <u>graduated with honors</u> and <u>studied broadcast journalism in college</u>.

Spelling
Concentration in this section will be on spelling plurals and possessives.
The multiplicity and complexity of spelling rules based on phonics, letter doubling, and exceptions to rules—not even mastered by adulthood—should be replaced by a good dictionary. As spelling mastery is also difficult for adolescents, our recommendation is the same. Learning the use of a dictionary and a thesaurus will be a more rewarding use of time.

Most plurals of nouns that end in hard consonants or hard consonant sounds followed by a silent *e* are made by adding *s*. Some words ending in vowels only add *s*.
    fingers, numerals, banks, bugs, riots, homes, gates, radios, bananas

Nouns that end in soft consonant sounds *s, j, x, z, ch*, and *sh* add *es*. Some nouns ending in *o* add *es*.
    dresses, waxes, churches, brushes, tomatoes, potatoes

Nouns ending in *y* preceded by a vowel just add *s*.
    boys, alleys

Nouns ending in *y* preceded by a consonant change the *y* to *i* and add *es*.
    babies, corollaries, frugalities, poppies

Some noun plurals are formed irregularly or remain the same.
    sheep, deer, children, leaves, oxen

Capitalization

Capitalize all proper names of persons (including specific organizations or agencies of government); places (countries, states, cities, parks, and specific geographical areas); and things (political parties, structures, historical and cultural terms, and calendar and time designations); and religious terms (any deity, revered person or group, and sacred writings).

> Percy Bysshe Shelley, Argentina, Mount Rainier National Park, Grand Canyon, League of Nations, the Sears Tower, Birmingham, Lyric Theater, Americans, Midwesterners, Democrats, Renaissance, Boy Scouts of America, Easter, God, Bible, Dead Sea Scrolls, Koran

Capitalize proper adjectives and titles used with proper names.

> California gold rush, President John Adams, French fries, Homeric epic, Romanesque architecture, Senator John Glenn

Note: Some words that represent titles and offices are not capitalized unless used with a proper name.

Capitalized	Not Capitalized
Congressman McKay	the congressman from Florida
Commander Alger	commander of the Pacific Fleet
Queen Elizabeth	the queen of England

Capitalize all main words in titles of works of literature, art, and music. The candidate for the certification exam should be cognizant of proper rules and conventions of punctuation, capitalization, and spelling. Competency exams will generally test the ability to apply the more advanced skills; thus, a limited number of more frustrating rules is presented here. Rules should be applied according to the American style of English, i.e. spelling *theater* instead of *theater* and placing terminal marks of punctuation almost exclusively within other marks of punctuation.

Punctuation

Quotation marks

In a quoted statement that is either declarative or imperative, place the period inside the closing quotation marks.

> "The airplane crashed on the runway during takeoff."

If the quotation is followed by other words in the sentence, place a comma inside the closing quotation marks and a period at the end of the sentence.

> "The airplane crashed on the runway during takeoff," said the announcer.

In most instances in which a quoted title or expression occurs at the end of a sentence, the period is placed before either the single or double quotation marks.

> "The middle school readers were unprepared to understand Bryant's poem 'Thanatopsis.'"

> Early book-length adventure stories like *Don Quixote* and *The Three Musketeers* were known as "picaresque novels."

In sentences that are interrogatory or exclamatory, the question mark or exclamation point should be positioned outside the closing quotation marks if the quote itself is a statement, command, or cited title.

> Who decided to lead us in the recitation of the "Pledge of Allegiance"?

> Why was Tillie shaking as she began her recitation, "Once upon a midnight dreary..."?

> I was embarrassed when Mrs. White said, "Your slip is showing"!

In sentences that are declarative but the quotation is a question or an exclamation, place the question mark or exclamation point inside the quotation marks.

> The hall monitor yelled, "Fire! Fire!"

> Cory shrieked, "Is there a mouse in the room?" (In this instance, the question supersedes the exclamation.)

Using periods with parentheses

Place the period inside the parentheses or brackets if they enclose a complete sentence that is independent of the other sentences around it.

> Stephen Crane was a confirmed alcohol and drug addict. (He admitted as much to other journalists in Cuba.)

If the parenthetical expression is a statement inserted within another statement, the period in the enclosure is omitted.

> Mark Twain used the character Indian Joe (he also appeared in *The Adventures of Tom Sawyer*) as a foil for Jim in *The Adventures of Huckleberry Finn*.

Commas

Separate two or more coordinate adjectives modifying the same word and three or more nouns, phrases, or clauses in a list.

Maggie's hair was dull, dirty, and lice-ridden.

Dickens portrayed the Artful Dodger as a skillful pickpocket, loyal follower of Fagin, and defendant of Oliver Twist.

Ellen daydreamed about getting out of the rain, taking a shower, and eating a hot dinner.

In Elizabethan England, Ben Johnson wrote comedy, Christopher Marlowe wrote tragedies, and William Shakespeare composed both.

Use commas to separate antithetical or complimentary expressions from the rest of the sentence.

The veterinarian, not his assistant, would perform the delicate surgery.

The more he knew about her, the less he wished he had known.

Randy hopes to, and probably will, get an appointment to the Naval Academy.

His thorough, though esoteric, scientific research could not easily be understood by high school students.

Semicolons

Use semicolons to separate independent clauses when the second clause is introduced by a transitional adverb. (These clauses may also be written as separate sentences, preferably by placing the adverb within the second sentence.)

The Elizabethans modified the rhyme scheme of the sonnet; thus, it was called the English sonnet.

or

The Elizabethans modified the rhyme scheme of the sonnet. It thus was called the English sonnet.

Use semicolons to separate items in a series that are long and complex or have internal punctuation.

The Italian Renaissance produced masters in the fine arts: Dante Alighieri, author of *The Divine Comedy;* Leonardo da Vinci, painter of *The Last Supper;* and Donatello, sculptor of the *Quattro Coronati,* the four saints.

The leading scorers in the WNBA were Haizhaw Zheng, averaging 23.9 points per game; Lisa Leslie, 22; and Cynthia Cooper, 19.5.

Colons

Place a colon at the beginning of a list of items. (Note its use in the sentence about Renaissance Italians on the previous page.)

The teacher directed us to compare Faulkner's three symbolic novels: *Absalom, Absalom; As I Lay Dying;* and *Light in August.*

Do **not** use a colon if the list is preceded by a verb.

Three of Faulkner's symbolic novels are *Absalom, Absalom; As I Lay Dying,* and *Light in August.*

Dashes

Place dashes to denote sudden breaks in thought.

Some periods in literature—the Romantic Age, for example—spanned different time periods in different countries.

Use dashes instead of commas if commas are already used elsewhere in the sentence for amplification or explanation.

The Fireside Poets included three Brahmans—James Russell Lowell, Henry David Wadsworth, Oliver Wendell Holmes—and John Greenleaf Whittier.

Use italics to punctuate the titles of long works of literature, names of periodical publications, musical scores, works of art and motion picture television, and radio programs. (When unable to write in italics, students should be instructed to underline in their own writing where italics would be appropriate.)

The Idylls of the King	*Hiawatha*	*The Sound and the Fury*
Mary Poppins	*Newsweek*	*The Nutcracker Suite*

Skill 3.5 **Analyze and revise written work in relation to organization, unity, clarity, and style (e.g., adding topic sentences, reordering sentences, deleting unnecessary information)**

Revise comes from the Latin word *revidere*, meaning, "to see again." Revision is probably the most important step for the writer in the writing process. Here, students examine their work and make changes in wording, details, and ideas. So many times, students write a draft and then feel they're done. On the contrary, students must be encouraged to develop, change, and enhance their writing as they go, as well as once they've completed a draft.

Therefore, effective teachers realize that revision and editing go hand-in-hand, and students often move back and forth between these stages during the course of one written work. Also, these stages must be practiced in small groups, pairs, and/or individually. Students must learn to analyze and improve their own work as well as the works of their peers. Some methods to use include:

1. Students, working in pairs, analyze sentences for variety.
2. Students work in pairs or groups to ask questions about unclear areas. in the writing or to help each other add details, information, etc.
3. Students perform a final edit.

Many teachers introduce Writer's Workshop to their students to maximize learning about the writing process. Writer's Workshops vary across classrooms, but the main idea is for students to become comfortable with the writing process to produce written work. A basic Writer's Workshop will include a block of classroom time committed to writing various projects (i.e., narratives, memoirs, book summaries, fiction, book reports, etc). Students use this time to write, meet with others to review/edit writing, make comments on writing, revise their own work, proofread, meet with the teacher, and publish their work.

Teachers who facilitate effective Writer's Workshops are able to meet with students one at a time and can guide that student in his or her individual writing needs. This approach allows the teacher to differentiate instruction for each student's writing level.

Students need to be trained to become effective at proofreading, revising, and editing strategies. Begin by training them using both desk-side and scheduled conferences. Listed below are some strategies to use to guide students through the final stages of the writing process (and these can easily be incorporated into Writer's Workshop).

- Provide some guide sheets or forms for students to use during peer responses.
- Allow students to work in pairs and limit the agenda.
- Model the use of the guide sheet or form for the entire class.

- Give students a time limit or number of written pieces to be completed in a specific amount of time.
- Have the students read their partners' papers and ask at least three who, what, when, why, and how questions. The students answer the questions and use them as a place to begin discussing the piece.
- At this point in the writing process, a mini-lesson that focuses on some of the problems your students are having would be appropriate.

To help students revise, provide students with a series of questions that will assist them in revising their writing.

1. Do the details give a clear picture? Add details that appeal to more than just the sense of sight.
2. How effectively are the details organized? Reorder the details if it is needed.
3. Are the thoughts and feelings of the writer included? Add personal thoughts and feelings about the subject.

As you discuss revision, you begin with discussing the definition of the word revise. Also, state that all writing must be revised to improve it. After students have revised their writing, it is time for the final editing and proofreading.

Writing Introductions

It's important to remember that in the writing process, the introduction should be written last. Until the body of the paper has been determined—thesis, development—it's difficult to make strategic decisions regarding the introduction. The Greek rhetoricians called this part of a discourse *exordium*, a "leading into." The basic purpose of the introduction, then, is to lead the audience into the discourse. It can let the reader know what the purpose of the discourse is, and it can condition the audience to be receptive to what the writer wants to say. It can be very brief or it can take up a large percentage of the total word count. Aristotle said that the introduction could be compared to the flourishes that flute players make before their performance, an overture in which the musicians display what they can play best in order to gain the favor and attention of the audience for the main performance.

In order to write an introduction, we must first of all know what we are going to say; who the readership is likely to be; what the social, political, economic, etc., climate is; what preconceived notions the audience is likely to have regarding the subject; and how long the discourse is going to be.

There are many ways to do this:
- Show that the subject is important.
- Show that although the points we are presenting may seem improbable, they are true.
- Show that the subject has been neglected, misunderstood, or misrepresented.
- Explain an unusual mode of development.
- Forestall any misconception of the purpose.
- Apologize for a deficiency.
- Arouse interest in the subject with an anecdotal lead-in.
- Ingratiate oneself with the readership.
- Establish one's own credibility.

The introduction often ends with the thesis, the point or purpose of the paper. However, this is not set in stone. The thesis may open the body of the discussion, or it may conclude the discourse. The most important thing to remember is that the purpose and structure of the introduction should be deliberate if it is to serve the purpose of "leading the reader into the discussion."

Writing Conclusions
It's easier to write a conclusion after the decisions regarding the introduction have been made. Aristotle taught that the conclusion should strive to do five things:
1. Inspire the reader with a favorable opinion of the writer.
2. Amplify the force of the points made in the body of the paper.
3. Reinforce the points made in the body.
4. Rouse appropriate emotions in the reader.
5. Restate in a summary way what has been said.

The conclusion may be short or it may be long depending on its purpose in the paper. Recapitulation, a brief restatement of the main points or certainly of the thesis, is the most common form of effective conclusions. A good example is the closing argument in a court trial.

Text Organization
In studies of professional writers and how they produce their successful works, it has been revealed that writing is a process that can be clearly defined, although in practice it must have enough flexibility to allow for creativity. The teacher must be able to define the various stages that a successful writer goes through in order to make a statement that has value. There must be a discovery stage when ideas, materials, supporting details, etc., are deliberately collected. These may come from many possible sources: the writer's own experience and observations, deliberate research of written sources, interviews of live persons, television presentations, or the Internet.

The next stage is organization, where the purpose, thesis, and supporting points are determined. Most writers will put forth more than one possible thesis, and in the next stage, the writing of the paper, settle on one as the result of trial and error. Once the paper is written, the editing stage is necessary and is probably the most important stage. This is not just the polishing stage. At this point, decisions must be made regarding whether the reasoning is cohesive: does it hold together? Is the arrangement the best possible one or should the points be rearranged? Are there holes that need to be filled in? What form will the introduction take? Does the conclusion lead the reader out of the discourse or is it inadequate or too abrupt, etc?

It's important to remember that the best writers engage in all of these stages recursively. They may go back to discovery at any point in the process. They may go back and rethink the organization, etc. To help students become effective writers, the teacher needs to give them adequate practice in the various stages and encourage them to engage deliberately in the creative thinking that makes writers successful.

Skill 3.6   Demonstrate knowledge of activities, instructional resources, and technologies for promoting students' writing competence and for integrating writing with the other language arts

In order to take students from where they are in English language arts to the next level of reading and writing, teachers need to know the individual levels of the students. Both formal and informal assessment should be a regular part of the classroom. Assessment for learning will help to lead the direction that the instruction needs to take. All students will not be at the same level or need the same supports. By using the balanced literacy model, teachers are better able to individualize their lessons to provide the instruction that all students need.

A comprehensive English language arts program should contain the following components:
1. Skills mini-lessons
2. Reading based on the skills lessons
3. Independent reading
4. Work with words
5. Shared and independent writing
6. Read alouds
7. Author and novel studies
8. Student projects
9. Language arts integration with the content areas
10. Student conferencing (with teacher and with peers)

Teachers should also be familiar with current research with regards to integrating all the components of language arts. The Internet is a valuable source of information in this regard with respect to the International Reading Association, best practices for teachers in language arts, and in specific grades. Two sites of interest are www.teachersfirst.com and www.literacyuconn.edu.

Strategies for Promoting Awareness of the Relationship between Spoken and Written Language

1. Write down what the children are saying on a chart.

2. Highlight and celebrate the meanings, uses, and print products found in the classroom. These products include: posters, labels, yellow sticky pad notes, labels on shelves and lockers, calendars, rule signs, and directions.

3. Intentionally read big-print and oversized books to teach print conventions such as directionality.

4. Practice exercises in reading to others (for K-1 or K-2), where young children practice how to handle a book, how to turn pages, how to find tops and bottoms of pages, and how to tell the difference between the front and back covers of a book.

5. Search and discuss adventures in word awareness and close observation, where children are challenged to identify and talk about the length, appearance, and boundaries of specific words and the letters which comprise them.

6. Have children match oral words to printed words by forming an echo chorus. As the teacher reads the story aloud, they echo the reading. Often this works best with poetry or rhymes.

7. Have the children combine, manipulate, switch, and move letters to change words and spelling patterns.

8. Work with letter cards to create messages and respond to the messages that they create.

Use of Reading and Writing Strategies for Teaching Letter-Sound Correspondence

Provide children with a sample of a single letter book (or create one from environmental sources, newspapers, coupons, circulars, magazines, or your own text ideas). Make sure that your already-published or created sample includes a printed version of the letter in both upper and lower case forms. Make certain that each page contains a picture of something that starts with that specific letter and also has the word for the picture. The book you select or create should be a predictable one in that when the picture is identified, the word can be read.

Once the children have been provided with your sample and have listened to it being read, challenge them to each make a one letter book. Often it is best to focus on familiar consonants for the single letter book or the first letter of the child's first name. Use of the first letter of the child's first name invites the child to develop a book which tells about him or her and the words that he or she finds. This is an excellent way to have the reading workshop aspect of the teacher's teaching of alphabetic principle complement and enhance the writing workshop. Encourage children to be active writers and readers by finding words for their book on the classroom word wall, in alphabet books in the special alphabet book bin, and in grade- and age-appropriate pictionaries (dictionaries for younger children which are filled with pictures).

Students need numerous opportunities to write for various purposes. Writing should be a daily activity in all classrooms, and students should be instructed in the writing process. The components of the writing process are:

- Prewriting – Brainstorming, webbing, story maps: these are a few ways that students can generate ideas for their writing. For younger writers, a picture can be the stimulus for writing. They draw a picture and then write a few sentences about the picture. For older writers, teachers can provide the picture or a prompt to generate ideas for writing.
- Drafting – Students get their ideas down on paper. Teachers should not worry about proper spelling or conventions. The main idea is to get the students writing. Correcting the mistakes is part of the editing process.
- Revising – In this stage of the writing process, students reread the writing to determine where they can add in ideas or delete some things. They can also change around parts of the writing so that it flows more smoothly.
- Editing – This section of the writing process sees the students correcting the writing for conventions of grammar and correct spelling.
- Publishing – In this component, the students prepare the writing to be displayed on a bulletin board or to be published in some other way. It is important to note that not all writing needs to be brought to this stage.

When students are given a writing assignment, the first instinct is to start writing. They also want to finish the piece and pass it in without reading it over or editing it. It is a chore to rewrite a draft, so teachers need to model this for them to teach them that rewriting is what all writers do.

Prewriting activities set the stage for writing in the classroom. Students need guidance in terms of how to plan for their writing and instruction in how to brainstorm and use a web, story map, or some other graphic organizer to help them organize their thoughts. Modelling by the teacher helps the students understand the steps they need to take to tackle different forms of writing. The instruction needs to be very explicit so that students can see and hear every action they should take with their own writing. The prewriting activities include planning the writing, considering the purpose, and in the case of a research project, they can consider where they will get the information they will need.

During the drafting stage, students will be putting their ideas on paper. The quality of the text should not be a concern at this point, as it is more important for the students to just write. Students may even use inventive spelling in this stage and not bother with capitalization or punctuation depending on their stage in the development of writing.

Revising and editing stages are the ones where teachers do have to spend the most time teaching the concepts. In revising, students have to look at the relationship of the sentences and decide whether or not the piece flows smoothly. They may have to read the text out loud, as this is when they can really hear where the text does not make sense. Teachers can work with students to revise their work by asking them to add in information to clarify a point or to help them see where certain sentences do not fit together. Modelling is crucial here, and the use of exemplars can really demonstrate how the students can improve their work.

Editing for grammatical structure, correct spelling, punctuation, and capitalization is another issue in teaching the stages of writing. Here students need plenty of practice. Many teachers have mini-lessons as the need arises in student writing and provide practice in the form of worksheets. However, the students may get all the answers correct on the worksheets and still not edit their own work. For this reason, teachers should look for only specific things in a piece of writing so as not to confuse the students. Instead of marking the paper with red ink, ask the students to look for all the places where they should have used capital letters. On another occasion, ask the students to underline all the words they think may be spelled incorrectly. Do not overload them with too much editing all at once.

Peer editing also helps with revising and editing. Providing opportunities for students to work together in small groups or pairs to edit each other's work not only helps the writer, but also helps the other student gain experience in editing and revising.

Once the writing has been revised and edited to the student's satisfaction, he/she can decide how to publish the work or even whether or not to publish. The student can rewrite the piece in good handwriting or even use a word processor. Colored paper and the use of colorful illustrations give the students the opportunity to take pride in their work and to display it for others to see.

COMPETENCY 4.0 UNDERSTAND EFFECTIVE COMMUNICATION THROUGH THE USE OF LISTENING AND SPEAKING SKILLS

Skill 4.1 Demonstrate understanding of concepts related to communication theory, language development, language diversity, and the role of language in learning (e.g., the cultural dimensions of communication, the significance of nonverbal cues in communication)

One of the most important things to know about the differences between L1 (first language) and L2 (second language) acquisition is that people usually will master L1, but they will almost never be fully proficient in L2. However, if children can be trained in L2 before about the age of seven, their chances at full mastery will be much higher. Children learn language with so little effort, which is why they can be babbling one year and speaking with complete, complex ideas just a few years later. It is important to know that language is innate, meaning that our brains are ready to learn a language from birth. Yet a lot of language learning is behavioral, meaning that children imitate adults' speech.

L2 acquisition is much harder for adults. Multiple theories of L2 acquisition have come about. Some of the more notable ones come from Jim Cummins. Cummins argues that there are two types of language that usually need to be acquired by students learning English as a second language: Basic Interpersonal Communication Skills (BICS) and Cognitive Academic Language Proficiency (CALP). BICS is general, everyday language used to communicate simple thoughts, whereas CALP is the more complex, academic language used in school. It is harder for students to acquire CALP, and many teachers mistakenly assume that students can learn complex academic concepts in English if they have already mastered BICS. The truth is that CALP takes much longer to master, and in some cases, particularly with little exposure in certain subjects, it may never be mastered.

Another set of theories is based on Stephen Krashen's research in L2 acquisition. Most people understand his theories based on five principles:

1. The acquisition-learning hypothesis: This states that there is a difference between learning a language and acquiring it. Children "acquire" a first language easily—it's natural. But adults often have to "learn" a language through coursework, studying, and memorizing. One can acquire a second language, but often it requires more deliberate and natural interaction within that language.
2. The monitor hypothesis: This is when the learned language "monitors" the acquired language. In other words, this is when a person's "grammar check" kicks in and keeps awkward, incorrect language out of a person's L2 communication.
3. The natural order hypothesis: This suggests that the learning of grammatical structures is predictable and follows a "natural order."

4. The input hypothesis: Some people call this "comprehensible input." This means that a language learner will learn best when the instruction or conversation is just above the learner's ability. That way, the learner has the foundation to understand most of the language, but still will have to figure out, often in context, what that extra more difficult element means.

5. The affective filter hypothesis: This suggests that people will learn a second language when they are relaxed, have high levels of motivation, and have a decent level of self-confidence.

Teaching students who are learning English as a second language poses some unique challenges, particularly in a standards-based environment. The key is realizing that no matter how little English a student knows, the teacher should teach with the student's developmental level in mind. This means that instruction should not be "dumbed-down" for ESOL students. Different approaches should be used, however, to ensure that these students (a) get multiple opportunities to learn and practice English, and (b) still learn content.

Many ESOL approaches are based on social learning methods. By being placed in mixed-level groups or by being paired with a student of another ability level, students will get a chance to practice English in a natural, non-threatening environment. Students should not be pushed in these groups to use complex language or to experiment with words that are too difficult. They should simply get a chance to practice with simple words and phrases.

In teacher-directed instructional situations, visual aids, such as pictures, objects, and video are particularly effective at helping students make connections between words and items they are already familiar with.

ESOL students may need additional accommodations with assessments, assignments, and projects. For example, teachers may find that written tests provide little to no information about a student's understanding of the content. Therefore, an oral test may be better suited for ESOL students. When students are somewhat comfortable and capable with written tests, a shortened test may actually be preferable; take note that they will need extra time to translate.

Nonverbal Communication

In the intercultural communication model, students are able to learn how different cultures engage in both verbal and nonverbal modes of communicating meaning. Students who become multilingual in understanding the stereotypes that have defined other cultures are able to create new bonding experiences that will typify a more integrated global culture. Students who understand how to effectively communicate with diverse cultural groups are able to maximize their own learning experiences by being able to transmit, both verbally and nonverbally, cues and expectations in project collaborations and in performance-based activities.

The learning curve for teachers in intercultural understanding is exponential in that they are able to engage all learners in the academic process and learning engagement. Teaching students how to incorporate learning techniques from a cultural aspect enriches the cognitive expansion experience, since students are able to expand their cultural knowledge bases.

Skill 4.2   Apply knowledge of listening strategies for various purposes and contexts (e.g., acquiring or analyzing information, appreciating literature read aloud, social interaction, personal response)

Informal and formal language is a distinction made on the basis of the occasion as well as the audience. At a "formal" occasion, such as a meeting of executives or of government officials, for example, even conversational exchanges are likely to be more formal. A cocktail party or a golf game is an example where the language is likely to be informal. Formal language uses fewer or no contractions, less slang, longer sentences, and more organization in longer segments.

Speeches delivered to executives, college professors, government officials, etc., are likely to be formal. Speeches made to fellow employees are likely to be informal. Sermons tend to be formal; Bible lessons will tend to be informal.

Different from the basic writing forms of discourse is the art of debating, discussion, and conversation. The ability to use language and logic to convince the audience to accept your reasoning and to side with you is an art. This form of writing/speaking is extremely confined/structured and logically sequenced, with supporting reasons and evidence. At its best, it is the highest form of propaganda. A position statement, evidence, reason, evaluation, and refutation are integral parts of this writing schema.

Interviewing provides opportunities for students to apply expository and informative communication. It teaches them how to structure questions to evoke fact-filled responses. Compiling the information from an interview into a biographical essay or speech helps students to list, sort, and arrange details in an orderly fashion.

Speeches that encourage students to describe persons, places, or events in their own lives or oral interpretations of literature help them sense the creativity and effort used by professional writers.

Skill 4.3   Recognize factors that affect children's development of listening skills and their ability to listen effectively and construct meaning in various situations, and strategies for addressing listening needs

Listening is not a skill that is talked about much, except when someone clearly does not listen. The truth is, though, that listening is a very specific skill for very specific circumstances. There are two aspects to listening that warrant attention. The first is comprehension. This is simply understanding what someone says, the purpose behind the message, and the context in which it is said. The second is purpose. While someone may completely understand a message, what is the listener supposed to do with it? Just nod and smile? Go out and take action? While listening comprehension is indeed a significant skill in itself that deserves a lot of focus in the classroom (much in the same way that reading comprehension does), we will focus on purpose here. Often, when we understand the purpose of listening in various contexts, comprehension will be much easier. Furthermore, when we know the purpose of listening, we can better adjust our comprehension strategies.

First, when complex or new information is provided to us orally, we must analyze and interpret that information. What is the author's most important point? How do the figures of speech impact meaning? How are conclusions arrived at? Often, making sense of this information can be tough when presented orally: first, because we have no place to go back and review material already stated; second, because oral language is so much less predictable and even than written language. However, when we focus on extracting the meaning, message, and speaker's purpose, rather than just "listen" and wait for things to make sense for us—in other words, when we are more "active" in our listening—we have greater success in interpreting speech.

Second, listening is often done for the purpose of enjoyment. We like to listen to stories; we enjoy poetry; we like radio dramas and theater. Listening to literature can also be a great pleasure. The problem today is that students have not learned how to extract great pleasure on a widespread scale from listening to literature, poetry, or language read aloud. Perhaps that is because we have not done a good enough job of showing students how listening to literature, for example, can indeed be more interesting than television or video games. In the classrooms of exceptional teachers, we will often find that students are captivated by the reading aloud of good literature. It is refreshing and enjoyable to just sit and soak in the language, story, and poetry of literature being read aloud. Therefore, we must teach students *how* to listen and enjoy such work. We do this by making it fun and giving many possibilities and alternatives to capture the wide array of interests in each classroom.

Finally, we will discuss listening in large and small group conversation. The difference here is that conversation requires more than just listening: It involves feedback and active involvement. This can be particularly challenging, as in our culture, we are trained to move conversations along, to discourage silence in a conversation, and to always get the last word in. This poses significant problems for the art of listening. In a discussion, for example, when we are instead preparing our next response—rather than listening to what others are saying—we do a large disservice to the entire discussion. Students need to learn how listening carefully to others in discussions actually promotes better responses on the part of subsequent speakers. One way teachers can encourage this in both large and small group discussions is to expect students to respond *directly* to the previous student's comments before moving ahead with their new comments. This will encourage them to pose their new comments in light of the comments that came just before them.

Strategies for active listening

Oral speech can be very difficult to follow. First, we have no written record in which to "reread" things we didn't hear or understand. Second, oral speech can be much less structured or even than written language. Yet, aside from re-reading, many of the skills and strategies that help us in reading comprehension can help us in listening comprehension. For example, as soon as we start listening to something new, we should tap into our prior knowledge in order to attach new information to what we already know. This will not only help us understand the new information more quickly, it will also assist us in remembering the material.

We can also look for transitions between ideas. Sometimes, in oral speech, this is pretty simple when voice tone or body language changes. Of course, we don't have the luxury of looking at paragraphs in oral language, but we do have the animation that comes along with live speech. Human beings have to try very hard to be completely non-expressive in their speech. Listeners should take advantage of this and notice how the speaker changes character and voice in order to signal a transition of ideas.

Speaking of animation of voice and body language, listeners can also better comprehend the underlying intents of authors when they notice nonverbal cues. Simply looking to see expression on the face of a speaker can do more to signal irony, for example, than trying to extract irony from actual words. And often in oral speech, unlike written text, elements like irony are not indicated by the actual words, but rather by the tone and nonverbal cues.

One good way to follow oral speech is to take notes and outline major points. Because oral speech can be more circular (as opposed to linear) than written text, it can be of great assistance to keep track of an author's message. Students can learn this strategy in many ways in the classroom: by taking notes of the teacher's oral messages as well as other students' presentations and speeches. Other classroom methods can help students learn good listening skills. For example, teachers can have students practice following complex directions. They can also have students orally retell stories, or retell (in writing or in oral speech) oral presentations of stories or other materials. These activities give students direct practice in the very important skill of listening. They provide students with outlets in which they can slowly improve their abilities to comprehend oral language and take decisive action based on oral speech.

Effective listening

Teachers should relate to students the specific purpose of their reading assignment. This will help them to:

- ASSOCIATE: Relate ideas to each other.
- VISUALIZE: Try to see pictures in your mind as you read.
- CONCENTRATE: Have a specific purpose for reading.
- REPEAT: Keep telling yourself important points and associate details to these points.

Oral language (listening and speaking) involves receiving and understanding messages sent by other people and also expressing our own feelings and ideas. Students must learn that listening is a communication process, and in order to be successful, it must be an active process. In other words, they must be an active participant in this communication process. In active listening, meaning and evaluation of a message must take place before a student can respond to the teacher.

Evaluating Messages

Analyzing the speech of others is a very good technique for helping students improve their own public speaking abilities. Because in most circumstances, students cannot view themselves as they give speeches and presentations, when they get the opportunity to critique, question, and analyze others' speeches, they begin to learn what works and what doesn't work in effective public speaking. However, a very important word of warning: DO NOT have students critique each others' public speaking skills. It could be very damaging to a student to have his or her peers point out what did not work in a speech. Instead, video is a great tool teachers can use. Any appropriate source of public speaking can be used in the classroom for students to analyze and critique.

Some of the things students can pay attention to include the following:

- Volume: A speaker should use an appropriate volume: not too loud to be annoying, but not too soft to be inaudible.
- Pace: The rate at which words are spoken should be appropriate: not too fast to make the speech non-understandable, but not too slow so as to put listeners to sleep.
- Pronunciation: A speaker should make sure words are spoken clearly. Listeners do not have a text to go back and reread things they didn't catch.
- Body language: While animated body language can help a speech, too much of it can be distracting. Body language should help convey the message, not detract from it.
- Word choice: The words speakers choose should be consistent with their intended purpose and the audience.
- Visual aids: Visual aids, like body language, should enhance a message. Many visual aids can be distracting, and that detracts from the message.

Overall, instead of telling students to keep these above factors in mind when presenting information orally, having them view speakers who do these things well and poorly will help them know and remember the next time they give a speech.

Responding to messages

How students respond to messages is more than communication going from one person's mouth to the teacher's ear. In addition to the words, messages are transferred by eye contact, physical closeness, tone of voice, visual cues, and overall body language. Language employs symbols— gestures, visual clues, or spoken sounds—to represent communication between the teacher and the student. Children first learn to respond to messages by listening to and understanding what they hear (supported by overall body language); next, they experiment with expressing themselves through speaking.

As children become proficient in language, they expect straight messages from the teacher. A straight message is one in which words, vocal expression, and body movements are all congruent. Students need to feel secure and safe. If the message is not straight; if the words say one thing but the tone and facial expression say another, the child is confused. When students are confused, they often feel threatened in the school environment.

Remembering message content

Reading is more than pronouncing the words correctly; the reader has to gain meaning from the words. A competent reader can pronounce the words on a page, remember what they mean, and learn information from them.

The processes that increase the student's ability to remember:

- ASSOCIATION: When you associate, you make the things you want to remember relate to each other in some way.
- VISUALIZATION: Visualization helps you to create a strong, vivid memory. Try to picture in your mind what you wish to remember.
- CONCENTRATION: Concentration can be defined as focusing attention on one thing and one thing only. How can you learn to concentrate better? Visualizing will help because it forces attention to one thing only. If you try to see specific pictures as you read, it will help you to concentrate. Making sure of your purpose is a third way to force concentration. When you read for a particular purpose, you will concentrate on what you read.
- REPETITION: When you have difficulty remembering textbook information, you should repeat the procedures for associating, visualizing, and concentration. The repetition will help retain the information in your memory.

Skill 4.4   Recognize strategies for organizing and presenting ideas and information for different audiences and purposes (e.g., to inform, persuade, entertain; to participate in group discussions)

In public speaking, not all speeches deserve the same type of speaking style. For example, when providing a humorous speech, it is important to utilize body language in order to accent humorous moments. However, when giving instructions, it is extremely important to speak clearly and slowly, carefully noting the mood of the audience, so that if there is general confusion on peoples' faces, the speaker can go back and review something. In group discussions, it is important for speakers to ensure that they are listening to other speakers carefully and tailoring their messages so that the messages fit into the general mood and location of the discussion at hand. When giving an oral presentation, the mood should be both serious and friendly. The speaker should focus on ensuring that the content is covered, while also relating to audience members as much as possible.

As students practice these skills, they can receive guidance and modeling from videos of various types of speeches appropriate to the types they are giving themselves. Also, the various attributes of each type of oral speaking strategy should be covered with students so that they can clearly hear the differences.

Skill 4.5 Recognize factors that affect children's development of speaking skills, signs that a child may be experiencing difficulties in language development, and strategies for addressing oral language needs

Some of the factors that can affect children's development in speaking skills include:

- The child has not received enough stimulation. From the earliest age, children need to be talked to and played with.
- Some children have developmental delay, a delay in the development of motor skills, or a delay in cognitive development.
- The first language may not be English, which will affect how well the child speaks and whether or not the child is reluctant to speak.
- There may be a medical problem involving the muscles needed for speech.
- There may be a lack of knowledge about how to communicate effectively.
- Hearing problems can cause problems with speech development.
- The child may not have enough opportunities to speak, such as having many siblings or one older sibling who is very dominant.
- A short attention span can result in speech problems, because the child's mind jumps from one idea to another.
- There may be a history of speech problems in the family.

Signs that the teacher can look for to indicate that a child is experiencing difficulties in language development include:

- Difficulty understanding speech
- The child distorts sounds
- Substitution of sounds
- Omission of sounds
- Adding extra sounds to words
- Confusing the sequence of sounds in words

Strategies to use when addressing oral language needs include:

-   Slow down the rate at which the teacher speaks in the classroom.
-   Maintain eye contact with the student.
-   Allow the student plenty of time to answer.
-   Model a low rate of speech, speaking distinctly.
-   Model the correct pronunciation when a student makes a mistake.
-   Don't ask open-ended questions if the student does have speech problems.
-   Encourage the student to use full sentences when answering questions, instead of one word answers.
-   Point out the sounds of letters.
-   Compare sounds with each other.
-   Teach the student how to position the tongue to make certain sounds.

COMPETENCY 5.0   UNDERSTAND LITERACY DEVELOPMENT AND HOW TO USE EFFECTIVE, DEVELOPMENTALLY APPROPRIATE STRATEGIES TO PROMOTE STUDENTS' LITERARY SKILLS

Skill 5.1   Demonstrate knowledge of children's literacy development, factors that influence the development of reading skills, signs that a child may be experiencing difficulties in reading, and strategies for addressing reading needs

If there were two words which could be synonymous with reading comprehension as far as the balanced literacy approach is concerned, they would be "Constructing Meaning."

Cooper, Taberski, Strickland, and other key theorists and classroom teachers conceptualize the reader as designating a specific meaning to the text using both clues in the text and his/her own prior knowledge. Comprehension for the balanced literacy theorists is a strategic process.

The reader interacts with the text and brings his/her prior knowledge and experience to it or LACK of prior knowledge and experience to it. Writing is interlaced with reading and is a mutually integrative and supportive parallel process. Hence the division of literacy learning by the balanced literacy folks into reading workshop and writing workshop, with the same anchor readings or books being used for both.

Consider the sentence,

"The test booklet was white with black print, but very scary looking."

According to the idea of constructing meaning as the reader reads this sentence, the schemata (generic information stored in the mind) of tests that he or she has personally activated by the author's ideas that tests are scary. Therefore the ultimate meaning that the reader derives from the page is from the reader's own responses and experiences with the ideas the author presents. The reader constructs a meaning that reflects the author's intent and also the reader's response to that intent.

It is also to be remembered that generally readings are fairly lengthy passages, comprised of paragraphs which in turn are comprised of more than one sentence. With each successive sentence, and in every new paragraph, the reader refocuses. The schemata are reconsidered, and a new meaning is constructed.

The purpose of reading is to convert visual images (the letters and words) into a message. Pronouncing the words is not enough; the reader must be able to extract the meaning of the text. When people read, they utilize four sources of background information to comprehend the meaning behind the literal text (Reid, pp.166-171).

1. *Word Knowledge:* Information about words and letters. One's knowledge about word meanings is *lexical knowledge*—a sort of dictionary. Knowledge about spelling patterns and pronunciations is *orthographic knowledge.* Poor readers do not develop the level of automatically in using orthographic knowledge to identify words and decode unfamiliar words.

2. *Syntax and Contextual Information:* When children encounter unknown words in a sentence, they rely on their background knowledge to choose a word that makes sense. Errors of younger children therefore are often substitutions of words in the same syntactic class. Poor readers often fail to make use of contextual clues to help them identify words or activate the background knowledge that would help them with comprehension. Poor readers also process sentences word by word, instead of "chunking" phrases and clauses, resulting in a slow pace that focuses on the decoding rather than comprehension. They also have problems answering wh- (who, what, where, when, why) questions as a result of these problems with syntax.

3. *Semantic Knowledge:* This includes the reader's background knowledge about a topic, which is combined with the text information as the reader tries to comprehend the material. New information is compared to the background information and incorporated into the reader's schema. Poor readers have problems with using their background knowledge, especially with passages that require inference or cause-and-effect.

4. *Text Organization:* Good readers are able to differentiate types of text structure, e.g., story narrative, exposition, compare-contrast, or time sequence. They use knowledge of text to build expectations and construct a framework of ideas on which to build meaning. Poor readers may not be able to differentiate types of text and miss important ideas. They may also miss important ideas and details by concentrating on lesser or irrelevant details.

Research on reading development has yielded information on the behaviors and habits of good readers vs. poor readers. Some of the characteristics of good readers are:

- They think about the information that they will read in the text, formulate questions that they predict will be answered in the text, and confirm those predictions from the information in the text.

- When faced with unfamiliar words, they attempt to pronounce them using analogies to familiar words.

- Before reading, good readers establish a purpose for reading, select possible text structure, choose a reading strategy, and make predictions about what will be in the reading.

- As they read, good readers continually test and confirm their predictions, go back when something does not make sense, and make new predictions.

Skill 5.2 **Recognize factors that affect a reader's construction of meaning through interactions with text (e.g., prior knowledge and experiences, reading rate, characteristics of the text)**

  o See Skill 1.3

Skill 5.3 **Demonstrate knowledge of print concepts (e.g., letter, word, and sentence representation; directionality; tracking); of ways to assess students' understanding of print; and of instructional strategies, activities, and materials for promoting students' interaction with print in varied and meaningful contexts**

Understanding that print carries meaning is demonstrated every day in the elementary classroom as the teacher holds up a selected book to read it aloud to the class. The teachers explicitly and deliberately think aloud about how to hold the book, how to focus the class on looking at its cover, where to start reading, and in what direction to begin.

Even in writing the morning message on the board, the teacher targets the children on the placement of the message and its proper place at the top of the board, to be followed by additional activities and a schedule for the rest of the day.

When the teacher challenges children to make letter posters of a single letter and identify the items in the classroom, their home, or their knowledge base which start with that letter, the children are making concrete the understanding that print carries meaning.

Teachers need to look for five basic behaviors in students:

- Do students know how to hold the book?
- Can students match speech to print?
- Do students know the difference between letters and words?
- Do students know that print conveys meaning?
- Can students track print from left to right?

In order for students to understand concepts of print, they must be able to recognize text and understand the various mechanics that text contains. This includes the following:

- All text contains a message.
- The English language has a specific structure.
- In order to decode words and read text, students must be able to understand that structure.

The structure of the English language consists of rules of grammar, capitalization, and punctuation. For younger children, this means being able to recognize letters and form words. For older children, it means being able to recognize different types of text, such as lists, stories, and signs, and know the purpose of each one.

When reading to children, teachers point to words as they read them. Illustrations and pictures also contribute to being able to understand the meaning of the text. Therefore, teachers should also discuss illustrations related to the text.

When reading to students, teachers also discuss the common characteristics of books (author, title page, table of contents, etc.). Asking students to predict what the story might be about is a good strategy to employ to help teach students about the cover and its importance to the story. Pocket charts, big books, and song charts provide ample opportunity for teachers to point to words as they read.

Instructional Strategies:

1. Using big books in the classroom

Gather the children around you in a group with the big book placed on a stand. This allows all children to see the words and pictures. As you read, point to each word. It is best to use a pointer so that you are not covering any other words or part of the page. When students read from the big book on their own, have them also use the pointer for each word.

When students begin reading from smaller books, have them transfer what they have learned about pointing to the words by using their finger to track the reading.

Observation is a key point in assessing students' ability to track words and speech.

2. A classroom rich in print

Having words from a familiar rhyme or poem in a pocket chart lends itself to an activity where the students arrange the words in the correct order and then read the rhyme. This is an instructional strategy that reinforces directionality of print. It also reinforces punctuation, capitalization, and matching print to speech.

Using highlighters or sticky tabs to locate upper- and lowercase letters or specific words can help students isolate words and learn about the structure of language, which they need to understand for reading.

There should be plenty of books in the classroom for children to read on their own or in small groups. As you observe each of these groups, take note of how the child holds the book in addition to how he/she tracks and reads the words.

3. Word wall

The use of a word wall is a great teaching tool for words in isolation and with writing. Each of the letters of the alphabet is displayed with words underneath, and each word begins with that letter. Students then find the letter on the wall and read the words under each one.

4. Sounds of the letters

In addition to teaching the letter names, students should learn the corresponding sound of each letter. This is a key feature of decoding when beginning to read. The use of rhyming words is an effective way to teach letter sounds so that children have a solid background in connecting sounds to letters.

Students should be exposed to daily opportunities for viewing and reading texts. Teachers can do this by engaging the students in discussions about books during shared, guided, and independent reading times. The teacher should draw the students' attention to the conventions of print and discuss with them the reasons for choosing different books. For example, teachers should let the students know that it is perfectly acceptable to return a book and select another if they think it is too hard for them.

Predictable books help engage the students in reading. Once the students realize what words are repeated in the text, they will eagerly chime in to repeat the words at the appropriate time during the reading. Rereading of texts helps the students learn the words and helps them to read these lines fluently.

Some things for teachers to observe during reading are:

- Students' responses during reading conferences, such as pointing to letters or words
- Students ability to say when they should begin reading and how they know to stop or pause depending on the punctuation
- Student behavior when holding a book (e.g., holding the book right side up or upside down, reading from left to right, stopping to look at the pictures to confirm meaning)

Skill 5.4   Demonstrate knowledge of spelling development and its significance for reading; of ways to assess students' spelling skills; and of effective instructional strategies, activities, and materials for promoting students' spelling skills

The Alphabetic Principle is sometimes called Graphophonemic Awareness. This multisyllabic technical reading foundation term details the understanding that written words are composed of patterns of letters which represent the sounds of spoken words.

There are basically two parts to the alphabetic principle:

- An understanding that words are made up of letters, and that each of these letters has a specific sound.
- The correspondence between sounds and letters leads to phonological reading. This consists of reading regular and irregular words and doing an advanced analysis of words.

Since the English language is dependent on the alphabet, being able to recognize and sound out letters is the first step for beginning readers. Relying simply on memorization for recognition of words is just not feasible as a way for children to learn to recognize words. Therefore decoding is essential. The most important goal of beginning reading teachers is to teach students to decode text so that they can read fluently and with understanding.

There are four basic features of the alphabetic principle:

1. Students need to be able to take spoken words apart and blend different sounds together to make new words.
2. Students need to apply letter sounds to all of their reading.
3. Teachers need to use a systematic, effective program in order to teach children to read.
4. The teaching of the alphabetic principle usually begins in kindergarten.

It is important to keep in mind that some children already know the letters and sounds before they come to school. Others may catch on to this quite quickly, and still others need to have one-on-one instruction in order to learn to read.

Critical skills that students need to learn are the following:

- Letter-sound correspondence
- How to sound out words
- How to decode text to make meaning

See also Skill 1.2.

Skill 5.5   Relate reading development to the development of skills in oral and written language

When students practice fluency, they practice reading connected pieces of text. In other words, instead of looking at a word as just a word, they might read a sentence straight through. The point of this is that in order for the student to comprehend what she is reading, she would need to be able to "fluently" piece words in a sentence together quickly. If a student is NOT fluent in reading, he or she would sound each letter or word out slowly and pay more attention to the phonics of each word. A fluent reader, on the other hand, might read a sentence out loud using appropriate intonations. The best way to test for fluency, in fact, is to have a student read something out loud, preferably a few sentences in a row—or more. Sure, most students just learning to read will probably not be very fluent right away; but with practice, they will increase their fluency. Even though fluency is not the same as comprehension, it is said that fluency is a good predictor of comprehension. Think about it: if you're focusing too much on sounding out each word, you're not going to be paying attention to the meaning.

During the preschool years, children acquire cognitive skills in oral language that they apply later on to reading comprehension. Reading aloud to young children is one of the most important things that an adult can do, because they are teaching children how to monitor, question, predict, and confirm what they hear in the stories. (Reid, 1988, p. 165) described four metalinguistic abilities that young children acquire through early involvement in reading activities:

1. *Word consciousness.* Children who have access to books first can tell the story through the pictures. Gradually they begin to realize the connection between the spoken words and the printed words. The beginning of letter and word discrimination begins in the early years.

2. *Language and conventions of print.* During this stage children learn the way to hold a book, where to begin to read, the left to right motion, and how to continue from one line to another.

3. *Functions of print.* Children discover that print can be used for a variety of purposes and functions, including entertainment and information.

The typical variation in literacy backgrounds that children bring to reading can make teaching more difficult. Often a teacher has to choose between focusing on the learning needs of a few students at the expense of the group, and focusing on the group at the risk of leaving some students behind academically. This situation is particularly critical for children with gaps in their literacy knowledge, who may be at risk in subsequent grades for becoming "diverse learners."

Areas of Emerging Evidence

1. Experiences with print (through reading and writing) help preschool children develop an understanding of the conventions, purpose, and functions of print. Children learn about print from a variety of sources and in the process come to realize that print carries the story. They also learn how text is structured visually (i.e., text begins at the top of the page, moves from left to right, and carries over to the next page when it is turned). While knowledge about the conventions of print enables children to understand the physical structure of language, the conceptual knowledge that printed words convey a message also helps children bridge the gap between oral and written language.

2. Phonological awareness and letter recognition contribute to initial reading acquisition by helping children develop efficient word recognition strategies (e.g., detecting pronunciations and storing associations in memory.) Phonological awareness and knowledge of print-speech relations play an important role in facilitating reading acquisition. Therefore, phonological awareness instruction should be an integral component of early reading programs. Within the emergent literacy research, viewpoints diverge on whether acquisition of phonological awareness and letter recognition are preconditions of literacy acquisition or whether they develop interdependently with literacy activities, such as story reading and writing.

3. Storybook reading affects children's knowledge about, strategies for, and attitudes towards reading. Of all the strategies intended to promote growth in literacy acquisition, none is as commonly practiced, nor as strongly supported across the emergent literacy literature, as storybook reading. Children in different social and cultural groups have differing degrees of access to storybook reading. For example, it is not unusual for a teacher to have students who have experienced thousands of hours of story reading time, along with other students who have had little or no such exposure.

Learning approach

Early theories of language development were formulated from learning theory research. The assumption was that language development evolved from learning the rules of language structures and applying them through imitation and reinforcement. This approach also assumed that language, cognitive, and social developments were independent of each other. Thus, children were expected to learn language from patterning after adults who spoke and wrote standard English. No allowance was made for communication through child jargon, idiomatic expressions, or grammatical and mechanical errors resulting from too strict adherence to the rules of inflection (*childs* instead of *children*) or conjugation (*runned* instead of *ran*). No association was made between physical and operational development and language mastery.

Linguistic approach

Studies spearheaded by Noam Chomsky in the 1950s formulated the theory that language ability is innate and develops through natural human maturation as environmental stimuli trigger acquisition of syntactical structures appropriate to each exposure level. The assumption of a hierarchy of syntax downplayed the significance of semantics. Because of the complexity of syntax and the relative speed with which children acquire language, linguists attributed language development to biological rather than cognitive or social influences.

Cognitive approach

Researchers in the 1970s proposed that language knowledge derives from both syntactic and semantic structures. Drawing on the studies of Piaget and other cognitive learning theorists, supporters of the cognitive approach maintained that children acquire knowledge of linguistic structures after they have acquired the cognitive structures necessary to process language. For example, joining words for specific meaning necessitates sensory motor intelligence. The child must be able to coordinate movement and recognize objects before she can identify words to name the objects or word groups to describe the actions performed with those objects. Children must have developed the mental abilities for organizing concepts as well as concrete operations, predicting outcomes, and theorizing before they can assimilate and verbalize complex sentence structures, choose vocabulary for particular nuances of meaning, and examine semantic structures for tone and manipulative effect.

Sociocognitive approach

Other theorists in the 1970s proposed that language development results from sociolinguistic competence. Language, cognitive, and social knowledges are interactive elements of total human development. Emphasis on verbal communication as the medium for language expression resulted in the inclusion of speech activities in most language arts curricula.

Unlike previous approaches, the sociocognitive allowed that determining the appropriateness of language in given situations for specific listeners is as important as understanding semantic and syntactic structures. By engaging in conversation, children at all stages of development have opportunities to test their language skills, receive feedback, and make modifications. As a social activity, conversation is as structured by social order as grammar is structured by the rules of syntax. Conversation satisfies the learner's need to be heard and understood and to influence others. Thus, his choices of vocabulary, tone, and content are dictated by his ability to assess the language knowledge of his listeners. He is constantly applying his cognitive skills to using language in a social interaction. If the capacity to acquire language is inborn, without an environment in which to practice language, a child would not pass beyond grunts and gestures, as did primitive man.

Of course, the varying degrees of environmental stimuli to which children are exposed at all age levels creates a slower or faster development of language. Some children are prepared to articulate concepts and recognize symbolism by the time they enter fifth grade because they have been exposed to challenging reading and conversations with well-spoken adults at home or in their social groups. Others are still trying to master the sight recognition skills and are not yet ready to combine words into complex patterns.

Skill 5.6 Demonstrate knowledge of the importance of independent reading and effective approaches for guiding students to select independent reading materials and for motivating students to read independently

As with any learning experience, it is important for students to connect learning with real-world experiences. Therefore with reading, students should be given opportunities to experience reading outside the classroom or traditional classroom methods.

Literature Circles involve a group discussion with no more than six children, but usually under four, who have read the same work of literature (narrative or expository text). They talk about key parts of the work, relate it to their own experience, listen to the responses of others, and discuss how parts of the text relate to the whole. Literature circles are excellent for the classroom setting, because they mimic book clubs while providing a format for the discussion meeting for students who are learning to discuss literature.

Book clubs are another excellent opportunity for students to discuss reading in an open setting. Whether it be at a local library, school library group, recess group, or parent-child evening reading program, book clubs promote reading in an enjoyable setting unattached from traditional homework assignments and book reports.

DOMAIN II.   MATHEMATICS

COMPETENCY 6.0   APPLY A VARIETY OF APPROACHES (e.g., ESTIMATION, MENTAL MATHEMATICS, FORMAL AND INFORMAL REASONING, MODELING, PATTERN RECOGNITION, TECHNOLOGY) TO SOLVE PROBLEMS; INVESTIGATE REAL-WORLD SITUATIONS; AND ANALYZE, INTERPRET, AND COMMUNICATE MATHEMATICAL IDEAS AND INFORMATION

Skill 6.1   Apply knowledge of appropriate mathematical strategies (e.g., mental computation; working backwards; numerical, geometric, and algebraic pattern recognition) to analyze mathematical ideas, solve problems, and investigate real-world situations

Successful math teachers introduce their students to multiple problem-solving strategies and create a classroom environment where free thought and experimentation are encouraged. Teachers can promote problem solving by allowing multiple attempts at problems, giving credit for reworking test or homework problems, and encouraging the sharing of ideas through class discussion. There are several specific problem-solving skills with which teachers should be familiar.

The **guess-and-check** strategy calls for students to make an initial guess at the solution, check the answer, and use the outcome to guide the next guess. With each successive guess, the student should get closer to the correct answer. Constructing a table from the guesses can help organize the data.

Example: There are 100 coins in a jar, and 10 are dimes. The rest are pennies and nickels. There are twice as many pennies as nickels. How many pennies and nickels are in the jar?

There are 90 total nickels and pennies in the jar (100 coins – 10 dimes).

There are twice as many pennies as nickels. Make guesses that fulfill the criteria and adjust based on the answer found. Continue until you find the correct answer: 60 pennies and 30 nickels.

Number of Pennies	Number of Nickels	Total Number of Pennies and Nickels
40	20	60
80	40	120
70	35	105
60	30	90

When solving a problem where the final result and the steps to reach the result are given, students must **work backwards** to determine what the starting point must have been.

Example:
John subtracted 7 from his age, and divided the result by 3. The final result was 4. What is John's age?

Work backward by reversing the operations:
$4 \times 3 = 12$
$12 + 7 = 19$
John is 19 years old.

Estimation and testing for **reasonableness** are related skills students should employ prior to and after solving a problem. These skills are particularly important when students use calculators to find answers.

Example:
Find the sum of 4387 + 7226 + 5893.

$4300 + 7200 + 5800 = 17300$	Estimation.
$4387 + 7226 + 5893 = 17506$	Actual sum.

By comparing the estimate to the actual sum, students can determine that their answer is reasonable.

Skill 6.2   Apply knowledge of formal and informal mathematical reasoning processes (e.g., evaluating solutions to problems, judging the validity of arguments, using logical reasoning to draw and justify conclusions from given information)

A valid argument is a statement made about a pattern or relationship between elements, thought to be true, which is subsequently justified through repeated examples and logical reasoning. Another term for a valid argument is a proof.

For example, the statement that the sum of two odd numbers is always even could be tested through actual examples.

Two Odd Numbers	Sum	Validity of Statement
1+1	2 (even)	Valid
1+3	4 (even)	Valid
61+29	90 (even)	Valid
135+47	182 (even)	Valid
253+17	270 (even)	Valid
1,945+2,007	3,952 (even)	Valid
6,321+7,851	14,172 (even)	Valid

Adding two odd numbers always results in a sum that is even. It is a valid argument based on the justifications in the table above.

Here is another example. The statement that a fraction of a fraction can be determined by multiplying the numerator by the numerator and the denominator by the denominator can be proven through logical reasoning. For example, one-half of one-quarter of a candy bar can be found by multiplying $\frac{1}{2} \times \frac{1}{4}$. The answer would be one-eighth. The validity of this argument can be demonstrated with a model.

The entire rectangle represents one whole candy bar. The top-half section of the model is shaded in one direction to demonstrate how much of the candy bar remains from the whole candy bar. The left quarter, shaded in a different direction, demonstrates that one-quarter of the candy bar has been given to a friend. Since the whole candy bar is not available to give out, the area that is double-shaded is the fractional part of the one-half candy bar that has been actually given away. That fractional part is one-eighth of the whole candy bar, as shown in both the sketch and the algorithm.

Skill 6.3   Apply knowledge of how to interpret mathematical terminology, symbols, and representations and how to convert among graphic, numeric, symbolic, oral, and written representations of mathematical ideas and relationships

Students of mathematics must be able to recognize and interpret the different representations of arithmetic operations.

First, there are many different verbal descriptions for the operations of addition, subtraction, multiplication, and division. The table below identifies several words and/or phrases that are often used to denote the different arithmetic operations.

Operation	Descriptive Words
Addition	"plus," "combine," "sum," "total," "put together"
Subtraction	"minus," "less," "take away," "difference"
Multiplication	"product," "times," "groups of"
Division	"quotient," "into," "split into equal groups"

Second, diagrams of arithmetic operations can present mathematical data in visual form. For example, we can use the number line to add and subtract.

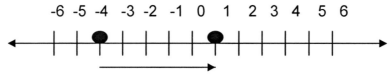

The addition of 5 to -4 on the number line: -4 + 5 = 1.

Finally, as shown in the examples below, we can use pictorial representations to explain all of the arithmetic processes.

Two groups of four equals eight, or 2 x 4 = 8 shown in picture form.

Adding three objects to two, or 2 + 3 = 5 shown in picture form.

See also Skill 8.2

Skill 6.4 **Apply knowledge of how to use graphic, numeric, symbolic, oral, and written representations to interpret and communicate mathematical information, reasoning, concepts, applications, and procedures**

o   See Skill 6.3

Skill 6.5 **Recognize common uses, benefits, and limitations of calculators and computers as tools for learning, exploration, and problem solving**

Calculators are an important tool. They should be encouraged in the classroom and at home. They do not replace basic knowledge, but they can relieve the tedium of mathematical computations, allowing students to explore more challenging mathematical directions. Students will be able to use calculators more intelligently if they are taught how. Students should always check their work by estimating. The goal of mathematics is to prepare the child to survive in the real world. Technology is a reality in today's society.

COMPETENCY 7.0   UNDERSTAND CONCEPTS AND SKILLS RELATED TO NUMBERS, NUMBER SENSE, AND NUMERATION (INCLUDING FRACTIONS, DECIMALS, RATIOS, AND PERCENTS) TO SUPPORT THE LEARNING OF MATHEMATICS

Skill 7.1   Apply knowledge of strategies for promoting the development of number sense in children and factors that can affect development

The real number system includes all rational and irrational numbers.

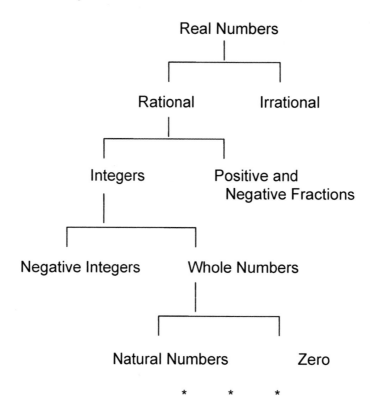

Rational numbers can be expressed as the ratio of two integers, $\frac{a}{b}$ where b ≠ 0. For example: $\frac{2}{3}$, $-\frac{4}{5}$, $5 = \frac{5}{1}$.

The rational numbers include integers, fractions and mixed numbers, terminating and repeating decimals. Every rational number can be expressed as a repeating or terminating decimal and can be shown on a number line.

Integers are positive and negative whole numbers and zero.
   ...-6, -5, -4, -3, -2, -1, 0, 1, 2, 3, 4, 5, 6, ...

Whole numbers are natural numbers and zero.
   0, 1, 2, 3, 4, 5 ,6 ...

Natural numbers are the counting numbers.

1, 2, 3, 4, 5, 6, ...

Irrational numbers are real numbers that cannot be written as the ratio of two integers. These are infinite non-repeating decimals.

Examples:

$\sqrt{5} = 2.2360..$, pi $=\prod = 3.1415927...$

Percent = per 100 (written with the symbol %). Thus $10\% = \dfrac{10}{100} = \dfrac{1}{10}$.

Decimals = deci = part of ten. To find the decimal equivalent of a fraction, use the denominator to divide the numerator as shown in the following examples.

Example:

Find the decimal equivalent of $\dfrac{7}{10}$.

$$
\begin{array}{r}
.7 \\
10\overline{)7.0} \\
70 \\
\hline
00
\end{array}
$$

Since 10 cannot divide into 7 evenly, put a decimal point in the answer row on top; put a zero behind 7 to make it 70. Continue the division process. If a remainder occurs, put a zero by the last digit of the remainder and continue the division.

Thus $\dfrac{7}{10} = 0.7$

It is a good idea to write a zero before the decimal point so that the decimal point is emphasized.

Example:

Find the decimal equivalent of $\dfrac{7}{125}$.

$$
\begin{array}{r}
.056 \\
125\overline{)7.000} \\
625 \\
\hline
750 \\
750 \\
\hline
0
\end{array}
$$

Example:
Convert 0.056 to a fraction.

Multiplying 0.056 by $\dfrac{1000}{1000}$ to get rid of the decimal point:

$$0.056 \times \dfrac{1000}{1000} = \dfrac{56}{1000} = \dfrac{7}{125}$$

Example:
Find 23% of 1000.

$$= \dfrac{23}{100} \times \dfrac{1000}{1} = 23 \times 10 = 230$$

Example:
Convert 6.25% to a fraction and to a mixed number.

$$6.25\% = 0.0625 = 0.0625 \times \dfrac{10000}{10000} = \dfrac{625}{10000} = \dfrac{1}{16}$$

Skill 7.2 Recognize and compare properties of whole numbers and the whole number system (e.g., commutative, distributive)

Real numbers exhibit the following addition and multiplication **properties**, where a, b, and c are real numbers.

Note: Multiplication is implied when there is no symbol between two variables. Thus, $a \times b$ can be written ab. Multiplication can also be indicated by a raised dot .

Closure
For all real numbers a and b,
$a + b$ is a unique real number.
ab is a unique real number.

Example:
Since 2 and 5 are both real numbers, 7 is also a real number.

Example:
Since 3 and 4 are both real numbers, 12 is also a real number.

Commutative

For all real numbers a and b,
a + b = b +a.
ab = ba.

Example:
5 + ⁻8 = ⁻8 + 5 = ⁻3

Example:
⁻2 × 6 = 6 × ⁻2 = ⁻12

Associative

For all real numbers a, b, and c,
(a + b) + c = a + (b + c).
(ab)c = a(bc).

Example:
(⁻2 + 7) + 5 = ⁻2 + (7 + 5)
    5 + 5 = ⁻2 + 12 = 10

Example:
(3 × ⁻7) × 5 = 3 × (⁻7 × 5)
    ⁻21 ×5 = 3 × ⁻35 = ⁻105

Additive Identity (Property of Zero)

There exists a unique real number 0 (zero) such that

a + 0 = 0 + a = a for every real number a.

Example:
17 + 0 = 17
The sum of any number and zero is that number.

Multiplicative Identity (Property of One)

There exists a unique nonzero real number 1 (one) such that $1 \cdot a = a \cdot 1 = a$.
$a \cdot 1 = a$

Example:
⁻34 × 1 = ⁻34
The product of any number and one is that number.

Additive Inverse (Property of Opposites)
For each real number *a*, there exists a real number –*a* (the opposite of *a*) such that the sum of any number and its opposite is zero. *a + (-a) = (-a) + a = 0.*

Example:
25 + ⁻25 = 0

Multiplicative Inverse (Property of Reciprocals)
For each nonzero real number, there exists a real number 1/*a* (the reciprocal of a) such that *a*(1/*a*) = (1/*a*)*a* = 1.

Example:
$5 \times \frac{1}{5} = 1$

The product of any number and its reciprocal is one.

Distributive
a (b + c) = ab + ac

Example:
6 × (⁻4 + 9) = (6 × ⁻4) + (6 × 9)
  6 × 5 = ⁻24 + 54 = 30

To multiply a sum by a number, multiply each addend by the number; then add the products.

Summary of the properties of operation

Property	Of Addition	Of Multiplication
Commutative	a + b = b + a	ab = ba
Associative	a + (b + c) = (a + b) + c	a(bc) = (ab)c
Identity	a + 0 = a	(a)(1) = a
Inverse	a + (-a) = 0	a· (1/a) = 1

Skill 7.3 Apply concepts of the number and numeration systems to compare, order, and round numbers

Whole Number Place Value
Consider the number 792. We can assign a place value to each digit.

Reading from left to right, the first digit (7) represents the hundreds' place. The hundreds' place tells us how many sets of one hundred the number contains. Thus, there are 7 sets of one hundred in the number 792.

The second digit (9) represents the tens' place. The tens' place tells us how many sets of ten the number contains. Thus, there are 9 sets of ten in the number 792.

The last digit (2) represents the ones' place. The ones' place tells us how many ones the number contains. Thus, there are 2 sets of one in the number 792.

Therefore, there are 7 sets of 100, plus 9 sets of 10, plus 2 ones in the number 792.

Decimal Place Value
More complex numbers have additional place values to both the left and right of the decimal point. Consider the number 374.8.

Reading from left to right, the first digit (3) is in the hundreds' place and tells us the number contains 3 sets of one hundred.

The second digit (7) is in the tens' place and tells us the number contains 7 sets of ten.

The third digit (4) is in the ones' place and tells us the number contains 4 ones.

Finally, the number after the decimal (8) is in the tenths' place and tells us the number contains 8 tenths.

Place Value for Older Students
Each digit to the left of the decimal point increases progressively in powers of ten. Each digit to the right of the decimal point decreases progressively in powers of ten.

Example:
12345.6789 occupies the following powers-of-ten positions:

10^4	10^3	10^2	10^1	10^0	0	10^{-1}	10^{-2}	10^{-3}	10^{-4}
1	2	3	4	5	.	6	7	8	9

Names of power-of-ten positions:

10^0 = ones (note that any nonzero base raised to power zero is 1).

10^1 = tens (number 1 and 1 zero or 10)

10^2 = hundred (number 1 and 2 zeros or 100)

10^3 = thousand (number 1 and 3 zeros or 1000)

10^4 = ten thousand (number 1 and 4 zeros or 10000)

$10^{-1} = \dfrac{1}{10^1} = \dfrac{1}{10}$ = tenths (1st digit after decimal point or 0.1)

$10^{-2} = \dfrac{1}{10^2} = \dfrac{1}{100}$ = hundredth (2nd digit after decimal point or 0.01)

$10^{-3} = \dfrac{1}{10^3} = \dfrac{1}{1000}$ = thousandth (3rd digit after decimal point or 0.001)

$10^{-4} = \dfrac{1}{10^4} = \dfrac{1}{10000}$ = ten thousandth (4th digit after decimal point or 0.0001)

Example:
Write 73169.00537 in expanded form.

We start by listing all the powers-of-ten positions.

$$10^4 \quad 10^3 \quad 10^2 \quad 10^1 \quad 10^0 \quad . \quad 10^{-1} \quad 10^{-2} \quad 10^{-3} \quad 10^{-4} \quad 10^{-5}$$

Multiply each digit by its power of ten. Add all the results.

$$\text{Thus } 73169.00537 = (7 \times 10^4) + (3 \times 10^3) + (1 \times 10^2) + (6 \times 10^1)$$
$$+ (9 \times 10^0) + (0 \times 10^{-1}) + (0 \times 10^{-2}) + (5 \times 10^{-3})$$
$$+ (3 \times 10^{-4}) + (7 \times 10^{-5})$$

Example:
Determine the place value associated with the underlined digit in 3.16<u>9</u>5.

$$10^0 \quad . \quad 10^{-1} \quad 10^{-2} \quad 10^{-3} \quad 10^{-4}$$
$$3 \quad . \quad 1 \quad 6 \quad 9 \quad 5$$

The place value for the digit 9 is 10^{-3} or $\dfrac{1}{1000}$.

Example:
Find the number that is represented by

$$(7 \times 10^3) + (5 \times 10^0) + (3 \times 10^{-3}).$$
$$= 7000 + 5 + 0.003$$
$$= 7005.003$$

Example:
Write 21×10^3 in standard form.

$$= 21 \times 1000 = 21{,}000$$

Example:
Write 739×10^{-4} in standard form.

$$= 739 \times \frac{1}{10000} = \frac{739}{10000} = 0.0739$$

Rounding numbers is a form of estimation that is very useful in many mathematical operations. For example, when estimating the sum of two three-digit numbers, it is helpful to round the two numbers to the nearest hundred prior to addition. We can round numbers to any place value.

Rounding Whole Numbers

To round whole numbers, you first find the place value you want to round to (the rounding digit) and look at the digit directly to the right. If the digit is less than five, do not change the rounding digit and replace all numbers after the rounding digit with zeroes. If the digit is greater than or equal to five, increase the rounding digit by one and replace all numbers after the rounding digit with zeroes.

Example:
Round 517 to the nearest ten.

1 is the rounding digit because it occupies the tens' place.

517 rounded to the nearest ten = 520; because 7 > 5 we add one to the rounding digit.

Example:
Round 15,449 to the nearest hundred.

The first 4 is the rounding digit because it occupies the hundreds' place.

15,449 rounded to the nearest hundred = 15,400; because 4 < 5 we do not add to the rounding digit.

Rounding Decimals

Rounding decimals is identical to rounding whole numbers except that you simply drop all the digits to the right of the rounding digit.

Example:
Round 417.3621 to the nearest tenth.

3 is the rounding digit because it occupies the tenths' place.

417.3621 rounded to the nearest tenth = 417.4; because 6 > 5 we add one to the rounding digit.

Skill 7.4   Recognize concepts and skills related to using integers, fractions, decimals, ratios, and percents to solve problems (e.g., finding equivalent forms of fractions, decimals, and percents)

A **decimal** can be converted to a **percent** by multiplying by 100, or merely moving the decimal point two places to the right. A **percent** can be converted to a **decimal** by dividing by 100, or moving the decimal point two places to the left.

Examples:
$$0.375 = 37.5\%$$
$$0.7 = 70\%$$
$$0.04 = 4\%$$
$$3.15 = 315\%$$
$$84\% = 0.84$$
$$3\% = 0.03$$
$$60\% = 0.6$$
$$110\% = 1.1$$
$$\tfrac{1}{2}\% = 0.5\% = 0.005$$

A **percent** can be converted to a **fraction** by placing it over 100 and reducing to simplest terms.

Examples:
$$32\% = \tfrac{32}{100} = \tfrac{8}{25}$$
$$6\% = \tfrac{6}{100} = \tfrac{3}{50}$$
$$111\% = \tfrac{111}{100} = 1\tfrac{11}{100}$$

COMMON EQUIVALENTS

$\frac{1}{2} = 0.5 = 50\%$

$\frac{1}{3} = 0.33\frac{1}{3} = 33\frac{1}{3}\%$

$\frac{1}{4} = 0.25 = 25\%$

$\frac{1}{5} = 0.2 = 20\%$

$\frac{1}{6} = 0.16\frac{2}{3} = 16\frac{2}{3}\%$

$\frac{1}{8} = 0.12\frac{1}{2} = 12\frac{1}{2}\%$

$\frac{1}{10} = 0.1 = 10\%$

$\frac{2}{3} = 0.66\frac{2}{3} = 66\frac{2}{3}\%$

$\frac{5}{6} = 0.83\frac{1}{3} = 83\frac{1}{3}\%$

$\frac{3}{8} = 0.37\frac{1}{2} = 37\frac{1}{2}\%$

$\frac{5}{8} = 0.62\frac{1}{2} = 62\frac{1}{2}\%$

$\frac{7}{8} = 0.87\frac{1}{2} = 87\frac{1}{2}\%$

$1 = 1.0 = 100\%$

Skill 7.5 **Demonstrate knowledge of how to select and use a wide range of manipulatives, instructional resources, and technologies to explore concepts and solve real-world problems involving number, number sense, and numeration**

The use of supplementary materials in the classroom can greatly enhance the learning experience by stimulating student interest and satisfying different learning styles. Manipulatives, models, and technology are examples of tools available to teachers.

Manipulatives are materials that students can physically handle and move. Manipulatives allow students to understand mathematical concepts by allowing them to see concrete examples of abstract processes. Manipulatives are attractive to students because they appeal to the students' visual and tactile senses. Available for all levels of math, manipulatives are useful tools for reinforcing operations and concepts. They are not, however, a substitute for the development of sound computational skills.

Models are another means of representing mathematical concepts by relating the concepts to real-world situations. Teachers must choose wisely when devising and selecting models because, to be effective, models must be applied properly. For example, a building with floors above and below ground is a good model for introducing the concept of negative numbers. It would be difficult, however, to use the building model in teaching the subtraction of negative numbers.

Finally, there are many forms of **technology** available to math teachers. For example, students can test their understanding of math concepts by working on skill-specific computer programs and websites. Graphing calculators can help students visualize the graphs of functions. Teachers can also enhance their lectures and classroom presentations by creating multimedia presentations.

COMPETENCY 8.0   UNDERSTAND AND APPLY CONCEPTS AND METHODS RELATED TO ALGEBRA AND GEOMETRY TO SUPPORT THE LEARNING OF MATHEMATICS

Skill 8.1   Recognize patterns in numbers, shapes, and data and how to use variables, expressions, equations, and inequalities to describe patterns and express relationships algebraically

Arithmetic Sequences

When given a set of numbers where the common difference between the terms is constant, use the following formula:

$a_n = a_1 + (n-1)d$
where a_1 = the first term
n = the nth term (general term)
d = the common difference between the term to be found and a_1

Example:
Find the eighth term of the arithmetic sequence 5, 8, 11, 14, ...

$a_n = a_1 + (n-1)d$
$a_1 = 5$　　　　　　　identify the 1st term
$d = 8 - 5 = 3$　　　　find d
$a_n = 5 + (8-1)3$　　substitute
$a_n = 26$

Example:
Given two terms of an arithmetic sequence, find a_1 and d.

$a_4 = 21$　　　　　　$a_6 = 32$
$a_n = a_1 + (n-1)d$　　$a_4 = 21, n = 4$
$21 = a_1 + (4-1)d$　　$a_6 = 32, n = 6$
$32 = a_1 + (6-1)d$

$21 = a_1 + 3d$　　　solve the system of equations
$32 = a_1 + 5d$

$21 = \ a_1 + 3d$
$\underline{-32 = -a_1 - 5d}$　　multiply by -1
$-11 = \quad -2d$　　　add the equations
$5.5 = d$

$21 = a_1 + 3(5.5)$　　substitute d = 5.5, into one of the equations
$21 = a_1 + 16.5$
$a_1 = 4.5$

The sequence begins with 4.5 and has a common difference of 5.5 between numbers.

Geometric Sequences

When using geometric sequences, consecutive numbers are compared to find the common ratio.

$$r = \frac{a_{n+1}}{a_n}$$

where r = common ratio
a = the nth term

The ratio is then used in the geometric sequence formula:

$$a_n = a_1 r^{n-1}$$

Example:
Find the 8th term of the geometric sequence 2, 8, 32, 128 ...

$r = \frac{a_{n+1}}{a_n}$ use common ratio formula to find ratio

$r = \frac{8}{2}$ substitute $a_n = 2$ $a_{n+1} = 8$

$r = 4$

$a_n = a_1 \times r^{n-1}$ use r = 4 to solve for the 8th term

$a_n = 2 \times 4^{8-1}$

$a_n = 32{,}768$

Congruent figures have the same size and shape. If one is placed above the other, it will fit exactly. Congruent lines have the same length. Congruent angles have equal measures.

The symbol for congruent is $\cong$.

Polygons (pentagons) *ABCDE* and *VWXYZ* are congruent. They are exactly the same size and shape.

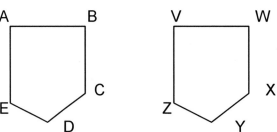

ABCDE $\cong$ *VWXYZ*

Corresponding parts are the congruent angles and congruent sides, that is:

corresponding angles	corresponding sides
$\angle A \leftrightarrow \angle V$	$AB \leftrightarrow VW$
$\angle B \leftrightarrow \angle W$	$BC \leftrightarrow WX$
$\angle C \leftrightarrow \angle X$	$CD \leftrightarrow XY$
$\angle D \leftrightarrow \angle Y$	$DE \leftrightarrow YZ$
$\angle E \leftrightarrow \angle Z$	$AE \leftrightarrow VZ$

Example: Given two similar quadrilaterals, find the lengths of sides x, y, and z.

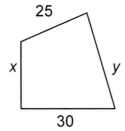 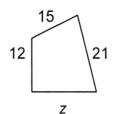

Since corresponding sides are proportional:

$$\frac{15}{25} = \frac{3}{5} \text{ so the scale is } \frac{3}{5}$$

$$\frac{12}{x} = \frac{3}{5} \qquad\qquad \frac{21}{y} = \frac{3}{5} \qquad\qquad \frac{z}{30} = \frac{3}{5}$$

$$3x = 60 \qquad\qquad 3y = 105 \qquad\qquad 5z = 90$$
$$x = 20 \qquad\qquad\quad y = 35 \qquad\qquad\quad z = 18$$

Similarity

Two figures that have the same shape are **similar.** Polygons are similar if and only if corresponding angles are congruent and corresponding sides are in proportion. Corresponding parts of similar polygons are proportional.

<u>Example</u>:
Given the rectangles below, compare the area and perimeter.

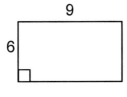
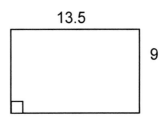

$A = LW$	$A = LW$	1. write formula
$A = (6)(9)$	$A = (9)(13.5)$	2. substitute known values
$A = 54$ sq. units	$A = 121.5$ sq. units	3. compute
$P = 2(L + W)$	$P = 2(L + W)$	1. write formula
$P = 2(6 + 9)$	$P = 2(9 + 13.5)$	2. substitute known values
$P = 30$ units	$P = 45$ units	3. compute

Notice that the areas relate to each other in the following manner:

Ratio of sides $9/13.5 = 2/3$

Multiply the first area by the square of the reciprocal $(3/2)^2$ to get the second area.
$54 \times (3/2)^2 = 121.5$

The perimeters relate to each other in the following manner:

Ratio of sides $9/13.5 = 2/3$

Multiply the perimeter of the first by the reciprocal of the ratio to get the perimeter of the second.

$30 \times 3/2 = 45$

Example:
Tommy draws and cuts out two triangles for a school project. One of them has sides of 3, 6, and 9 inches. The other triangle has sides of 2, 4, and 6 inches. Is there a relationship between the two triangles?

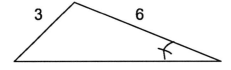   

Take the proportion of the corresponding sides.

$$\frac{2}{3} \qquad \frac{4}{6} = \frac{2}{3} \qquad \frac{6}{9} = \frac{2}{3}$$

The smaller triangle is 2/3 the size of the large triangle.

The union of all points on a simple closed surface and all points in its interior form a space figure called a **solid.** The five regular solids, or **polyhedra,** are the cube, tetrahedron, octahedron, icosahedron, and dodecahedron. A **net** is a two-dimensional figure that can be cut out and folded up to make a three-dimensional solid. Below are models of the five regular solids with their corresponding face polygons and nets.

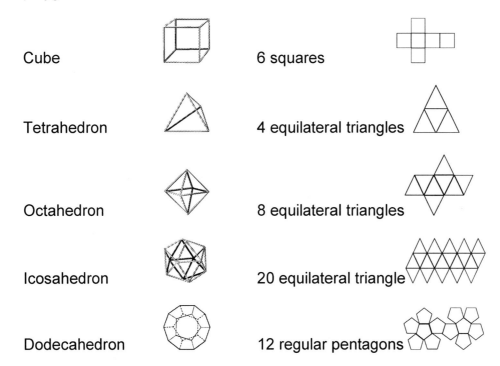

Cube   6 squares

Tetrahedron   4 equilateral triangles

Octahedron   8 equilateral triangles

Icosahedron   20 equilateral triangle

Dodecahedron   12 regular pentagons

Other examples of solids:

Sphere

Cone

<u>Example</u>:
Conjecture about the pattern presented in tabular form.

Kepler discovered a relationship between the average distance of a planet from the Sun and the time it takes the planet to orbit the Sun.

The following table shows the data for the six planets closest to the Sun:

	Mercury	Venus	Earth	Mars	Jupiter	Saturn
Average distance, x	0.387	0.723	1	1.523	5.203	9.541
x^3	0.058	0.378	1	3.533	140.852	868.524
Time, y	0.241	0.615	1	1.881	11.861	29.457
y^2	0.058	0.378	1	3.538	140.683	867.715

Looking at the data in the table, we see that $x^3 \simeq y^2$. We can conjecture the following function for Kepler's relationship: $y = \sqrt{x^3}$.

Representation of patterns using symbolic notation

<u>Example</u>:
Find the recursive formula for the sequence 1, 3, 9, 27, 81…

We see that any term other than the first term is obtained by multiplying the preceding term by 3. Then, we may express the formula in symbolic notation as

$a_n = 3a_{n-1}, \ a_1 = 1$,

where a represents a term, the subscript n denotes the place of the term in the sequence, and the subscript $n-1$ represents the preceding term.

Identification of patterns of change created by functions (e.g., linear, quadratic, exponential)

A **linear function** is a function defined by the equation $f(x) = mx + b$.

Example:
A model for the distance traveled by a migrating monarch butterfly looks like $f(t) = 80t$, where t represents time in days. We interpret this to mean that the average speed of the butterfly is 80 miles per day, and distance traveled may be computed by substituting the number of days traveled for t. In a linear function, there is a **constant** rate of change.

The standard form of a **quadratic function** is $f(x) = ax^2 + bx + c$.

Example:
What patterns appear in a table for $y = x^2 - 5x + 6$?

x	y
0	6
1	2
2	0
3	0
4	2
5	6

We see that the values for y are **symmetrically** arranged.

An **exponential function** is a function defined by the equation $y = ab^x$, where a is the starting value, b is the growth factor, and x tells how many times to multiply by the growth factor.

Example:

$$y = 100(1.5)^x$$

x	y
0	100
1	150
2	225
3	337.5
4	506.25

This is an **exponential** or multiplicative pattern of growth.

Iterative and recursive functional relationships (e.g., Fibonacci numbers)

The **iterative process** involves repeated use of the same steps. A **recursive function** is an example of the iterative process. A recursive function is a function that requires the computation of all previous terms in order to find a subsequent term. Perhaps the most famous recursive function is the **Fibonacci sequence.** This is the sequence of numbers 1,1,2,3,5,8,13,21,34 … for which the next term is found by adding the previous two terms.

Skill 8.2   Identify different types of functions (e.g., linear, nonlinear) and uses of patterns and functions to model real-world situations and make predictions

A relationship between two quantities can be shown using a table, graph, or rule. In this example, the equation y = 9x describes the relationship between the total amount earned, y, and the total amount of $9 sunglasses sold, x. A table using this equation would appear as:

number of sunglasses sold	1	5	10	15
total dollars earned	9	45	90	135

Each *(x,y)* relationship between a pair of values is called a coordinate pair and can be plotted on a graph. The coordinate pairs *(1,9)*, *(5,45)*, *(10,90)*, and *(15,135)* are plotted on the graph below.

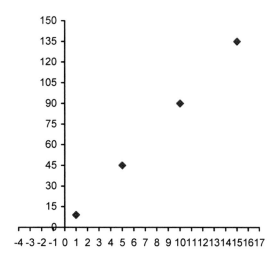

The graph above shows a linear relationship. A linear relationship is one in which two quantities are proportional to each other. Doubling *x* also doubles *y*. On a graph, a straight line depicts a linear relationship.

Another type of relationship is a nonlinear relationship. This is one in which change in one quantity does not affect the other quantity to the same extent. Nonlinear graphs have a curved line such as the graph below.

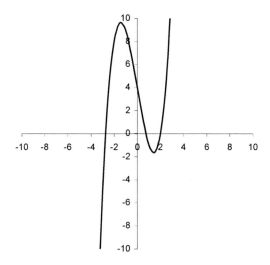

We can represent any two-dimensional geometric figure in the **Cartesian** or **rectangular coordinate system.** The Cartesian or rectangular coordinate system is formed by two perpendicular axes (coordinate axes): the x-axis and the y-axis. If we know the dimensions of a two-dimensional, or planar, figure, we can use this coordinate system to visualize the shape of the figure.

Example:
Represent an isosceles triangle with two sides of length 4.

Draw the two sides along the x- and y- axes and connect the points (vertices).

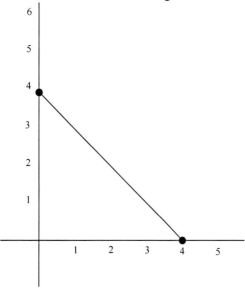

We refer to three-dimensional figures in geometry as **solids.** A solid is the union of all points on a simple closed surface and all points in its interior. A **polyhedron** is a simple closed surface formed from planar polygonal regions. Each polygonal region is called a **face** of the polyhedron. The vertices and edges of the polygonal regions are called the **vertices** and **edges** of the polyhedron.

We may form a cube from three congruent squares. However, if we tried to put four squares about a single vertex, their interior angle measures would add up to 360°; i.e., four edge-to-edge squares with a common vertex lie in a common plane and therefore cannot form a corner figure of a regular polyhedron.

There are five ways to form corner figures with congruent regular polygons:

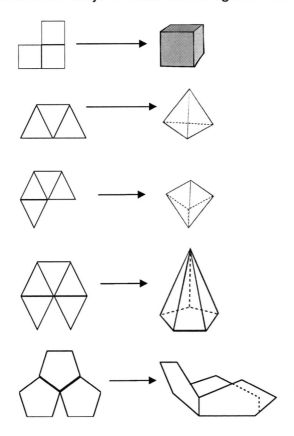

When creating a three-dimensional figure, if we know any two values of the vertices, faces, and edges, we can find the remaining value by using **Euler's Formula:** $V + F = E + 2$.

<u>For example:</u>

We want to create a pentagonal pyramid, and we know it has six vertices and six faces. Using Euler's Formula, we compute:

$$V + F = E + 2$$
$$6 + 6 = E + 2$$
$$12 = E + 2$$
$$10 = E$$

Thus, we know that our figure should have 10 edges.

In order to represent three-dimensional figures, we need three coordinate axes (X, Y, and Z) which are all mutually perpendicular to each other. Since we cannot draw three mutually perpendicular axes on a two-dimensional surface, we use oblique representations.

Example:
Represent a cube with sides of 2.

Once again, we draw three sides along the three axes to make things easier.

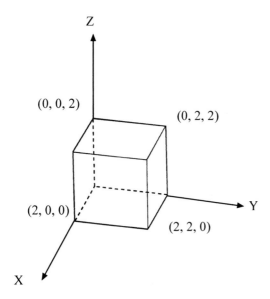

Each point has three coordinates (x, y, z).

Skill 8.3 Recognize types of geometric figures in one, two, and three dimensions and their properties (e.g., symmetry)

Symmetry is exact similarity between two parts or halves, as if one were a mirror image of the other.

A **Tessellation** is an arrangement of closed shapes that completely covers the plane without overlapping or leaving gaps. Unlike **tilings,** tessellations do not require the use of regular polygons. In art the term is used to refer to pictures or tiles mostly in the form of animals and other life forms, which cover the surface of a plane in a symmetrical way without overlapping or leaving gaps. M. C. Escher is known as the "father" of modern tessellations. Tessellations are used for tiling, mosaics, quilts, and art.

If you look at a completed tessellation, you will see the original motif repeats in a pattern. There are seventeen possible ways that a pattern can be used to tile a flat surface or "wallpaper."

There are four basic transformational symmetries that can be used in tessellations: **translation, rotation, reflection,** and **glide reflection.** The transformation of an object is called its image. If the original object were labeled with letters, such as *ABCD*, the image may be labeled with the same letters followed by a prime symbol, *A'B'C'D'* .

A **translation** is a transformation that "slides" an object a fixed distance in a given direction. The original object and its translation have the same shape and size, and they face in the same direction.

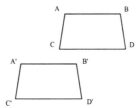

An example of a translation in architecture would be stadium seating. The seats are the same size and the same shape and face in the same direction.

A **rotation** is a transformation that turns a figure about a fixed point called the center of rotation. An object and its rotation are the same shape and size, but the figures may be turned in different directions. Rotations can occur in either a clockwise or a counterclockwise direction.

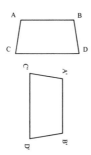

Rotations can be seen in wallpaper and art, and a Ferris wheel is an example of rotation.

An object and its **reflection** have the same shape and size, but the figures face in opposite directions.

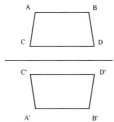

The line (where a mirror may be placed) is called the **line of reflection.** The distance from a point to the line of reflection is the same as the distance from the point's image to the line of reflection.

A **glide reflection** is a combination of a reflection and a translation.

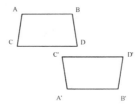

The tessellation below is a combination of the four types of transformational symmetry we have discussed:

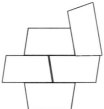

Skill 8.4   Solve problems involving perimeter, area, volume, geometric transformations (e.g., reflections, translations), and coordinate systems (e.g., using coordinate systems on lines and planes to solve problems)

The **perimeter** of any polygon is the sum of the lengths of the sides.
    P = sum of sides

Since the opposite sides of a rectangle are congruent, the perimeter of a rectangle equals twice the sum of the length and width, or
    P_{rect} = 2L + 2W or 2(L + W)

Similarly, since all the sides of a square have the same measure, the perimeter of a square equals four times the length of one side, or
    P_{square} = 4s

The **area** of a polygon is the number of square units covered by the figure.
    A_{rect} = L × W
    A_{square} = s^2

Example:
Find the perimeter and the area of this rectangle.

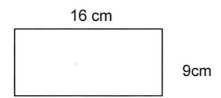

16 cm

9cm

$P_{rect} = 2L + 2W$
$= 2(16) + 2(9)$
$= 32 + 18 = 50$ cm

$A_{rect} = L \times W$
$= 16(9)$
$= 144$ cm^2

Example:
Find the perimeter and area of this square.

3.6 in.

$P_{square} = 4s$
$= 4(3.6)$
$= 14.4$ in.

$A_{square} = s^2$
$= (3.6)(3.6)$
$= 12.96$ in^2

In the following formulas, b = the base and h = the height of an altitude drawn to the base.

$A_{parallelogram} = bh$
$A_{triangle} = \frac{1}{2}bh$
$A_{trapezoid} = \frac{1}{2}h(b_1 + b_2)$

Example:
Find the area of a parallelogram whose base is 6.5 cm, and the height of the altitude to that base is 3.7 cm.

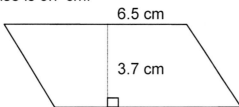

6.5 cm

3.7 cm

$A_{parallelogram} = bh$
$= (3.7)(6.5)$
$= 24.05$ cm^2

Example:
Find the area of this triangle.

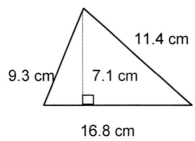

$A_{triangle} = \frac{1}{2}bh$
$= 0.5(16.8)(7.1)$
$= 59.64 \text{ cm}^2$

Note that the altitude is drawn to the base measuring 16.8 cm. The lengths of the other two sides is unnecessary information.

Skill 8.5   **Apply knowledge of how to use various geometric and algebraic concepts (e.g., similarity, congruence, spatial relationships, patterns, functions, variables), models, materials, methods, and technologies to represent and solve real-world problems involving algebra and geometry**

Many algebraic procedures are similar to and rely upon number operations and algorithms. Two examples of this similarity are the adding of rational expressions and division of polynomials.

Addition of rational expressions is similar to fraction addition. The basic algorithm of addition for both fractions and rational expressions is the common denominator method. Consider an example of the addition of numerical fractions.

$$\frac{3}{5}+\frac{2}{3}=\frac{3(3)}{5(3)}+\frac{2(5)}{3(5)}=\frac{9}{15}+\frac{10}{15}=\frac{19}{15}$$

To complete the sum, we first find the least common denominator.

Now, consider an example of rational expression addition.

$$\frac{(x+5)}{(x+1)}+\frac{2x}{(x+3)}=\frac{(x+3)(x+5)}{(x+3)(x+1)}+\frac{(x+1)2x}{(x+1)(x+3)}$$
$$=\frac{x^2+8x+15}{(x+3)(x+1)}+\frac{2x^2+2x}{(x+3)(x+1)}=\frac{3x^2+10x+15}{(x+3)(x+1)}$$

Note the similarity to fractional addition. The basic algorithm, finding a common denominator and adding the numerators, is the same.

Division of polynomials follows the same algorithm as numerical long division. Consider an example of numerical long division.

$$6\overline{)4321} \quad \begin{array}{r} 720 \\ \hline \end{array}$$

$$\begin{array}{r} \underline{42} \\ 12 \\ \underline{12} \\ 01 \end{array} \longrightarrow 720\ ^1/_6 = \text{final quotient}$$

Compare the process of numerical long division to polynomial division.

$$x+1\overline{)x^2 - 8x - 9} \quad \begin{array}{r} x - 9 \\ \hline \end{array}$$

$$\begin{array}{r} \underline{-x^2 - x} \\ -9x - 9 \\ \underline{+9x + 9} \\ 0\ +\ 0 \end{array} \longrightarrow x - 9 = \text{final quotient}$$

Note that the step-by-step process is identical in both cases.

Concrete and visual representations can help demonstrate the logic behind operational algorithms. Blocks or other objects modeled on the base ten system are useful concrete tools. Base ten blocks represent ones, tens, and hundreds. For example, modeling the partial sums algorithm with base ten blocks helps clarify the thought process. Consider the sum of 242 and 193. We represent 242 with two one-hundred blocks, four ten blocks and two one blocks. We represent 193 with one one-hundred block, nine ten blocks and three one blocks. In the partial sums algorithm, we manipulate each place value separately and total the results. Thus, we group the hundred blocks, ten blocks and one blocks and derive a total for each place value. We combine the place values to complete the sum.

An example of a visual representation of an operational algorithm is the modeling of a two-term multiplication as the area of a rectangle. For example, consider the product of 24 and 39. We can represent the product in geometric form. Note that the four sections of the rectangle equate to the four products of the partial products method.

	30	9
20	A = 600	A = 180
4	A = 120	A = 36

Thus, the final product is the sum of the areas, or 600 + 180 + 120 + 36 = 936.

Word problems can sometimes be solved by using a system of two equations with two unknowns. This system can then be solved using **substitution,** or the **addition-subtraction method.**

Example:
Farmer Greenjeans bought 4 cows and 6 sheep for $1700. Mr. Ziffel bought 3 cows and 12 sheep for $2400. If all the cows were the same price and all the sheep were another price, find the price charged for a cow or for a sheep.

Let x = price of a cow
Let y = price of a sheep
Then Farmer Greenjeans' equation would be: $4x + 6y = 1700$
Mr. Ziffel's equation would be: $3x + 12y = 2400$

To solve by **addition-subtraction:**
Multiply the first equation by $^-2$: $\quad ^-2(4x + 6y = 1700)$
Keep the other equation the same : $(3x + 12y = 2400)$
By doing this, the equations can be added to each other to eliminate one variable and solve for the other variable.

$$^-8x - 12y = {}^-3400$$
$$\underline{3x + 12y = 2400} \quad \text{Add these equations.}$$
$$^-5x \qquad = {}^-1000$$

$x = 200 \leftarrow$ The price of a cow was $200.
Solving for y, $y = 150 \leftarrow$ The price of a sheep, $150.

To solve by **substitution:**

Solve one of the equations for a variable. (Try to make an equation without fractions if possible.) Substitute this expression into the equation that you have not yet used. Solve the resulting equation for the value of the remaining variable.

$$4x + 6y = 1700$$
$$3x + 12y = 2400 \leftarrow \text{ Solve this equation for } x.$$

It becomes $x = 800 - 4y$. Now substitute $800 - 4y$ in place of x in the OTHER equation. $4x + 6y = 1700$ now becomes:

$$4(800 - 4y) + 6y = 1700$$
$$3200 - 16y + 6y = 1700$$
$$3200 - 10y = 1700$$
$$^{-}10y = {}^{-}1500$$
$$y = 150, \text{ or \$150 for a sheep.}$$

Substituting 150 back into an equation for y, find x.
$$4x + 6(150) = 1700$$
$$4x + 900 = 1700$$
$$4x = 800$$
$$x = 200, \text{ or \$200 for a cow.}$$

Word problems can sometimes be solved by using a system of three equations with three unknowns. This system can then be solved using either **substitution** or the **addition-subtraction method.**

To solve by **substitution**:

Example:
Mrs. Allison bought 1 pound of potato chips, a 2 pound beef roast, and 3 pounds of apples for a total of $8.19. Mr. Bromberg bought a 3 pound beef roast and 2 pounds of apples for $9.05. Kathleen Kaufman bought 2 pounds of potato chips, a 3 pound beef roast, and 5 pounds of apples for $13.25. Find the per pound price of each item.

Let x = price of a pound of potato chips
Let y = price of a pound of roast beef
Let z = price of a pound of apples

Mrs. Allison's equation would be: $1x + 2y + 3z = 8.19$
Mr. Bromberg's equation would be: $3y + 2z = 9.05$
K. Kaufman's equation would be: $2x + 3y + 5z = 13.25$

Take the first equation and solve it for x. (This was chosen because x is the easiest variable to isolate in this set of equations.) This equation would become:

$$x = 8.19 - 2y - 3z$$

Substitute this expression into the other equations in place of the letter x:

$3y + 2z = 9.05 \leftarrow$ equation 2
$2(8.19 - 2y - 3z) + 3y + 5z = 13.25 \leftarrow$ equation 3

Simplify the equation by combining like terms:

$3y + 2z = 9.05 \leftarrow$ equation 2
$^-1y - 1z = {}^-3.13 \leftarrow$ equation 3

Solve equation 3 for either y or z:

$^*y = 3.13 - z$

Substitute this into equation 2 for y:
$3(3.13 - z) + 2z = 9.05 \leftarrow$ equation 2
$^-1y - 1z = {}^-3.13 \leftarrow$ equation 3

Combine like terms in equation 2:

$$9.39 - 3z + 2z = 9.05$$
$$z = .34 = \text{per pound price of bananas}$$

Substitute .34 for z in the starred equation above to solve for y:

$$y = 3.13 - z \text{ becomes } y = 3.13 - .34 \text{, so}$$
$$y = 2.79 = \text{per pound price of roast beef}$$

Substituting .34 for z and 2.79 for y in one of the original equations, solve for x:

$$1x + 2y + 3z = 8.19$$
$$1x + 2(2.79) + 3(.34) = 8.19$$
$$x + 5.58 + 1.02 = 8.19$$
$$x + 6.60 = 8.19$$
$$x = 1.59 = \text{per pound price of potato chips}$$

$$(x, y, z) = (1.59, 2.79, .34)$$

To solve by **addition-subtraction**:

Choose a letter to eliminate. Since the second equation is already missing an x, let's eliminate x from equations 1 and 3.

1) $1x + 2y + 3x = 8.19 \leftarrow$ Multiply by $^-2$ below.
2) $3y + 2z = 9.05$
3) $2x + 3y + 5z = 13.25$

$$^-2(1x + 2y + 3z = 8.19) \quad = \quad ^-2x - 4y - 6z = ^-16.38$$
$$\text{Keep equation 3 the same :} \quad 2x + 3y + 5z = 13.25$$

By doing this, the equations can be added to each other to eliminate one variable.

$$^-y - z = ^-3.13 \leftarrow \text{equation 4}$$

The equations left to solve are equations 2 and 4:

$$^-y - z = ^-3.13 \leftarrow \text{equation 4}$$
$$3y + 2z = 9.05 \leftarrow \text{equation 2}$$

Multiply equation 4 by 3: $\quad 3(^-y - z = ^-3.13)$
Keep equation 2 the same: $\quad 3y + 2z = 9.05$

$$^-3y - 3z = ^-9.39$$
$$3y + 2z = 9.05 \qquad \text{Add these equations.}$$

$$^-1z = ^-.34$$
$$z = .34 \leftarrow \text{the per pound price of bananas}$$

solving for y, $y = 2.79 \leftarrow$ the per pound price of roast beef

solving for x, $x = 1.59 \leftarrow$ potato chips, per pound price

To solve by **substitution:**

Solve one of the three equations for a variable. (Try to make an equation without fractions if possible.) Substitute this expression into the other two equations that you have not yet used.

1) $1x + 2y + 3z = 8.19 \leftarrow$ Solve for x.
2) $3y + 2z = 9.05$
3) $2x + 3y + 5z = 13.25$

Equation 1 becomes $x = 8.19 - 2y - 3z$.

Substituting this into equations 2 and 3, they become:

2) $3y + 2z = 9.05$
3) $2(8.19 - 2y - 3z) + 3y + 5z = 13.25$
$16.38 - 4y - 6z + 3y + 5z = 13.25$
$^-y - z = {}^-3.13$

The equations left to solve are :

$3y + 2z = 9.05$

$^-y - z = {}^-3.13 \leftarrow$ Solve for either y or z.

It becomes $y = 3.13 - z$

Now substitute $3.13 - z$ in place of y in the OTHER equation. $3y + 2z = 9.05$ now becomes:

$3(3.13 - z) + 2z = 9.05$
$9.39 - 3z + 2z = 9.05$
$9.39 - z = 9.05$
$^-z = {}^-.34$
$z = .34$, or $.34$/lb of bananas

Substituting .34 back into an equation for z, find y.

$3y + 2z = 9.05$
$3y + 2(.34) = 9.05$
$3y + .68 = 9.05$
$y = 2.79$, or 2.79/lb of roast beef

Substituting .34 for z and 2.79 for y into one of the original equations, it becomes:

$$2x + 3y + 5z = 13.25$$
$$2x + 3(2.79) + 5(.34) = 13.25$$
$$2x + 8.37 + 1.70 = 13.25$$
$$2x + 10.07 = 13.25$$
$$x = 1.59, \text{ or } \$1.59/\text{lb of potato chips}$$

COMPETENCY 9.0   UNDERSTAND AND APPLY PRINCIPLES, CONCEPTS, AND PROCEDURES RELATED TO MEASUREMENT, STATISTICS, AND PROBABILITY TO SUPPORT THE LEARNING OF MATHEMATICS

Skill 9.1   Recognize appropriate measurement instruments, units, and procedures for various measurement problems (e.g., involving length, area, angles, volume, mass, temperature)

Examining the change in area or volume of a given figure requires first finding the existing area given the original dimensions and then finding the new area given the increased dimensions.

Sample problem:
Given the rectangle below determine the change in area if the length is increased by 5 and the width is increased by 7.

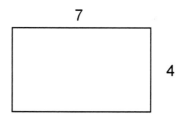

Draw and label a sketch of the new rectangle.

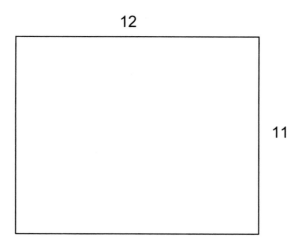

Find the areas.

Area of original = LW
= (7)(4)
= 28 units^2

Area of enlarged = LW
= (12)(11)
= 132 units^2

The change in area is 132 – 28 = 104 units^2.

Rates

First write the equation. To solve it, multiply each term by the LCD of all fractions. This will cancel out all of the denominators and give an equivalent algebraic equation that can be solved.

1. The denominator of a fraction is 2 less than 3 times the numerator. If 3 is added to both the numerator and denominator, the new fraction equals $1/2$.

original fraction: $\dfrac{x}{3x-2}$ revised fraction: $\dfrac{x+3}{3x+1}$

$$\dfrac{x+3}{3x+1} = \dfrac{1}{2}$$ cross multiply

$2x + 6 = 3x + 1$ solve for x

$x = 5$

original fraction: $\dfrac{5}{13}$

2. Elly Mae can feed the animals in 15 minutes. Jethro can feed them in 10 minutes. How long will it take them if they work together?

Solution: If Elly Mae can feed the animals in 15 minutes, then she could feed $1/15$ of them in 1 minute, $2/15$ of them in 2 minutes, and $x/15$ of them in x minutes. In the same fashion Jethro could feed $x/10$ of them in x minutes. Together they complete 1 job. The equation is:

$$\dfrac{x}{15} + \dfrac{x}{10} = 1$$

Multiply each term by the LCD, 30:

$2x + 3x = 30$

$x = 6$ minutes

3. A salesman drove 480 miles from Pittsburgh to Hartford. The next day he returned the same distance to Pittsburgh in half an hour less time than his original trip took, because he increased his average speed by 4 mph. Find his original speed.

Since distance = rate x time, then time = $\dfrac{\text{distance}}{\text{rate}}$

original time $- 1/2$ hour $=$ shorter return time

$$\frac{480}{x} - \frac{1}{2} = \frac{480}{x+4}$$

Multiplying by the LCD of $2x(x+4)$, the equation becomes:

$$480\left[2(x+4)\right] - 1\left[x(x+4)\right] = 480(2x)$$

$$960x + 3840 - x^2 - 4x = 960x$$

$$x^2 + 4x - 3840 = 0$$

$$(x+64)(x-60) = 0$$

$x = 60$ 60 mph is the original speed

                    64 mph is the faster return speed

Angles

The classifying of angles refers to the angle measure. The naming of angles refers to the letters or numbers used to label the angle.

Sample Problem:

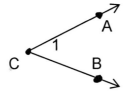

$\overrightarrow{CA}$ (read ray CA) and $\overrightarrow{CB}$ are the sides of the angle.
The angle can be called $\angle ACB$, $\angle BCA$, $\angle C$ or $\angle 1$.

Angles are classified according to their size as follows:

acute:	greater than 0 and less than 90 degrees
right:	exactly 90 degrees
obtuse:	greater than 90 and less than 180 degrees
straight:	exactly 180 degrees

Angles can be classified in a number of ways. Some of those classifications are outlined here.

Adjacent angles have a common vertex and one common side but no interior points in common.

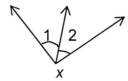

Complimentary angles add up to 90 degrees.

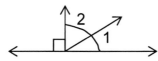

Supplementary angles add up to 180 degrees.

Vertical angles have sides that form two pairs of opposite rays.

Corresponding angles are in the same corresponding position on two parallel lines cut by a transversal.

Alternate interior angles are diagonal angles on the inside of two parallel lines cut by a transversal.

Alternate exterior angles are diagonal on the outside of two parallel lines cut by a transversal.

Skill 9.2   Apply knowledge of procedures for estimating and converting measurements within the customary and metric systems and for using measurements to describe and compare phenomena

Measurements of length (English system)

12 inches (in)	=	1 foot (ft)
3 feet (ft)	=	1 yard (yd)
1760 yards (yd)	=	1 mile (mi)

Measurements of length (metric system)

kilometer (km)	=	1000 meters (m)
hectometer (hm)	=	100 meters (m)
decameter (dam)	=	10 meters (m)
meter (m)	=	1 meter (m)
decimeter (dm)	=	1/10 meter (m)
centimeter (cm)	=	1/100 meter (m)
millimeter (mm)	=	1/1000 meter (m)

Conversion of length from English to metric

1 inch	=	2.54 centimeters
1 foot	≈	30 centimeters
1 yard	≈	0.9 meter
1 mile	≈	1.6 kilometers

Measurements of weight (English system)

28 grams (g)	=	1 ounce (oz)
16 ounces (oz)	=	1 pound (lb)
2000 pounds (lb)	=	1 ton (t) (short ton)
1.1 tons (t)	=	1 ton (t)

Measurements of weight (metric system)

kilogram (kg)	=	1000 grams (g)
gram (g)	=	1 gram (g)
milligram (mg)	=	1/1000 gram (g)

Conversion of weight from English to metric

1 ounce	≈	28 grams
1 pound	≈	0.45 kilogram

Measurement of volume (English system)

8 fluid ounces (oz)	=	1 cup (c)
2 cups (c)	=	1 pint (pt)
2 pints (pt)	=	1 quart (qt)
4 quarts (qt)	=	1 gallon (gal)

Measurement of volume (metric system)

kiloliter (kl)	=	1000 liters (l)
liter (l)	=	1 liter (l)
milliliter (ml)	=	1/1000 liter (ml)

Conversion of volume from English to metric

1 teaspoon (tsp)	≈	5 milliliters
1 fluid ounce	≈	15 milliliters
1 cup	≈	0.24 liter
1 pint	≈	0.47 liter
1 quart	≈	0.95 liter
1 gallon	≈	3.8 liter

Note: (') represents feet and (") represents inches.

Square units can be derived with knowledge of basic units of length by squaring the equivalent measurements.

> 1 square foot (sq. ft.) = 144 sq. in.
> 1 sq. yd. = 9 sq. ft.
> 1 sq. yd. = 1296 sq. in.

Example:
14 sq. yd. = _____ sq. ft.
          14 × 9 = 126 sq. ft.

Skill 9.3   Apply knowledge of basic concepts and principles of statistics and probability (e.g., mean, median, mode, range)

Mean, median, and mode are three measures of central tendency. The **mean** is the average of the data items. The **median** is found by putting the data items in order from smallest to largest and selecting the item in the middle (or the average of the two items in the middle). The **mode** is the most frequently occurring item.

Range is a measure of variability. It is found by subtracting the smallest value from the largest value.

Sample problem:

Find the mean, median, mode, and range of the test scores listed below:

85	77	65
92	90	54
88	85	70
75	80	69
85	88	60
72	74	95

Mean (X) = sum of all scores ÷ number of scores = 78

Median = put numbers in order from smallest to largest. Pick middle number.
54, 60, 65, 69, 70, 72, 74, 75, 77, 80, 85, 85, 85, 88, 88, 90, 92, 95
                                    -- --
Both 77 and 80 are in middle, therefore, median is average of two numbers in the middle, or 78.5

Mode = most frequent number = 85

Range = largest number minus smallest number = 95 − 54 = 41

Different situations require different information. If we examine the circumstances under which an ice cream store owner may use statistics collected in the store, we find different uses for different information.

Over a 7-day period, the store owner collected data on the ice cream flavors sold. He found that the mean number of scoops sold was 174 per day. The most frequently sold flavor was vanilla. This information was useful in determining how much ice cream to order in all, and in what amounts for each flavor.

In the case of the ice cream store, the median and range had little business value for the owner. Consider the set of test scores from a math class: 0, 16, 19, 65, 65, 65, 68, 69, 70, 72, 73, 73, 75, 78, 80, 85, 88, and 92. The mean is 64.06 and the median is 71. Since out of the 18 scores, there are only 3 scores less than the mean, the median (71) would be a more descriptive score.

Retail store owners may be most concerned with the most common dress size, so that they may order more of that size than any other. Therefore, knowing the mode would be most helpful for them.

An understanding of the definitions is important in determining the validity and uses of statistical data. All definitions and applications in this section apply to ungrouped data.

Data item: each piece of data represented by the letter, X

Mean: the average of all data represented by the symbol, $\overline{X}$

Range: the difference between the highest and lowest value of data items

Sum of the Squares: the sum of the squares of the differences between each item and the mean $Sx^2 = (X - \overline{X})^2$

Variance: the sum of the squares divided by the number of items. (The lowercase Greek letter sigma squared (σ^2) represents variance.)
$$\frac{Sx^2}{N} = \sigma^2$$
The larger the value of the variance, the larger the spread.

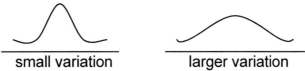

| small variation | larger variation |

Standard Deviation: the square root of the variance. (The lowercase Greek letter sigma (σ) is used to represent standard deviation.) $\sigma = \sqrt{\sigma^2}$

Most statistical calculators have standard deviation keys on them and should be used when asked to calculate statistical functions. It is important to become familiar with the calculator and the location of the keys needed.

Sample Problem:
Given the ungrouped data below, calculate the mean, range, standard deviation, and variance.

| 15 | 22 | 28 | 25 | 34 | 38 |
| 18 | 25 | 30 | 33 | 19 | 23 |

Mean ($\overline{X}$) = 25.8333333
Range: $38 - 15 = 23$
Standard deviation (σ) = 6.6936952
Variance (σ^2) = 44.805556

Skill 9.4   Identify various methods (e.g., surveys, tables, graphs) of systematically collecting, organizing, describing, and analyzing data

To make a **bar graph** or a **pictograph,** determine the scale to be used for the graph. Then determine the length of each bar on the graph or determine the number of pictures needed to represent each item of information. Be sure to include an explanation of the scale in the legend.

Example:
A class had the following grades: 4 A's, 9 B's, 8 C's, 1 D, 3 F's.
Graph these on a bar graph and a pictograph.

Pictograph

Bar graph

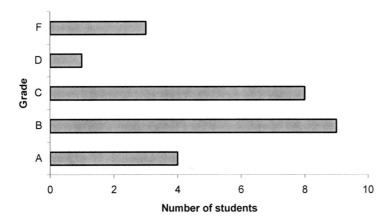

To make a **line graph,** determine appropriate scales for both the vertical and horizontal axes (based on the information to be graphed). Describe what each axis represents and mark the scale periodically on each axis. Graph the individual points and connect the points on the graph from left to right.

Example:
Graph the following information using a line graph.

The number of National Merit finalists/school year

	90-'91	91-'92	92-'93	93-'94	94-'95	95-'96
Central	3	5	1	4	6	8
Wilson	4	2	3	2	3	2

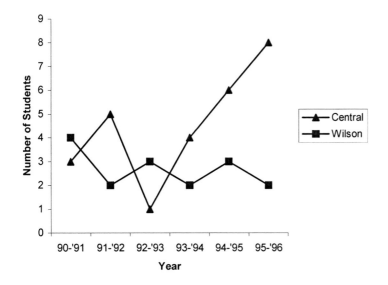

To make a **circle graph,** total all the information that is to be included on the graph. Determine the central angle to be used for each sector of the graph using the following formula:

$$\frac{\text{information}}{\text{total information}} \times 360° = \text{degrees in central } \angle$$

Lay out the central angles to these sizes, label each section, and include its percent.

Example:
Graph this information on a circle graph:

Monthly expenses:

Rent, $400
Food, $150
Utilities, $75
Clothes, $75
Church, $100
Misc., $200
Total, $1,000

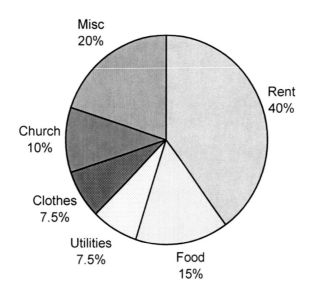

*   *   *

To read a bar graph or a pictograph, read the explanation of the scale that was used in the legend. Compare the length of each bar with the dimensions on the axes and calculate the value each bar represents. On a pictograph count the number of pictures used in the chart and calculate the value of all the pictures.

To read a circle graph, find the total of the amounts represented on the entire circle graph. To determine the actual amount that each sector of the graph represents, multiply the percent in a sector times the total amount number.

Scatter plots compare two characteristics of the same group of things or people and usually consist of a large body of data. They show how much one variable is affected by another. The relationship between the two variables is their **correlation.** The closer the data points come to making a straight line when plotted, the closer the correlation.

Stem and leaf plots are visually similar to line plots. The **stems** are the digits in the greatest place value of the data values, and the **leaves** are the digits in the next greatest place values. Stem and leaf plots are best suited for small sets of data and are especially useful for comparing two sets of data. The column on the left represents the "stem" or the tens digit and the left column represents the "leaves" or the ones digits. The following is an example using test scores. In the first row, the number 49 is represented, in the second row, 54 and 59 are shown:

4	9
5	4 9
6	1 2 3 4 6 7 8 8
7	0 3 4 6 6 6 7 7 7 8 8 8 8
8	3 5 5 7 8
9	0 0 3 4 5
10	0 0

Histograms are used to summarize information from large sets of data that can be naturally grouped into intervals. The vertical axis indicates **frequency** (the number of times any particular data value occurs), and the horizontal axis indicates data values, or ranges of data values. The number of data values in any interval is the **frequency of the interval.**

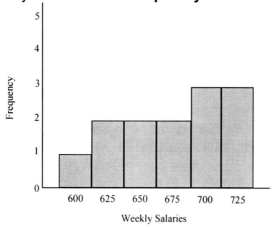

Weekly Salaries

Skill 9.5 Apply knowledge of how to interpret graphic and nongraphic representations of statistical data (e.g., frequency distributions, percentiles)

Percentiles divide data into 100 equal parts. A person whose score falls in the 65th percentile has outperformed 65 percent of all those who took the test. This does not mean that the score was 65 percent out of 100, nor does it mean that 65 percent of the questions answered were correct. It means that the grade was higher than 65 percent of all those who took the test.

Stanine "standard nine" scores combine the understandability of percentages with the properties of the normal curve of probability. Stanines divide the bell curve into nine sections, the largest of which stretches from the 40th to the 60th percentile and is the "Fifth Stanine" (the average of taking into account error possibilities).

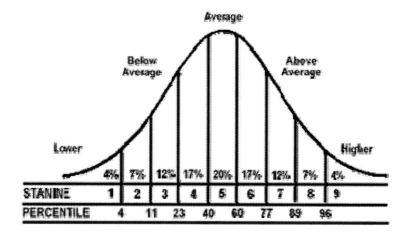

Quartiles divide the data into four parts. To find the quartiles, first find the median of the data set (Q2); then find the median of the upper (Q3) and lower (Q1) halves of the data set. If there are an odd number of values in the data set, include the median value in both halves when finding quartile values. For example, given the data set,{1, 4, 9, 16, 25, 36, 49, 64, 81}, first find the median value, which is 25. This is the second quartile. Since there are an odd number of values in the data set (9), we include the median in both halves. To find the quartile values, we must find the medians of {1, 4, 9, 16, 25} and {25, 36, 49, 64, 81}.

Since each of these subsets had an odd number of elements (5), we use the middle value. Thus the first quartile value is 9 and the third quartile value is 49. If the data set had an even number of elements, average the middle two values. The quartile values are always either one of the data points or exactly halfway between two data points.

Sample problem:
1. Given the following set of data, find the percentile of the score 104.

      70, 72, 82, 83, 84, 87, 100, 104, 108, 109, 110, 115

Solution: Find the percentage of scores below 104.

      7/12 of the scores are less than 104. This is 58.333%; therefore, the score of 104 is in the 58th percentile.

2. Find the first, second, and third quartile for the data listed.

      6, 7, 8, 9, 10, 12, 13, 14, 15, 16, 18, 23, 24, 25, 27, 29, 30, 33, 34, 37

      Quartile 1: The 1st Quartile is the median of the lower half of the data set, which is 11.

      Quartile 2: The median of the data set is the 2nd Quartile, which is 17.

      Quartile 3: The 3rd Quartile is the median of the upper half of the data set, which is 28.

Basic statistical concepts can be applied without computations. For example, inferences can be drawn from a graph or from statistical data. After a school fundraiser, a bar graph could display which grade level collected the most money. Statistical data such as student test scores would enable the teacher to determine which units need remedial instruction.

Random sampling supplies every combination of items from the frame, or stratum, as a known probability of occurring. A large body of statistical theory quantifies the risk and thus enables an appropriate sample size to be chosen.

Systematic sampling selects items in the frame according to the kth sample. The first item is chosen to be the rth, where r is a random integer in the range $1,...,k-1$.

There are three stages to *Cluster* or *Area sampling*: the target population is divided into many regional clusters (groups); a few clusters are randomly selected for study; a few subjects are randomly chosen from within a cluster.

Convenience sampling is the method of choosing items arbitrarily and in an unstructured manner from the frame.

Skill 9.6   Recognize how to use a variety of materials, models, and methods (e.g., combinations, theoretical probability) to represent and solve problems involving probability and mathematical expectations

Counting Procedures
So far, in all the problems we dealt with, the Sample Space was given or can be easily obtained. In many real-life situations, the sample space and events within it are very large and difficult to find. There are three techniques to help find the number of elements in one event, or a sample space: counting principle, permutations, and combinations.

The Counting Principle: In a sequence of two distinct events, in which the first one has n number of outcomes or possibilities, and the second one has m number of outcomes or possibilities, the total number or possibilities of the sequence will be

$$n \cdot m$$

Example:
A car dealership has three Mazda models, and each model comes in a choice of four colors. How many Mazda cars are available at the dealership?

Number of available Mazda cars = (3)(4) = 12

Example:
If a license plate consists of three digits followed by three letters, find the possible number of licenses if

a) repetition of letters and digits is **not** allowed.

b) repetition of letters and digits **is** allowed.

a) Since we have 26 letters and 10 digits, using the counting principle, we get

possible # of licenses = (26)(25)(24)(10)(9)(8)
= 11,232,000

b) Since repetitions are allowed, we get

possible # of licenses = (26)(26)(26)(10)(10)(10)
= 17,576,000

The Addition Principle of Counting states:
If A and B are events, $n(AorB) = n(A) + n(B) - n(A \cap B)$.

Example:
In how many ways can you select a black card or a jack from an ordinary deck of playing cards?

Let B denote the set of black cards and let J denote the set of jacks. Then,
$n(B \text{ or } J) = 26, n(B) = 4, n(J) = 4, n(B \cap J) = 2$ and
$= 26 + 4 - 2$
$= 28.$

The Addition Principle of Counting for Mutually Exclusive Events states:
If A and B are mutually exclusive events, $n(AorB) = n(A) + n(B)$.

Example:
A travel agency offers 40 possible trips: 14 to Asia, 16 to Europe, and 10 to South America. In how many ways can you select a trip to Asia or Europe through this agency?

Let A denote trips to Asia and let E denote trips to Europe. Then,
$A \cap E = \varnothing$ and $n(AorE) = 14 + 16 = 30.$

Therefore, the number of ways you can select a trip to Asia or Europe is 30.

The Multiplication Principle of Counting for Dependent Events states:
Let A be a set of outcomes of Stage 1 and B a set of outcomes of Stage 2. Then the number of ways $n(AandB)$ that A and B can occur in a two-stage experiment is given by: $n(AandB) = n(A)n(B|A)$, where $n(B|A)$ denotes the number of ways B can occur given that A has already occurred.

Example:
How many ways can two jacks be drawn in succession from and ordinary deck of 52 cards if the first card is drawn but not replaced in the deck, and then the second card is drawn?

> This is a two-stage experiment for which we wish to compute $n(AandB)$, where A is the set of outcomes for which a jack is obtained on the first draw, and B is the set of outcomes for which a jack is obtained on the second draw.

> If the first card drawn is a jack, then there are only three remaining jacks left to choose from on the second draw. Thus, drawing two cards without replacement means the events A and B are dependent.
> $n(AandB) = n(A)n(B|A) = 4 \cdot 3 = 12$

The Multiplication Principle of Counting for Independent Events states:
Let A be a set of outcomes of Stage 1 and B a set of outcomes of Stage 2. If A and B are independent events, then the number of ways $n(AandB)$ that A and B can occur in a two-stage experiment is given by: $n(AandB) = n(A)n(B)$.

Example:
How many six-letter code "words" can be formed if repetition of letters is not allowed?

> Since these are code words, a word does not have to look like a word; for example, abcdef could be a code word. Since we must choose a first letter *and* a second letter *and* a third letter *and* a fourth letter *and* a fifth letter *and* a sixth letter, this experiment has six stages.

> Since repetition is not allowed, there are 26 choices for the first letter; 25 for the second; 24 for the third; 23 for the fourth; 22 for the fifth; and 21 for the sixth. Therefore, we have:

> n (six-letter code words without repetition of letters)
> $= 26 \cdot 25 \cdot 24 \cdot 23 \cdot 22 \cdot 21$
> $= 165,765,600$

Permutations

In order to understand **Permutations**, the concept of factorials must be addressed.

n factorial, written n!, is represented by n ! = n(n-1)(n-2) . . . . . (2)(1)

$5! = (5)(4)(3)(2)(1) = 120$

$3! = 3(2)(1) = 6$

By definition: $0! = 1$
$1! = 1$

$\dfrac{6!}{6!} = 1$ but $\dfrac{6!}{2!} \neq 3!$

$\dfrac{6!}{2!} = \dfrac{6 \cdot 5 \cdot 4 \cdot 3 \cdot 2!}{2!} = 6 \cdot 5 \cdot 4 \cdot 3 = 360$

The number of permutations represents the number of ways r items can be selected from n items and arranged in a specific order. It is written as $_nP_r$ and is calculated using the following relationship:

$$_nP_r = \frac{n!}{(n-r)!}$$

When calculating permutations, order counts. For example, 2, 3, 4 and 4, 3, 2 are counted as two different permutations. Calculating the number of permutations is not valid with experiments where replacement is allowed.

Example:
How many different ways can a president and a vice president be selected from a math class if seven students are available?

We know we are looking for the number of permutations, since the positions of president and vice president are not equal.

$$_7P_2 = \frac{7!}{(7-2)!} = \frac{7!}{5!} = \frac{7 \cdot 6 \cdot 5!}{5!} = 7 \cdot 6 = 42$$

It is important to recognize that the number of permutations is a special case of the counting principle. Unless we are specifically asked to use the permutation relationship, we use the counting principle to solve problems dealing with the number of permutations. For instance, in this example we have seven available students to choose a president from. After a president is chosen, we have six available students to choose a vice president from.

Hence, using the counting principle, the ways a president and a vice president can be chosen are 7 x 6 = 42

Combinations

When dealing with the number of **combinations,** the order in which elements are selected is not important. For instance, the numbers

2, 3, 4 and 4, 2, 3 are considered one combination.

The number of combinations represents the number of ways r elements are selected from n elements (in no particular order). The number of combinations is represented by $_nC_r$ and can be calculated using the following relationship:

$$_nC_r = \frac{n!}{(n-r)r!}$$

Example:
In how many ways can two students be selected from a class of seven students to represent the class?

Since both representatives have the same position, the order is not important, and we are dealing with the number of combinations.

$$_nC_r = \frac{7!}{(7-2)!2!} = \frac{7 \cdot 6 \cdot 5!}{5! 2 \cdot 1} = 21$$

Example:
In a club there are six women and four men. A committee of two women and one man is to be selected. How many different committees can be selected?

This problem has a sequence of two events. The first event involves selecting two women out of six women, and the second event involves selecting one man out of four men. We use the combination relationship to find the number of ways in events 1 and 2 and the counting principle to find the number of ways the sequence can happen.

# of committees = $_6C_2 \cdot {}_4C_1$

$$\frac{6!}{(6-2)!2!} x \frac{4!}{(4-1)!1!}$$
$$= \frac{6 \cdot 5 \cdot 4!}{4! \cdot 2 \cdot 1} x \frac{4 \cdot 3!}{3! \cdot 1}$$
$$= (15) x (4) = 60$$

Using Tables

Example:

The results of a survey of 47 students are summarized in the table below.

	Black Hair	Blonde Hair	Red Hair	Total
Male	10	8	6	24
Female	6	12	5	23
Total	16	20	11	47

Use the table to answer questions a - c.

a)   If one student is selected at random, find the probability of selecting a male student.

$$\frac{\text{Number of male students}}{\text{Number of students}} = \frac{24}{47}$$

b)   If one student is selected at random, find the probability of selecting a female with red hair.

$$\frac{\text{Number of red-haired females}}{\text{Number of students}} = \frac{5}{47}$$

c)   If one student is selected at random, find the probability of selecting a student that does not have red hair.

$$\frac{\text{Red-haired students}}{\text{Number of students}} = \frac{11}{47}$$

$$1 - \frac{11}{47} = \frac{36}{47}$$

Skill 9.7   Demonstrate knowledge of how to select and use various age-appropriate simulations, manipulatives, materials, and technologies to explore concepts and solve real-world problems involving measurement, data analysis, statistics, and probability

See Skill 9.3.

DOMAIN III.   SCIENCE

COMPETENCY 10.0 UNDERSTAND AND APPLY FUNDAMENTAL CONCEPTS AND PRINCIPLES OF LIFE AND ENVIRONMENTAL SCIENCE TO INTERPRET, ANALYZE, AND EXPLAIN PHENOMENA

Skill 10.1   Recognize basic processes and concepts related to cells and the characteristics, needs, and organization of living things

The organization of living systems builds by levels from small to increasingly more large and complex. All aspects, whether it be a cell or an ecosystem, have the same requirements to sustain life. Life is organized from simple to complex in the following way:

Organelles make up **cells** that make up **tissues** that make up **organs**. Groups of organs make up **organ systems**. Organ systems work together to provide life for the **organism.**

Several characteristics have been described to identify living versus nonliving substances.

1. **Living things are made of cells;** they grow, are capable of reproduction, and respond to stimuli.
2. **Living things must adapt to environmental changes or perish**.
3. **Living things carry on metabolic processes**. They use and make energy.

All organic life has a common element: carbon. Carbon is recycled through the ecosystem through both biotic and abiotic means. It is the link between biological processes and the chemical makeup of life.

The cell is the basic unit of all living things. The two types of cells are prokaryotic and eukaryotic. **Prokaryotic** cells consist only of bacteria and blue-green algae. Bacteria were most likely the first cells and date back in the fossil record to 3.5 billion years ago. The important things that put these cells in their own group are:

1. They have no defined nucleus or nuclear membrane. The DNA and ribosomes float freely within the cell.
2. They have a thick cell wall. This is for protection, to give shape, and to keep the cell from bursting.
3. The cell walls contain amino sugars (glycoproteins). Penicillin works by disrupting the cell wall, which is bad for the bacteria, but will not harm the host.
4. Some have a capsule made of polysaccharides, which make the bacteria sticky.
5. 5. Some have pili, which is a protein strand. This also allows for attachment of the bacteria and may be used for sexual reproduction (conjugation).
6. Some have flagella for movement.

Eukaryotic cells are found in protists, fungi, plants, and animals. Some features of eukaryotic cells include:

1. They are usually larger than prokaryotic cells.
2. They contain many organelles, which are membrane-bound areas for specific cell functions.
3. They contain a cytoskeleton, which provides a protein framework for the cell.
4. They contain cytoplasm to support the organelles and contain the ions and molecules necessary for cell function.

Parts of Eukaryotic Cells

1. Nucleus - The brain of the cell. The nucleus contains:

- **chromosomes** - DNA, RNA, and proteins tightly coiled to conserve space while providing a large surface area.
- **chromatin** - loose structure of chromosomes. Chromosomes are called chromatin when the cell is not dividing.
- **nucleoli** -where ribosomes are made. These are seen as dark spots in the nucleus.
- **nuclear membrane** - contains pores which let RNA out of the nucleus. The nuclear membrane is continuous with the endoplasmic reticulum, which allows the membrane to expand or shrink if needed.

2. Ribosomes - The site of protein synthesis. Ribosomes may be free floating in the cytoplasm or attached to the endoplasmic reticulum. There may be up to a half a million ribosomes in a cell, depending on how much protein is made by the cell.

3. Endoplasmic Reticulum - These are folded and provide a large surface area. They are the "roadway" of the cell and allow for transport of materials. The lumen of the endoplasmic reticulum helps to keep materials out of the cytoplasm and headed in the right direction. The endoplasmic reticulum is capable of building new membrane material. There are two types:

1. **Smooth Endoplasmic Reticulum** - contain no ribosomes on their surface.
2. **Rough Endoplasmic Reticulum** - contain ribosomes on their surface. This form of ER is abundant in cells that make many proteins, like in the pancreas, which produces many digestive enzymes.

4. Golgi Complex or Golgi Apparatus - This structure is stacked to increase surface area. The Golgi Complex functions to sort, modify, and package molecules that are made in other parts of the cell. These molecules are either sent out of the cell or to other organelles within the cell.

5. Lysosomes - Tound mainly in animal cells. These contain digestive enzymes that break down food, substances not needed, viruses, damaged cell components, and eventually the cell itself. It is believed that lysosomes are responsible for the aging process.

6. Mitochondria - Large organelles that make ATP to supply energy to the cell. Muscle cells have many mitochondria because they use a great deal of energy. The folds inside the mitochondria are called cristae. They provide a large surface where the reactions of cellular respiration occur. Mitochondria have their own DNA and are capable of reproducing themselves if a greater demand is made for additional energy. Mitochondria are found only in animal cells.

7. Plastids - Found in photosynthetic organisms only. They are similar to the mitochondria due to their double-membrane structure. They also have their own DNA and can reproduce if increased capture of sunlight becomes necessary. There are several types of plastids:

- **Chloroplasts** – green, function in photosynthesis.. They are capable of trapping sunlight.
- **Chromoplasts** - make and store yellow and orange pigments; they provide color to leaves, flowers, and fruits.
- **Amyloplasts** - store starch and are used as a food reserve. They are abundant in roots like potatoes.

8. Cell Wall - Found in plant cells only; it is composed of cellulose and fibers. It is thick enough for support and protection, yet porous enough to allow water and dissolved substances to enter. Cell walls are cemented to each other.

9. Vacuoles - Hold stored food and pigments. Vacuoles are very large in plants. This allows them to fill with water in order to provide turgor pressure. Lack of turgor pressure causes a plant to wilt.

10. Cytoskeleton - composed of protein filaments attached to the plasma membrane and organelles. They provide a framework for the cell and aid in cell movement. They constantly change shape and move about. Three types of fibers make up the cytoskeleton:

- **Microtubules** - Largest of the three; make up cilia and flagella for locomotion. Flagella grow from a basal body. Some examples are sperm cells and tracheal cilia. Centrioles are also composed of microtubules. They form the spindle fibers that pull the cell apart into two cells during cell division. Centrioles are not found in the cells of higher plants.
- **Intermediate Filaments** - They are smaller than microtubules but larger than microfilaments. They help the cell to keep its shape.
- **Microfilaments** - Smallest of the three; they are made of actin and small amounts of myosin (like in muscle cells). They function in cell movement such as cytoplasmic streaming, endocytosis, and ameboid movement. This structure pinches the two cells apart after cell division, forming two cells.

Carolus Linnaeus is termed the father of taxonomy. **Taxonomy** is the science of classification. Linnaeus based his system on morphology (study of structure). Later on, evolutionary relationships (phylogeny) were also used to sort and group species. The modern classification system uses binomial nomenclature. This consists of a two-word name for every species. The genus is the first part of the name and the species is the second part. Notice, in the levels explained below, that Homo sapiens is the scientific name for humans. Starting with the kingdom, the groups get smaller and more alike as one moves down the levels in the classification of humans:

Kingdom: Animalia, **Phylum:** Chordata, **Subphylum:** Vertebrata, **Class:** Mammalia, **Order:** Primate, **Family:** Hominidae, **Genus:** Homo, **Species:** sapiens

Species are defined by the ability to successfully reproduce with members of their own kind.

- **Kingdom Monera** - bacteria and blue-green algae, prokaryotic, has no true nucleus, unicellular.
- **Kingdom Protista** - eukaryotic, unicellular, some are photosynthetic, some are consumers.
- **Kingdom Fungi** - eukaryotic, multicellular, absorptive consumers, contain a chitin cell wall.

Bacteria are classified according to their morphology (shape). **Bacilli** are rod-shaped, **cocci** are round, and **spirillia** are spiral-shaped. The **gram stain** is a staining procedure used to identify bacteria. Gram-positive bacteria pick up the stain and turn purple. Gram-negative bacteria do not pick up the stain and are pink in color. To classify protista, microbiologists use methods of locomotion, reproduction, and the process of obtaining food.

Methods of locomotion – Flagellates have a flagellum, ciliates have cilia, and ameboids move through use of pseudopodia.

Methods of reproduction - Binary fission is simply dividing in half and is asexual. All new organisms are exact clones of the parent. Sexual modes provide more diversity. Bacteria can reproduce sexually through conjugation, where genetic material is exchanged.

Methods of obtaining nutrition - Photosynthetic organisms, or producers, convert sunlight to chemical energy; consumers, or heterotrophs, eat other living things. Saprophytes are consumers that live off dead or decaying material.

MAJOR GROUPS OF PLANTS

NONVASCULAR PLANTS - small in size; they do not require vascular tissue (xylem and phloem) because individual cells are close to their environment. The nonvascular plants have no true leaves, stems, or roots.

- **Division Bryophyta** - Mosses and liverworts; these plants have a dominant gametophyte generation. They possess rhizoids, which are root-like structures. Moisture in their environment is required for reproduction and absorption.

VASCULAR PLANTS - The development of vascular tissue enable these plants to grow in size. Xylem and phloem allow for the transport of water and minerals up to the top of the plant, as well as the transport of food manufactured in the leaves to the bottom of the plant. All vascular plants have a dominant sporophyte generation.

- **Division Lycophyta** - Club mosses; these plants reproduce with spores and require water for reproduction.
- **Division Sphenophyta** - Horsetails; they also reproduce with spores. These plants have small, needle-like leaves and rhizoids. They require moisture for reproduction.
- **Division Pterophyta** - Ferns; reproduce with spores and flagellated sperm. These plants have a true stem and need moisture for reproduction.
- **Gymnosperms** - The word means "naked seed." These were the first plants to evolve with seeds, which made them less dependent on water to assist in reproduction. Their seeds could travel by wind. Pollen from the male was also easily carried by the wind. Gymnosperms have cones which protect the seeds.
- **Division Cycadophyta** - Cycads; these plants look like palms with cones.
- **Divison Ghetophyta** - Desert dwellers.
- **Division Coniferophyta** - Pines; these plants have needles and cones.
- **Divison Ginkgophyta** - The Ginkgo is the only member of this division.
- **Angiosperms (Division Anthophyta)** - Angiosperms are the largest group in the plant kingdom. They are the flowering plants and produce true seeds for reproduction.

MAJOR GROUPS OF ANIMALS

Annelida - the segmented worms. The Annelida have specialized tissue. The circulatory system is more advanced in these worms and is a closed system with blood vessels. The nephridia are their excretory organs. They are hermaphrodidic, and each worm fertilizes the other upon mating. They support themselves with a hydrostatic skeleton and have circular and longitudinal muscles for movement.

Mollusca - clams, octopus, and soft bodied animals. These animals have a muscular foot for movement. They breathe through gills and most are able to make a shell for protection from predators. They have an open circulatory system, with sinuses bathing the body regions.

Arthropoda - insects, crustaceans, and spiders; this is the largest group of the animal kingdom. Phylum arthropoda accounts for about 85 percent of all the animal species. Animals in the phylum arthropoda possess an exoskeleton made of chitin. They must molt to grow. Insects, for example, go through four stages of development. They begin as an egg, hatch into a larva, form a pupa, and then emerge as an adult. Arthropods breathe through gills, trachea, or book lungs. Movement varies, with members being able to swim, fly, and crawl. There is a division of labor among the appendages (legs, antennae, etc.). This is an extremely successful phylum, with members occupying diverse habitats.

Echinodermata - sea urchins and starfish; these animals have a spiny skin. Their habitat is marine. They have tube feet for locomotion and feeding.

Chordata - all animals with a notocord or a backbone. The classes in this phylum include Agnatha (jawless fish), Chondrichthyes (cartilage fish), Osteichthyes (bony fish), Amphibia (frogs and toads; gills which are replaced by lungs during development), Reptilia (snakes, lizards; the first to lay eggs with a protective covering), Aves (birds; warm-blooded with wings consisting of a particular shape and composition designed for flight), and Mammalia (warm blooded animals with body hair that bear their young alive and possess mammary glands for milk production).

Skill 10.2   Recognize the basic structures and functions of the human body in comparison to those of other organisms

Muscular System - functions in movement. There are three types of muscle tissue. Skeletal muscle is voluntary. These muscles are attached to bones. Smooth muscle is involuntary. It is found in organs and enables functions such as digestion and respiration. Cardiac muscle is a specialized type of smooth muscle and is found in the heart. Muscles can only contract; therefore they work in antagonistic pairs to allow backward and forward movement. Muscle fibers are made of groups of myofibrils, which are made of groups of sarcomeres. Actin and myosin are proteins which make up the sarcomere.

Nervous System - The neuron is the basic unit of the nervous system. It consists of an axon, which carries impulses away from the cell body; the dendrite, which carries impulses toward the cell body; and the cell body, which contains the nucleus. Synapses are spaces between neurons. Chemicals called neurotransmitters are found close to the synapse. The myelin sheath, composed of Schwann cells, covers the neurons and provides insulation.

Digestive System - The function of the digestive system is to break down food and absorb it into the blood stream, where it can be delivered to all cells of the body for use in cellular respiration. As animals evolved, digestive systems changed from simple absorption to a system with a separate mouth and anus, capable of allowing the animal to become independent of a host.

Respiratory System - This system functions in the gas exchange of oxygen (needed) and carbon dioxide (waste). It delivers oxygen to the bloodstream and picks up carbon dioxide for release out of the body. Simple animals diffuse gases from and to their environment. Gills allow aquatic animals to exchange gases in a fluid medium by removing dissolved oxygen from the water. Lungs maintain a fluid environment for gas exchange in terrestrial animals.

Circulatory System - The function of the circulatory system is to carry oxygenated blood and nutrients to all cells of the body and return carbon dioxide waste to be expelled from the lungs. Animals evolved from an open system to a closed system, with vessels leading to and from the heart.

The **axial skeleton** consists of the bones of the skull and vertebrae. The **appendicular skeleton** consists of the bones of the legs, arms, tail, and shoulder girdle. Bone is a connective tissue. Parts of the bone include compact bone which gives strength, spongy bone which contains red marrow to make blood cells, yellow marrow in the center of long bones to store fat cells, and the periosteum, which is the protective covering on the outside of the bone.

PERIOSTEUM,
PROTECTIVE COVERING
ON OUTSIDE OF BONE.

BONE

yellow

COMPACT
GIVES STRENGTH

RED MARROW
RED MAKES blood cells

YELLOW MARROW IN
CENTER OF LONG BONES
STORE FAT CELLS

A **joint** is defined as a place where two bones meet. Joints enable movement. **Ligaments** attach bone to bone. **Tendons** attach bones to muscles.

Physiology of muscle contraction - A nerve impulse strikes a muscle fiber. This causes calcium ions to flood the sarcomere. Calcium ions allow ATP to expend energy. The myosin fibers creep along the actin, causing the muscle to contract. Once the nerve impulse has passed, calcium is pumped out and the contraction ends.

Physiology of the nerve impulse - Nerve action depends on depolarization and an imbalance of electrical charges across the neuron. A polarized nerve has a positive charge outside the neuron. A depolarized nerve has a negative charge outside the neuron. Neurotransmitters turn off the sodium pump, which results in depolarization of the membrane. This wave of depolarization (as it moves from neuron to neuron) carries an electrical impulse. This is actually a wave of opening and closing gates that allows for the flow of ions across the synapse. Nerves have an action potential. There is a threshold of the level of chemicals that must be met or exceeded in order for muscles to respond. This is called the "all or none" response.

The **reflex arc** is the simplest nerve response. The brain is bypassed. When a stimulus (like touching a hot stove) occurs, sensors in the hand send the message directly to the spinal cord. This stimulates motor neurons that contract the muscles to move the hand.

Voluntary nerve responses involve the brain. Receptor cells send the message to sensory neurons that lead to association neurons. The message is taken to the brain. Motor neurons are stimulated and the message is transmitted to effector cells that cause the end effect.

Organization of the Nervous System - The somatic nervous system is controlled consciously. It consists of the central nervous system (brain and spinal cord) and the peripheral nervous system (nerves that extend from the spinal cord to the muscles). The autonomic nervous system is unconsciously controlled by the hypothalamus of the brain. Smooth muscles, the heart, and digestion are some processes controlled by the autonomic nervous system. The sympathetic nervous system works opposite of the parasympathetic nervous system. For example, if the sympathetic nervous system stimulates an action, the parasympathetic nervous system would end that action.

Neurotransmitters - These are chemicals released by exocytosis. Some neurotransmitters stimulate, while others inhibit, action.

Acetylcholine - The most common neurotransmitter; it controls muscle contraction and heartbeat. The enzyme acetylcholinesterase breaks it down to end the transmission.

Epinephrine - Responsible for the "fight or flight" reaction. It causes an increase in heart rate and blood flow to prepare the body for action. It is also called adrenaline.

Endorphins and Enkephalins - These are natural pain killers and are released during serious injury and childbirth.

Digestive System - The function of the digestive system is to break food down and absorb it into the blood stream, where it can be delivered to all cells of the body for use in cellular respiration. The teeth and saliva begin digestion by breaking food down into smaller pieces and lubricating it so it can be swallowed. The lips, cheeks, and tongue form a bolus (ball) of food. It is carried down the pharynx by the process of peristalsis (wave-like contractions) and enters the stomach through the cardiac sphincter which closes to keep food from going back up. In the stomach, pepsinogen and hydrochloric acid form pepsin, the enzyme that breaks down proteins. The food is broken down further by this chemical action and is turned into chyme. The pyloric sphincter muscle opens to allow the food to enter the small intestine. Most nutrient absorption occurs in the small intestine. Its large surface area, accomplished by its length and protrusions called villi and microvilli, allow for a great absorptive surface. Upon arrival into the small intestine, chyme is neutralized to allow the enzymes found there to function. Any food left after the trip through the small intestine enters the large intestine. The large intestine functions to reabsorb water and produce vitamin K. The feces, or remaining waste, are passed out through the anus.

Accessory Organs - Although not part of the digestive tract, these organs function in the production of necessary enzymes and bile. The pancreas makes many enzymes to break down food in the small intestine. The liver makes bile, which breaks down and emulsifies fatty acids.

Respiratory System - This system functions in the gas exchange of oxygen (needed) and carbon dioxide (waste). It delivers oxygen to the bloodstream and picks up carbon dioxide for release out of the body. Air enters the mouth and nose, where it is warmed, moistened, and filtered of dust and particles. Cilia in the trachea trap unwanted material in mucus, which can be expelled. The trachea splits into two bronchial tubes, and the bronchial tubes divide into smaller and smaller bronchioles in the lungs. The internal surface of the lung is composed of alveoli, which are thin-walled air sacs. These allow for a large surface area for gas exchange. The alveoli are lined with capillaries. Oxygen diffuses into the bloodstream and carbon dioxide diffuses out to be exhaled. The oxygenated blood is carried to the heart and delivered to all parts of the body.

The thoracic cavity holds the lungs. A muscle, the diaphragm, below the lungs is an adaptation that makes inhalation possible. As the volume of the thoracic cavity increases, the diaphragm muscle flattens out and inhalation occurs. When the diaphragm relaxes, exhalation occurs.

(handwritten margin note: PATH OF BLOOD FROM HEART → LUNGS → HEART → BODY → HEART)

Circulatory System - The function of the circulatory system is to carry oxygenated blood and nutrients to all cells of the body and return carbon dioxide waste to be expelled from the lungs. Be familiar with the parts of the heart and the path blood takes from the heart to the lungs, through the body, and back to the heart. Unoxygenated blood enters the heart through the inferior and superior vena cava. The first chamber it encounters is the right atrium. It goes through the tricuspid valve to the right ventricle, on to the pulmonary arteries, and then to the lungs, where it is oxygenated. It returns to the heart through the pulmonary vein into the left atrium. It travels through the bicuspid valve to the left ventricle, where it is pumped to all parts of the body through the aorta.

Sinoatrial node (SA node) - The pacemaker of the heart. Located on the right atrium, it is responsible for the contraction of the right and left atrium.

Atrioventricular node (AV node) - Located on the left ventricle; it is responsible for contraction of the ventricles.

Blood vessels include:

- **arteries** - Lead away from the heart. All arteries carry oxygenated blood except the pulmonary artery going to the lungs. Arteries are under high pressure.
- **arterioles** - Arteries branch off to form these smaller passages.
- **capillaries** - Arterioles branch off to form tiny capillaries, which reach every cell. Blood moves slowest here due to the small size of the capillaries; only one red blood cell may pass at a time to allow for diffusion of gases into and out of cells. Nutrients are also absorbed by the cells from the capillaries.
- **venules** – Capillaries combine to form larger venules. The vessels are now carrying waste products from the cells
- **veins** - Venules combine to form larger veins, leading back to the heart. Veins and venules have thinner walls than arteries because they are not under as much pressure. Veins contain valves to prevent the backward flow of blood due to gravity.

Components of the blood include:

- **plasma** – Sixty percent of the blood is plasma. It contains salts called electrolytes, nutrients, and waste. It is the liquid part of blood.
- **erythrocytes** - Also called red blood cells; they contain hemoglobin which carries oxygen molecules.
- **leukocytes** - Also called white blood cells. White blood cells are larger than red cells. They are phagocytic and can engulf invaders. White blood cells are not confined to the blood vessels and can enter the interstitial fluid between cells.
- **platelets** - Assist in blood clotting. Platelets are made in the bone marrow.
- **blood clotting** - The neurotransmitter that initiates blood vessel constriction following an injury is called serotonin. A material called prothrombin is converted to thrombin with the help of thromboplastin. The thrombin is then used to convert fibrinogen to fibrin, which traps red blood cells to form a scab and stop blood flow.

Lymphatic System (Immune System)

Nonspecific defense mechanisms – They do not target specific pathogens, but are a whole-body response. Results of nonspecific mechanisms are seen as symptoms of an infection. These mechanisms include the skin, mucous membranes, and cells of the blood and lymph (i.e., white blood cells, macrophages). Fever is a result of an increase of white blood cells. Pyrogens are released by white blood cells, which set the body's thermostat to a higher temperature. This inhibits the growth of microorganisms. It also increases metabolism to increase phagocytosis and body repair.

Specific defense mechanisms - They recognize foreign material and respond by destroying the invader. These mechanisms are specific in purpose and diverse in type. They are able to recognize individual pathogens. They are able to differentiate between foreign material and self. Memory of the invaders provides immunity upon further exposure.

- **antigen** - Any foreign particle that invades the body.
- **antibody** - Manufactured by the body, they recognize and latch onto antigens, hopefully destroying them.
- **immunity** - This is the body's ability to recognize and destroy an antigen before it causes harm. Active immunity develops after recovery from an infectious disease (chicken pox) or after a vaccination (mumps, measles, and rubella). Passive immunity may be passed from one individual to another. It is not permanent. A good example is the immunities passed from mother to nursing child.

Excretory System - The function of the excretory system is to rid the body of nitrogenous wastes in the form of urea. The functional unit of excretion is the nephrons, which make up the kidneys. Anti-diuretic hormone (ADH), which is made in the hypothalamus and stored in the pituitary, is released when differences in osmotic balance occur. This will cause more water to be reabsorbed. As the blood becomes more dilute, ADH release ceases.
The Bowman's capsule contains the glomerulus, a tightly packed group of capillaries. The glomerulus is under high pressure. Waste and fluids leak out due to pressure. Filtration is not selective in this area. Selective secretion by active and passive transport occurs in the proximal convoluted tubule. Unwanted molecules are secreted into the filtrate. Selective secretion also occurs in the loop of Henle. Salt is actively pumped out of the tube, and much water is lost due to the hyperosmosity of the inner part (medulla) of the kidney. As the fluid enters the distal convoluted tubule, more water is reabsorbed. Urine forms in the collecting duct which leads to the ureter and then to the bladder where it is stored. Urine is passed from the bladder through the urethra. The amount of water reabsorbed back into the body is dependent upon how much water or fluids an individual has consumed. Urine can be very dilute or very concentrated if dehydration is present.

Endocrine System - The function of the endocrine system is to manufacture proteins called hormones. Hormones are released into the bloodstream and are carried to a target tissue where they stimulate an action. Hormones may build up over time to cause their effect, as in puberty or the menstrual cycle.

Hormone activation - Hormones are specific and fit receptors on the target tissue cell surface. The receptor activates an enzyme which converts ATP to cyclic AMP. Cyclic AMP (cAMP) is a second messenger from the cell membrane to the nucleus. The genes found in the nucleus turn on or off to cause a specific response.

There are two classes of hormones.

1. **Steroid hormones** come from cholesterol. Steroid hormones cause sexual characteristics and mating behavior. Hormones include estrogen and progesterone in females and testosterone in males.
2. **Peptide hormones** are made in the pituitary, adrenal glands (kidneys), and the pancreas. They include the following:
   - **Follicle-stimulating hormone (FSH)** - production of sperm or egg cells
   - **Luteinizing hormone (LH)** - functions in ovulation
   - **Luteotropic hormone (LTH)** - assists in production of progesterone
   - **Growth hormone (GH)** - stimulates growth
   - **Antidiuretic hormone (ADH)** - assists in retention of water
   - **Oxytocin** - stimulates labor contractions at birth and let-down of milk
   - **Melatonin** - regulates circadian rhythms and seasonal changes
   - **Epinephrine (adrenaline)** - causes fight or flight reaction of the nervous system
   - **Thyroxin** - increases metabolic rate
   - **Calcitonin** - removes calcium from the blood
   - **Insulin** - decreases glucose level in blood
   - **Glucagon** - increases glucose level in blood

Hormones work on a feedback system. The increase or decrease in one hormone may cause the increase or decrease in another. Release of hormones causes a specific response.

Reproductive System - Sexual reproduction greatly increases diversity due to the many combinations possible through meiosis and fertilization. Gametogenesis is the production of the sperm and egg cells. Spermatogenesis begins at puberty in the male. One spermatozoa produces four sperm. The sperm mature in the seminiferous tubules located in the testes. Oogenesis, the production of egg cells is usually complete by the birth of a female. Egg cells are not released until menstruation begins at puberty. Meiosis forms one ovum with all the cytoplasm and three polar bodies which are reabsorbed by the body. The ovum are stored in the ovaries and released each month from puberty to menopause.

Path of the sperm - Sperm are stored in the seminiferous tubules in the testes, where they mature. Mature sperm are found in the epididymis located on top of the testes. After ejaculation, the sperm travels up the vas deferens, where they mix with semen made in the prostate and seminal vesicles and travel out the urethra.

Path of the egg - Eggs are stored in the ovaries. Ovulation releases the egg into the fallopian tubes, which are ciliated to move the egg along. Fertilization normally occurs in the fallopian tube. If pregnancy does not occur, the egg passes through the uterus and is expelled through the vagina during menstruation. Levels of progesterone and estrogen stimulate menstruation. In the event of pregnancy, hormonal levels are affected by the implantation of a fertilized egg, so menstruation does not occur.

Pregnancy - If fertilization occurs, the zygote implants in about two to three days in the uterus. Implantation promotes secretion of human chorionic gonadotropin (HCG). This is what is detected in pregnancy tests. The HCG keeps the level of progesterone elevated to maintain the uterine lining in order to feed the developing embryo until the umbilical cord forms. Labor is initiated by oxytocin, which causes labor contractions and dilation of the cervix. Prolactin and oxytocin cause the production of milk.

Skill 10.3   Recognize the processes by which energy and nutrients cycle through ecosystems and are used by organisms (e.g., photosynthesis, respiration)

Essential elements are recycled through an ecosystem. At times, the element needs to be "fixed" in a useable form. Cycles are dependent on plants, algae, and bacteria to fix nutrients for use by animals.

Water cycle – Two percent of all the available water is fixed and held in ice or in the bodies of organisms. Available water includes surface water (lakes, oceans, and rivers) and ground water (aquifers, wells). Ninety-six percent of all available water is from ground water. Water is recycled through the processes of evaporation and precipitation. The water present now is the water that has been here since our atmosphere formed.

Carbon cycle - Ten percent of all available carbon in the air (from carbon dioxide gas) is fixed by photosynthesis. Plants fix carbon in the form of glucose; animals eat the plants and are able to obtain their source of carbon. When animals release carbon dioxide through respiration, the plants again have a source of carbon to fix.

Nitrogen cycle - Eighty percent of the atmosphere is in the form of nitrogen gas. Nitrogen must be fixed and taken out of the gaseous form to be incorporated into an organism. Only a few genera of bacteria have the correct enzymes to break the triple bond between nitrogen atoms. These bacteria live within the roots of legumes (peas, beans, alfalfa) and add bacteria to the soil, so it may be taken up by the plant. Nitrogen is necessary to make amino acids and the nitrogenous bases of DNA.

Phosphorus cycle - Phosphorus exists as a mineral and is not found in the atmosphere. Fungi and plant roots have structures called mycorrhizae that are able to fix insoluble phosphates into useable phosphorus. Urine and decayed matter returns phosphorus to the Earth, where it can be fixed in the plant. Phosphorus is needed for the backbone of DNA and for the manufacture of ATP.

Important Processes in Plants

Photosynthesis is the process by which plants make carbohydrates from the energy of the Sun, carbon dioxide, and water. Oxygen is a waste product. Photosynthesis occurs in the chloroplast, where the pigment chlorophyll traps Sun energy. It is divided into two major steps:

Light Reactions - Sunlight is trapped, water is split, and oxygen is given off. ATP is made and hydrogens reduce NADP to $NADPH_2$. The light reactions occur in light. The products of the light reactions enter into the dark reactions (Calvin cycle).

Dark Reactions - Carbon dioxide enters during the dark reactions, which can occur with or without the presence of light. The energy transferred from $NADPH_2$ and ATP allows for the fixation of carbon into glucose.

Respiration - During times of decreased light, plants break down the products of photosynthesis through cellular respiration. Glucose, with the help of oxygen, breaks down and produces carbon dioxide and water as waste. Approximately 50 percent of the products of photosynthesis are used by the plant for energy.

Transpiration - Water travels up the xylem of the plant through the process of transpiration. Water sticks to itself (cohesion) and to the walls of the xylem (adhesion). As it evaporates through the stomata of the leaves, the water is pulled up the column from the roots. Environmental factors such as heat and wind increase the rate of transpiration. High humidity will decrease the rate of transpiration.

Reproduction - Angiosperms are the largest group in the plant kingdom. They are the flowering plants and produce true seeds for reproduction. They arose about seventy million years ago when the dinosaurs were disappearing. The land was drying up and their ability to produce seeds that could remain dormant until conditions became acceptable allowed for their success. When compared to other plants, they also had more advanced vascular tissue and larger leaves for increased photosynthesis. Angiosperms reproduce through a method of **double fertilization**. An ovum is fertilized by two sperm. One sperm produces the new plant; the other forms the food supply for the developing plant.

Seed dispersal – The success of plant reproduction involves the seed moving away from the parent plant to decrease competition for space, water, and minerals. Seeds may be carried by wind (maple trees use this method), water (palm trees), animals (burrs), or ingested by animals and released in their feces in another area.

Important Processes in Animals

Animal respiration takes in oxygen and gives off waste gases. For instance a fish uses its gills to extract oxygen from the water. Bubbles are evidence that waste gases are expelled. Respiration without oxygen is called anaerobic respiration. Anaerobic respiration in animal cells is also called lactic acid fermentation. The end product is lactic acid.

Animal reproduction can be asexual or sexual. Geese lay eggs. Animals such as bear cubs, deer, and rabbits are born alive. Some animals reproduce frequently while others do not. Some animals only produce one baby, yet others produce many (clutch size).

Animal digestion – Some animals only eat meat (carnivores), while others only eat plants (herbivores). Many animals do both (omnivores). Nature has created animals with structural adaptations so they may obtain food through sharp teeth or long facial structures. Digestion's purpose is to break down carbohydrates, fats, and proteins. Many organs are needed to digest food. The process begins with the mouth. Certain animals, such as birds, have beaks to puncture wood or to allow for large fish to be consumed. The tooth structure of a beaver is designed to cut down trees. Tigers are known for their sharp teeth, used to rip hides from their prey. Enzymes are catalysts that help speed up chemical reactions by lowering effective activation energy. Enzyme rate is affected by temperature, pH, and the amount of substrate. Saliva is an enzyme that changes starches into sugars.

Animal circulation – The blood temperature of all mammals stays constant regardless of the outside temperature. This is called warm-blooded, while cold-blooded animals' (amphibians') circulation will vary with the temperature.

Skill 10.4   Analyze how organisms interact with one another and with their environment

Ecology is the study of organisms, where they live, and their interactions with the environment. A **population** is a group of the same species in a specific area. A **community** is a group of populations residing in the same area. Communities that are ecologically similar in regards to temperature, rainfall, and the species that live there are called **biomes**. Specific biomes include:

Marine - Covers 75 percent of the Earth. This biome is organized by the depth of the water. The intertidal zone is from the tide line to the edge of the water. The littoral zone is from the water's edge to the open sea. It includes coral reef habitats and is the most densely populated area of the marine biome. The open sea zone is divided into the epipelagic zone and the pelagic zone. The epipelagic zone receives more Sunlight and has a larger number of species. The ocean floor is called the benthic zone and is populated with bottom feeders.

Tropical Rain Forest - Temperature is constant (25 degrees C); rainfall exceeds 200 cm per year. Located around the area of the equator, the rain forest has abundant, diverse species of plants and animals.

Savanna - Temperatures range from 0 to 25 degrees C depending on the location. Rainfall is from 90 to 150 cm per year. Plants include shrubs and grasses. The savanna is a transitional biome between the rain forest and the desert.

Desert - Temperatures range from 10 to 38 degrees C. Rainfall is under 25 cm per year. Plant species include xerophytes and succulents. Lizards, snakes, and small mammals are common animals.

Temperate Deciduous Forest - Temperature ranges from -24 to 38 degrees C. Rainfall is between 65 to 150 cm per year. Deciduous trees are common, as well as deer, bear, and squirrels.

Taiga - Temperatures range from -24 to 22 degrees C. Rainfall is between 35 to 40 cm per year. Taigas are located very north and very south of the equator, close to the poles. Plant life includes conifers and plants that can withstand harsh winters. Animals include weasels, mink, and moose.

Tundra - Temperatures range from -28 to 15 degrees C. Rainfall is limited, ranging from 10 to 15 cm per year. The tundra is located even further north and south than the taiga. Common plants include lichens and mosses. Animals include polar bears and musk ox.

Polar or Permafrost - Temperature ranges from -40 to 0 degrees C. It rarely gets above freezing. Rainfall is below 10 cm per year. Most water is bound up as ice. Life is limited.

Succession - Succession is an orderly process of replacing a community that has been damaged or beginning one where no life previously existed. Primary succession occurs after a community has been totally wiped out by a natural disaster or where life never existed before, as in a flooded area. Secondary succession takes place in communities that were once flourishing but were disturbed by some source, either man or nature, but were not totally stripped. A climax community is a community that is established and flourishing.

Definitions of feeding relationships:

- **Parasitism** - Two species that occupy a similar place; the parasite benefits from the relationship, while the host is harmed.
- **Commensalism** - Two species that occupy a similar place; neither species is harmed or benefits from the relationship.
- **Mutualism (symbiosis)** - Two species that occupy a similar place; both species benefit from the relationship.
- **Competition** - Two species that occupy the same habitat or eat the same food are said to be in competition with each other.
- **Predation** - Animals that eat other animals are called predators. The animals they feed on are called prey. Population growth depends upon competition for food, water, shelter, and space. The amount of predators determines the amount of prey, which in turn affects the number of predators.
- **Carrying Capacity** - This is the total amount of life a habitat can support. Once the habitat runs out of food, water, shelter, or space, the carrying capacity decreases, and then stabilizes.

Ecological Problems

Nonrenewable resources are fragile and must be conserved for use in the future. Man's impact and knowledge of conservation will control our future.

Biological magnification - Chemicals and pesticides accumulate along the food chain. Tertiary consumers have more accumulated toxins than animals at the bottom of the food chain.

Simplification of the food web - Three major crops feed the world (rice, corn, wheat). The planting of these foods wipes out habitats and pushes animals residing there into other habitats, causing overpopulation or extinction.

Fuel sources - Strip mining and the overuse of oil reserves have depleted these resources. At the current rate of consumption, conservation or alternate fuel sources will guarantee our future fuel sources.

Pollution - Although technology gives us many advances, pollution is a side effect of production. Waste disposal and the burning of fossil fuels have polluted our land, water, and air. Global warming and acid rain are two results of the burning of hydrocarbons and sulfur.

Global warming – Rain forest depletion and the use of fossil fuels and aerosols have caused an increase in carbon dioxide production. This leads to a decrease in the amount of oxygen, which is directly proportional to the amount of ozone. As the ozone layer depletes, more heat enters our atmosphere and is trapped. This causes an overall warming effect, which may eventually melt polar ice caps, causing a rise in water levels and changes in climate which will affect weather systems worldwide.

Endangered species – The construction of homes to house people in our overpopulated world has caused the destruction of habitat for other animals, leading to their extinction.

Overpopulation - The human race is still growing at an exponential rate. Carrying capacity has not been met due to our ability to use technology to produce more food and housing. Space and water cannot be manufactured, and eventually our nonrenewable resources will reach a crisis state. Our overuse affects every living thing on this planet.

All living organisms respond and adapt to their environments. Homeostasis is the result of regulatory mechanisms that help maintain an organism's internal environment within tolerable limits.

The molecular composition of the immediate environment outside of the organism is not the same as it is inside, and the temperature outside may not be optimal for metabolic activity within the organism. Homeostasis is the control of these differences between internal and external environments. There are three **homeostatic systems** to regulate these differences.

Osmoregulation deals with maintenance of the appropriate level of water and salts in body fluids for optimum cellular functions.

Excretion is the elimination of metabolic waste products from the body, including excess water.

Thermoregulation maintains the internal, or core, body temperature of the organism within a tolerable range for metabolic and cellular processes. For example, in humans and mammals, constriction and dilation of blood vessels near the skin help maintain body temperature.

Skill 10.5   Apply knowledge of the principles of genetics and evolutionary theory to understand how organisms change over time

The purpose of cell division is to provide growth and repair cells in the body (somatic), and to replenish or create sex cells for reproduction. There are two forms of cell division. Mitosis is the division of somatic cells, and **meiosis** is the division of sex cells (eggs and sperm). The table below summarizes the major differences between the two processes.

MITOSIS
1. Division of somatic cells.
2. Two cells result from each division.

3. Chromosome number is identical. to parent cells.
4. For cell growth and repair.

MEIOSIS
1. Division of sex cells.
2. Four cells, or polar bodies, result from each division.

3. Chromosome number is half the number of parent cells.
4. Recombinations provide genetic diversity.

Some terms to know:
*   **gamete** - sex cell or germ cell; eggs and sperm.
*   **chromatin** - loose chromosomes; this state is found when the cell is not dividing.
*   **chromosome** - tightly coiled, visible chromatin; this state is found when the cell is dividing.
*   **homologues** - chromosomes that contain the same information. They are of the same length and contain the same genes.
*   **diploid** - 2n number; diploid chromosomes are a pair of chromosomes (somatic cells).
*   **haploid** - 1n number; haploid chromosomes are a half of a pair (sex cells).

MITOSIS

The cell cycle is the life cycle of the cell. It is divided into two stages: **interphase** and the **mitotic division,** where the cell is actively dividing. Interphase is divided into three steps: G1 (growth) period, where the cell is growing and metabolizing, S period (synthesis), where new DNA and enzymes are being made, and the G2 phase (growth), where new proteins and organelles are being made to prepare for cell division. The mitotic stage consists of the stages of mitosis and the division of the cytoplasm.

The stages of mitosis and their events are as follows. Be sure to know the correct order of steps. (IPMAT)

1. **Interphase** - Chromatin is loose, chromosomes are replicated, and cell metabolism is occurring. Interphase is technically <u>not</u> a stage of mitosis.

2. **Prophase** - Once the cell enters prophase, it proceeds through the following steps continuously, with no stopping. The chromatin condenses to become visible chromosomes. The nucleolus disappears and the nuclear membrane breaks apart. Mitotic spindles form which will eventually pull the chromosomes apart. They are composed of microtubules. The cytoskeleton breaks down and the spindles are pushed to the poles, or opposite ends of the cell, by the action of centrioles.

3. **Metaphase** - Kinetechore fibers attach to the chromosome, which causes the chromosomes to line up in the center of the cell (think **m**iddle for **m**etaphase).

4. **Anaphase** - Centromeres split in half, and homologous chromosomes separate. The chromosomes are pulled to the poles of the cell, with identical sets at either end.

5. 5.   **Telophase** - Two nuclei form with a full set of DNA that is identical to the parent cell. The nucleoli become visible and the nuclear membrane reassembles. A cell plate is visible in plant cells, whereas a cleavage furrow is formed in animal cells. The cell is pinched into two cells. Cytokinesis, or division, of the cytoplasm and organelles occurs.

MEIOSIS

Meiosis contains the same five stages as mitosis, but is repeated in order to reduce the chromosome number by one half. This way, when the sperm and egg join during fertilization, the haploid number is reached. The steps of meiosis are as follows:

Major function of Meiosis I - Chromosomes are replicated; cells remain diploid.

Prophase I - Replicated chromosomes condense and pair with homologues. This forms a tetrad. Crossing over (the exchange of genetic material between homologues to further increase diversity) occurs during Prophase I.

Metaphase I - Homologous sets attach to spindle fibers after lining up in the middle of the cell.

Anaphase I - Sister chromatids remain joined and move to the poles of the cell.

Telophase I - Two new cells are formed; chromosome number is still diploid

Major function of Meiosis II - to reduce the chromosome number in half.

Prophase II - Chromosomes condense.

Metaphase II - Spindle fibers form again; sister chromatids line up in center of cell; centromeres divide and sister chromatids separate.

Anaphase II - Separated chromosomes move to opposite ends of cell.

Telophase II - Four haploid cells form for each original sperm germ cell. One viable egg cell gets all the genetic information and three polar bodies form with no DNA. The nuclear membrane reforms and cytokinesis occurs.

Since it's not a perfect world, mistakes happen. Inheritable changes in DNA are called **mutations**. Mutations may be errors in replication or a spontaneous rearrangement of one or more segments by factors like radioactivity, drugs, or chemicals. The amount of the change is not as critical as where the change is. Mutations may occur on somatic or sex cells. Usually the ones on sex cells are more dangerous, since they contain the basis of all information for the developing offspring. Mutations are not always bad. They are the basis of evolution, and if they make a more favorable variation that enhances the organism's survival, then they are beneficial. But, mutations may also lead to abnormalities, birth defects, and even death. There are several types of mutations; let's suppose a normal sequence was as follows:

- **Normal** -   A B C D E F
- **Duplication** - One gene is repeated.   A B C C D E F
- **Inversion** - A segment of the sequence is flipped around.   A E D C B F
- **Deletion** - A gene is left out.   A B C E F
- **Insertion or Translocation** - A segment from another place on the DNA is inserted in the wrong place.   A B C R S D E F
- **Breakage** - A piece is lost.   A B C (DEF is lost.)
- **Non-disjunction** – This occurs during meiosis when chromosomes fail to separate properly. One sex cell may get both genes and another may get none. Depending on the chromosomes involved, this may or may not be serious. Offspring end up with either an extra chromosome or are missing one. An example of non-disjunction is Down Syndrome, where three of chromosome #21 are present.

Gregor Mendel is recognized as the father of genetics. His work in the late 1800s is the basis of our knowledge of genetics. Although unaware of the presence of DNA or genes, Mendel realized there were factors (now known as genes) that were transferred from parents to their offspring. Mendel worked with pea plants and fertilized the plants himself, keeping track of subsequent generations, which led to the Mendelian laws of genetics. Mendel found that two "factors" governed each trait, one from each parent. Traits or characteristics came in several forms, known as alleles. For example, the trait of flower color had white alleles and purple alleles. Mendel formed three laws:

1. **Law of dominance** - In a pair of alleles, one trait may cover up the allele of the other trait. Example: brown eyes are dominant to blue eyes.
2. **Law of segregation** - Only one of the two possible alleles from each parent is passed on to the offspring from each parent. (During meiosis, the haploid number insures that half the sex cells get one allele, and half get the other.)
3. **Law of independent assortment** - Alleles sort independently of each other. (Many combinations are possible depending on which sperm ends up with which egg. Compare this to the many combinations of hands possible when dealing a deck of cards.)

Monohybrid cross - A cross using only one trait.

Dihybrid cross - A cross using two traits. More combinations are possible.

Punnet squares - These are used to show the possible ways that genes combine and indicate probability of the occurrence of a certain genotype or phenotype. One parent's genes are put at the top of the box and the other parent at the side of the box. Genes combine on the square just like numbers that are added in the addition tables we learned in elementary school.

Example: Monohybrid Cross - four possible gene combinations
Example: Dihybrid Cross - sixteen possible gene combinations

Darwin defined the theory of Natural Selection in the mid-1800s. Through the study of finches on the Galapagos Islands, Darwin theorized that nature selects the traits that are advantageous to the organism. Those that do not possess the desirable trait die and do not pass on their genes. Those more fit to survive reproduce, thus increasing that gene in the population. Darwin listed four principles to define natural selection:

1. The individuals in a certain species vary from generation to generation.
2. Some of the variations are determined by the genetic makeup of the species.
3. More individuals are produced than will survive.
4. Some genes allow for better survival of an animal.

Causes of evolution - Certain factors increase the chances of variability in a population, thus leading to evolution. Items that increase variability include mutations, sexual reproduction, immigration, and large population. Items that decrease variation would be natural selection, emigration, small population, and random mating.

Sexual selection - Genes that happen to come together determine the makeup of the gene pool. Animals that use mating behaviors may be successful or unsuccessful. An animal that lacks attractive plumage or has a weak mating call will not attract the female, thereby eventually limiting that gene in the gene pool. Mechanical isolation, where sex organs do not fit the female, has an obvious disadvantage.

Skill 10.6   **Apply knowledge of how to use major concepts, processes, and themes of life science (e.g., those related to heredity, flow of energy, systems, interactions) and the interconnections of life, physical, environmental, Earth, and space sciences to interpret, analyze, and explain everyday phenomena**

See Skills 10.1, 10.4 and 10.5

Skill 10.7   **Recognize relationships among life and environmental science, technology, and society in historical and contemporary contexts**

Humans have been engaging in science since prehistoric times. We have much documentation of scientific experiments and discoveries from classical times. Additionally, feats of engineering show that technology was highly developed in ancient Greek, Roman, Egyptian, Chinese, and other civilizations. However, modern Western science is typically thought to have begun during the Scientific Revolution of the 16th and 17th centuries. This is when the more modern version of the scientific method began to be practiced. Since that time several trends in science and technology have emerged.

First, science is increasingly used to serve the public good. Most early science was largely "pure research science." That is, its only aim was to increase our knowledge of the natural world. As the Industrial Revolution dawned, more and more scientific discoveries were put to use in emerging technologies. This trend has continued and resulted in the development of modern conveniences and necessities ranging from automobiles to computers to high-tech medicine. The continuation of this trend means that now nearly all science is application-driven; most research much at least have the potential to provide a practical advance for humanity. Therefore, unfortunately, there is little funding for pure science in the present day.

Second, science has become increasingly specialized and expensive to perform. During the 16th and 17th century, most scientists were largely hobbyists who had trained under other scientists as apprentices. Additionally, they likely performed research in all scientific areas. As universities sprang up and people wished to investigate phenomena in more detail, scientists began to require more formal training. In modern times, most scientists have advanced degrees, work in high-tech labs with expensive equipment, and may spend entire careers focused on a single problem.

Finally, as communication has improved and technological developments have increased, science has become more and more a part of our everyday lives. Just a few hundred years ago, many people were unable to read, and most knew little about current scientific discoveries. Now, it is easy for most of us to learn more about new science being performed, and we've become accustomed to the constant emergence of new inventions. This has also had the effect of making people less reluctant to accept new technologies and ideas. Historically, individuals and organizations were often highly opposed to the new findings of scientists. As the potential for these discoveries to improve our lives has increased, so has people's willingness to embrace them.

Skill 10.8 Identify a wide range of instructional resources and technologies to support the learning of life and environmental science

While a certain amount of information will always be presented in lecture form or using traditional written materials (i.e., textbooks), there are also many alternative resources available for teaching science at the elementary level. Several examples are listed below:

Hands-on experiments and games

Some simple experiments in the life and environmental sciences may be appropriate for elementary-aged students. For instance, they might examine samples of pond water under a microscope or assist with dissection of plants or lower animals. Students can also model environmental scenarios, perhaps with students playing either predatory or prey animals. Such interactive experiences help students visualize principles explained elsewhere and help them become more engaged with the subject matter.

Software and simulations

When hands-on experiments are costly, complicated, dangerous, or otherwise not possible, students may benefit from software programs that simulate them. Multimedia software packages can be used to expose students to the sounds of the life forms and the environmental settings they are studying. The following website lists many publishers of such software:
http://www.educational-software-directory.net/science/

Natural history museums, zoos, and wildlife preserves

Visits to facilities that aim to spread information about the life and environmental sciences, such as museums and zoos, can be an exciting change from classroom learning. Wildlife preserves and similar facilities often provide educational opportunities and allow students to observe living things in their native environment.

Professional scientists and state/ national government employees

Research scientists and other professionals may be a good resource to teach students more about certain subjects. This is especially true when they can present demonstrations or invite students to their labs, etc. In some cases an agency such as the Department of Natural Resources, Environmental Protection Agency, or state Extension Service may also be a resource.

Finally, there are many websites for science teachers that list more resources, including the following:

http://sciencepage.org/teachers.htm
http://www.nbii.gov/education/
http://www.biologycorner.com/

COMPETENCY 11.0 UNDERSTAND AND APPLY FUNDAMENTAL CONCEPTS AND PRINCIPLES OF PHYSICAL SCIENCE TO INTERPRET, ANALYZE, AND EXPLAIN PHENOMENA

Skill 11.1   Apply knowledge of basic concepts related to matter and energy (e.g., composition and structure of matter, conservation of energy)

Everything in our world is made up of **matter,** whether it is a rock, a building, an animal, or a person. Matter is defined by its characteristics: It takes up space and it has mass.

Mass is a measure of the amount of matter in an object. Two objects of equal mass will balance each other on a simple balance scale, no matter where the scale is located. For instance, two rocks with the same amount of mass that are in balance on Earth will also be in balance on the Moon. They will feel heavier on Earth than on the Moon, however, because of the gravitational pull of the Earth. So, although the two rocks have the same mass, they will have different **weight.**

Weight is the measure of the Earth's pull of gravity on an object. It can also be defined as the pull of gravity between other bodies. The units of weight measurement commonly used are the pound (English measure) and the kilogram (metric measure).

In addition to mass, matter also has the property of volume. **Volume** is the amount of cubic space that an object occupies. Volume and mass together give a more exact description of the object. Two objects may have the same volume, but different mass, or the same mass but different volumes, etc. For instance, consider two cubes that are each one cubic centimeter: one made from plastic, one from lead. They have the same volume, but the lead cube has more mass. The measure that we use to describe the cubes takes into consideration both the mass and the volume. **Density** is the mass of a substance contained per unit of volume. If the density of an object is less than the density of a liquid, the object will float in the liquid. If the object is denser than the liquid, then the object will sink.

Density is stated in grams per cubic centimeter (g/cm^3) where the gram is the standard unit of mass. To find an object's density, you must measure its mass and its volume. Then divide the mass by the volume ($D = m/V$). To discover an object's density, first use a balance to find its mass. Then calculate its volume. If the object is a regular shape, you can find the volume by multiplying the length, width, and height together. However, if it is an irregular shape, you can find the volume by seeing how much water it displaces. Measure the water in the container before and after the object is submerged. The difference will be the volume of the object.

Specific gravity is the ratio of the density of a substance to the density of water. For instance, the specific density of one liter of turpentine is calculated by comparing its mass (0.81 kg) to the mass of one liter of water (1 kg):

$$\frac{\text{mass of 1 L alcohol}}{\text{mass of 1 L water}} = \frac{0.81 \text{ kg}}{1.00 \text{ kg}} = 0.81$$

An **atom** is a nucleus surrounded by a cloud with moving electrons.

The **nucleus** is the center of the atom. The positive particles inside the nucleus are called **protons.** The mass of a proton is about 2,000 times that of the mass of an electron. The number of protons in the nucleus of an atom is called the **atomic number**. All atoms of the same element have the same atomic number.

Neutrons are another type of particle in the nucleus. Neutrons and protons have about the same mass, but neutrons have no charge. Neutrons were discovered because scientists observed that not all atoms in neon gas have the same mass. They had identified isotopes. **Isotopes** of an element have the same number of protons in the nucleus, but have different masses. Neutrons explain the difference in mass. They have mass but no charge.

The mass of matter is measured against a standard mass such as the gram. Scientists measure the mass of an atom by comparing it to that of a standard atom. The result is relative mass. The **relative mass** of an atom is its mass expressed in terms of the mass of the standard atom. The isotope of the element carbon is the standard atom. It has six (6) neutrons and is called carbon-12.It is assigned a mass of 12 atomic mass units (amu). Therefore, the **atomic mass unit (amu)** is the standard unit for measuring the mass of an atom. It is equal to the mass of a carbon atom.

The **mass number** of an atom is the sum of its protons and neutrons. In any element, there is a mixture of isotopes, some having slightly more or slightly fewer protons and neutrons. The **atomic mass** of an element is an average of the mass numbers of its atoms. The following table summarizes the terms used to describe atomic nuclei:

Term	Example	Meaning	Characteristic
Atomic Number	# protons (p)	same for all atoms of a given element	Carbon (C) atomic number = 6 (6p)
Mass number	# protons + # neutrons (p + n)	changes for different isotopes of an element	C-12 (6p + 6n) C-13 (6p + 7n)
Atomic mass	average mass of the atoms of the element	usually not a whole number	atomic mass of carbon equals 12.011

Each atom has an equal number of electrons (negative) and protons (positive). Therefore, atoms are neutral. Electrons orbiting the nucleus occupy energy levels that are arranged in order, and the electrons tend to occupy the lowest energy level available. A **stable electron arrangement** is an atom that has all of its electrons in the lowest possible energy levels.

Each energy level holds a maximum number of electrons. However, an atom with more than one level does not hold more than eight electrons in its outermost shell.

Level	Name	Max. # of Electrons
First	K shell	2
Second	L shell	8
Third	M shell	18
Fourth	N shell	32

This can help explain why chemical reactions occur. Atoms react with each other when their outer levels are unfilled. When atoms either exchange or share electrons with each other, these energy levels become filled, and the atom becomes more stable.

As an electron gains energy, it moves from one energy level to a higher energy level. The electron cannot leave one level until it has enough energy to reach the next level. **Excited electrons** are electrons that have absorbed energy and have moved farther from the nucleus.

Electrons can also lose energy. When they do, they fall to a lower level. However, they can only fall to the lowest level that has room for them. This explains why atoms do not collapse.

An **element** is a substance that cannot be broken down into other substances. To date, scientists have identified 109 elements: 89 are found in nature and 20 are synthetic.

An **atom** is the smallest particle of the element that retains the properties of that element. All of the atoms of a particular element are the same. The atoms of each element are different from the atoms of other elements.

Elements are assigned an identifying symbol of one or two letters. The symbol for oxygen is O and stands for one atom of oxygen. However, because oxygen atoms in nature are joined together in pairs, the symbol O_2 represents oxygen. This pair of oxygen atoms is a molecule. A **molecule** is the smallest particle of substance that can exist independently and have all of the properties of that substance. A molecule of most elements is made up of one atom. However, oxygen, hydrogen, nitrogen, and chlorine molecules are made of two atoms each.

A **compound** is made of two or more elements that have been chemically combined. Atoms join together when elements are chemically combined. The result is that the elements lose their individual identities when they are joined. The compound that they become has different properties.

We use a formula to show the elements of a chemical compound. A **chemical formula** is a shorthand way of showing what is in a compound by using symbols and subscripts. The letter symbols let us know what elements are involved and the number subscript tells how many atoms of each element are involved. No subscript is used if there is only one atom involved. For example, carbon dioxide is made up of one atom of carbon (C) and two atoms of oxygen (O_2), so the formula would be represented as CO_2.

Substances can combine without a chemical change. A **mixture** is any combination of two or more substances in which the substances keep their own properties. A fruit salad is a mixture. So is an ice cream sundae, although you might not recognize each part if it is stirred together. Colognes and perfumes are the other examples. You may not readily recognize the individual elements. However, they can be separated.

Compounds and **mixtures** are similar in that they are made up of two or more substances. However, they have the following opposite characteristics:

Compounds:
- Made up of one kind of particle
- Formed during a chemical change
- Broken down only by chemical changes
- Properties are different from its parts
- Has a specific amount of each ingredient

Mixtures:
- Made up of two or more particles
- Not formed by a chemical change
- Can be separated by physical changes
- Properties are the same as its parts
- Does not have a definite amount of each ingredient

Conservation of Energy
The law of conservation of energy states that energy is neither created nor destroyed. Thus, energy changes form when energy transactions occur in nature. The following are the major forms energy can take.

Thermal energy is the total internal energy of objects created by the vibration and movement of atoms and molecules. Heat is the transfer of thermal energy.

Acoustical energy, or sound energy, is the movement of energy through an object in waves. Energy that forces an object to vibrate creates sound.

Radiant energy is the energy of electromagnetic waves. Light, visible and otherwise, is an example of radiant energy.

Electrical energy is the movement of electrical charges in an electromagnetic field. Examples of electrical energy are electricity and lightning.

Chemical energy is the energy stored in the chemical bonds of molecules. For example, the energy derived from gasoline is chemical energy.

Mechanical energy is the potential and kinetic energy of a mechanical system. Rolling balls, car engines, and body parts in motion exemplify mechanical energy.

Nuclear energy is the energy present in the nucleus of atoms. Division, combination, or collision of nuclei release nuclear energy.

Because the total energy in the universe is constant, energy continually transitions between forms. For example, an engine burns gasoline, converting the chemical energy of the gasoline into mechanical energy; a plant converts the radiant energy of the Sun into chemical energy found in glucose, or a battery converts chemical energy into electrical energy.

Skill 11.2 Recognize the physical and chemical properties of matter (e.g., mass, boiling point, pH)

Physical properties and chemical properties of matter describe the appearance or behavior of a substance. A **physical property** can be observed without changing the identity of a substance. For instance, you can describe the color, mass, shape, and volume of a book. **Chemical properties** describe the ability of a substance to be changed into new substances. Baking powder goes through a chemical change as it changes into carbon dioxide gas during the baking process.

Matter constantly changes. A **physical change** is a change that does not produce a new substance. The freezing and melting of water is an example of physical change. A **chemical change** (or chemical reaction) is any change of a substance into one or more other substances. Burning materials turn into smoke; a seltzer tablet fizzes into gas bubbles.

The **phase of matter** (solid, liquid, or gas) is identified by its shape and volume.

A **solid** has a definite shape and volume. A **liquid** has a definite volume, but no shape. A **gas** has no shape or volume because it will spread out to occupy the entire space of whatever container it is in.

While plasma is really a type of gas, its properties are so unique that it is considered a unique phase of matter. **Plasma is a gas that has been ionized,** meaning that at least one electron has been removed from some of its atoms. Plasma shares some characteristics with gas, specifically, the **high kinetic energy** of its molecules. Thus, plasma exists as a diffuse "cloud," though it sometimes includes tiny grains (this is termed dusty plasma). What most distinguishes plasma from gas is that it is **electrically conductive** and exhibits a strong response to electromagnetic fields. This property is a consequence of the **charged particles that result from the removal of electrons** from the molecules in the plasma.

Energy is the ability to cause change in matter. Applying heat to a frozen liquid changes it from solid back to liquid. Continue heating it and it will boil and give off steam, a gas.

Evaporation is the change in phase from liquid to gas. **Condensation** is the change in phase from gas to liquid.

Common compounds are **acids, bases, salts**, and **oxides** and are classified according to their characteristics.

An **acid** contains one element of hydrogen (H). Although it is never wise to taste a substance to identify it, acids have a sour taste. Vinegar and lemon juice are both acids, and acids occur in many foods in a weak state. Strong acids can burn skin and destroy materials. Common acids include:

Sulfuric acid (H_2SO_4)	-	Used in medicines, alcohol, dyes, and car batteries.
Nitric acid (HNO_3)	-	Used in fertilizers, explosives, and cleaning materials.
Carbonic acid (H_2CO_3)	-	Used in soft drinks.
Acetic acid ($HC_2H_3O_2$)	-	Used in making plastics, rubber, photographic film, and as a solvent.

Bases have a bitter taste, and the stronger ones feel slippery. Like acids, strong bases can be dangerous and should be handled carefully. All bases contain the elements oxygen and hydrogen (OH). Many household cleaning products contain bases. Common bases include:

Sodium hydroxide	NaOH	-	Used in making soap, paper, vegetable oils, and refining petroleum.
Ammonium hydroxide	NH_4OH	-	Making deodorants, bleaching compounds, and cleaning compounds.
Potassium hydroxide	KOH	-	Making soaps, drugs, dyes, alkaline batteries, and purifying industrial gases.
Calcium hydroxide	$Ca(OH)_2$	-	Making cement and plaster

An **indicator** is a substance that changes color when it comes in contact with an acid or a base. Litmus paper is an indicator. Blue litmus paper turns red in an acid. Red litmus paper turns blue in a base.

A substance that is neither acid nor base is **neutral.** Neutral substances do not change the color of litmus paper.

Salt is formed when an acid and a base combine chemically. Water is also formed. The process is called **neutralization.** Table salt (NaCl) is an example of this process. Salts are also used in toothpaste, epsom salts, and cream of tartar. Calcium chloride ($CaCl_2$) is used on frozen streets and walkways to melt the ice. **Oxides** are compounds that are formed when oxygen combines with another element. Rust is an oxide formed when oxygen combines with iron.

The **periodic table of elements** is an arrangement of the elements in rows and columns so that it is easy to locate elements with similar properties. The elements of the modern periodic table are arranged in numerical order by atomic number.

The **periods** are the rows down the left side of the table. They are called first period, second period, etc. The columns of the periodic table are called **groups,** or **families.** Elements in a family have similar properties.

There are three types of elements that are grouped by color: metals, nonmetals, and metalloids.

Element Key

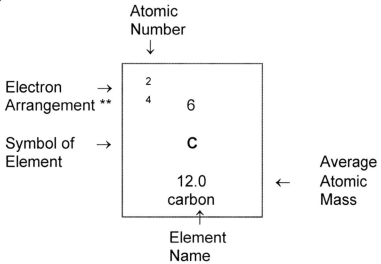

** Number of electrons on each level. Top number represents the innermost level.

The periodic table arranges metals into families with similar properties. The periodic table has its columns marked IA - VIIIA. These are the traditional group numbers. Arabic numbers 1 to 18 are also used, as suggested by the Union of Physicists and Chemists. The Arabic numerals will be used in this text.

Metals:

With the exception of hydrogen, all elements in Group 1 are **alkali metals.** These metals are shiny, softer, and less dense than other metals, and are the most chemically active.

Group 2 metals are the **alkaline earth metals.** They are harder, denser, have higher melting points, and are chemically active.

The **transition elements** can be found by finding the periods (rows) from 4 to 7 under the groups (columns) 3 to 12. They are metals that do not show a range of properties as you move across the chart. They are hard and have high melting points. Compounds of these elements are colorful, such as silver, gold, and mercury.

Elements can be combined to make metallic objects. An **alloy** is a mixture of two or more elements having properties of metals. The elements do not have to be all metals. For instance, steel is made up of the metal iron and the nonmetal carbon.

Nonmetals:

Nonmetals are not as easy to recognize as metals because they do not always share physical properties. However, in general the properties of nonmetals are the opposite of metals. They are dull, brittle, and are not good conductors of heat and electricity.

Nonmetals include solids, gases, and one liquid (bromine).

Nonmetals have four to eight electrons in their outermost energy levels and tend to attract electrons. As a result, the outer levels are usually filled with eight electrons. This difference in the number of electrons is what causes the differences between metals and nonmetals. The outstanding chemical property of nonmetals is that they react with metals.

The **halogens** can be found in Group 17. Halogens combine readily with metals to form salts. Table salt, fluoride toothpaste, and bleach all have an element from the halogen family.

The **noble gases** got their name from the fact that they did not react chemically with other elements, much like the nobility did not mix with the masses. These gases (found in Group 18) will only combine with other elements under very specific conditions. They are **inert** (inactive). In recent years, however, scientists have found this to be only generally true, since chemists have been able to prepare compounds of krypton and xenon.

Metalloids:

Metalloids have properties in between metals and nonmetals. They can be found in Groups 13 to 16, but do not occupy the entire group. They are arranged in stair steps across the groups.

Physical Properties:
- All are solids having the appearance of metals.
- All are white or gray, but not shiny.
- They will conduct electricity, but not as well as a metal.

Chemical Properties:
- They have some characteristics of metals and nonmetals.
- Their properties do not follow patterns like metals and nonmetals. Each must be studied individually.

Boron is the first element in Group 13. It is a poor conductor of electricity at low temperatures. However, increase its temperature and it becomes a good conductor. By comparison, metals, which are good conductors, lose their ability as they are heated. It is because of this property that boron is so useful. Boron is a semiconductor. **Semiconductors** are used in electrical devices that have to function at temperatures too high for metals.

Silicon is the second element in Group 14. It is also a semiconductor and is found in great abundance in the Earth's crust. Sand is made of a silicon compound, silicon dioxide. Silicon is also used in the manufacture of glass and cement.

Skill 11.3   Apply knowledge of characteristics of different forms of energy (e.g., sound, heat)

The **pitch** of a sound depends on the **frequency** that the ear receives. High-pitched sound waves have high frequencies. High notes are produced by an object that is vibrating at a greater number of times per second than one that produces a low note.

The **intensity** of a sound is the amount of energy that crosses a unit of area in a given unit of time. The loudness of the sound is subjective and depends upon the effect on the human ear. Two tones of the same intensity but different pitches may appear to have different loudness. The intensity level of sound is measured in decibels. Normal conversation is about 60 decibels. A power saw is about 110 decibels.

The **amplitude** of a sound wave determines its loudness. Loud sound waves have large amplitudes. The larger the sound wave, the more energy is needed to create the wave.

An oscilloscope is useful in studying waves because it gives a picture of the wave that shows the crest and trough of the wave. **Interference** is the interaction of two or more waves that meet. If the waves interfere constructively, the crest of each one meets the crests of the others. They combine into a crest with greater amplitude. As a result, you hear a louder sound. If the waves interfere destructively, then the crest of one meets the trough of another. They produce a wave with lower amplitude that produces a softer sound.

If you have two tuning forks that produce different pitches, then one will produce sounds of a slightly higher frequency. When you strike the two forks simultaneously, you may hear beats. **Beats** are a series of loud and soft sounds. This is because when the waves meet, the crests combine at some points and produce loud sounds. At other points, they nearly cancel each other out and produce soft sounds.

Sound waves are produced by a vibrating body. The vibrating object moves forward and compresses the air in front of it and then reverses direction so that the pressure on the air is lessened and expansion of the air molecules occurs. One compression and expansion creates one longitudinal wave. Sound can be transmitted through any gas, liquid, or solid. However, it cannot be transmitted through a vacuum, because there are no particles present to vibrate and bump into their adjacent particles to transmit the wave.

The vibrating air molecules move back and forth parallel to the direction of motion of the wave as they pass the energy from adjacent air molecules (closer to the source) to air molecules farther away from the source.

Electromagnetic waves are transverse waves, similar to water waves in the ocean or the waves seen on a guitar string. This is very different from the compression waves of sound. The amplitude of electromagnetic waves relates to its intensity, or brightness (as in the case of visible light). With visible light, the brightness is usually measured in lumens. With other wavelengths the intensity of the radiation, which is power per unit area or watts per square meter, is used. The square of the amplitude of a wave is the intensity. The wavelengths of electromagnetic waves go from extremely long to extremely short and everything in between. The wavelengths determine how matter responds to the electromagnetic wave, and those characteristics determine the name we give that particular group of wavelengths. The velocity of electromagnetic waves in a vacuum is approximately 186,000 miles per second, or 300,000 kilometers per second, the same as the speed of light. When these waves pass through matter, they slow down slightly, according to their wavelength. The frequency of any waveform equals the velocity divided by the wavelength. The units of measurement are in cycles per second, or Hertz.

Seismic Waves are body waves that travel through the solid Earth. Primary Waves (P Waves) are the fastest traveling and the first to arrive, hence "primary." They are conducted as pressure differential and travel through any material. Secondary Waves (S Waves) are slower than P waves, "second" to arrive, hence "secondary." They are conducted as a shearing motion and will not travel through liquids or gas because these materials lack shear strength.

There are three factors that cause different materials to conduct seismic waves differently.

- **Density**: Seismic energy passing through more dense materials must displace more mass than seismic waves passing through a less dense material. All other factors being equal, higher densities slow down the propagation of seismic waves. Rocks in the deeper Earth are denser because the weight of the overlying materials compresses the atoms closer together.

- **Incompressibility:** Seismic waves are propagated by a rebounding action similar to the basketball: as P-wave energy hits a material, it causes rapid compression, and then the material rebounds (springs back) and passes the energy along. The faster the material rebounds, the faster seismic waves can travel through it. All materials have some compressive strength, but gases are more compressible than liquids, and liquids are more compressible than solids. Thus P waves travel through gases very slowly (called sound waves), and they travel through solids rapidly.

- **Rigidity**: Rigidity, or shear strength, is the material's resistance to shearing force--bending. Rigidity is measured in dynes/cm^2. You can tell that water has zero rigidity. Try turning a jar of water with a fish in it: the jar turns, the water does not, and the fish is still facing the same direction. This is because the sides of the jar slide across the water without affecting it: water has no shear strength. Put gelatin into the jar and you have a material with shear strength, and the fish will turn with the jar. Also consider the act of diving into the water: you put your hands in front to break the water, and, if you do it right, you slide right into the water without pain, again because water has no shear strength. If you do it wrong and face an area of your body toward the water, you confront the incompressibility of the water. The change in rigidity will affect the conduction of the seismic waves.

Water Waves

Everything from earthquakes to ship wakes creates waves; however, the most common cause is wind. As wind passes over the water's surface, friction forces it to ripple. The strength of the wind, the distance the wind blows (fetch), and the length of the gust (duration) determine how big the ripples will become. Waves are divided into several parts. The crest is the highest point on a wave, while the trough or valley between two waves is the lowest point. Wavelength is the horizontal distance, either between the crests or between the troughs of two consecutive waves. Wave height is a vertical distance between a wave's crest and the next trough. Wave period measures the size of the wave in time. A wave period can be measured by picking a stationary point and counting the seconds it takes for two consecutive crests or troughs to pass it.

In deep water, a wave is a forward motion of energy, not the motion of water. In fact, the water does not even move forward with a wave. If we followed a single drop of water during a passing wave, we would see it move in a vertical circle, returning to a point near its original position at the wave's end. These vertical circles are more obvious at the surface. As depth increases, their effects slowly decrease until completely disappearing about half a wavelength below the surface.

Electrostatics is the study of stationary electric charges. A plastic rod that is rubbed with fur or a glass rod that is rubbed with silk will become electrically charged and will attract small pieces of paper. The charge on the plastic rod rubbed with fur is negative and the charge on glass rod rubbed with silk is positive.

Electrically charged objects share these characteristics:

1. Like charges repel one another.
2. Opposite charges attract each other.
3. Charge is conserved. A neutral object has no net change. If the plastic rod and fur are initially neutral, when the rod becomes charged by the fur, a negative charge is transferred from the fur to the rod. The net negative charge on the rod is equal to the net positive charge on the fur.

Materials through which electric charges can easily flow are called conductors. On the other hand, an **insulator** is a material through which electric charges do not move easily, if at all. A simple device used to indicate the existence of a positive or negative charge is called an **electroscope.** An electroscope is made up of a conducting knob, and attached to it are very lightweight conducting leaves usually made of foil (gold or aluminum). When a charged object touches the knob, the leaves push away from each other because like charges repel. It is not possible to tell whether the charge is positive or negative.

Charging by induction:
Touch the knob with a finger while a charged rod is nearby. The electrons will be repulsed and flow out of the electroscope through the hand. If the hand is removed while the charged rod remains close, the electroscope will retain the charge.

When an object is rubbed with a charged rod, the object will take on the same charge as the rod. However, charging by induction gives the object the opposite charge as that of the charged rod.

Grounding charge:
Charge can be removed from an object by connecting it to the Earth through a conductor. The removal of static electricity by conduction is called **grounding.**

An **electric circuit** is a path along which electrons flow. A simple circuit can be created with a dry cell, wire, a bell, or a light bulb. When all are connected, the electrons flow from the negative terminal through the wire to the device and back to the positive terminal of the dry cell. If there are no breaks in the circuit, the device will work. The circuit is closed. Any break in the flow will create an open circuit and cause the device to shut off.

The device (bell, bulb) is an example of a **load.** A load is a device that uses energy. Suppose that you also add a buzzer so that the bell rings when you press the buzzer button. The buzzer is acting as a **switch.** A switch is a device that opens or closes a circuit. Pressing the buzzer makes the connection complete and the bell rings. When the buzzer is not engaged, the circuit is open and the bell is silent.

A **series circuit** is one where the electrons have only one path along which they can move. When one load in a series circuit goes out, the circuit is open. An example of this is a set of Christmas tree lights that is missing a bulb. None of the bulbs will work.

A **parallel circuit** is one where the electrons have more than one path to move along. If a load goes out in a parallel circuit, the other load will still work because the electrons can still find a way to continue moving along the path.

When an electron goes through a load, it does work and therefore loses some of its energy. The measure of how much energy is lost is called the **potential difference.** The potential difference between two points is the work needed to move a charge from one point to another.

Potential difference is measured in a unit called the volt. **Voltage** is potential difference. The higher the voltage, the more energy the electrons have. This energy is measured by a device called a voltmeter. To use a voltmeter, place it in a circuit parallel with the load you are measuring.

Current is the number of electrons per second that flow past a point in a circuit. Current is measured with a device called an ammeter. To use an ammeter, put it in the series with the load you are measuring.

As electrons flow through a wire, they lose potential energy. Some is changed into heat energy because of resistance. **Resistance** is the ability of the material to oppose the flow of electrons through it. All substances have some resistance, even if they are a good conductor, such as copper. This resistance is measured in units called **ohms.** A thin wire will have more resistance than a thick one because it will have less room for electrons to travel. In a thicker wire, there will be more possible paths for the electrons to flow. Resistance also depends upon the length of the wire. The longer the wire, the more resistance it will have.

Potential difference, resistance, and current form a relationship know as **Ohm's Law.** Current **(I)** is measured in amperes and is equal to potential difference **(V)** divided by resistance **(R).**

$$I = V / R$$

If you have a wire with resistance of 5 ohms and a potential difference of 75 volts, you can calculate the current by

I = 75 volts / 5 ohms
I = 15 amperes

A current of 10 or more amperes will cause a wire to get hot. Twenty-two amperes is about the maximum for a house circuit. Anything above 25 amperes can start a fire.

Skill 11.4   Analyze the interactions of matter and energy in a system, including transfers and transformations of energy and changes in matter

The **kinetic theory** states that matter consists of molecules, possessing kinetic energies, in continual random motion. The state of matter (solid, liquid, or gas) depends on the speed of the molecules and the amount of kinetic energy the molecules possess. The molecules of solid matter merely vibrate, allowing strong intermolecular forces to hold the molecules in place. The molecules of liquid matter move freely and quickly throughout the body, and the molecules of gaseous matter move randomly and at high speeds.

Matter changes state when energy is added or taken away. The addition of energy, usually in the form of heat, increases the speed and kinetic energy of the component molecules. Faster moving molecules more readily overcome the intermolecular attractions that maintain the form of solids and liquids. In conclusion, as the speed of molecules increases, matter changes state from solid to liquid to gas (melting and evaporation).

As matter loses heat energy to the environment, the speed of the component molecules decreases. Intermolecular forces have greater impact on slower moving molecules. Thus, as the speed of molecules decreases, matter changes from gas to liquid to solid (condensation and freezing).

Heat and temperature are different physical quantities. **Heat** is a measure of energy. **Temperature** is the measure of how hot (or cold) a body is with respect to a standard object.

Two concepts are important in the discussion of temperature changes. Objects are in thermal contact if they can affect each other's temperatures. Set a hot cup of coffee on a desk top. The two objects are in thermal contact with each other and will begin affecting each other's temperatures. The coffee will become cooler and the desktop warmer. Eventually, they will have the same temperature. When this happens, they are in **thermal equilibrium.**

We cannot rely on our sense of touch to determine temperature because the heat from a hand may be conducted more efficiently by certain objects, making them feel colder. **Thermometers** are used to measure temperature. A small amount of mercury in a capillary tube will expand when heated. The thermometer and the object whose temperature it is measuring are put in contact long enough for them to reach thermal equilibrium. Then the temperature can be read from the thermometer scale.

Three temperature scales are used:

1. **Celsius:** The freezing point of water is set at 0 and the steam (boiling) point is 100. The interval between the two is divided into 100 equal parts called degrees Celsius.

2. **Fahrenheit:** The freezing point of water is 32 degrees and the boiling point is 212. The interval between is divided into 180 equal parts called degrees Fahrenheit.

   Temperature readings can be converted from one to the other as follows.

i. Fahrenheit to Celsius	Celsius to Fahrenheit
$C = 5/9 (F - 32)$	$F = (9/5) C + 32$

3. **Kelvin Scale** has degrees the same size as the Celsius scale, but the zero point is moved to the triple point of water. Water inside a closed vessel is in thermal equilibrium in all three states (ice, water, and vapor) at 273.15 degrees Kelvin. This temperature is equivalent to .01 degrees Celsius. Because the degrees are the same in the two scales, temperature changes are the same in Celsius and Kelvin.

   Temperature readings can be converted from Celsius to Kelvin:

Celsius to Kelvin	Kelvin to Celsius
$K = C + 273.15$	$C = K - 273.15$

Heat is a measure of energy. If two objects that have different temperatures come into contact with each other, heat flows from the hotter object to the cooler.

The **heat capacity** of an object is the amount of heat energy that it takes to raise the temperature of the object by one degree.

Heat capacity (C) per unit mass (m) is called **specific heat** (c):

$$c = \frac{C}{m} = \frac{Q/\Delta}{m}$$

Specific heats for many materials have been calculated and can be found in tables.
There are a number of ways that heat is measured. In each case, the measurement is dependent upon raising the temperature of a specific amount of water by a specific amount. These conversions of heat energy and work are called the **mechanical equivalent of heat.**

The **calorie** is the amount of energy that it takes to raise one gram of water one degree Celsius.

The **kilocalorie** is the amount of energy that it takes to raise one kilogram of water by one degree Celsius. Food calories are kilocalories.

In the International System of Units **(SI),** the calorie is equal to 4.184 **joules.**

A **British thermal unit (BTU)** = 252 calories = 1.054 kJ

Heat energy that is transferred into or out of a system is **heat transfer.** The temperature change is positive for a gain in heat energy and negative when heat is removed from the object or system.

The formula for heat transfer is $Q = mc\Delta T$, where Q is the amount of heat energy transferred, m is the amount of substance (in kilograms), c is the specific heat of the substance, and ΔT is the change in temperature of the substance. It is important to assume that the objects in thermal contact are isolated and insulated from their surroundings.

If a substance in a closed container loses heat, then another substance in the container must gain heat.

A **calorimeter** uses the transfer of heat from one substance to another to determine the specific heat of the substance.

When an object undergoes a change of phase, it goes from one physical state (solid, liquid, or gas) to another. For instance, water can go from liquid to solid (freezing) or from liquid to gas (boiling). The heat that is required to change from one state to the other is called **latent heat.**

The **heat of fusion** is the amount of heat that it takes to change from a solid to a liquid or the amount of heat released during the change from liquid to solid.

The **heat of vaporization** is the amount of heat that it takes to change from a liquid to a gaseous state.

Heat is transferred in three ways: **conduction, convection, and radiation.**

1. **Conduction** occurs when heat travels through the heated solid.
2. The transfer rate is the ratio of the amount of heat per amount of time it takes to transfer heat from one area of an object to another. For example, if you place an iron pan on a flame, the handle will eventually become hot. How fast the handle gets too hot to touch is a function of the amount of heat and how long it is applied. Because the change in time is in the denominator of the function, the shorter the amount of time it takes to heat the handle, the greater the transfer rate.
3. **Convection** is heat transported by the movement of a heated substance.
4. Warmed air rising from a heat source such as a fire or electric heater is a common example of convection. Convection ovens make use of circulating air to more efficiently cook food.
5. **Radiation** is heat transfer as the result of electromagnetic waves. The Sun warms the Earth by emitting radiant energy.

An example of all three methods of heat transfer occurs in the thermos bottle, or Dewar flask. The bottle is constructed of double walls of Pyrex glass that have a space in between. Air is evacuated from the space between the walls and the inner wall is silvered. The lack of air between the walls lessens heat loss by convection and conduction. The heat inside is reflected by the silver, cutting down heat transfer by radiation. Hot liquids remain hotter and cold liquids remain colder for longer periods of time.

Dynamics is the study of the relationship between motion and the forces affecting motion. **Force** causes motion.

Mass and weight are not the same quantities. An object's **mass** gives it a resistance to changing its current state of motion. It is also the measure of an object's resistance to acceleration. The force that the Earth's gravity exerts on an object with a specific mass is called the object's weight on Earth. Weight is a force that is measured in Newtons. Weight (W) = mass times acceleration due to gravity **(W = mg).** To illustrate the difference between mass and weight, picture two rocks of equal mass on a balance scale. If the scale is balanced in one place, it will be balanced everywhere, regardless of the gravitational field. However, the weight of the stones would vary on a spring scale, depending upon the gravitational field. In other words, the stones would be balanced both on Earth and on the Moon. However, the weight of the stones would be greater on Earth than on the Moon.

Surfaces that touch each other have a certain resistance to motion. This resistance is **friction,** a force that can be described by the following characteristics:

- The materials that make up the surfaces will determine the magnitude of the frictional force.
- The frictional force is independent of the area of contact between the two surfaces.
- The direction of the frictional force is opposite to the direction of motion.
- The frictional force is proportional to the normal force between the two surfaces in contact.

Static friction describes the force of the friction of two surfaces that are in contact but do not have any motion relative to each other, such as a block sitting on an inclined plane. **Kinetic friction** describes the force of the friction of two surfaces in contact with each other when there is relative motion between the surfaces.

When an object moves in a circular path, a force must be directed toward the center of the circle in order to keep the motion going. This constraining force is called **centripetal force.** Gravity is the centripetal force that keeps a satellite circling the Earth.

Electrical force is the influential power resulting from electricity as an attractive or repulsive interaction between two charged objects. The electric force is determined using Coulomb's law. As shown below, the appropriate unit of charge is the Coulomb (C), and the appropriate unit of distance is meters (m). Use of these units will result in a force expressed in units of Newtons. The demand for these units emerges from the units of Coulomb's constant.

$$F_{elect} = k \cdot Q_1 \cdot Q_2 / d^2$$

There is something of a mystery as to how objects affect each other when they are not in mechanical contact. Newton wrestled with the concept of "action-at-a-distance" (as Electrical Force is now classified), and eventually concluded that it was necessary for there to be some form of ether, or intermediate medium, which made it possible for one object to transfer force to another. We now know that no ether exists. It is possible for objects to exert force on one another without any medium to transfer the force. From our fluid notion of electrical forces, however, we still associate forces as being due to the exchange of something between the two objects. The electrical field force acts between two charges in the same way that the gravitational field force acts between two masses.

Magnetic Force - Magnetized items interact with other items in very specific ways. If a magnet is brought close enough to a ferromagnetic material (that is not magnetized itself), the magnet will strongly attract the ferromagnetic material, regardless of orientation. Both the north and south pole of the magnet will attract the other item with equal strength. In opposition, diamagnetic materials weakly repel a magnetic field. This occurs regardless of the north/south orientation of the field. Paramagnetic materials are weakly attracted to a magnetic field. This also occurs regardless of the north/south orientation of the field. **Calculating** the attractive or repulsive magnetic force between two magnets is, in the general case, an extremely complex operation, as it depends on the shape, magnetization, orientation, and separation of the magnets.

In the **Nuclear Force** the protons in the nucleus of an atom are positively charged. If protons interact, they are usually pushed apart by the electromagnetic force. However, when two or more nuclei come VERY close together, the nuclear force comes into play. The nuclear force is a hundred times stronger than the electromagnetic force, so the nuclear force may be able to "glue" the nuclei together so that fusion can happen. The nuclear force is also known as the strong force. The nuclear force keeps together the most basic of elementary particles, the quarks. Quarks combine to form the protons and neutrons in the atomic nucleus.

The **force of gravity** is the force at which the Earth, Moon, or other massively large object attracts another object towards itself. By definition, this is the weight of the object. All objects upon Earth experience a force of gravity that is directed "downward" towards the center of the Earth. The force of gravity on Earth is always equal to the weight of the object, as found by the equation:

Fgrav = m * g

where g = 9.8 m/s^2 (on Earth)
and m = mass (in kg)

Newton's laws of motion:

Newton's first law of motion is also called the law of inertia. It states that an object at rest will remain at rest, and an object in motion will remain in motion at a constant velocity unless acted upon by an external force.

Newton's second law of motion states that if a net force acts on an object, it will cause the acceleration of the object. The relationship between force and motion is the following: force equals mass times acceleration. **(F = ma.)**

Newton's third law of motion states that for every action, there is an equal and opposite reaction. Therefore, if an object exerts a force on another object, that second object exerts an equal and opposite force on the first.

Newton's laws of motion have practical applications. For example, they help us to assess frictional forces, determine the forces acting on a pendulum, and analyze nonlinear motion. Let's look at a pendulum.

The motion of a **pendulum** is an example of mechanical energy conservation. A pendulum is made up of a bob attached to a pivot point by a string. The pendulum sweeps outward in a circular arc, moving back and forth in a periodic fashion. There are only two forces acting upon the bob. Gravity is one force, acting in a downward direction and doing work on the bob. However, gravity is a conservative, or internal, force and does not change the total amount of mechanical energy of the bob. Tension is the other force acting upon the bob. It is an external force, which does not do work on the bob because it always acts in a direction perpendicular to the bob. The angle between the force of tension and its instantaneous displacement is always 90 degrees at all points in the trajectory of the bob. [F*d*cos (90°) = 0 Joules.] Thus, the force of tension does not do work upon the bob.

There are no external forces doing work, so the total mechanical energy of the pendulum bob is conserved. The falling motion of the bob is accompanied by an increase in speed. As the bob loses height and potential energy, it gains speed and kinetic energy. The sum of potential energy and kinetic energy remains constant; the total of the two forms of mechanical energy is conserved.

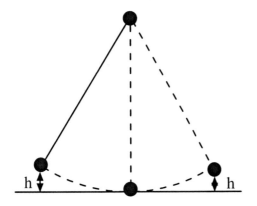

Skill 11.5 **Apply knowledge of how to use major concepts, processes, and themes of physical science (e.g., those related to motion of objects, waves and vibrations, changes in matter), as well as the interconnections of physical, life, environmental, Earth, and space sciences to interpret, analyze, and explain everyday phenomena**

The relationship between heat, forms of energy, and work (mechanical, electrical, etc.) are the **Laws of Thermodynamics.** These laws deal strictly with systems in thermal equilibrium and not those within the process of rapid change or in a state of transition. Systems that are nearly always in a state of equilibrium are called **reversible systems.**

The first law of thermodynamics is a restatement of the conservation of energy. The change in heat energy supplied to a system (Q) is equal to the sum of the change in the internal energy (U) and the change in the work done by the system against internal forces. $\Delta Q = \Delta U + \Delta W$

The second law of thermodynamics is stated in two parts:

1. No machine is 100 percent efficient. It is impossible to construct a machine that only absorbs heat from a heat source and performs an equal amount of work, because some heat will always be lost to the environment.
2. Heat cannot spontaneously pass from a colder to a hotter object. An ice cube sitting on a hot sidewalk will melt into a little puddle, but it will never spontaneously cool and form the same ice cube. Certain events have a preferred direction called the **arrow of time.**

Entropy is the measure of how much energy, or heat, is available for work. Work occurs only when heat is transferred from hotter to cooler objects. Once this is done, no more work can be extracted. The energy is still being conserved but is not available for work as long as the objects are the same temperature. Theory has it that eventually, all things in the universe will reach the same temperature. If this happens, energy will no longer be usable.

Electricity can be used to change the chemical composition of a material. For instance, when electricity is passed through water, it breaks the water down into hydrogen gas and oxygen gas.

Circuit breakers in a home monitor the electric current. If there is an overload, the circuit breaker will create an open circuit, stopping the flow of electricity. Computers can be made small enough to fit inside a plastic credit card by creating what is known as a solid state device. In this device, electrons flow through solid material such as silicon.

Resistors are used to regulate volume on a television or radio or through a dimmer switch for lights.

A bird can sit on an electrical wire without being electrocuted because the bird and the wire have about the same potential. However, if that same bird would touch two wires at the same time, he would not have to worry about flying south next year.

When caught in an electrical storm, a car is a relatively safe place from lightening because of the resistance of the rubber tires. A metal building would not be safe unless there were a lightening rod that would attract the lightening and conduct it into the ground.

Telegraphs use electromagnets to work. When a telegraph key is pushed, current flows through a circuit, turning on an electromagnet which attracts an iron bar. The iron bar hits a sounding board, which responds with a click. Release the key and the electromagnet turns off. Messages can be sent around the world in this way.

Scrap metal can be removed from waste materials by the use of a large electromagnet that is suspended from a crane. When the electromagnet is turned on, the metal in the pile of waste will be attracted to it. All other materials will stay on the ground.

Air conditioners, vacuum cleaners, and washing machines use electric motors. An electric motor uses an electromagnet to change electric energy into mechanical energy.

Skill 11.6   **Recognize relationships among physical science, technology, and society in historical and contemporary contexts**

    o   See Skill 10.7

Skill 11.7   **Identify a wide range of instructional resources and technologies to support the learning of physical science**

    o   See Skill 10.8

COMPETENCY 12.0 UNDERSTAND AND APPLY FUNDAMENTAL CONCEPTS AND PRINCIPLES OF EARTH AND SPACE SCIENCE TO INTERPRET, ANALYZE, AND EXPLAIN PHENOMENA

Skill 12.1 Apply knowledge of the geological composition and history of the Earth

The biological history of the Earth is partitioned into four major Eras, which are further divided into major periods. The major periods are refined into groupings called Epochs.

Earth's history extends over more than four billion years and is reckoned in terms of a scale. Paleontologists who study the history of the Earth have divided this huge period of time into four large time units, called eons. Eons are divided into smaller units of time called eras. An era refers to a time interval in which particular plants and animals were dominant, or present in great abundance. The end of an era is most often characterized by (1) a general uplifting of the crust, (2) the extinction of the dominant plants or animals, and (3) the appearance of new life-forms.

Each era is divided into several smaller divisions of time called periods. Some periods are divided into smaller time units called epochs.

Era	Period	Time	Characteristics
Cenozoic	Quaternary	1.6 million years ago to the present	The Ice Age occurred, and human beings evolved.
	Tertiary	65-1.64 million years ago	Mammals and birds evolved to replace the great reptiles and dinosaurs that had just become extinct. Forests gave way to grasslands, and the climate became cooler.
Mesozoic	Cretaceous	135-65 million years ago	Reptiles and dinosaurs roamed the Earth. Most of the modern continents had split away from the large landmass, Pangaea, and many were flooded by shallow chalk seas.
	Jurassic	350-135 million years ago	Reptiles were beginning to evolve. Pangaea started to break up. Deserts gave way to forests and swamps.
	Triassic		

Paleozoic	Permian	350-250 million years ago	Continents came together to form one big landmass, Pangaea. Forests (that formed today's coal) grew on deltas around the new mountains, and deserts formed.
	Carboniferous		
	Devonian	410-355 million years ago	Continents started moving toward each other. The first land animals, such as insects and amphibians, existed. Many fish swam in the seas.
	Silurian	510-410 million years ago	Sea life flourished, and the first fish evolved. The earliest land plants began to grow around shorelines and estuaries.
	Ordovician		
	Cambrian	570-510 million years ago	No life on land, but all kinds of sea animals existed.
Precambrian	Proterozoic	Beginning of the Earth to 570 million years ago (seven-eighths of the Earth's history)	Some sort of life existed.
	Archaean		No life.

Infer the history of an area using geologic evidence

The determination of the age of rocks by cataloging their composition has been outmoded since the middle 1800s. Today a sequential history can be determined by the fossil content (principle of fossil succession) of a rock system as well as its superposition within a range of systems. This classification process was termed stratigraphy and permitted the construction of a Geologic Column, in which rock systems are arranged in their correct chronological order.

Principles of catastrophism and uniformitarianism

Uniformitarianism - is a fundamental concept in modern geology. It simply states that the physical, chemical, and biological laws that operated in the geologic past operate in the same way today. The forces and processes that we observe presently shaping our planet have been at work for a very long time. This idea is commonly stated as "the present is the key to the past."

Catastrophism - the concept that the Earth was shaped by catastrophic events of a short-term nature.

Skill 12.2   Analyze the major features of the Earth in terms of the natural processes that shape them (e.g., plate tectonics, erosion, volcanic activity)

Orogeny is the term given to natural mountain building.

A mountain is terrain that has been raised high above the surrounding landscape by volcanic action, or some form of tectonic plate collisions. The plate collisions could be intercontinental or ocean floor collisions with a continental crust (subduction). The physical composition of mountains would include igneous, metamorphic, or sedimentary rocks; some may have rock layers that are tilted or distorted by plate collision forces.

There are many different types of mountains. The physical attributes of a mountain range depends upon the angle at which plate movement thrusts layers of rock to the surface. Many mountains (Adirondacks, Southern Rockies) were formed along high angle faults.

Folded mountains (Alps, Himalayas) are produced by the folding of rock layers during their formation. The Himalayas are the highest mountains in the world and contain Mount Everest, which rises almost 9 km above sea level. The Himalayas were formed when India collided with Asia. The movement which created this collision is still in process at the rate of a few centimeters per year.

Fault-block mountains (Utah, Arizona, and New Mexico) are created when plate movement produces tension forces instead of compression forces. The area under tension produces normal faults, and rock along these faults is displaced upward.

Dome mountains are formed as magma tries to push up through the crust but fails to break the surface. Dome mountains resemble a huge blister on the Earth's surface.

Upwarped mountains (Black Hills of South Dakota) are created in association with a broad arching of the crust. They can also be formed by rock thrust upward along high-angle faults.

Volcanism is the term given to the movement of magma through the crust and its emergence as lava onto the Earth's surface. Volcanic mountains are built up by successive deposits of volcanic materials.

An active volcano is one that is presently erupting or building to an eruption. A dormant volcano is one that is between eruptions but still shows signs of internal activity that might lead to an eruption in the future. An extinct volcano is said to be no longer capable of erupting. Most of the world's active volcanoes are found along the rim of the Pacific Ocean, which is also a major earthquake zone. This curving belt of active faults and volcanoes is often called the Ring of Fire.

The world's best known volcanic mountains include Mount Etna in Italy and Mount Kilimanjaro in Africa. The Hawaiian Islands are actually the tops of a chain of volcanic mountains that rise from the ocean floor.

There are three types of volcanic mountains: shield volcanoes, cinder cones, and composite volcanoes.

Shield Volcanoes are associated with quiet eruptions. Lava emerges from the vent, or opening, in the crater and flows freely out over the Earth's surface until it cools and hardens into a layer of igneous rock. A repeated lava flow builds this type of volcano into the largest volcanic mountain. Mauna Loa, found in Hawaii, is the largest volcano on Earth.

Cinder Cone Volcanoes are associated with explosive eruptions, as lava is hurled high into the air in a spray of droplets of various sizes. These droplets cool and harden into cinders and particles of ash before falling to the ground. The ash and cinder pile up around the vent to form a steep, cone-shaped hill called the cinder cone. Cinder cone volcanoes are relatively small but may form quite rapidly.

Composite Volcanoes are described as being built by both lava flows and layers of ash and cinders. Mount Fuji in Japan, Mount St. Helens in Washington, USA, and Mount Vesuvius in Italy are all famous composite volcanoes.

Mechanisms of producing mountains
Mountains are produced by different types of mountain-building processes. Most major mountain ranges are formed by the processes of folding and faulting.

Folded Mountains are produced by the folding of rock layers. Crustal movements may press horizontal layers of sedimentary rock together from the sides, squeezing them into wavelike folds. Up-folded sections of rock are called anticlines; down-folded sections of rock are called synclines. The Appalachian Mountains are an example of folded mountains with long ridges and valleys in a series of anticlines and synclines formed by folded rock layers.

Faults are fractures in the Earth's crust, which have been created by either tension or compression forces transmitted through the crust. These forces are produced by the movement of separate blocks of crust.

Faultings are categorized on the basis of the relative movement between the blocks on both sides of the fault plane. The movement can be horizontal, vertical, or oblique.

A dip-slip fault occurs when the movement of the plates is vertical and opposite. The displacement is in the direction of the inclination, or dip, of the fault. Dip-slip faults are classified as normal faults when the rock above the fault plane moves down relative to the rock below.

Reverse faults are created when the rock above the fault plane moves up relative to the rock below. Reverse faults having a very low angle to the horizontal are also referred to as thrust faults.

Faults in which the dominant displacement is horizontal movement along the trend, or strike (length), of the fault are called **strike-slip faults.** When a large strike-slip fault is associated with plate boundaries, it is called a **transform fault.** The San Andreas Fault in California is a well-known transform fault.

Faults that have both vertical and horizontal movement are called **oblique-slip faults.**

When lava cools, igneous rock is formed. This formation can occur either above ground or below ground.

Intrusive rock includes any igneous rock that was formed below the Earth's surface. Batholiths are the largest structures of intrusive-type rock and are composed of near-granite materials; they are the core of the Sierra Nevada Mountains.

Extrusive rock includes any igneous rock that was formed at the Earth's surface.

Dikes are old lava tubes formed when magma entered a vertical fracture and hardened. Sometimes magma squeezes between two rock layers and hardens into a thin horizontal sheet called a **sill.** A **laccolith** is formed in much the same way as a sill, but the magma that creates a laccolith is very thick and does not flow easily. It pools and forces the overlying strata, creating an obvious surface dome.

A **caldera** is normally formed by the collapse of the top of a volcano. This collapse can be caused by a massive explosion that destroys the cone and empties most, if not all, of the magma chamber below the volcano. The cone collapses into the empty magma chamber, forming a caldera.

An inactive volcano may have magma solidified in its pipe. This structure, called a volcanic neck, is resistant to erosion and today may be the only visible evidence of the past presence of an active volcano.

Glaciation

A continental glacier covered a large part of North America during the most recent ice age. Evidence of this glacial coverage remains as abrasive grooves, large boulders from northern environments dropped in southerly locations, glacial troughs created by the rounding out of steep valleys by glacial scouring, and the remains of glacial sources, called **cirques,** that were created by frost wedging the rock at the bottom of the glacier. Remains of plants and animals found in warm climates and discovered in the moraines and out-wash plains help to support the theory of periods of warmth during the past ice ages.

The Ice Age began about 2 to 3 million years ago. This age saw the advancement and retreat of glacial ice over millions of years. Theories relating to the origin of glacial activity include Plate Tectonics, where it can be demonstrated that some continental masses, now in temperate climates, were at one time blanketed by ice and snow. Another theory involves changes in the Earth's orbit around the Sun, changes in the angle of the Earth's axis, and the wobbling of the Earth's axis. Support for the validity of this theory has come from deep-ocean research that indicates a correlation between climatic sensitive micro-organisms and the changes in the Earth's orbital status.

About 12,000 years ago, a vast sheet of ice covered a large part of the northern United States. This huge, frozen mass had moved southward from the northern regions of Canada as several large bodies of slow-moving ice, or glaciers. A time period in which glaciers advance over a large portion of a continent is called an ice age. A glacier is a large mass of ice that moves or flows over the land in response to gravity. Glaciers form among high mountains and in other cold regions.

There are two main types of glaciers: valley glaciers and continental glaciers. Erosion by valley glaciers is characteristic of U-shaped erosion. This type of erosion produces sharp, peaked mountains such as the Matterhorn in Switzerland. Erosion by continental glaciers often rides over mountains in their paths leaving smoothed, rounded mountains and ridges.

Data obtained from many sources led scientists to develop the theory of plate tectonics. This theory is the most current model that explains not only the movement of the continents, but also the changes in the Earth's crust caused by internal forces.

Plates are rigid blocks of Earth's crust and upper mantle. These rigid, solid blocks make up the lithosphere. The Earth's lithosphere is broken into nine large sections and several small ones. These moving slabs are called plates. The major plates are named after the continents they are "transporting."

The plates float on and move with a layer of hot, plastic-like rock in the upper mantle. Geologists believe that the heat currents circulating within the mantle cause this plastic zone of rock to slowly flow, carrying along the overlying crustal plates.

Movement of these crustal plates creates areas where the plates diverge as well as areas where the plates converge. A major area of divergence is located in the Mid-Atlantic. Currents of hot mantle rock rise and separate at this point of divergence, creating new oceanic crust at the rate of 2 to 10 centimeters per year. Convergence is when the oceanic crust collides with either another oceanic plate or a continental plate. The oceanic crust sinks, forming an enormous trench and generating volcanic activity. Convergence also includes continent-to-continent plate collisions. When two plates slide past one another, a transform fault is created.

These movements produce many major features of the Earth's surface, such as mountain ranges, volcanoes, and earthquake zones. Most of these features are located at plate boundaries, where the plates interact by spreading apart, pressing together, or sliding past each other. These movements are very slow, averaging only a few centimeters a year.

Boundaries form between spreading plates where the crust is forced apart in a process called rifting. Rifting generally occurs at mid-ocean ridges. Rifting can also take place within a continent, splitting the continent into smaller landmasses that drift away from each other, thereby forming an ocean basin between them. The Red Sea is a product of rifting. As the seafloor spreading takes place, new material is added to the inner edges of the separating plates. In this way the plates grow larger, and the ocean basin widens. This is the process that broke up the super continent, Pangaea, and created the Atlantic Ocean.

Boundaries between plates that are colliding are zones of intense crustal activity. When a plate of ocean crust collides with a plate of continental crust, the more dense oceanic plate slides under the lighter continental plate and plunges into the mantle. This process is called **subduction,** and the site where it takes place is called a subduction zone. A subduction zone is usually seen on the sea floor as a deep depression called a trench.

The crustal movement which is identified by plates sliding sideways past each other produces a plate boundary characterized by major faults that are capable of unleashing powerful earthquakes. The San Andreas Fault forms such a boundary between the Pacific Plate and the North American Plate.

Erosion is the inclusion and transportation of surface materials by another moveable material, usually water, wind, or ice. The most important cause of erosion is running water. Streams, rivers, and tides are constantly at work removing weathered fragments of bedrock and carrying them away from their original location.

A stream erodes bedrock by the grinding action of the sand, pebbles, and other rock fragments. This grinding against each other is called abrasion.
Streams also erode rocks by dissolving or absorbing their minerals. Limestone and marble are readily dissolved by streams.

The breaking down of rocks at or near the Earth's surface is known as **weathering.** Weathering breaks down these rocks into smaller and smaller pieces. There are two types of weathering: physical weathering and chemical weathering.

Physical weathering is the process by which rocks are broken down into smaller fragments without undergoing any change in chemical composition. Physical weathering is mainly caused by the freezing of water, the expansion of rock, and the activities of plants and animals.

Frost wedging is the cycle of daytime thawing and refreezing at night. This cycle causes large rock masses, especially the rocks exposed on mountain tops, to be broken into smaller pieces.

The peeling away of the outer layers from a rock is called exfoliation. Rounded mountain tops are called exfoliation domes and have been formed in this way. Chemical weathering is the breaking down of rocks through changes in their chemical composition. An example would be the change of feldspar in granite to clay. Water, oxygen, and carbon dioxide are the main agents of chemical weathering. When water and carbon dioxide combine chemically, they produce a weak acid that breaks down rocks.

Deposition, also known as sedimentation, is the term for the process by which material from one area is slowly deposited into another area. This is usually due to the movement of wind, water, or ice containing particles of matter. When the rate of movement slows down, particles filter out and remain behind, causing a build-up of matter. Note that this is a result of matter being eroded and removed from another site.

Skill 12.3   Demonstrate understanding of the water cycle

Water that falls to Earth in the form of rain and snow is called **precipitation.** Precipitation is part of a continuous process, in which water at the Earth's surface evaporates, condenses into clouds, and returns to Earth. This process is termed the **water cycle.** The water located below the surface is called groundwater.

The impacts of altitude upon climatic conditions are primarily related to temperature and precipitation. As altitude increases, climatic conditions become increasingly drier and colder. Solar radiation becomes more severe as altitude increases, while the effects of convection forces are minimized. Climatic changes as a function of latitude follow a similar pattern (as a reference, latitude moves either north or south from the equator). The climate becomes colder and drier as the distance from the equator increases. Proximity to land or water masses produces climatic conditions based upon the available moisture. Dry and arid climates prevail where moisture is scarce; lush tropical climates can prevail where moisture is abundant. Climate, as described above, depends upon the specific combination of conditions making up an area's environment. Man impacts all environments by producing pollutants in Earth, air, and water. It follows then, that man is a major player in world climatic conditions.

Skill 12.4   Recognize fundamental weather processes and phenomena (e.g., storms, atmospheric circulation) and factors that influence them

World weather patterns are greatly influenced by ocean surface currents in the upper layer of the ocean. These currents continuously move along the ocean surface in specific directions. Ocean currents that flow deep below the surface are called sub-surface currents. These currents are influenced by such factors as the location of landmasses in the current's path and the Earth's rotation.

Surface currents are caused by winds and are classified by temperature. Cold currents originate in the polar regions and flow through surrounding water that is measurably warmer. Those currents with a higher temperature than the surrounding water are called warm currents and can be found near the equator. These currents follow swirling routes around the ocean basins and the equator.

The Gulf Stream and the California Current are the two main surface currents that flow along the coastlines of the United States. The Gulf Stream is a warm current in the Atlantic Ocean that carries warm water from the equator to the northern parts of the Atlantic Ocean. Benjamin Franklin studied and named the Gulf Stream. The California Current is a cold current that originates in the Arctic regions and flows southward along the west coast of the United States.

Differences in water density also create ocean currents. Water found near the bottom of oceans is the coldest and the densest. Water tends to flow from a denser area to a less dense area. Currents that flow because of a difference in the density of the ocean water are called density currents. Water with a higher salinity is denser than water with a lower salinity. Water that has a salinity different from the surrounding water may form a density current.

Air masses moving toward or away from the Earth's surface are called air currents. Air moving parallel to the Earth's surface is called **wind.** Weather conditions are generated by winds and air currents carrying large amounts of heat and moisture from one part of the atmosphere to another. Wind speeds are measured by instruments called anemometers.

The wind belts in each hemisphere consist of convection cells that encircle Earth like belts. There are three major wind belts on Earth: (1) trade winds, (2) prevailing westerlies, and (3) polar easterlies. Wind belt formation depends on the differences in air pressures that develop in the doldrums, the horse latitudes, and the polar regions. The Doldrums surround the equator. Within this belt heated air usually rises straight up into Earth's atmosphere. The Horse latitudes are regions of high barometric pressure with calm and light winds, and the Polar Regions contain cold dense air that sinks to the Earth's surface.

Winds caused by local temperature changes include sea breezes and land breezes.

Sea breezes are caused by the unequal heating of the land and an adjacent, large body of water. Land heats up faster than water. The movement of cool ocean air toward the land is called a sea breeze. Sea breezes usually begin blowing about mid-morning, ending about sunset.

A breeze that blows from the land to the ocean or a large lake is called a **land breeze.**

Monsoons are huge wind systems that cover large geographic areas and that reverse direction seasonally. The monsoons of India and Asia are examples of these seasonal winds. They alternate wet and dry seasons. As denser, cooler air over the ocean moves inland, a steady seasonal wind called a summer or wet monsoon is produced.

The air temperature at which water vapor begins to condense is called the **dew point.**

Relative humidity is the actual amount of water vapor in a certain volume of air compared to the maximum amount of water vapor this air could hold at a given temperature.

Knowledge of types of storms

A **thunderstorm** is a brief, local storm produced by the rapid upward movement of warm, moist air within a cumulo-nimbus cloud. Thunderstorms always produce lightning and thunder, and are accompanied by strong wind gusts and heavy rain or hail.

A severe storm with swirling winds that may reach speeds of hundreds of km per hour is called a **tornado.** Such a storm is also referred to as a "twister." The sky is covered by large cumulo-nimbus clouds and violent thunderstorms; a funnel-shaped swirling cloud may extend downward from a cumulo-nimbus cloud and reach the ground. Tornadoes are storms that leave a narrow path of destruction on the ground.

A swirling, funnel-shaped cloud that extends downward and touches a body of water is called a **waterspout.**

Hurricanes are storms that develop when warm, moist air carried by trade winds rotates around a low-pressure "eye." A large, rotating, low-pressure system accompanied by heavy precipitation and strong winds is called a tropical cyclone (better known as a hurricane). In the Pacific region, a hurricane is called a typhoon.

Storms that occur only in the winter are known as blizzards, or ice storms. A **blizzard** is a storm with strong winds, blowing snow, and frigid temperatures. An **ice storm** consists of falling rain that freezes when it strikes the ground, covering everything with a layer of ice.

Skill 12.5   Apply knowledge of the basic components and structure of the solar system

There are eight established planets in our solar system: Mercury, Venus, Earth, Mars, Jupiter, Saturn, Uranus, and Neptune. Pluto was an established planet in our solar system, but as of the summer of 2006, its status is being reconsidered. The planets are divided into two groups based on their distance from the Sun. The inner planets include Mercury, Venus, Earth, and Mars. The outer planets include Jupiter, Saturn, Uranus, and Neptune.

Planets

Mercury -- the closest planet to the Sun. Its surface has craters and rocks. The atmosphere is composed of hydrogen, helium, and sodium. Mercury was named after the Roman messenger god.

Venus -- has a slow rotation when compared to Earth. Venus and Uranus rotate in opposite directions from the other planets. This opposite rotation is called retrograde rotation. The surface of Venus is not visible due to the extensive cloud cover. The atmosphere is composed mostly of carbon dioxide. Sulfuric acid droplets in the dense cloud cover give Venus a yellow appearance. Venus has a greater greenhouse effect than observed on Earth. The dense clouds combined with carbon dioxide trap heat. Venus was named after the Roman goddess of love.

Earth -- considered a water planet with 70 percent of its surface covered by water. Gravity holds the masses of water in place. The different temperatures observed on Earth allow for the different states (solid, liquid, gas) of water to exist. The atmosphere is composed mainly of oxygen and nitrogen. Earth is the only planet that is known to support life.

Mars -- the surface of Mars contains numerous craters, active and extinct volcanoes, ridges, and valleys with extremely deep fractures. Iron oxide found in the dusty soil makes the surface seem rust-colored and the skies seem pink in color. The atmosphere is composed of carbon dioxide, nitrogen, argon, oxygen, and water vapor. Mars has polar regions with ice caps composed of water. Mars has two satellites. Mars was named after the Roman war god.

Jupiter -- largest planet in the solar system. Jupiter has sixteen Moons. The atmosphere is composed of hydrogen, helium, methane, and ammonia. There are white-colored bands of clouds indicating rising gases and dark-colored bands of clouds indicating descending gases. The gas movement is caused by heat resulting from the energy of Jupiter's core. Jupiter has a Great Red Spot that is thought to be a hurricane-type cloud. Jupiter has a strong magnetic field.

Saturn -- the second largest planet in the solar system. Saturn has rings of ice, rock, and dust particles circling it. Saturn's atmosphere is composed of hydrogen, helium, methane, and ammonia. Saturn has twenty-plus satellites. Saturn was named after the Roman god of agriculture.

Uranus -- the second largest planet in the solar system with retrograde revolution. Uranus is a gaseous planet. It has ten dark rings and fifteen satellites. Its atmosphere is composed of hydrogen, helium, and methane. Uranus was named after the Greek god of the heavens.

Neptune -- another gaseous planet with an atmosphere consisting of hydrogen, helium, and methane. Neptune has three rings and two satellites. Neptune was named after the Roman sea god because its atmosphere is the same color as the seas.

Pluto – once considered the smallest planet in the solar system; its status as a planet is being reconsidered. Pluto's atmosphere probably contains methane, ammonia, and frozen water. Pluto has one satellite. Pluto revolves around the Sun every 250 years. Pluto was named after the Roman god of the underworld.

Comets, asteroids, and meteors

Astronomers believe that rocky fragments may have been the remains of the birth of the solar system that never formed into a planet. **Asteroids** are found in the region between Mars and Jupiter.

Comets are masses of frozen gases, cosmic dust, and small rocky particles. Astronomers think that most comets originate in a dense comet cloud beyond Pluto. A comet consists of a nucleus, a coma, and a tail. A comet's tail always points away from the Sun. The most famous comet, **Halley's Comet,** is named after the person who first discovered it in 240 B.C. It returns to the skies near Earth every 75 to 76 years.

Meteoroids are composed of particles of rock and metal of various sizes. When a meteoroid travels through the Earth's atmosphere, friction causes its surface to heat up and it begins to burn. The burning meteoroid falling through the Earth's atmosphere is called a **meteor** (also known as a "shooting star").

Meteorites are meteors that strike the Earth's surface. A physical example of a meteorite's impact on the Earth's surface can be seen in Arizona. The Barringer Crater is a huge meteor crater. There are many other meteor craters throughout the world.

Oort Cloud and Kuiper Belt

The **Oort Cloud** is a hypothetical spherical cloud surrounding our solar system. It extends approximately three light years, or thirty trillion kilometers from the Sun. The cloud is believed to be made up of materials ejected out of the inner solar system because of interaction with Uranus and Neptune, but is gravitationally bound to the Sun. It is named the Oort Cloud after Jan Oort, who suggested its existence in 1950. Comets from the Oort Cloud exhibit a wide range of sizes, inclinations, and eccentricities and are often referred to as Long-Period Comets because they have a period of greater than 200 years.

It seems that the Oort Cloud objects were formed closer to the Sun than the Kuiper Belt objects. Small objects formed near the giant planets would have been ejected from the solar system by gravitational encounters. Those that didn't escape entirely formed the distant Oort Cloud. Small objects formed farther out had no such interactions and remained as the Kuiper Belt objects.

The **Kuiper Belt** is the name given to a vast population of small bodies orbiting the Sun beyond Neptune. There are more than 70,000 of these small bodies with diameters larger than 100 km extending outwards from the orbit of Neptune to 50AU. They exist mostly within a ring, or belt, surrounding the Sun. It is believed that the objects in the Kuiper Belt are primitive remnants of the earliest phases of the solar system. It is also believed that the Kuiper Belt is the source of many Short-Period Comets (periods of less then 200 years). It is a reservoir for the comets in the same way that the Oort Cloud is a reservoir for long-period comets.

Occasionally the orbit of a Kuiper Belt object will be disturbed by the interactions of the giant planets in such a way as to cause the object to cross the orbit of Neptune. It will then very likely have a close encounter with Neptune, sending it out of the solar system or into an orbit crossing those of the other giant planets, or even into the inner solar system. Prevailing theory states that scattered disk objects began as Kuiper Belt objects, which were scattered through gravitational interactions with the giant planets.

The **Sun** is considered the nearest star to Earth that produces solar energy. By the process of nuclear fusion, hydrogen gas is converted to helium gas. Energy flows out of the core to the surface, and then radiation escapes into space.

Parts of the Sun include: (1) **core:** the inner portion of the Sun where fusion takes place, (2) **photosphere:** the surface of the Sun which produces **Sunspots** (cool, dark areas that can be seen on its surface), (3) **chromosphere:** hydrogen gas causes this portion to be red in color (also found here are solar flares-- sudden brightness of the chromosphere--and solar prominences, gases that shoot outward from the chromosphere), and (4) **corona**, the transparent area of Sun visible only during a total eclipse.

Solar radiation is energy traveling from the Sun that radiates into space. **Solar flares** produce excited protons and electrons that shoot outward from the chromosphere at great speeds, reaching Earth. These particles disturb radio reception and also affect the magnetic field on Earth.

A star is a ball of hot, glowing gas that is hot enough and dense enough to trigger nuclear reactions, which fuel the star. In comparing the mass, light production, and size of the Sun to other stars, astronomers find that the Sun is a perfectly ordinary star. It behaves exactly the way they would expect a star of its size to behave. The main difference between the Sun and other stars is that the Sun is much closer to Earth.

Most stars have masses similar to that of the Sun. The majority of stars' masses are between 0.3 to 3.0 times the mass of the Sun. Theoretical calculations indicate that in order to trigger nuclear reactions and to create its own energy—that is, to become a star—a body must have a mass greater than 7 percent of the mass of the Sun. Astronomical bodies that are less massive than this become planets or objects called brown dwarfs. The largest accurately determined stellar mass is of a star called V382 Cygni and is twenty-seven times that of the Sun.

The range of brightness among stars is much larger than the range of mass. Astronomers measure the brightness of a star by measuring its magnitude and luminosity. Magnitude allows astronomers to rank how bright, comparatively, different stars appear to humans. Because of the way our eyes detect light, a lamp ten times more luminous than a second lamp will appear less than ten times brighter to human eyes. This discrepancy affects the magnitude scale, as does the tradition of giving brighter stars lower magnitudes. The lower a star's magnitude, the brighter it is. Stars with negative magnitudes are the brightest of all.

Magnitude is given in terms of absolute and apparent values. Absolute magnitude is a measurement of how bright a star would appear if viewed from a set distance away. Astronomers also measure a star's brightness in terms of its luminosity. A star's absolute luminosity, or intrinsic brightness, is the total amount of energy radiated by the star per second. Luminosity is often expressed in units of watts.

Astronomers use groups or patterns of stars called **constellations** as reference points to locate other stars in the sky. Familiar constellations include Ursa Major (also known as the big bear) and Ursa Minor (known as the little bear). Within the Ursa Major, the larger constellation, The Big Dipper is found. Within the Ursa Minor, the smaller constellation, The Little Dipper is found.

Different constellations appear as the Earth continues its revolution around the Sun with the seasonal changes.

Magnitude stars are twenty-one of the brightest stars that can be seen from Earth. These are the first stars noticed at night. In the Northern Hemisphere there are fifteen commonly observed first-magnitude stars.

A vast collection of stars is defined as a **galaxy.** Galaxies are classified as irregular, elliptical, and spiral. An irregular galaxy has no real structured appearance; most are in their early stages of life. An elliptical galaxy consists of smooth ellipses, containing little dust and gas, but composed of millions or trillions of stars. Spiral galaxies are disk-shaped and have extending arms that rotate around their dense centers. Earth's galaxy is found in the Milky Way, and it is a spiral galaxy.

A **pulsar** is defined as a variable radio source that emits signals in very short, regular bursts, and is believed to be a rotating neutron star.

A **quasar** is defined as an object that photographs like a star but has an extremely large redshift and a variable energy output; it is believed to be the active core of a very distant galaxy.

A **black hole** is defined as an object that has collapsed to such a degree that light cannot escape from its surface; light is trapped by the intense gravitational field.

Origin of the Solar System

Two main hypotheses of the origin of the solar system are (1) **the tidal hypothesis,** and (2) **the condensation hypothesis.**

The tidal hypothesis proposes that the solar system began with a near collision of the Sun and a large star. Some astronomers believe that as these two stars passed each other, the great gravitational pull of the large star extracted hot gases out of the Sun. The mass from the hot gases started to orbit the Sun, which began to cool, and then the mass condensed into the nine planets. (Few astronomers support this hypothesis.)

The condensation hypothesis proposes that the solar system began with rotating clouds of dust and gas. Condensation occurred in the center, forming the Sun, and the smaller parts of the cloud formed the nine planets. (This example is widely accepted by many astronomers.)

Two main theories to explain the origins of the universe include (1) **The Big Bang Theory,** and (2) **The Steady State Theory.**

The Big Bang Theory has been widely accepted by many astronomers. It states that the universe originated from a magnificent explosion, spreading mass, matter, and energy into space. The galaxies formed from this material as it cooled during the next half-billion years.

The Steady State Theory is the least accepted theory. It states that the universe is continuously being renewed. Galaxies move outward, and new galaxies replace the older galaxies. Astronomers have not found any evidence to prove this theory.

The future of the universe is hypothesized with the Oscillating Universe Hypothesis. It states that the universe will oscillate, or expand and contract. Galaxies will move away from one another and will in time slow down and stop. Then a gradual moving toward each other will again activate the explosion, or the big bang theory.

The stages of life for a star start with a mass of gas and dust that becomes a nebula and then a main sequence star. Next it becomes a red giant, then a nova, and then in its final stages, a white dwarf (the dying core of a giant star), a neutron star, or a black hole.

The forces of gravity acting on particles of gas and dust in a cloud in an area of space produce stars. This cloud is called a nebula. Particles in this cloud attract each other, and as the cloud grows, its temperature increases. With the increased temperature the star begins to glow. Fusion occurs in the core of the star, releasing radiant energy at the star's surface.

When hydrogen becomes exhausted in a small, or even an average star, its core will collapse and cause its temperature to rise. This released heat causes nearby gases to heat, contract, carry out fusion, and produce helium. Stars at this stage are nearing the end of their life. These stars are called red giants; also called supergiants. A white dwarf is the dying core of a giant star. A nova is an ordinary star that experiences a sudden increase in brightness and then fades back to its original brightness. A supernova radiates even greater light energy. A neutron star is the result of mass left behind after a supernova. A black hole is a star with condensed matter and gravity so intense that light cannot escape.

Skill 12.6   Apply principles and concepts of Earth and space science to describe the composition, motions, and interactions of objects in the universe

Earth is the third planet away from the Sun in our solar system. Earth's numerous types of motion and states of orientation greatly affect global conditions, such as seasons, tides, and lunar phases. The Earth orbits the Sun within a period of 365 days. During this orbit, the average distance between the Earth and Sun is ninty-three million miles. The shape of the Earth's orbit around the Sun deviates only slightly from the shape of a circle. This deviation, known as the Earth's eccentricity, has a very small affect on the Earth's climate. The Earth is closest to the Sun at perihelion, occurring around January 2nd of each year, and farthest from the Sun at aphelion, occurring around July 2nd. Because the Earth is closest to the Sun in January, the northern winter is slightly warmer than the southern winter.

Seasons

The rotation axis of the Earth is not perpendicular to the orbital (ecliptic) plane. The axis of the Earth is tilted approximately 23.5 degrees from perpendicular. The tilt of the Earth's axis is known as the obliquity of the ecliptic, and is mainly responsible for the four seasons of the year by influencing the intensity of solar rays received by the Northern and Southern Hemispheres. The four seasons, spring, summer, fall, and winter, are extended periods of characteristic average temperature, rainfall, storm frequency, and vegetation growth, or dormancy. The effect of the Earth's tilt on climate is best demonstrated at the solstices, the two days of the year when the Sun is farthest from the Earth's equatorial plane.

At the Summer Solstice (June Solstice), the Earth's tilt on its axis causes the Northern Hemisphere to lean toward the Sun, while the Southern Hemisphere leans away. Consequently, the Northern Hemisphere receives more intense rays from the Sun and experiences summer during this time, while the Southern Hemisphere experiences winter. At the Winter Solstice (December Solstice), it is the Southern Hemisphere that leans toward the Sun and thus experiences summer. Spring and fall are produced by varying degrees of the same leaning toward or away from the Sun.

Tides

The orientation of the Earth and Moon and their gravitational interaction are responsible for the ocean tides that occur on Earth. The term "tide" refers to the cyclic rise and fall of large bodies of water. Gravitational attraction is defined as the force of attraction between all bodies in the universe. At the location on Earth closest to the Moon, the gravitational attraction of the Moon draws seawater toward the Moon in the form of a tidal bulge. On the opposite side of the Earth, another tidal bulge forms in the direction away from the Moon because at this point, the Moon's gravitational pull is the weakest. "Spring tides" are especially strong tides that occur when the Earth, Sun, and Moon are in line, allowing both the Sun and the Moon to exert gravitational force on the Earth and increase tidal bulge height. These tides occur during the full Moon and the new Moon. "Neap tides" are especially weak tides, occurring when the gravitational forces of the Moon and the Sun are perpendicular to one another. These tides occur during quarter Moons.

Lunar Phases

The Earth's orientation in respect to the solar system is also responsible for our perception of the phases of the Moon. As the Earth orbits the Sun within a period of 365 days, the Moon orbits the Earth every twenty-seven days. As the Moon circles the Earth, its shape in the night sky appears to change. The changes in the appearance of the Moon from Earth are known as "lunar phases." These phases vary cyclically according to the relative positions of the Moon, the Earth, and the Sun. At all times, half of the Moon is facing the Sun and is thus illuminated by reflecting the Sun's light. As the Moon orbits the Earth and the Earth orbits the Sun, the half of the Moon that faces the Sun changes. However, the Moon is in synchronous rotation around the Earth, meaning that nearly the same side of the Moon faces the Earth at all times. This side is referred to as the near side of the Moon. Lunar phases occur as the Earth and Moon orbit the Sun, and the fractional illumination of the Moon's near side changes.

When the Sun and Moon are on opposite sides of the Earth, observers on Earth perceive a "full Moon," meaning the Moon appears circular because the entire illuminated half of the Moon is visible. As the Moon orbits the Earth, the Moon "wanes," and the amount of the illuminated half of the Moon that is visible from Earth decreases. A gibbous Moon is between a full Moon and a half Moon, or between a half Moon and a full Moon. When the Sun and the Moon are on the same side of Earth, the illuminated half of the Moon is facing away from Earth, and the Moon appears invisible. This lunar phase is known as the "new Moon." The time between each full Moon is approximately 29.53 days.

A list of all lunar phases includes:
- New Moon: The Moon is invisible, or the first signs of a crescent appear.
- Waxing Crescent: The right crescent of the Moon is visible.
- First Quarter: The right quarter of the Moon is visible.
- Waxing Gibbous: Only the left crescent is not illuminated.
- Full Moon: The entire illuminated half of the Moon is visible.
- Waning Gibbous: Only the right crescent of the Moon is not illuminated.
- Last Quarter: The left quarter of the Moon is illuminated.
- Waning Crescent: Only the left crescent of the Moon is illuminated.

Viewing the Moon from the Southern Hemisphere would cause these phases to occur in the opposite order.

Skill 12.7 **Apply knowledge of how to use major processes and themes of Earth and space science (e.g., those related to weather, the water cycle, patterns of change), as well as the interconnections of Earth, space, physical, life, and environmental sciences to interpret, analyze, and explain everyday phenomena**

When we look at the various phenomena in geology and meteorology, we can see manifestations of many scientific principles. It is not simply that certain examples exist in the natural world. Rather it is the reverse; scientists observed natural phenomena to formulate and refine the theories and laws of science.

First, there are many simple chemical and physical principles that underlie the various phenomena discussed in this section. For instance, basic principles of radioactive decay are exploited to allow carbon dating. Chemical laws also dictate the dissolution and precipitation that govern the formation of many rocks. Chemical principles are important in various processes involving water: the dissolution of carbonic acid that causes acid rain; reactions between rock and water leading to karst topography; and solubility rules that govern what compounds leach out of soil and into groundwater. The laws of thermodynamics are also extremely important in the natural world, since they predict everything from how weather systems move to how water flows to the ultimate heat death of the universe.

- See also Skill 10.6

Skill 12.8 **Recognize interrelationships among Earth and space science, technology, and society in historical and contemporary contexts**

Two main theories have been developed to explain the origins of the universe. These are: (1) **The Big Bang Theory,** and (2) **The Steady State Theory.**

The Big Bang Theory has been widely accepted by many astronomers. It states that the universe originated from a magnificent explosion spreading mass, matter, and energy into space. The galaxies were formed from this material as it cooled during the next half-billion years.

The Steady State Theory is the least accepted theory. It states that the universe is continuously being renewed. Galaxies move outward and new galaxies replace the older galaxies. Astronomers have not found any evidence to prove this theory.

The Oscillating Universe Hypothesis has been developed to describe the future of the universe. It states that the universe will oscillate, or expand and contract. Galaxies will move away from one another and will, in time, slow down and stop moving. Then a gradual moving toward a common center will again result in another explosion in a repeat of the big bang theory.

Space exploration programs

Though outer space has been a subject of fascination throughout human history, space exploration refers particularly to the travel into outer space to discover new features and facts. Though space exploration continues today, it was at its height in the late 20th century, when much progress was made over just a few years.

Telescopes are one of the oldest technologies used to gain information about space. Most telescopes are optical, though spectrum telescopes for gathering all types of electromagnetic radiation also exist. Optical telescopes have been used for hundreds of years to observe bodies and phenomena in outer space. As technology has allowed telescopes to be launched into outer space, even more detailed information has been obtained. Particularly, these telescopes have allowed observation unhindered by the interference of the Earth's atmosphere. The Hubble telescope, which is in orbit around Earth, is one famous optical telescope that has been utilized in this manner. The Chandra X-ray observatory is another famous telescope, though it collects X-rays. These and other telescopes have gleaned much information about distant bodies in outer space.

Some of the earliest forays into true space exploration were unmanned missions involving space probes. The probes are controlled remotely from Earth and have been shot into outer space and immediately returned, placed into orbit around our planet, and sent to and past the other planets in our solar system. The first was the USSR's Sputnik I in October of 1957. It was the first man-made object ever launched into space. This was the beginning of the "space race" between the USSR and the U.S.A. The U.S.A.'s first successful launch of a space probe occurred with Vanguard I in December of 1957. A few early, unmanned missions were space probes carrying animals, such as the Soviet dog Laika that became the first animal in orbit in November of 1957. Animals are included only for research purposes in current missions. Space probes are still used for certain applications where risk, cost, or duration makes manned missions impractical. The Voyager probes are among the most famous probes. They were launched to take advantage of the favorable planetary alignment in the late 1970s. They returned data and fascinating pictures from Jupiter and Saturn, as well as information from beyond our solar system. It is hoped that, as technology continues to improve, space probes will allow us to investigate space even farther away from Earth.

The first manned mission occurred in 1961, when the USSR launched Yuri Gagarin aboard Vostok I into space. A year later, the American John Glenn became the first man to orbit the Earth. The U.S.A. finally pulled well ahead in the space race in 1969, when Neil Armstrong and Buzz Aldrin became the first men to reach the Moon aboard Apollo 11. Reusable space shuttles were a large step forward in allowing manned missions. The first space shuttle to enter outer space was the Columbia, though other famous U.S. shuttles include the Challenger, Atlantis, and Endeavour. Shuttles are now used to conduct experiments and to transport astronauts to and from space stations. Space stations now serve as key tools in space exploration.

A space station is any artificial structure designed to house, but not transport, humans living in space. The first space station was Salyut 1, launched by the USSR in 1971. This, like all space stations up to the present, was a low Earth-orbital station. Other space stations include Skylab, Salyuts 2-7, Mir, and the International Space Station. Only the International Space Station is currently in use. Space stations offer an excellent environment to run long-term experiments in outer space. However, they are not suitable for human life beyond a few months because of the low gravity, high radiation, and other less-understood factors. Much progress needs to be made before human beings will be able to live permanently in space. In fact, the future of manned missions is somewhat uncertain, as there is some debate about how necessary they are. Many speculate that significant cost and risk could be avoided with the use of robots. Currently, humans in space perform many experiments and conduct necessary repairs on equipment.

Benefits of Space Exploration

Space exploration, like all scientific endeavors, provides the expansion of our knowledge about how the universe works. However, given the relatively high cost of space exploration, further justification is needed. Firstly, money spent on space research creates many jobs and so has economic benefits. Secondly, as space exploration has become an increasingly international affair, it has served to increase cooperation between nations and generate goodwill. Note that such cooperation also decreases the financial burden for individual countries. However, one of the greatest benefits of space exploration is the potential for transfer of technology. A vast array of technologies developed to further space exploration has found broader applications. These include communication devices, satellite operations, electronics, fabrics, and other materials. For instance, the technology used in smoke detectors was developed for NASA's Skylab spacecraft in the 1970s, and quartz timing crystals used in nearly all wristwatches were developed as timing devices for the Apollo lunar missions.

Skill 12.9 Identify a wide range of instructional resources and technologies to support the learning of physical science

While a certain amount of information will always be presented in lecture form or using traditional written materials (i.e., textbooks), there are also many alternative resources available for teaching the physical sciences at the elementary level. Several examples are listed below:

Hands-on experiments and games

Some simple experiments in the physical sciences may be appropriate for elementary-aged students. For instance, they might experiment with a gyroscope, perform simple acid-base reactions (baking and vinegar, etc.), or make a potato battery. Such interactive experiences help students visualize principles explained elsewhere and help them become more engaged with the subject matter.

Software and simulations

See section 10.8 for additional information on these resources.

Museums of science and technology, observatories, and planetariums

Facilities such as these offer a different environment for students to be exposed to concepts and objects, particularly when exhibits allow students to touch, feel, and gain first-hand experience with the manifestations of the principles of the physical sciences.

Professional scientists, engineers, and inventors

Research scientists and other professionals may be a good resource to teach students more about certain subjects. This especially true when they can present demonstrations or invite students to their labs, etc. Most engineers and inventors also rely on the principles of physical science. Demonstrations and presentations about the development of new technology may also be applicable.

Finally, there are many websites for science teachers to that list more resources, including the following::
http://sciencepage.org/teachers.htm
http://www.anachem.umu.se/eks/pointers.htm
http://www.csun.edu/science/

COMPETENCY 13.0 UNDERSTAND THE PRINCIPLES AND PROCESSES OF SCIENTIFIC INVESTIGATION AND HOW TO PROMOTE STUDENTS' DEVELOPMENT OF SCIENTIFIC KNOWLEDGE AND SKILLS, INCLUDING THEIR USE OF SCIENTIFIC THINKING, INQUIRY, REASONING, AND INVESTIGATION

Skill 13.1   Determine the type of scientific investigation (e.g., experimentation, systematic observation) that best addresses a given question or hypothesis

Science may be defined as a body of knowledge that is systematically derived from study, observations, and experimentation. Its goal is to identify and establish principles and theories that may be applied to solve problems. Pseudoscience, on the other hand, is a belief that is not warranted. There is no scientific methodology or application. Some of the more classic examples of pseudoscience include witchcraft, alien encounters, or any topics that are explained by hearsay.

Scientific inquiry starts with observation. Observation is a very important skill by itself, since it leads to experimentation and finally to communicating the experimental findings to society/the public. After observing, a question is formed, which starts with "why" or "how." To answer these questions, experimentation is necessary. Between observation and experimentation, there are three more important steps. These are gathering information (or researching about the problem), hypothesis, and designing the experiment.

Designing an experiment is very important, since it involves identifying control variables, constants, independent variables, and dependent variables. A control/standard is something we compare our results with at the end of the experiment. It is like a reference. Constants are the factors we have to keep constant in an experiment to get reliable results. Independent variables are factors we change in an experiment. It is very important to bear in mind that there should be more constants than variables to obtain reproducible results in an experiment.

Classifying is grouping items according to their similarities. It is important for students to realize relationships and similarities as well as differences in order to reach a reasonable conclusion in a lab experiment.

After the experiment is done, it is repeated and results are graphically presented. The results are then analyzed and conclusions drawn.

It is the responsibility of the scientists to share the knowledge they obtain through their research.

After the conclusion is drawn, the final step is communication. In this age, a lot of emphasis is put on the method of communication. The conclusions must be communicated by clearly describing the information using accurate data, visual presentation like graphs (bar/line/pie), tables/charts, diagrams, artwork, and other appropriate media, like power-point presentation. Modern technology must be used whenever necessary. The method of communication must be suitable to the audience.

Written communication is as important as oral communication. This is essential for submitting research papers to scientific journals, newspapers, other magazines, etc.

Skill 13.2 **Demonstrate knowledge of considerations and procedures, including safety practices, related to designing and conducting experiments (e.g., formulation of hypothesis; use of control and experimental groups; recognition of variables being held constant, those being manipulated, and those responding in an experiment)**

The scientific method is the basic process behind science. It involves several steps beginning with hypothesis formulation and working through to the conclusion.

Posing a question
Although many discoveries happen by chance, the standard thought process of a scientist begins with forming a question to research. The more limited the question, the easier it is to set up an experiment to answer it.

Forming a hypothesis
Once the question is formulated take an educated guess about the answer to the problem or question. This 'best guess' is your hypothesis.

Doing the test
To make a test fair, data from an experiment must have a **variable,** or any condition that can be changed, such as temperature or mass. A good test will try to manipulate as few variables as possible so as to see which variable is responsible for the result. This requires a second example of a **control**. A control is an extra setup in which all the conditions are the same except for the variable being tested.

Observing and recording the data
Reporting of the data should state specifics of how the measurements were calculated. A graduated cylinder needs to be read with proper procedures. As beginning students, technique must be part of the instructional process so as to give validity to the data.

Drawing a conclusion

After recording data, you compare your data with that of other groups. A conclusion is the judgment derived from the data results.

Graphing data

Graphing utilizes numbers to demonstrate patterns. The patterns offer a visual representation, making it easier to draw conclusions.

Applying knowledge of designing and performing investigations

Normally, knowledge is integrated in the form of a lab report. A report has many sections. It should include a specific **title** and tell exactly what is being studied. The **abstract** is a summary of the report written at the beginning of the paper. The **purpose** should always be defined and will state the problem. The purpose should include the **hypothesis** (educated guess) of what is expected from the outcome of the experiment. The entire experiment should relate to the problem, or purpose.

It is important to describe exactly what was done to prove or disprove a hypothesis. A **control** is necessary to prove that the results occurred from the changed conditions and would not have happened normally. Only one variable should be manipulated at a time. **Observations** and **results** of the experiment should be recorded, including all results from data. Drawings, graphs and illustrations should be included to support information. Observations are objective, whereas analysis and interpretation are subjective. A **conclusion** should explain why the results of the experiment either proved or disproved the hypothesis.

A scientific theory is an explanation of a set of related observations based on a proven hypothesis. A scientific law usually lasts longer than a scientific theory and has more experimental data to support it.

Skill 13.3 **Recognize how to use methods, tools, technologies, and measurement units to gather and organize data, compare and evaluate data, and describe and communicate the results of investigations in various formats**

Science uses the metric system as it is accepted worldwide and allows easier comparison among experiments done by scientists around the world. Learn the following basic units and prefixes:

meter - measure of length
liter - measure of volume
gram - measure of mass

deca-(meter, liter, gram)= 10X the base unit   **deci** = 1/10 the base unit
hecto-(meter, liter, gram)= 100X the base unit   **centi** = 1/100 the base unit
kilo-(meter, liter, gram) = 1000X the base unit   **milli** = 1/1000 the base unit

Graphing is an important skill to visually display collected data for analysis. The two types of graphs most commonly used are the **line graph** and the **bar graph** (histogram). Line graphs are set up to show two variables represented by one point on the graph. The x-axis is the horizontal axis and represents the independent variable. Independent variables are those that would be present independently of the experiment. A common example of an independent variable is time. Time proceeds regardless of anything else occurring. The y-axis is the vertical axis and represents the dependent variable. Dependent variables are manipulated by the experiment, such as the amount of light, or the height of a plant. Graphs should be calibrated at equal intervals. If one space represents one day, the next space may not represent ten days. A "best fit" line is drawn to join the points and may not include all the points in the data. Axes must always be labeled for the graph to be meaningful. A good title will describe both the dependent and the independent variable. Bar graphs are set up similarly in regards to axes, but points are not plotted. Instead, the dependent variable is set up as a bar where the x-axis intersects with the y-axis. Each bar is a separate item of data and is not joined by a continuous line.

Moles = mass X 1 mole/molecular weight
For example, to determine the moles of 20 grams of water, you would take the mass of the water (20 g) and multiply it by 1 mole of water divided by the molecular weight of a molecule of water (18 g).

Percent solutions and **proportions** are basically the same thing. To find percent volume, divide the grams of the substance by the amount of the solvent. For example, 20 grams of salt divided by 100 ml of water would result in a 20% solution of saltwater. To determine percent mass, divide the ml of substance being mixed by the amount of solvent. Percent mass is not used as often as percent volume.

Rate is determined by dividing the change in distance (or the independent variable) by the change in time. If a plant grew four inches in two days, the rate of growth would be two inches per day.

CURRENT TECHNOLOGY

Chromatography uses the principles of capillary action to separate substances such as plant pigments. Molecules of a larger size will move more slowly up the paper, whereas smaller molecules will move more quickly, producing lines of pigments.

Spectrophotometry uses the percent of light absorbance to measure a color change, thus giving qualitative data a quantitative value.

Centrifugation involves spinning substances at a high speed. The more dense part of a solution will settle to the bottom of the test tube, while the lighter material will stay on top. Centrifugation is used to separate blood into blood cells and plasma, with the heavier blood cells settling to the bottom.

Electrophoresis uses electrical charges of molecules to separate them according to their size. The molecules, such as DNA or proteins, are pulled through a gel towards either the positive end of the gel box (if the material has a negative charge) or the negative end of the gel box (if the material has a positive charge).

Computer technology has greatly improved the collection and interpretation of scientific data. Molecular findings have been enhanced through the use of computer images. Technology has revolutionized access to data via the Internet and shared databases. The manipulation of data is enhanced by sophisticated software capabilities. Computer engineering advances have produced such products as MRIs and CT scans in medicine. Laser technology has numerous applications with refining precision.

Satellites have improved our ability to communicate and transmit radio and television signals. Navigational abilities have been greatly improved through the use of satellite signals. Sonar uses sound waves to locate objects and is especially useful underwater. The sound waves bounce off the object and are used to assist in location. Seismographs record vibrations in the Earth and allow us to measure earthquake activity.

Dissections - Animals which are not obtained from recognized sources should not be used. Decaying animals or those of unknown origin may harbor pathogens and/or parasites. Specimens should be rinsed before handling. Latex gloves are desirable. If gloves are not available, students with sores or scratches should be excused from the activity. Formaldehyde is a carcinogen and should be avoided or disposed of according to district regulations. Students objecting to dissections for moral reasons should be given an alternative assignment.

Live specimens - No dissections may be performed on living mammalian vertebrates or birds. Lower order life and invertebrates may be used. Biological experiments may be done with all animals except mammalian vertebrates or birds. No physiological harm may result to the animal. All animals housed and cared for in the school must be handled in a safe and humane manner. Animals are not to remain on school premises during extended vacations unless adequate care is provided. Many state laws stipulate that any instructor who intentionally refuses to comply with the laws may be suspended or dismissed.

Microbiology - Pathogenic organisms must never be used for experimentation. Students should adhere to the following rules at all times when working with microorganisms to avoid accidental contamination:

1. Treat all microorganisms as if they were pathogenic.
2. Maintain sterile conditions at all times.

If you are taking a national-level exam, you should check the Department of Education for your state for safety procedures. You will want to know what your state expects of you, not only for the test, but also for performance in the classroom and for the welfare of your students.

Bunsen burners - Hot plates should be used whenever possible to avoid the risk of burns or fire. If Bunsen burners are used, the following precautions should be followed:

1. Know the location of fire extinguishers and safety blankets and train students in their use. Long hair and long sleeves should be secured and out of the way.
2. Turn the gas all the way on and make a spark with the striker. The preferred method to light burners is to use strikers rather than matches.
3. Adjust the air valve at the bottom of the Bunsen burner until the flame shows an inner cone.
4. Adjust the flow of gas to the desired flame height by using the adjustment valve.
5. Do not touch the barrel of the burner (it is hot).

Graduated Cylinder - These are used for precise measurements. They should always be placed on a flat surface. The surface of the liquid will form a meniscus (lens-shaped curve). The measurement is read at the bottom of this curve.

Balance - Electronic balances are easier to use, but more expensive. An electronic balance should always be tarred (returned to zero) before measuring and should be used on a flat surface. Substances should always be placed on a piece of paper to avoid spills and/or damage to the instrument. Triple-beam balances must be used on a level surface. There are screws located at the bottom of the balance to make any adjustments. Start with the largest counterweight first and proceed toward the last notch that does not tip the balance. Do the same with the next largest, etc. until the pointer remains at zero. The total mass is the total of all the readings on the beams. Again, use paper under the substance to protect the equipment.

Buret – A buret is used to dispense precisely measured volumes of liquid. A stopcock is used to control the volume of liquid being dispensed at a time.

Light microscopes are commonly used in laboratory experiments. Several procedures should be followed to properly care for this equipment:

1. Clean all lenses with lens paper only.
2. Carry microscopes with two hands: one on the arm and one on the base.
3. Always begin focusing on low power; then switch to high power.
4. Store microscopes with the low power objective down.
5. Always use a coverslip when viewing wet mount slides.
6. Bring the objective down to its lowest position; then focus by moving it up to avoid breaking the slide or scratching the lens.

Wet mount slides should be made by placing a drop of water on the specimen and then putting a glass coverslip on top of the drop of water. Dropping the coverslip at a forty-five degree angle will help in avoiding air bubbles. Total magnification is determined by multiplying the ocular (usually 10X) and the objective (usually 10X on low, 40X on high).

Skill 13.4 Recognize the values inherent in science (e.g., reliance on verifiable evidence, reasoning, logic, avoidance of bias) and strategies for helping students discover new knowledge through the use of scientific thinking and reasoning

Many scientists and employees in the field embarked upon their careers or began conducting specific research because their curiosity was piqued by a strange event, a puzzling question, or some other occurrence during early exploration of scientific topics. In the same way, teachers of science can help inspire students to become active learners by motivating them with open-ended questions, puzzles, and paradoxes. Students at the elementary level can benefit from the use of scientific thinking and reasoning if the activities are appropriate to their level of cognitive understanding.

Inquiry as a tool for scientific teaching and learning is the creation of a classroom where students are engaged in open-ended, student-centered, hands-on activities for learning. It is a method that engages students in lessons that are based on real science. They learn about how scientists work and what tools are used in research. Students are encouraged to ask questions and are involved in experiments. The teacher is the primary source of information, instead of a textbook. Such exposure to real science increases students' enthusiasm for science. Their ability to ask questions and get real answers increases their knowledge as well as their curiosity.

Each lesson begins with questions to stimulate students' thinking, to find out their prior knowledge or misconceptions, and to get them excited about the topic. Examples or analogies are used to help students relate the topics to their experiences. Lessons are conducted in an experimental way to show students how scientists would do research. This includes hypothesizing about outcomes and explaining results of each experiment or observation. At the end of each lesson, students express their observations and are encouraged to ask questions. To assess the effectiveness of lessons, students are given pre- and post-lesson questions.

Scientific thinking includes observing, investigating, questioning, and predicting. The teaching methodology should be student-centered. A child's physical, social, emotional, and cognitive development are closely related. Therefore student learning experiences should be organized in ways that help children develop optimally in all areas. For example, the use of a continuously changing learning center fosters all of the domains. Children must construct their own knowledge. Therefore, science activities should require active learning, drawing on prior knowledge in all the domains. Social and cultural expression is not separated from the science. At the early elementary level play is an important vehicle for development in the domains, and activities should involve water, sand, moving vehicles across different surfaces, blowing bubbles, taking things apart, etc., exploring the five senses. Books on science content should be readily available and regularly "read."

Skill 13.5 Demonstrate knowledge of strategies to engage students in discovering new knowledge through the use of scientific thinking and reasoning (e.g., exploration labs, learning cycle approach)

Learning can be broadly divided into two kinds: active and passive. Active learning involves, as the name indicates, a learning atmosphere full of action, whereas in passive learning students are taught in a nonstimulating and inactive atmosphere. Active learning involves and draws students into it, thereby interesting them to the point of participating and purposely engaging in learning.

It is crucial that students are actively engaged, not entertained. They should be taught the answers for "How" and "Why" questions and should be encouraged to be inquisitive and interested.
Active learning is conceptualized as follows:

A Model of Active Learning

Experience of	Dialogue with
Doing	Self
Observing	Others

This model suggests that all learning activities involve some kind of experience or some kind of dialogue. The two main kinds of dialogue are "Dialogue with self" and "Dialogue with others." The two main kinds of experience are "Observing" and "Doing."

Dialogue with self: This is what happens when learners think reflectively about a topic. They ask themselves a number of things about the topic.

Dialogue with others: When the students are listening to a book being read by another student or when the teacher is teaching, a partial dialogue takes place because the dialogue is only one-sided. When they are listening to an adult and when there is an exchange of ideas back and forth, it is said to be a dialogue with others.

Observing: This is a most important skill in science. This occurs when a learner is carefully watching or observing someone else doing an activity or experiment. This is a good experience, although it is not quite like doing it independently.

Doing: This refers to any activity where a learner actually does something, giving the learner a firsthand experience that is very valuable.

Inquiry is invaluable to teaching in general and to teaching science, especially. The steps involved in scientific inquiry are discussed in the following section.

The scientific attitude is to be curious, open to new ideas, and skeptical. In science, there are always new research, new discoveries, and new theories proposed. Sometimes, old theories are disproved. To view these changes rationally, one must have much openness, curiosity, and skepticism. (Skepticism is a Greek word, meaning a method of obtaining knowledge through systematic doubt and continual testing. A scientific skeptic is one who refuses to accept certain types of claims without subjecting them to a systematic investigation.)

The students may not have these attitudes inherently, but it is the responsibility of the teacher to encourage, nurture, and practice these attitudes so that students will have a good role model.

There are many common misconceptions about science. The following are a few scientific misconceptions that are or have been common in the past:

- The Earth is the center of the solar system.
- The Earth is the largest object in the solar system.
- Rain comes from the holes in the clouds.
- Acquired characters can be inherited.
- The eye receives upright images.
- Energy is a thing.
- Heat is not energy.

Some strategies to uncover and dispel misconceptions include:

1. Planning appropriate activities, so that the students will see for themselves where there are misconceptions.

2. Web search is a very useful tool to dispel misconceptions. Students need to be guided in how to look for answers on the Web, and if necessary, the teacher should explain scientific literature to help the students understand it.

3. Science journals are a great source of information. Recent research is highly beneficial for the senior science students.

4. Critical thinking and reasoning are two important skills that the students should be encouraged to use to discover facts--for example, that heat is a form of energy. Here, the students have to be challenged to use their critical thinking skills to reason that heat can cause change--for example, causing water to boil--and so it is not a thing but a form of energy, since only energy can cause change.

COMPETENCY 14.0 UNDERSTAND THE STRUCTURES AND FUNCTIONS OF GOVERNMENT; THE RIGHTS AND RESPONSIBILITIES OF CITIZENSHIP IN THE UNITED STATES; AND THE SKILLS, KNOWLEDGE, AND ATTITUDES NECESSARY FOR SUCCESSFUL PARTICIPATION IN CIVIC LIFE

Skill 14.1   Recognize basic purposes and concepts of government, including the constitutional principles and democratic foundations of U.S. government

Historically the functions of government, or people's concepts of government and its purpose and function, have varied considerably. In the theory of political science, the function of government is to secure the common welfare of the members of the given society over which it exercises control. In different historical eras, governments have attempted to achieve the common welfare by various means in accordance with the traditions and ideology of the given society. Among *primitive peoples,* systems of control were rudimentary at best. They arose directly from the ideas of right and wrong that had been established in the group and was common in that particular society. Control was exercised most often by means of group pressure, usually in the forms of taboos and superstitions and in many cases by ostracism, or banishment from the group. Thus, in most cases, because of the extreme tribal nature of society in those early times, this led to very unpleasant circumstances for the individual so treated. Without the protection of the group, a lone individual was most often in for a sad, and very short, fate. (No other group would accept such an individual into their midst, and survival alone was extremely difficult if not impossible.)

Among more *civilized peoples,* governments began to assume more institutional forms. They rested on a well-defined legal basis. They imposed penalties on violators of the social order. They used force, which was supported and sanctioned by their people. The government was charged to establish the social order and was supposed to do so in order to be able to discharge its functions.

Eventually the ideas of government, who should govern and how, came to be considered by various thinkers and philosophers. The most influential of these, and those who had the most influence on our present society, were the ancient Greek philosophers such as Plato and Aristotle.

Aristotle's conception of government was based on a simple idea. The function of government was to provide for the general welfare of its people. A good government, and one that should be supported, was one that did so in the best way possible, with the least pressure on the people. Bad governments were those that subordinated the general welfare to that of the individuals who ruled. At no time should any function of any government be that of personal interest of any one individual, no matter who that individual was. This does not mean that Aristotle had no sympathy for the individual or individual happiness (as at times Plato has been accused by those who read his **"Republic,"** which was the first important philosophical text to explore these issues). Rather, Aristotle believed that a society is greater than the sum of its parts, or that "the good of the many outweighs the good of the few and also of the one."

Yet, a good government and one that is carrying out its functions well will always weigh the relative merits of what is good for a given individual in society and what is good for the society as a whole.

This basic concept has continued to our own time and has found its fullest expression in the idea of representative democracy and political and personal freedom. In addition, a government that maintains good social order, while allowing the greatest possible exercise of autonomy for individuals to achieve

Skill 14.2   Demonstrate knowledge of the basic structures and functions of federal, state, and local government in the United States (e.g., the branches of federal government and their roles, key aspects of government in Illinois)

In the United States, the three branches of the federal government mentioned earlier, the **Executive**, the **Legislative**, and the **Judicial**, divide up their powers thus:

Legislative – Article 1 of the Constitution established the legislative or law-making branch of the government called the Congress. It is made up of two houses, the House of Representatives and the Senate. Voters in all states elect the members who serve in each respective House of Congress. The legislative branch is responsible for making laws, raising and printing money, regulating trade, establishing the postal service and federal courts, approving the president's appointments, declaring war, and supporting the armed forces. The Congress also has the power to change the Constitution itself and to *impeach* (bring charges against) the president. Charges for impeachment are brought by the House of Representatives and are then tried in the Senate.

Executive – Article 2 of the Constitution created the executive branch of the government, headed by the president, who leads the country, recommends new laws, and can veto bills passed by the legislative branch. As the chief of state, the president is responsible for carrying out the laws of the country and the treaties and declarations of war passed by the legislative branch. The president also appoints federal judges and is commander-in-chief of the military when it is called into service. Other members of the executive branch include the vice president, also elected, and various cabinet members as he might appoint: ambassadors, presidential advisors, members of the armed forces, and other appointed and civil servants of government agencies, departments, and bureaus. Though the president appoints them, they must be approved by the legislative branch.

Judicial – Article 3 of the Constitution established the judicial branch of the government, headed by the Supreme Court. The Supreme Court has the power to rule that a law passed by the legislature, or an act of the executive branch is illegal and unconstitutional. Citizens, businesses, and government officials can, in an appeal capacity, ask the Supreme Court to review a decision made in a lower court if someone believes that the ruling by a judge is unconstitutional. The judicial branch also includes lower federal courts known as federal district courts that have been established by the Congress. These courts try lawbreakers and review cases referred from other courts.

<u>**Powers delegated to the federal government**</u>

1. To tax
2. To borrow and coin money
3. To establish postal service
4. To grant patents and copyrights
5. To regulate interstate & foreign commerce
6. To establish courts
7. To declare war
8. To raise and support the armed forces
9. To govern territories
10. To define and punish felonies and piracy on the high seas
11. To fix standards of weights and measures
12. To conduct foreign affairs

<u>**Powers reserved to the states**</u>

1. To regulate intrastate trade
2. To establish local governments
3. To protect general welfare
4. To protect life and property
5. To ratify amendments
6. To conduct elections
7. To make state and local laws

<u>Concurrent powers of the federal government and states.</u>

1. Both Congress and the states may tax.
2. Both may borrow money.
3. Both may charter banks and corporations.
4. Both may establish courts.
5. Both may make and enforce laws.
6. Both may take property for public purposes.
7. Both may spend money to provide for the public welfare.

<u>Implied powers of the federal government.</u>

1. To establish banks or other corporations implied from delegated powers to tax, borrow, and to regulate commerce
2. To spend money for roads, schools, health, insurance, etc. implied from powers to establish post roads, to tax to provide for general welfare and defense, and to regulate commerce
3. To create military academies, implied from powers to raise and support an armed force
4. To locate and generate sources of power and sell surplus, implied from powers to dispose of government property, commerce, and war powers
5. To assist and regulate agriculture, implied from power to tax and spend for general welfare and regulate commerce

The government of the **state of Illinois** is modeled upon the federal government. The executive branch, headed by the governor, consists of the secretary of state, the treasurer, the lieutenant governor, the comptroller, and the attorney general. It includes the following departments: state board of elections, bureau of the budget, department of education, civil administrative code departments, department of military affairs, and other boards, agencies, and authorities. The legislative branch is composed of the house of representatives (with 118 members), the senate (with 59 senators), and the auditor general. The house of representatives has a clerk of the house and various committees and staff. The senate has a secretary of the senate and various committees and staff. This branch of state government also includes various legislative support agencies. The judicial branch is composed of three courts: the circuit court, the appellate court, and a supreme court. This branch also includes a courts commission, which oversees a judicial inquiry board and an Administrative Office of Illinois Courts, including the state board of law examiners, the attorney registration and disciplinary commission, and the office of the state appellate defender.

Skill 14.3 **Demonstrate knowledge of basic democratic principles and rights (e.g., due process, equal protection) and fundamental democratic values and beliefs (e.g., majority rule, individual participation) and their significance for individuals, groups, and society**

The Declaration of Independence is an outgrowth of both ancient Greek ideas of democracy and individual rights and the ideas of the European Enlightenment and the Renaissance, especially the ideology of the political thinker, *John Locke.* Thomas Jefferson (1743-1826), the principle author of the Declaration, borrowed much from Locke's theories and writings.

Essentially, Jefferson applied Locke's principles to the contemporary American situation. Jefferson argued that the currently reigning King George III had repeatedly violated the rights of the colonists as subjects of the British Crown. Disdaining the colonial petition for redress of grievances (a right guaranteed by the Declaration of Rights of 1689), the king seemed bent upon establishing an "absolute tyranny" over the colonies. Such disgraceful behavior itself violated the reasons for which government had been instituted. The American colonists were left with no choice. Wrote Thomas Jefferson, *"It is their right, it is their duty, to throw off such a government, and to provide new guards for their future security."*

Yet, though his fundamental principles were derived from Locke's, Jefferson was bolder than his intellectual mentor was. He went farther in that his view of natural rights was much broader than Locke's and less tied to the idea of property rights.

For instance, though both Jefferson and Locke believed very strongly in property rights, especially as a guard for individual liberty, the famous line in the Declaration about people being endowed with the inalienable right to "life, liberty, and the pursuit of happiness" was originally Locke's idea. It was "life, liberty, and *private property."* Jefferson didn't want to tie the idea of rights to any one particular circumstance, however; thus, he changed Locke's original specific reliance on property and substituted the more general idea of human happiness as being a fundamental right that is the duty of a government to protect.

Locke and Jefferson both stressed that the individual citizen's rights are prior to and more important than any obligation to the state. Government is the servant of the people. The officials of government hold their positions at the sufferance of the people. Their job is to ensure that the rights of the people are preserved and protected by that government. The citizen come first, the government comes second. The Declaration thus produced turned out to be one of the most important and historic documents that expounded the inherent rights of all peoples: a document still looked up to as an ideal and an example.

Due process of law is the principal that government must normally respect all of a person's legal rights when the government deprives a person of life, liberty, or property. This principle also limits the interpretation of laws and legal proceedings in order to guarantee basic justice and liberty to all citizens. Due process is guaranteed by the Fifth Amendment to the Constitution.

The **Equal Protection Clause,** which guarantees to all people equal protection of the law, is contained in the Fourteenth Amendment to the Constitution. The Fourteenth Amendment protects the rights of citizens from invasion or abridgement by both the federal government and by state and local governments.

Majority Rule is the principal or law that requires that more than half (a simple majority) of those voting on an issue must support the issue or law being voted on. The essential belief is that the majority of those voting represent the preference or decision of the majority of the people.

Skill 14.4   Apply knowledge of the responsibilities of U.S. citizens, including classroom, school, and community applications (e.g., respecting others' rights, obeying laws and rules, voting in class elections) and the skills, knowledge, and attitudes necessary for successful participation in civic life (e.g., compromise, consensus building, cooperation)

Many of the core values in the U.S. democratic system can be found in the opening words of the Declaration of Independence, including the belief in equality and the rights of citizens to "life, liberty, and the pursuit of happiness."

The Declaration was a condemnation of the British king's tyrannical government, and these words emphasized the American colonists' belief that a government receives its authority to rule from the people, and its function should not be to suppress the governed, but to protect the rights of the governed, including protection from the government itself. These two ideals, **popular sovereignty** and the **rule of law** are basic core values.

Popular sovereignty grants citizens the ability to directly participate in their own government by voting and running for public office. This ideal is based on a belief of **equality** that holds that all citizens have an equal right to engage in their own governance. The ideal of equality has changed over the years, as women and nonwhite citizens were not always allowed to vote or bring suit in court. Now all U.S. citizens above the age of eighteen are allowed to vote. This expansion of rights since the adoption of the Constitution demonstrates an American value of **respect for minority rights.** The democratic system of election and representation is based on **majority rule.** In the case of most public elections, the candidate receiving the most votes is awarded the office. Majority rule is also used to pass legislation in Congress. Majority rule is meant to ensure that authority cannot be concentrated in one small group of people.

The rule of law is the ideal that the law applies not only to the governed, but to the government as well. This core value gives authority to the justice system, which grants citizens protection from the government by requiring that any accusation of a crime be proven by the government before a person is punished. This is called **due process** and ensures that any accused person will have an opportunity to confront his accusers and provide a defense. Due process follows from the core value of a right to liberty. The government cannot take away a citizen's liberty without reason or without proof. The correlating ideal is also a core value: that someone who does harm to another or breaks a law will receive **justice** under the democratic system. The ideal of justice holds that a punishment will fit the crime, and that any citizen can appeal to the judicial system if he feels he has been wronged.

Central to the ideal of justice is an expectation that citizens will act in a way that promotes the **common good,** that they will treat one another with **honesty** and respect, and that they will exercise **self-discipline** in their interactions with others. These are among the basic responsibilities of a citizen of a democracy.

Skill 14.5 Recognize the role of law in the Illinois and U.S. constitutional systems

The State Courts - Each state has an independent system of courts operating under the laws and constitution of that particular individual state. Broadly speaking, the state courts are based on the English judicial system as it existed in colonial times, but as modified by succeeding statues. The character and names of the various courts differ from state to state, but the state courts as a whole have general jurisdiction, except in cases in which exclusive jurisdiction has by law been vested in the federal courts. In cases involving the United States Constitution or federal laws or treaties and such, the state courts are governed by the decisions of the Supreme Court of the United States, and their decisions are subject to review by it.

Cases involving the federal Constitution, federal laws, or treaties and the like, may be brought to either the state courts or the federal courts. Ordinary **civil suits** not involving any of the aforementioned elements can be brought only to the state courts, except in cases of different state citizenship between the parties, in which case the suit may be brought to a federal court. By an act of Congress, however, suits involving different federal questions or different state citizenship may be brought to a federal court only when it is a civil suit that involves $3,000 or more. All such cases that involve a smaller amount must be brought to a state court only. In accordance with a congressional law, a suit brought before a state court may be removed to a federal court at the option of the defendant.

Bearing in mind that any statements about state courts that is trying to give a typical explanation of all of them is subject to many exceptions. The following may be taken as a general comprehensive description of their respective jurisdictions, functions, and organization.

County courts of general original jurisdiction exercise both criminal and civil jurisdictions in most states. A few states maintain separate courts of criminal and civil law inherited from the English judicial system. Between the lower courts and the supreme appellate courts of each state in a number of states, are intermediate appellate courts which, like the federal courts of appeals, provide faster justice for individuals by disposing of a large number of cases which would otherwise be added to the overcrowded calendars of the higher courts. Courts of last resort, the highest appellate courts for the states in criminal and civil cases, are usually called **State Supreme Courts**.

The state court system also includes a number of minor, local courts with limited jurisdictions; these courts dispose of minor offenses and relatively small civil actions. Included in this classification are police and municipal courts in various cities and towns, and the courts presided over by justices of the peace in rural areas.

Bail - Money left with the court in order for an individual to be released from jail pending trial. When an individual returns for trial the money is returned. If the person flees the money is forfeited.

Civil - A lawsuit brought before a court usually to recover monetary funds, as opposed to a criminal action brought for a penal offense.

Criminal - A penal crime, one that normally results in an imposition of a term of imprisonment, or of a monetary fine by the state or both.

Double Jeopardy - Subjecting an accused person to repeated trials for the same criminal offense. This is forbidden by the Fifth Amendment to the Constitution.

Due Process - The right of a defendant to go through the established legal system before imprisonment, i.e. trial, legal counsel, and a verdict rendered in a court of law.

Equity - A branch of civil law that provides remedial justice when there is no remedy in common or prescribed law.

Grand Jury - As specified in the Constitution, it is a body of persons called to hear complaints of the commission of criminal offenses and to determine if enough evidence is available for a criminal indictment. It is normally composed of twelve to twenty-four individuals who hear the evidence and deliberate in private.

Habeas Corpus - The right to appear in court in order to determine if an imprisonment is lawful. Also known as a *"Writ of Habeas Corpus."*

Exclusionary Rule - As defined from the Fourth and Fifth Amendments, it is the inability of evidence seized unlawfully or statements gathered wrongly, to be brought into a court of law.

Ex Post Facto Law - A law created to punish an act after it has been committed. Prohibited by the Constitution; i.e., you cannot prosecute someone for an act if it was legal at the time, although a law was subsequently enacted against it.

Impeach - To bring charges against an official in the government such as the president. In the case of the president, the House of Representatives is the only branch of government empowered to bring such charges. They are then tried in the Senate.

Judicial Review - The right of the court to review laws and acts of the legislature and executive branches and to declare them unconstitutional. (Established in *"Marbury* vs. *Madison* " *1803)*.

Judiciary - The legal system, including but not limited to, courts of law and appeal.

Judiciary Act - Law that organized the federal court system into federal and circuit courts in 1789.

Jurisprudence - Relating to, or pertaining to, the law or the legal system and its practice or exercise thereof.

Miranda Warning - As defined from the Fifth and Sixth Amendments. The right to remain silent so one does not incriminate oneself and the right to legal counsel during questioning.

Penal - Having to do with punishment, most often in regards to imprisonment and incarceration by the state.

Tort - A private or civil action brought before a court of law, i.e., a civil lawsuit.

Skill 14.6   Identify a wide range of instructional resources and technologies to support the learning of the structures and functions of government

Historical data can come from a wide range of sources beginning with libraries: small local ones or very large university **libraries.** Records and guides are almost universally digitally organized and available for instant searching by era, topic, event, personality, or area. Libraries offer resources such as survey information from various departments and bureaus of the federal and state government; magazines and periodicals in a wide range of topics; artifacts, encyclopedias and other reference materials; and usually access to the Internet.

The **Internet** offers unheard-of possibilities for finding even the most obscure information. However, even with all these resources available, nothing is more valuable than a visit to the site being researched, including a visit to historical societies, local libraries, and sometimes even local schools. A historian was searching for an answer to the question as to why her great-great-grandfather had enlisted in the Union army even though he lived in the deep South, so for lack of a formal historical society, she went to the site where he grew up and found the answer in the historical records stored in the local school house. The residents of the little town were also able to answer her question. She would never have found that historical information if she hadn't visited the site.

The same things could be said about geographical data. It's possible to find a map of almost any area online; however, the best maps will be available locally, as will knowledge and information about the development of the area. For example, a court house had been moved from one small town to another in a county in Tennessee for no apparent reason. However, the local old-timers can tell you. The railroad wanted to come through town, and the farmers in the area surrounding the previous court house didn't want to raise the $100,000 it would take; they were also concerned that the trains would scare their cows. This information is not in a history book, yet it would be very important to a study of the geography of the area.

The **scientific method** is the process by which researchers over time endeavor to construct an accurate (that is, reliable, consistent, and nonarbitrary) representation of the world. Recognizing that personal and cultural beliefs influence both our perceptions and our interpretations of natural phenomena, standard procedures and criteria minimize those influences when developing a theory.

The scientific method has four steps:
1. Observation and description of a phenomenon or group of phenomena
2. Formulation of a hypothesis to explain the phenomena
3. Use of the hypothesis to predict the existence of other phenomena or to predict quantitatively the results of new observations
4. Performance of experimental tests of the predictions by several independent experimenters and properly performed experiments

While the researcher may bring certain biases to the study, it's important that bias not be permitted to enter into the interpretation. It's also important that data that doesn't fit the hypothesis not be ruled out. This is unlikely to happen if the researcher is open to the possibility that the hypothesis might turn out to be null. Another important caution is to be certain that the methods for analyzing and interpreting are flawless. Abiding by these mandates is important if the discovery is to make a contribution to human understanding.

The phenomena that interest social scientists are usually complex. Capturing that complexity more fully requires the assessment of simultaneous covariations along the following dimensions: the units of observation, their characteristics, and time. This is how behavior occurs. For example, to obtain a richer and more accurate picture of the progress of school children means measuring changes in their attainment over time together with changes in the school over time. This acknowledges that changes in one arena of behavior are usually contingent on changes in other areas. Models used for research in the past were inadequate to handle the complexities suggested by multiple covariations. However, the evolution of computerized data processing has taken away that constraint.

While descriptions of the research project and presentation of outcomes along with analysis must be a part of every report, graphs, charts, and sometimes maps are necessary to make the results clearly understandable.

Demography is the branch of the science of statistics most concerned with the social well-being of people. **Demographic tables** may include (1) Analysis of the population on the basis of age, parentage, physical condition, race, occupation and civil position, giving the actual size and the density of each separate area, (2) Changes in the population as a result of birth, marriage, and death, (3) Statistics on population movements and their effects and their relations to given economic, social, and political conditions, (4) Statistics of crime, illegitimacy, and suicide, and (5) Levels of education and economic and social statistics.

Such information is also similar to that area of science known as **vital statistics,** and as such is indispensable in studying social trends and making important legislative, economic, and social decisions. Such demographic information is gathered from census and registrar reports and the like, and by state laws such information, especially the vital kind, is kept by physicians, attorneys, funeral directors, member of the clergy, and similar professional people. In the United States such demographic information is compiled, kept, and published by the Public Health Service of the United States Department of Health, Education, and Welfare.

The most important element of this information is the so-called **rate,** which customarily represents the average of births and deaths for a unit of 1000 population over a given calendar year. These general rates are called **crude rates,** which are then subdivided into *sex, color, age, occupation, locality, etc.* They are then known as **refined rates.**

In examining **statistics** and the sources of statistical data, one must also be aware of the methods of statistical information gathering. For instance, there are many good sources of raw statistical data. Books such as *The Statistical Abstract of the United States,* published by the United States Chamber of Commerce, *The World Fact Book,* published by the Central Intelligence Agency, or *The Monthly Labor Review,* published by the United States Department of Labor, are excellent examples that contain much raw data. Many such yearbooks and the like on various topics are readily available from any library, or from the government itself. However, knowing how that data and information was gathered is at least equally as important as the figures themselves. Only by having knowledge of statistical language and methodology can one really be able to gauge the usefulness of any given piece of data presented. Thus we must first understand just what statistics are and what they can, and cannot, tell us.

Simply put, statistics is the mathematical science that deals with the collection, organization, presentation, and analysis of various forms of numerical data and with the problems such as interpreting and understanding such data. The raw materials of statistics are sets of numbers obtained from enumerations or measurements collected by various methods of extrapolation, such as census-taking, interviews, and observations.

In collecting any such statistical information and data, care and adequate precautions must always be taken in order to assure that the knowledge obtained is complete and accurate. It is also important to be aware of just how much data is necessary to collect in order to establish the idea that is attempting to be formulated. One important idea to understand is that statistics usually deal with a specific **model, hypothesis,** or **theory** that is being attempted to be proven.

One should be aware that a theory can never actually be proven correct; it can only be corroborated. (**Corroboration** means that the data presented is more consistent with this theory than with any other theory, so it makes sense to use this theory.) One should also be aware that what is known as **correlation** (the joint movement of various data points) does not infer **causation** (the change in one of those data points caused the other data points to change). It is important that one take these aspects into account so that one can be in a better position to appreciate what the collected data is really saying.

Once collected, data must then be arranged, tabulated, and presented to permit ready and meaningful analysis and interpretation. Often tables, charts, or graphs will be used to present the information in a concise easy-to-see manner, with the information sometimes presented in raw numerical order as well. **Tests of reliability** are used, bearing in mind the manner in which the data has been collected and the inherent biases of any artificially created model to be used to explain real-world events. Indeed the methods used and the inherent biases and reasons for actually doing the study by the individual(s) involved must never be discounted.

COMPETENCY 15.0 UNDERSTAND THE INTERRELATIONSHIPS OF ECONOMIC AND POLITICAL PRINCIPLES, CONCEPTS, AND SYSTEMS AND THEIR RELATIONSHIP TO HISTORICAL AND CONTEMPORARY DEVELOPMENTS IN ILLINOIS, THE UNITED STATES, AND THE WORLD

Skill 15.1   Demonstrate understanding of fundamental concepts and principles of economics (e.g., supply and demand) and key features of different economic systems (e.g., command, market, mixed)

Economic systems refer to the arrangements a society has devised to answer what are known as the Three Questions: What goods to produce, How to produce the goods, and For Whom the goods are being produced, or how the allocation of the output is determined. Different economic systems answer these questions in different ways. These are the different "isms" that exist that define the method of resource and output allocation.

A **market economy** answers these questions in terms of **supply** and **demand** and the use of **markets.** Consumers vote for the products they want with their dollar spending. Goods acquiring enough dollar votes are profitable, signaling to the producers that society wants their scarce resources used in this way. This is how the "What" question is answered. The producer then hires inputs in accordance with the goods consumers want, looking for the most efficient or lowest-cost method of production. The lower the firm's costs for any given level of revenue, the higher the firm's profits. This is the way in which the "How" question is answered in a market economy. The "For Whom" question is answered in the marketplace by the determination of the equilibrium price. Price serves to ration the good to those who can and will transact at the market price or better. Those who can't or won't are excluded from the market. The United States has a market economy.

The opposite of the market economy is called the **centrally planned economy**. This used to be called communism, even though the term is not correct in a strict Marxian sense. In a planned economy, the means of production are publicly owned, with little, if any, public ownership. Instead of the three questions being solved by markets, a communist society has a planning authority that makes the decisions in place of markets. The planning authority decides what will be produced and how. Since most planned economies direct resources into the production of capital and military goods, there is little remaining for consumer goods, and the result is chronic shortages. Price functions as an accounting measure and does not reflect scarcity. The former Soviet Union and most of the Eastern Bloc countries were planned economies of this sort.

In between the two extremes is **market socialism.** This is a mixed economic system that uses both markets and planning. Planning is usually used to direct resources at the upper levels of the economy, with markets being used to determine prices of consumer goods and wages. This kind of economic system answers the three questions with planning and markets. The former Yugoslavia was a market socialist economy.

You can put each nation of the world on a continuum in terms of these characteristics and rank them from most capitalistic to most planned. The United States would probably rank as the most capitalistic and North Korea would probably rank as the most planned, but this doesn't mean that the United States doesn't engage in planning or that economies like mainland China don't use markets.

Skill 15.2   Recognize major features of the U.S. economic system, including the roles of consumers and producers and types of economic resources and activities in various regions, including Illinois

Free enterprise, individual entrepreneurship, competitive markets and consumer sovereignty are all parts of a **market economy**. Individuals have the right to make their own decisions as to what they want to do as a career. The financial incentives are there for individuals who are willing to take the risk. A successful venture earns profit. It is these financial incentives that serve to motivate inventors and small businesses. The same is true for businesses. They are free to determine what production technique they want to use and what output they want to produce within the confines of the legal system. They can make investments based on their own decisions. Nobody is telling them what to do. Competitive markets, relatively free from government interference are also a manifestation of the freedom that the U.S. economic system is based on. These markets function on the basis of supply and demand to determine output mix and resource allocation. There is no commissar dictating what is produced and how. Since consumers buy the goods and services that give them satisfaction, this means that, for the most part, they don't buy the goods and services that they don't want that don't give them satisfaction.

Consumers are, in effect, voting for the goods and services that they want with the dollars or what is called dollar voting. Consumers are basically signaling firms as to how they want society's scarce resources used with their dollar votes. A good that society wants acquires enough dollar votes for the producer to experience profits – a situation where the firm's revenues exceed the firm's costs. The existence of profits indicate to the firm that it is producing the goods and services that consumers want and that society's scarce resources are being used in accordance with consumer preferences. When a firm does not have a profitable product, it is because that product is not tabulating enough dollar votes of consumers. Consumers don't want the good or service and they don't want society's scarce resources being used in its production.

This process where consumers vote with their dollars is called **consumer sovereignty.** Consumers are basically directing the allocation of scarce resources in the economy with the dollar spending. Firms, who are in business to earn profit, then hire resources, or inputs, in accordance with consumer preferences. This is the way in which resources are allocated in a market economy. This is the manner in which society achieves the output mix that it desires.

The fact that resources are scarce is the basis for the existence of economics. Economics is defined as a study of how scarce resources are allocated to satisfy unlimited wants. Resources refer to the four factors of production: **labor, capital, land and entrepreneurship.** The fact that the supply of these resources is finite means that society cannot have as much of everything that it wants. There is a constraint on production and consumption and on the kinds of goods and services that can be produced and consumed. **Scarcity** means that choices have to be made. If society decides to produce more of one good, this means that there are fewer resources available for the production of other goods. Assume a society can produce two goods, good A and good B. The society uses resources in the production of each good. If producing one unit of good A results in an amount of resources used to produce three units of good B then producing one more unit of good A results in a decrease in 3 units of good B. In effect, one unit of good A "costs" three units of good B. This cost is referred to as opportunity cost. **Opportunity cost** is the value of the sacrificed alternative, the value of what had to be given up in order to have the output of good A. Opportunity cost does not just refer to production. Your opportunity cost of studying with this guide is the value of what you are not doing because you are studying, whether it is watching TV, spending time with family, working, or whatever. Every choice has an opportunity cost.

Illinois developed as a slave-free state. Its rich fertile land is attractive for farmers. The state benefited from canal building and railroads. Chicago, with its strategic location in the nation and on Lake Michigan developed as a center of industry, commerce, and transportation. It was a railroad hub prior to the Civil War. Commerce and industry develops and grows where there are transportation facilities. The waterways and railroads were conducive to Illinois' economic development and growth as grain elevators and other agricultural necessities were constructed along these transportation routes. Chicago was also the center for grain trading, which led to the establishment of the futures contracts and the Chicago Board of Trade in 1850. Seed experimentation and advances in agricultural technology, like threshers and reapers, etc., increased agricultural output and yields per acre and made the Midwest the breadbasket of the nations.

Chicago grew, as did other cities, because it offered jobs. Chicago had a population of over two million before World War I. As the cities grew, so did urban problems. Working conditions in the factory meant long hours, low pay, no benefits, and often unsafe working conditions. Even children worked long, hard hours. The labor movement began in the 1860s. Groups came together in support of a common goal and then disbanded. The American Federation of Labor (AFL) was established in the 1880s and became the first permanent labor union. It wanted to improve the working conditions for its members. This grew and eventually merged with the Congress of Industrial Organizations (AFL-CIO) in 1955.

The United States engaged in trade but remained basically isolationist until World War I. The end of the war began a period of prosperity that lasted until 1929. The "Roaring Twenties" wasn't just a period of speakeasies and bootleggers. The economy, freed from its wartime restraints, had to satisfy the pent-up demand caused by the war. Mass production satisfied mass demand and supplied the wages for the people to buy the output. Manufacturing output doubled during this period. The building sector experienced a boom that eventually faded. The financial sector was making loans for all the buildings. The stock market was booming, with almost unlimited buying and selling on margin. When the stock prices fell, many speculators could not meet their margin calls. This led to the onset of the Great Depression. The New Deal policies of public spending and the onset of World War II brought the economy slowly out of the Great Depression.

The United States, along with the Soviet Union, emerged as the new world powers after World War II. The European economies were shattered by the war, as was their infrastructure. America embarked on a program of massive aid called the Marshall Plan to help the war-devastated economies rebuild. The Bretton Woods System was established to provide stable exchange rates. GATT and other trade organizations were established to help lower trade barriers. This system worked well, and the world economies recovered from the war. Under the Bretton Woods System, the U.S. dollar was expressed in terms of gold, at $35 per ounce, and all other world currencies were expressed in terms of the dollar. Nations were required to keep their currency values within a specified range, and nations would settle their balance of payments imbalances at the end of the year. This system worked well until the 1960s, when the world kept experiencing exchange-rate crises, which were resulting in the exchange markets closing. The situation continued until 1973, when world exchange rates began to float. This eliminated the need for the settlement of payments imbalances, because the exchange rate adjusts to eliminate payments disequilibrium. A deficit results in currency depreciation and surplus results in currency appreciation. As firms and traders became more adept at hedging, currency problems were eliminated, and international trade continued to grow.

In today's world, all nations are members of a national economy. What happens in one nation affects the other nations, because they are all related through international trade and finance. For example, if one nation lowers its interest rates to stimulate its domestic economy, the lower interest rates cause an outflow of dollars to a foreign country with higher interest rates. This results in dollar depreciation and an appreciation of the foreign currency. The cheaper dollar (due to the lower dollar value) makes U.S. exports more attractive to foreigners. The result is that foreigners buy more U.S. exports. The higher value of the foreign currency makes foreign imports more expensive to U.S. citizens, so they buy fewer foreign imports. The result is higher employment levels in the U.S. and more unemployment in the foreign country. A nation cannot act in isolation in today's world.

Skill 15.3   Recognize key features and historical developments associated with different types of political systems; the interrelationships of economic and political systems; and their relationship to historical and contemporary developments in Illinois, the United States and the world

Forms of Government are listed below:

Anarchism – A political movement believing in the elimination of all government and its replacement by a cooperative community of individuals. Sometimes it has involved political violence, such as assassinations of important political or governmental figures. The historical banner of the movement is a black flag.

Communism - A belief as well as a political system characterized by the ideology of class conflict and revolution, one party state and dictatorship, repressive police apparatus, and government ownership of the means of production and distribution of goods and services. A revolutionary ideology preaching the eventual overthrow of all other political orders and the establishment of one world communist government. Same as Marxism. The historical banner of the movement is a red flag and a variation of stars, hammer, and sickles, representing the various types of workers.

Dictatorship - The rule by an individual or small group of individuals (oligarchy) that centralizes all political control in itself and enforces its will with a terrorist police force.

Fascism - A belief as well as a political system, opposed ideologically to communism, though similar in basic structure, with a one party state, centralized political control, and a repressive police system. It, however, tolerates private ownership of the means of production, though it maintains tight overall control. Central to its belief is the idolization of the leader, a "cult of personality," and most often an expansionist ideology. Examples have been German Nazism and Italian Fascism.

Monarchy - The rule of a nation by a monarch, (a nonelected, usually hereditary leader), most often a king or queen. It may or may not be accompanied by some measure of democratic open institutions and elections at various levels. A modern example is Great Britain, where it is called a constitutional monarchy.

Parliamentary System - A system of government with a legislature, usually involving a multiplicity of political parties and often coalition politics. There is division between the head of state and head of government. Head of government is usually known as a prime minister, who is also usually the head of the largest party. The head of government and cabinet usually both sit and vote in the parliament. Head of state is most often an elected president, (though in the case of a constitutional monarchy, like Great Britain, the sovereign may take the place of a president as head of state). A government may fall when a majority in parliament votes "no confidence" in the government.

Presidential System - A system of government with a legislature, can involve few or many political parties, no division between head of state and head of government. The president serves in both capacities. The president is elected either by direct or indirect election. A president and cabinet usually do not sit or vote in the legislature, and the president may or may not be the head of the largest political party. A president can thus rule even without a majority in the legislature. He can only be removed from office before an election for major infractions of the law.

Socialism - Political belief and system in which the state takes a guiding role in the national economy and provides extensive social services to its population. It may or may not own outright means of production, but even where it does not, it exercises tight control. It usually promotes democracy (Democratic Socialism), though the heavy state involvement produces excessive bureaucracy and usually inefficiency. Taken to an extreme it may lead to communism as government control increases and democratic practice decreases. Ideologically the two movements are very similar in both belief and practice, as socialists also preach the superiority of their system to all others, claiming that it will become the eventual natural order. It is considered, for that reason, a variant of Marxism as well. It has also used a red flag as a symbol.

Democracy is a much more familiar system to most. In the United States, it is the system under which we live. The term comes from the Greek "for the rule of the people," and that is just what it is. The two most prevalent types are **direct** and **indirect** democracy. Direct democracy usually involves all the people in a given area coming together to vote and decide on issues that will affect them. It is used only when the population involved is relatively small, for instance a local town meeting. An **indirect democracy** involves much larger areas and populations and involves the sending of representatives to a legislative body to vote on issues affecting the people. Such a system can be comprised of a **Presidential** or **Parliamentary** system. In the United States, we follow an indirect, or representative, democracy of the presidential type.

Many different factors affect and influence politics; of them **geography**, **economics,** and **culture** are among the most important. Looking at geography, we should realize that the geographic location of a particular country (that is the type of politics we will examine: those that take place on a national level) would greatly affect its politics. Both domestic and foreign policy are determined by a given country's location. For instance, in an area like Europe, where there are many independent countries in close proximity to each other, the development of rivalries and conflicts was bound to arise. The main struggles involved boundaries and control of the limited amount of land that was available for each national group. We can see historically how these conflicts have arisen throughout history whenever two or more countries in close proximity to each other engage in warfare. It is a fact of human experience that a majority of wars throughout history has begun for the most part over the issue of land, later spreading to other lands in a continuing competition.

In a country like the United States, for instance, separate for the most part from other nations by the wide oceans, the chances for conflict is greatly diminished. In the case of the United States, it started small as colonies established along a wide coast. With its independence, it had the ability to expand throughout a large land area straight across to the other side of the continent. This has been the most important fact in both America's growth from small, lightly-populated former colonies, to the strongest major power in the world. The policies of every American administration since independence have also focused on this idea: the right and obligation for America to expand and control the entire area between its two coasts. This is an idea called **"Manifest Destiny,"** or its "obvious" destiny. The fact that this massive expansion was able to occur with little or no real conflict helped the extent and speed by which it did occur.

The ability of America to expand so much so fast was directly related to its having no real enemies or rivals for power on the continent. The native Indian populations were too unorganized and too weak to be able to stop it. In addition, the European powers were similarly forced out of the continent, a process that accelerated with the defeat of Great Britain in the American Revolution. With America's growing power, it was able to proclaim the **"Monroe Doctrine,"** which told the Europeans that they will stay out of this area of the world. The only other countries that could possibly compete with the United States for hegemony on this continent, Mexico and Canada, are much less strong than the United States. Canada was then a semicolony of Great Britain, even after it gained most of its independence. It remained sparsely populated, and in any case, it has a similar culture and a similar economy to the United States. It also has a large area of uninhabited land in which to develop. The only other power in this hemisphere, Mexico, poses no real problem for the United States. Though there was a conflict with Mexico in the middle of the 1800s over land issues owing to America's expansionist policy, it was no real contest. America was and remains a stronger nation than Mexico.

Throughout history, thus, we see that geographic location has been of supreme importance. It has been a major factor in a nation's ability to advance its interests, even in the modern era, and looking at continuing world events, this fact is not likely to change.

Looking at economics, we must consider what is known as Political Economy, that is, the interrelationship between politics and economics. They are closely tied together. In fact, it has been stated by many different theorists that politics itself is just the particular method that people have adapted in order to solve their economic problems.

Among the most prominent of these theorists has been Karl Marx. Another important theorist on the subject of how politics and economics interact was Adam Smith, with his most famous work, "The Wealth of Nations" (1776). In it, he promoted the idea of "Laissez Faire," or letting an economy run itself with little or no government interference. Also important was Thomas Malthus, who wrote about population problems over available food, land, and resources. John Maynard Keynes studied the business cycle, and his observations gave rise to an economic theory that bears his name.

The most important fact in economics is the question of the ordering of the economy, and as stated, politics is how the economy is set up. Two of the most prominent methods are the **market** and **central planning.** The market is most closely associated with democratic free enterprise as it is practiced in the United States. Central planning is an important feature of socialist, communist, and to an extent, fascist systems. Whatever system is in place, all economies have to answer the basic questions of what to produce, how to produce it, and for whom to produce it.

Calvin Coolidge once said, "The business of America is business." He may have been overstating it, but generally, this can be said to be true, and not only for the United States, but also more and more for all nations.

The third major component we will examine in politics is **culture.** Though it may be examined third, it is by no means third in importance. In fact, all three things we are examining can be, at times, of equal importance. The first two, **geography** and **economics,** are more or less external forces. People choose (usually) the type of government and what type of economic policy they will follow.

In addition, a country can try to lessen geographic pressure. This can be done by staying neutral like Switzerland, or by maintaining superior and powerful armed forces capable of repelling aggression directed against it, like Israel. Israel is a nation with no strategic geographic territory in an area where it is outnumbered, outgunned, and surrounded by aggressive neighbors. Its survival has been a matter of sheer superior capabilities. Alternatively, a nation can simply be fortunate to live with large oceans for borders, like the United States.

However, a nation's culture is something that is immutable and intrinsically a part of a people. Thus, all of its politics will be naturally defined by it. The fact is that all peoples are different from each other. This is not a value judgment; it is not a question of superiority or inferiority. Terms like "Social Darwinism" (the struggle among peoples, in which only the strong survive) or "White Man's Burden," the presumed justification for colonial expansion, have historically been used to justify ideas of national or cultural superiority. (The white Europeans felt they had a burden or obligation to "civilize" the world.)

Culture simply means those attitudes and beliefs that a nation holds that affect their political and economic decisions. It is a fact of history that at certain times, specific peoples and cultures have found themselves in positions of importance or power that gave them an advantage over others. Usually this is because those cultures found themselves *better able to adapt to changing circumstances and times.* Examples of cultures that maximized their advantages have been the Roman Empire, Great Britain, Germany, Japan, and the United States. Each one of these arose from simple beginnings to positions of immense power in the world. This is directly traceable to their cultures, which proved themselves up to the challenges they were presented with. Thus, the key word historically for success is adaptability.

The differences between democracy vs. totalitarianism and authoritarianism are an easier comparison to make, since most understand the general differences, if not the specifics. The differences between totalitarianism and authoritarianism are not as readily apparent; indeed most do not understand that there is a difference. That being the case, on the political spectrum democracy stands on one side and totalitarianism and authoritarianism on the other. We will consider the differences between totalitarianism and authoritarianism first. The difference between the two of them and democracy is in actuality a very great difference. That is why there are two different expressions; they are names for two different ideas, and that is where we will start.

Consider the two names. We see that totalitarianism is derived from the word **total,** while authoritarianism is derived from the word **authority.** The essential idea is that while many may use the two expressions together and interchangeably, in regards to political movements such as fascism, communism, and similar types of regimes, there are really two different ideas. The difference is that a totalitarian system doesn't recognize the right for any aspect of society to be outside the influence of the state. Such a government sees itself as having a legitimate concern with all levels of human existence. Not only in regards to freedom of speech, or press, but even to social and religious institutions, it tries to achieve a complete conformity to its ideals. Thus, those ideologies that presume to speak to all of society's ills, such as communism and fascism, look to this model for what they attempt to create in society. As Benito Mussolini said, "*nothing outside of the state, nothing instead of the state.*"

Those regimes that conform to the **authoritarian** model never presume to seek such a complete reordering of society. Thus, those dictatorships that arise without this social pretension can best be described as authoritarian. They do usually leave some autonomous institutions, such as the Church, alone as long as they do not interfere with the state authority. This model can be seen in the history of Central and South America, where regimes, usually representing the interests of the upper classes, came to power and instituted dictatorships that sought to concentrate all political power into a few hands.

In authoritarianism, no overall embracing ideology of control is even thought about, let alone attempted. This is seen in many of these countries. The Church soon becomes an institution of opposition to the state authority after an initial period of acceptance, if the state was originally seen as providing order in the society and fighting communism. The only regimes where the drive for total society-changing control was attempted were those regimes in Cuba and Nicaragua that held to the Marxist-communist world view.

Skill 15.4   Demonstrate knowledge of the political processes and the role of political parties in the United States

The U.S. electoral process has many and varied elements, from simple voting to complex campaigning for office. Everything in between is complex and detailed.

First of all, American citizens vote. They vote for laws, statues, referenda, and elected officials. They have to register in order to vote, and at that time they can declare their intended membership in a political party. America has a large list of political parties, which have varying degrees of membership. The Democratic and Republican Parties are the two with the most money and power, but other political parties abound. In some cases, people who are registered members of a political party are allowed to vote only for members of that political party. This takes place in many cases in primary elections, when, for example, a number of people are running to secure the nomination of one political party for a general election. If you are a registered Democrat, then in the primary election, you will be able to vote only for Democratic candidates; this restriction will be listed for the general election, in which the Democratic Party will expect you to vote for that party's candidate, but in which you can also vote for whomever you want. A potential voter need not register for a political party, however.

Candidates affiliate themselves with political parties (or sometimes not: some candidates run unaffiliated, but they usually have trouble raising enough money to adequately campaign against their opponents). Candidates then go about the business of campaigning, which includes getting the word out on their candidacy, what they believe in, and what they will do if elected. All of this costs money, of course, unless a candidate relies entirely on word of mouth or some sort of email campaign. Candidates sometimes get together for debates to showcase their views on important issues of the day and to portray how those views differ from those of their opponents. Candidates give public speeches, attend public functions, and spout their views to reporters for coverage in newspapers and magazines and on radio and television. On Election Day, candidates cross their fingers and hope that what they've done is enough.

The results of elections are made known very quickly, sometimes instantly, thanks to computerized vote tallying. Once results are finalized, winning candidates give victory speeches and losing candidates give concession speeches. Losing candidates go back to the lives they were leading, and winning candidates get ready to take their places in the local, state, or national government.

Elections take place regularly, so voters know just how long it will be before the next election. Some candidates begin planning their next campaign the day after their victory or loss. Voters technically have the option to **recall** elected candidates; such a measure, however, is drastic and requires a large pile of signatures to get the motion on the ballot and then a large number of votes to have the measure approved. As such, recalls of elected candidates are relatively rare. One widely publicized recall in recent years was that of California Governor Gray Davis, who was replaced by movie star Arnold Schwarzenegger.

Another method of removing public officials from office is **impeachment.** This is also rare but still a possibility. Both houses of the state or federal government get involved, and both houses have to approve the impeachment measures by a large margin. In the case of the federal government, the House of Representatives votes to impeach a federal official, and the Senate votes to convict or acquit. Conviction means that the official must leave office immediately; acquittal results in no penalties or fines.

Article II of the Constitution lists the specifics of the Electoral College. The Founding Fathers included the Electoral College as one of the famous "checks and balances" for two reasons: 1) to give states with small populations more of an equal weight in the presidential election, and 2) they didn't trust the common man (women couldn't vote then) to be able to make an informed decision on which candidate would make the best president.

First of all, the same theory that created the U.S. Senate's practice of giving two senators to each state created the Electoral College. The large-population states had their populations reflected in the House of Representatives. New York and Pennsylvania, two of the states with the largest populations, had the highest number of members of the House of Representatives. But these two states still had only two senators, the exact same number that small-population states like Rhode Island and Delaware had. This was true as well in the Electoral College: Each state had just one vote, regardless of how many members of the House represented that state. So, the one vote that the state of New York cast would be decided by an initial vote of New York's representatives. (If that initial vote was a tie, then that deadlock would have to be broken.)

Secondly, when the Constitution was being written, not many people knew a whole lot about government, politics, or presidential elections. A large number of people were farmers or lived in rural areas, where they were far more concerned with making a living and providing for their families than they were with who was running for which office. Many of these "common people" could not read or write, either, and wouldn't be able to read a ballot in any case. Like it or not, the Founding Fathers thought that even if these "common people" could vote, they wouldn't necessarily make the best decision for who would make the best president. So, the Electoral College was born.

Technically, the electors do not have to vote for anyone. The Constitution does not require them to do so. And throughout the history of presidential elections, some have indeed voted for someone else. But tradition holds that the electors vote for the candidate chosen by their state, and so the vast majority of electors do just that. The Electoral College meets a few weeks after the presidential election. Mostly, their meeting is a formality. When all the electoral votes are counted, the president with the most votes wins. In most cases, the candidate who wins the popular vote also wins in the Electoral College. However, this has not always been the case.

Most recently, in the year 2000 in Florida, the election was decided by the Supreme Court. The Democratic Party's nominee was Vice President Al Gore, former Vice President to President Bill Clinton. As such, he was both a champion of Clinton's successes and a reflection of his failures. The Republican Party's nominee was George W. Bush, governor of Texas and son of former President George Bush. He campaigned on a platform of a strong national defense and an end to questionable ethics in the White House. The election was hotly contested, and many states went down to the wire, being decided by only a handful of votes. The one state that seemed to be flip-flopping as Election Day turned into Election Night was Florida. In the end, Gore won the popular vote by nearly 540,000 votes. But he didn't win the electoral vote. The vote was so close in Florida that a recount was necessary under federal law. Eventually, the Supreme Court weighed in and stopped all the recounts. The last count had Bush winning by less than a thousand votes. That gave him Florida and the White House.

Because of these irregularities, especially the last one, many have taken up the cry to eliminate the Electoral College, which they see as archaic and capable of distorting the will of the people. After all, they argue, elections these days come down to one or two key states, as if the votes of the people in all the other states don't matter. Proponents of the Electoral College point to the tradition of the entity and all of the other elections in which the electoral vote mirrored the popular vote. Eliminating the Electoral College would no doubt take a constitutional amendment, and those are certainly hard to come by. The debate crops up every four years; in the past decade, though, the debate has lasted longer in between elections.

Skill 15.5   Analyze political relationships between the United States and other nations; the role of the United States in world affairs; and global patterns of trade, exchange, and interdependence among individuals, businesses, and governments

Current national and international issues and controversies involve **employment** and **trade** issues. In today's world, markets are international. Nations are all part of a global economy. No nation exists in isolation or is totally independent of other nations. **Isolationism** is referred to as autarky, or a closed economy. No one nation has all of the resources needed to be totally self-sufficient in everything it produces and consumes. Even a nation with such a well-diversified resource base like the United States has to import items like coffee, tea, and other items. The United States is not as dependent on trade as are other nations, but trade is needed for goods and items that we either can't produce domestically or that we can't produce as cheaply as other nations can.

Trade barriers are a way in which economic problems are caused in other countries. Suppose the domestic government is confronted with rising unemployment in the domestic industry due to cheaper foreign imports. Consumers are buying the cheaper foreign import instead of the higher-priced domestic good. In order to protect domestic labor, government imposes a tariff, thus raising the price of the more efficiently produced foreign good. The result of the tariff is that consumers buy more of the domestic good and less of the foreign good. A decrease in the demand for the foreign good means foreign producers don't need as much labor, so they lay off workers in the foreign country. The result of the trade barrier is that unemployment has been exported from the domestic country to the foreign country. As trade barriers are lowered or eliminated, this causes changes in labor and output markets.

GATT, NAFTA, WTO, and EU are all forms of trade liberalization. The GATT was founded in 1947 and today, as the WTO, has 147 member nations. It was based on three principles. The first was most favored national status for all members. This means trade based on comparative advantage without tariffs or trade barriers. The second principle was elimination of quotas, and third, reduction of trade barriers through multilateral trade negotiations. The WTO is the successor to the GATT and came into being in 1995. Its object is to promote free trade. As such it administers trade agreements, settles disputes, and provides a forum for trade discussions and negotiations.

NAFTA and the EU are both forms of regional economic integration. Economic integration is a method of trade liberalization on a regional basis. NAFTA represents the lowest form, or first step, in the regional trade integration process. A free trade area consists of two or more countries that abolish tariffs and other trade barriers among themselves but maintain their own trade barriers against the rest of the world. A free trade area allows for specialization and trade on the basis of comparative advantage within the area. The next stage in the integration process is a customs union, which is a free trade area that has common external tariffs against nonmembers. The third stage is a common market, which is a customs union with free-factor mobility within the area. Factors migrate where they find the best payment within the area. The fourth stage is economic union, where the common market members have common or coordinated economic and social policies. The final stage is monetary union, where the area has a common currency. This is what Europe is working toward. They have a common market with elements of the fourth and fifth stages of integration.

The WTO does not change or blur the significance of political borders and territorial sovereignty in the same way that economic integration does, although the WTO is a way of settling trade disputes that arise from the different integration agreements. In the advanced stages of economic integration, the political borders remain, but economic and social policies are common or coordinated, and in monetary union, there is one common currency. Each nation is its own independent entity, but nations give up some sovereignty in the interest of having a successful union.

Trade agreements proliferate in the world today. The Smoot Hawley Tariffs and the rounds of retaliation in the 1930s are what laid the basis for today's WTO and EU. The GATT and the beginnings of what is now the EU came into being as organizations trying to undo the effects of the Great Depression and the world war. Free trade without trade barriers results in the most efficient use of resources, with higher consumption, employment, and income levels for all participants. This is why there are so many free trade agreements being negotiated in today's world.

*   *   *

The United States is a leader in international affairs. As the nation with the single largest economy it is the economic and political leader in the world.

Globalism is defined as the principle of the interdependence of all the world's nations and their peoples. Within this global community, every nation, in some way to a certain degree, is dependent on other nations. Since no one nation has all of the resources needed for production, trade with other nations is required to obtain what is needed for production, to sell what is produced, or to buy finished products and earn money to maintain and strengthen the nation's economic system.

Developing nations receive technical assistance and financial aid from developed nations. Many international organizations have been set up to promote and encourage cooperation and economic progress among member nations. Through the elimination of such barriers to trade as tariffs, trade is stimulated, resulting in increased productivity, economic progress, and increased cooperation and understanding on diplomatic levels.

Those nations not part of an international trade organization not only must make those economic decisions of what to produce and how and for whom, but must also deal with the problem of tariffs and quotas on imports. Regardless of international trade memberships, economic growth and development are vital and affect all trading nations. Businesses, labor, and governments share common interests and goals in a nation's economic status. International systems of banking and finance have been devised to assist governments and businesses in setting the policy and guidelines for the exchange of currencies.

The global economy had its origins in the early 20th century with the advent of the airplane, which made travel and trade easier and less time-consuming than ever. With the recent advent of the Internet, the world might be better termed a global neighborhood.

Airplanes travel the fastest of any mode of transportation on the planet. They can reduce days-long trips to hours-long adventures, resulting in not only shorter tourist trips but also shorter trade trips, meaning that goods (especially perishable foods) can travel farther and wider than ever before. Being able to ship goods quickly and efficiently means that businesses can conduct business overseas much more efficiently than ever before. Trucks, trains, and ships carry cargo all over the world. Trains travel faster than ever, as do ships. Roads are more prevalent and usually in better repair than they have ever been, making truck and even car travel not the dead-end option that it once was.

With all of this capability has come increasing demand. People traditionally had gotten their goods using their own means or from traders who lived nearby. As technology improved, trade routes got longer and demand for things from overseas grew. This demand feeds the economic imperative of creating more supply, and vice versa. As more people discovered goods from overseas, the demand for those foreign goods increased. Because people could get goods from overseas with relative ease, they continued to get them and demand more. Suppliers were only too happy to supply the goods.

An incredible increase in demand for something is not always a good thing, however, especially if what is being demanded is in limited supply. A good example is wood, paper, and other goods that are made from trees. The demand for paper, especially these days, is staggering. In order to fulfill that demand, companies are cutting down more and more trees. Forests around the world are disappearing at an alarming rate, especially in the precious rain forests of South America. Recycling of paper is very much a focus for many people today, but it can't keep up with clear-cutting.

Nonrenewable resources like coal and oil are in worldwide demand these days, and the supplies won't last forever. Making it easier to ship goods all over the world has made demand grow at an unbelievable rate, raising concerns about supply. Because resources like this have a limited supply (even though the day when that limit is reached seems far away still), they are in danger of becoming extinct.

Globalization has also brought about welcome and unwelcome developments in the field of epidemiology. Vaccines and other cures for diseases can be shipped relatively quickly all around the world. This has made it possible for HIV vaccines to reach the remotest areas of the world, for example. Unfortunately, the preponderance of global travel has also meant that the threat of spreading a disease to the world by an infected person traveling on an international flight is quite real.

The most recent example of technology contributing to globalization is the development of the Internet. Instant communication between people millions of miles apart is possible just by plugging in a computer and connecting to the Net. The Internet is an extension of the telephone and cell phone revolutions; all three are developments that have brought faraway places closer together. All three allow people to communicate no matter the distance. This communication can facilitate friendly chatter and, of course, trade. A huge number of businesses use cell phones and the Internet to do business these days, also using computers to track goods and receipts quickly and efficiently.

Globalization has brought financial and cultural exchange on a worldwide scale as well. A large number of businesses have investments in countries around the world. Financial transactions are conducted using a variety of currencies. The cultures of the countries of the world are increasingly viewed by people elsewhere in the world through the wonders of television and the Internet. Not only goods but also belief systems, customs, and practices are being exchanged.

With this exchange of money, goods, and culture has come an increase in immigration. Many people who live in less-developed nations see what is available in other places and want to move there in order to fully take advantage of all that those more-developed nations have to offer. This can conceivably create an increase in immigration. Depending on the numbers of people who want to immigrate and the resources available, this could become a problem. The technological advances in transportation and communication have made such immigration easier than ever.

Skill 15.6   Identify a wide range of instructional resources and technologies to support learning about economic and political systems

There are many resources available for the teaching of social science concepts. The resources used should be appropriate to the learning objectives specified. The teacher wants to use different kinds of resources in order to make the subject matter more interesting to the student and to appeal to different learning styles. First of all a good textbook is required. This gives the student something that they can refer to and something to study from. Students generally like to have a text to refer to. The use of audio-video aides is also beneficial in the classroom environment. Most people are visual learners and will retain information better when it is in visual form. Audio-visual presentations, like movies, give them concepts in pictures that they will easily retain.

Library projects are good for students also. The library has an abundance of resources that students should become familiar with at an early age, so they should learn to use the library. There are books and magazines that they can look through and read to expand their knowledge beyond the textbooks. Younger children, particularly, like to look at pictures. The computer also offers abundant opportunities as a teaching tool and resource. The Internet provides a wealth of information on all topics, and something can be found that is suitable for any age group. Children like to play games, so presenting the material in a game-like format is also a good teaching tool. Making little puzzles for vocabulary or letting them present the information in the form of a story or even a play helps them learn and retain various concepts. Field trips, if possible, are a good way to expose children to various aspects of social science. Trips to the stock markets, the Federal Reserve, etc., are things children enjoy and remember. Today's world of technology makes a myriad of resources available to the teacher. The teacher should make use of as many of them as possible to keep the material more interesting for the student and to aid in their retention of the material.

Assessment methods are always important in teaching. Assessment methods are ways to determine if the student has sufficiently learned the required material. There are different ways of accomplishing this. Assessment methods basically mean asking a question in some way and receiving a response in some way from the student, whether it is written or verbal. The test is the usual method, where the student answers questions on the material he has studied. Tests, of course, can be written or verbal. Tests for younger children can be game-like. They can be asked to draw lines connecting various associated symbols or to pick a picture representing a concept. Other methods involve writing essays on various topics. They don't have to be long, but just long enough for the student to demonstrate that he has adequate knowledge of a subject. Verbal reports can accomplish the same goal.

Assigning projects for students to do is another good way of reinforcing learning. Projects can require students to obtain information about a subject and organize that information into some sort of report, whether it is written or verbal. Children can use their imaginations in putting together the information and can be assessed on the quality and depth of the information included in the report.

Libraries of all sorts are valuable when conducting research, and nowadays almost all have digitized search systems to assist in finding information on almost any subject. Even so, the Internet, with powerful search engines like Google readily available, can retrieve information that doesn't exist in libraries, or if it does exist, is much more difficult to retrieve.

Conducting a research project once involved the use of punch cards, microfiche, and other manual means of storing the data in a retrievable fashion. No more. With high-powered computers available to anyone who chooses to conduct research, the organizing of the data in a retrievable fashion has been revolutionized. Creating multilevel folders, copying and pasting into the folders, making ongoing additions to the bibliography at the time that a source is consulted, and using search-and-find functions make this stage of the research process go much faster, with less frustration and a decrease in the likelihood that important data might be overlooked.

Serious research requires high-level analytical skills when it comes to processing and interpreting data. A degree in statistics or at least a graduate-level concentration is very useful. However, a team approach to a research project will include a statistician, in addition to those members who are knowledgeable in the social sciences.

COMPETENCY 16.0 UNDERSTAND FROM MULTIPLE PERSPECTIVES THE SIGNIFICANT ERAS, THEMES, EVENTS, AND CULTURAL DEVELOPMENTS IN THE HISTORY OF ILLINOIS, THE UNITED STATES, AND THE WORLD

Skill 16.1   Demonstrate knowledge of significant eras, themes, events, and people in the history of Illinois, the United States, and the world

Illinois was inhabited by Native Americans, among them the powerful **Illini.** This word was actually a French mangling of "Hileni," or "Illiniwek," as Illinois. This "name" notwithstanding, the Illini built one of the most powerful confederations ever seen on the continent.

The five most populous tribes were the **Peoria, Kaskaskia, Tamaroa, Cahokia, and Michigamea.** They grew pumpkins, squash, and maize. They caught fish from the Illinois River and participated in annual buffalo hunts.

Jacques Marquette and **Louis Joliet** explored much of the area in 1673. Also entering the picture in the late 17th century was René-Robert Cavelier, Sieur de La Salle. These explorers built forts and went on missions throughout what is now Illinois and claimed most of it for France.

In 1712, the Illinois River became the boundary of France's Louisiana Territory. For many years, the Illini Confederation fought the French. These struggles weakened both sides, making the British victory in the French and Indian War even easier.

After the British victory, the Illinois territory changed hands, from France to Great Britain. In 1771, the people of Illinois met at **Kaskaskia** and demanded a form of self-government; Great Britain refused, continuing to insist that all officials must be appointed by the British king.

The territory was soon part of a battle again, during the Revolutionary War. George Rogers Clark captured Kaskaskia, Cahokia, and Vincennes, all strategic locations. After the American victory in 1783, Virginia claimed Illinois; one year later, the state turned it over to the federal government.

The Northwest Territory, formed in 1787, included Illinois. So did the Indiana Territory, formed in 1800. Three years later, **Fort Dearborn** was built near what is now Chicago. In 1809, the Illinois Territory was officially created, with Kaskaskia as its capital. Fur trappers and other settlers began to put down roots in the new territory, which included all of Wisconsin except the northern part of the Green Bay Peninsula, a large part of Michigan, and all of Minnesota east of the Mississippi.

Illinois was also a battleground during the War of 1812. Native Americans killed many Americans at Fort Dearborn. With the American victory in 1814, Illinois was secure. The territory had, with the permission of the U.S. Congress in 1812, chosen a representative assembly and elected a territorial delegate to Congress. Eager to keep Kaskaskia, Vincennes, and other important cities in American hands, the United States put Illinois statehood on the fast track.

On December 3, 1818, Illinois became the twenty-first state. Its capital was Kaskaskia. The period after statehood was full of growing pains and war. The Black War in 1832 caused a great deal of strife. Mormons fled the state in 1844 after their leader, Joseph Smith, was killed.

Illinois was the scene of a famous series of political discussions known as the Lincoln-Douglas Debates. Senator **Stephen A. Douglas** and his challenger, **Abraham Lincoln,** traveled the state, debating the issues of the day. Douglas won re-election in 1858, but Lincoln became president two years later. Lincoln's election prompted a large handful of Southern states to secede. This, and the attack on Fort Sumter, began the Civil War. Illinois was still part of the Union during the war, even though many citizens had Southern loyalties. Illinois contributed large numbers of men, weapons, iron, and food to the war effort.

Despite the Civil War death toll, the Great Chicago Fire of 1871, and other 19th century disasters, Illinois was, by 1880, the fourth most populous state in the Union. Chicago and the rest of the state continued to grow. The state became a focal point for labor as well. The Haymarket Square riot and the Pullman strike emphasized the need for full disclosure on working conditions and salaries.

The dawn of the 20th century brought continued industrialization and progress in Illinois. Meatpacking industries, in particular, were a big business. Workplace reforms and outside competition eventually led to a decline in this industry. Chicago was known for its bootlegging and gangsters during the Roaring Twenties. The state itself was known as a major manufacturing center during both world wars. The World's Fair in 1933 and the opening of the St. Lawrence Seaway in 1959 made Chicago a household name around the world. The erection of the Sears Tower, in 1973, helped in this regard as well.

The civil rights movement of the 1950s and 1960s was a particularly difficult time in Illinois history. Large populations of African-Americans living in Chicago and other urban centers met with resistance to their drive toward equality (although this resistance was not as determined or fierce as that in the South).

Chicago and Illinois today are very much symbols of their surroundings. More so Chicago and the state's inner cities, but also the rest of the state is a Melting Pot of ethnicities and industries, chugging ahead into the 21st century.

Skill 16.2   Analyze ways in which cultural groups have affected and been affected by U.S. society and ways in which cultural heritage and diversity have influenced historical developments in the United States

Numerous conflicts, often called the "Indian Wars," broke out between the U.S. army and many different native tribes. Many treaties were signed with the various tribes, but most were broken by the government for a variety of reasons. Two of the most notable battles were the Battle of Little Bighorn in 1876, in which native people defeated General Custer and his forces, and the massacre of Native Americans in 1890 at Wounded Knee. In 1876, the U.S. government ordered all surviving Native Americans to move to reservations.

This forced migration of the Native Americans to lands that were deemed marginal, combined with the near-extermination of the buffalo, caused a downturn in prairie culture, which relied on the horse for hunting, trading, and traveling.

In the late 19th century, the avid reformers of the day instituted a practice of trying to "civilize" Indian children by educating them in Indian boarding schools. The children were forbidden to speak their native languages, they were forced to convert to Christianity, and generally forced to give up all aspects of their native culture and identity. There are numerous reports of abuse of the Indian children at these schools. During World War I, a large number of Native Americans were drafted into military service. Most served heroically. This fact, combined with a growing desire to see the native peoples effectively merged into mainstream society, led to the enactment of The Indian Citizenship Act of 1924, by which Native Americans were granted U.S. citizenship.

During World War II, the experiences and contributions of American fighting forces included the role of minorities.

Internment of people of Japanese ancestry. From the turn of the 20th century, there was tension between Caucasians and Japanese in California. A series of laws had been passed discouraging Japanese immigration and prohibiting land ownership by Japanese. The Alien Registration Act of 1940 (the Smith Act) required the fingerprinting and registration of all aliens over the age of fourteen. Aliens were also required to report any change of address within five days. Almost five million aliens registered under the provisions of this act. The Japanese attack on Pearl Harbor (December 7, 1941) raised suspicion that Japan was planning a full-scale attack on the West Coast. Many believed that American citizenship did not necessarily imply loyalty. Some authorities feared sabotage of both civilian and military facilities within the country.

By February, 1942, Presidential Executive Orders had authorized the arrest of all aliens suspected of subversive activities and permitted the creation of exclusion zones where people could be isolated from the remainder of the population and kept where they could not damage national infrastructure. These War Relocation Camps were used to isolate about 120,000 Japanese and Japanese Americans (62 percent were citizens) during World War II.

Women and minorities accepted remarkable new roles and served them with great distinction during WWII, both in military operations and at home. Within the military, women and minorities filled a number of new roles. Women served in the military as drivers, nurses, communications operators, clerks, etc. The Flight Nurses Corps was created at the beginning of the war. Among the most notable minority groups in the military were the following:

The Tuskegee Airmen were a group of African-American aviators who made a major contribution to the war effort. Although they were not considered eligible for the gold wings of a navy pilot until 1948, these men completed standard army-flight classroom instruction and the required flying time. This was the first group of African-Americans permitted to fly for the military. They flew more than 15,000 missions, destroyed over 1,000 German aircraft, and earned more than 150 Distinguished Flying Crosses and hundreds of Air Medals.

The 442nd Regimental Combat Team was a unit composed of Japanese Americans who fought in Europe. This unit was the most highly decorated unit of its size and length of service in the history of the U.S. Army. This self-sufficient force served with great distinction in North Africa, Italy, southern France, and Germany. The medals earned by the group include twenty-one Congressional Medals of Honor (the highest award given). The unit was awarded 9,486 purple hearts (for being wounded in battle). The casualty rate, combining those killed in action, missing in action, and wounded and removed from action, was 93 percent.

The Navajo Code Talkers have been credited with saving countless lives and accelerating the end of the war. There were over 400 Navajo Indians who served in all six Marine divisions from 1942 to 1945. At the time of WWII, less than thirty non-Navajos understood the Navajo language. Because it was a very complex language and because it was not a code, it was unbreakable by the Germans or the Japanese. The job of these men was to talk and transmit information on tactics, troop movements, orders, and other vital military information. Not only was the enemy unable to understand the language, but it was far faster than translating messages into Morse code. It is generally accepted that without the Navajo Code Talkers, Iwo Jima could not have been taken.

Until recent years, the policy of the federal government was to segregate and marginalize Native Americans. Their religion, arts, and culture have been largely ignored until recent years. Safely restricted to reservations in the "Indian territory," various attempts were made to strip them of their inherited culture, just as they were stripped of their ancestral lands. Life on the reservations has been difficult for most Native Americans. The policies of extermination and relocation as well as the introduction of disease among them significantly decimated their numbers by the end of the 19th century.

Skill 16.3   Analyze the influence of science, technology, economic activity, and religious and philosophical ideas on contemporary societies and societies throughout history

The **Scientific Revolution** was characterized by a shift in scientific approach and ideas. Near the end of the 16th century Galileo Galilei introduced a radical approach to the study of motion. He moved from attempts to explain why objects move the way they do and began to use experiments to describe precisely how they move. He also used experimentation to describe how forces affect nonmoving objects. Other scientists continued in the same approach. Outstanding scientists of the period included Johannes Kepler, Evangelista Torricelli, Blaise Pascal, Isaac Newton, and Gottfried Leibniz. This was the period when experiments dominated scientific study. This method of experimentation was particularly applied to the study of physics.

The **Agricultural Revolution** occurred first in England. It was marked by experimentation that resulted in increased production of crops from the land and a new and more technical approach to the management of agriculture. The revolution in agricultural management and production was hugely enhanced by the industrial revolution and the invention of the steam engine. The introduction of steam-powered tractors greatly increased crop production and significantly decreased labor costs. Developments in agriculture were also enhanced by the scientific revolution and the learning from experimentation that led to philosophies of crop rotation and soil enrichment. Improved systems of irrigation and harvesting contributed to the growth of agricultural production.

The **Industrial Revolution,** which began in Great Britain and spread elsewhere, was the development of power-driven machinery (fueled by coal and steam) leading to the accelerated growth of industry, with large factories replacing homes and small workshops as work centers. The lives of people changed drastically, and a largely agricultural society changed to an industrial one. In Western Europe, the period of empire and colonialism began. The industrialized nations seized and claimed parts of Africa and Asia in an effort to control and provide the raw materials needed to feed the industries and machines in the "mother country." Later developments included power based on electricity and internal combustion replacing coal and steam.

The Information Revolution refers to the sweeping changes during the latter half of the 20th century as a result of technological advances and a new respect for the knowledge or information provided by trained, skilled, and experienced professionals in a variety of fields. This approach to understanding a number of social and economic changes in global society arose from the ability to make computer technology both accessible and affordable. In particular, the development of the computer chip has led to such technological advances as the Internet, the cell phone, Cybernetics, wireless communication, and the related ability to disseminate and access a massive amount of information quite readily.

In terms of economic theory and segmentation, it is now very much the norm to think of three basic economic sectors: agriculture and mining, manufacturing, and "services." Indeed, labor is now often divided between manual labor and informational labor. The fact that businesses are involved in the production and distribution and processing and transmission of information has, according to some, created a new business sector.

Social and political movements are group actions in which large informal groups or persons and organizations focus on specific social or political issues and work for either implementing or undoing some form of change. The social movement originated in England and North America during the first decades of the 19th century.

Several types of social and political movements are often identified and distinguished by the following key factors:

1. Distinguished by *Scope*
    (a) reform movements aim to change some norms
    (b) radical movements seek to change some value systems
2. Distinguished by *Type of Change*
    (a) innovation movements attempt to introduce new norms or values
    (b) conservative movements want to preserve existing norms or values
3. Distinguished by *Target Group*
    (a) group-focus movements attempt to affect either society in general or specific groups
    (b) individual-focused movements seek to transform individuals
4. Distinguished by *Method of Action*
    (a) peaceful movements
    (b) violent movements
5. Distinguished by *Time*
    (a) old movements – prior to the 20th century
    (b) new movements – since the second half of the 20th century
6. Distinguished by *Range*
    (a) global movements
    (b) local movements

The role of religion in political movements or as a basis for political action can be quite varied, depending upon the religion and the exigencies of the time. In general, one's interpretation of how people should act within the political sphere will take one of three approaches: (1) withdrawal from politics (and sometimes from the world), (2) quietism, and (3) activism.

Religion has always been a factor in American life. Many early settlers came to America in search of religious freedom. Religion, particularly Christianity, was an essential element of the value and belief structure shared by the Founding Fathers. Yet the Constitution prescribes a separation of church and state. Religion is a basis for the actions of believers, no matter which religion is practiced or embraced. Because religion determines values and ethics, it influences the actions of individuals and groups to work to change conditions that are perceived to be wrong.

The **First Great Awakening** was a religious movement within American Protestantism in the 1730s and 1740s. This was primarily a movement among Puritans seeking a return to strict interpretation of morality and values as well as emphasizing the importance and power of personal religious or spiritual experience. Many historians believe the First Great Awakening unified the people of the original colonies and supported the independence of the colonists.

The **Second Great Awakening** (the Great Revival) was a broad movement within American Protestantism that led to several kinds of activities that were distinguished by region and denominational tradition. In general terms, the Second Great Awakening, which began in the 1820s, was a time of recognition that "awakened religion" must weed out sin on both a personal and a social level. It inspired a wave of social activism. In New England, the Congregationalists established missionary societies to evangelize the West. Publication and education societies arose, most notably the American Bible Society. This social activism gave rise to the temperance movement, prison reform efforts, and help for the handicapped and mentally ill. This period was particularly notable for the abolition movement. In the Appalachian region, the camp meeting was used to revive religion. The camp meeting became a primary method of evangelizing new territory.

The **Third Great Awakening** (the Missionary Awakening) gave rise to the Social Gospel movement. This period (1858 to 1908) resulted in a massive growth in membership of all major Protestant denominations through their missionary activities. This movement was partly a response to claims that the Bible was fallible. Many churches attempted to reconcile or change biblical teaching to fit scientific theories and discoveries. Colleges associated with Protestant churches began to appear rapidly throughout the nation. In terms of social and political movements, the Third Great Awakening was the most expansive and profound. Coinciding with many changes in production and labor, it won battles against child labor and stopped the exploitation of women in factories. Compulsory elementary education for children came from this movement, as did the establishment of a set work day. Much was also done to protect and rescue children from abandonment and abuse, to improve the care of the sick, to prohibit the use of alcohol and tobacco, and to address numerous other "social ills."

Skill 16.4 **Recognize how economic, political, cultural, geographic, and social processes interact to shape patterns of human population, cooperation, and conflict**

Human communities subsisted initially as gatherers--gathering berries, leaves, etc. With the invention of tools it became possible to dig for roots, hunt small animals, and catch fish from rivers and oceans. Humans observed their environments and soon learned to plant seeds and harvest crops. As people migrated to areas in which game and fertile soil were abundant, communities began to develop. When people had the knowledge to grow crops and the skills to hunt game, they began to understand division of labor. Some of the people in the community tended to agricultural needs while others hunted game.

As habitats attracted larger numbers of people, environments became crowded and there was competition. The concept of division of labor and sharing of food soon came, in more heavily populated areas, to be managed. Groups of people focused on growing crops while others concentrated on hunting. Experience led to the development of skills and of knowledge that made the work easier. Farmers began to develop new plant species and hunters began to protect animal species from other predators for their own use. This ability to manage the environment led people to settle down, to guard their resources, and to manage them.

Camps soon became villages. Villages became year-round settlements. Animals were domesticated and gathered into herds that met the needs of the village. With the settled life it was no longer necessary to "travel light." Pottery was developed for storing and cooking food.

By 8000 BCE, culture was beginning to evolve in these villages. Agriculture was developed for the production of grain crops, which led to a decreased reliance on wild plants. Domesticating animals for various purposes decreased the need to hunt wild game. Life became more settled. It was then possible to turn attention to such matters as managing water supplies, producing tools, making cloth, etc. There were both the social interaction and the opportunity to reflect upon existence. Mythologies and various kinds of belief systems arose. Rituals arose that re-enacted the mythologies that gave meaning to life.

As farming and animal husbandry skills increased, the dependence upon wild game and food gathering declined. With this change came the realization that a larger number of people could be supported on the produce of farming and animal husbandry.

Two things seem to have come together to produce cultures and civilizations: a society and culture based on agriculture and the development of centers of the community with literate social and religious structures. The members of these civilizations then managed water supply and irrigation, ritual and religious life, and exerted their own right to use a portion of the goods produced by the community for their own subsistence in return for their management.

Sharpened skills, development of more sophisticated tools, commerce with other communities, and increasing knowledge of their environment--the resources available to them and responses to the needs to share goods, order community life, and protect their possessions from outsiders--led to further division of labor and community development.

As trade routes developed and travel between cities became easier, trade led to specialization. Trade enables a people to obtain the goods they desire in exchange for the goods they are able to produce. This, in turn, leads to increased attention to refinements of technique and the sharing of ideas. The knowledge of a new discovery or invention provides knowledge and technology that increases the ability to produce goods for trade.

As each community learns the value of the goods it produces and improves its ability to produce the goods in greater quantity, industry is born.

Competition for control of areas of the Earth's surface is a common trait of human interaction throughout history. This competition has resulted in both destructive conflict and peaceful and productive cooperation. Societies and groups have sought control of regions of the Earth's surface for a wide variety of reasons, including religion, economics, politics, and administration. Numerous wars have been fought through the centuries for the control of territory for each of these reasons.

At the same time, groups of people, even societies, have peacefully worked together to establish boundaries around regions or territories that serve specific purposes in order to sustain the activities that support life and social organization.

Individuals and societies have divided the Earth's surface through conflict for a number of reasons:

- The domination of peoples or societies, e.g., colonialism
- The control of valuable resources, e.g., oil
- The control of strategic routes, e.g., the Panama Canal

Conflicts can be spurred by religion, political ideology, national origin, language, and race. Conflicts can result from disagreement over how land, ocean, or natural resources will be developed, shared, and used. Conflicts have resulted from trade, migration, and settlement rights. Conflicts can occur between small groups of people, between cities, between nations, between religious groups, and between multinational alliances.

Today, the world is primarily divided by political/administrative interests into state sovereignties. A particular region is recognized to be controlled by a particular government, including its territory, population, and natural resources. The only area of the Earth's surface that today is not defined by state or national sovereignty is Antarctica.

Alliances are developed among nations on the basis of political philosophy, economic concerns, cultural similarities, religious interests, or for military defense. Some of the most notable alliances today are:
- The United Nations
- The North Atlantic Treaty Organization
- The Caribbean Community
- The Common Market
- The Council of Arab Economic Unity
- The European Union

Large companies and multinational corporations also compete for control of natural resources for manufacturing, development, and distribution.

Throughout human history there have been conflicts on virtually every scale over the right to divide the Earth according to differing perceptions, needs, and values. These conflicts have ranged from tribal conflicts to urban riots, to civil wars, to regional wars, and to world wars. While these conflicts have traditionally centered on control of land surfaces, new disputes are beginning to arise over the resources of the oceans and space.

On a smaller scale, conflicts have created divisions between rival gangs over the use of zones in cities, water supply, and school districts; economic divisions include franchise areas and trade zones.

During World War II Americans found it advisable to cede to the federal government a greater degree of control over the economy, key institutions and services, and the assurance of both their personal welfare and their security. This led to a significant growth in both the reach and the size of the federal government. The nation had faced two major crises: The Great Depression and World War I. The government had assumed greater responsibility for ensuring the basic needs of its citizens, promoting economic opportunity for all, and managing economic growth. The government had also taken on the role of providing for the military safety and security of the nation against foreign enemies.

This marked the culmination of a major change in the role of the federal government that many have called "the rise of the welfare state." Since the First World War, regulatory agencies had been created to control the actions of big business, to protect labor, and to protect the rights and privileges of minorities. In addition, a truly national culture had emerged from shared hardships, the growth of the railroad and the radio, the introduction of the automobile, and the war effort itself. These factors had smoothed out many of the regional differences that previously divided the social and cultural interests of the American people.

New challenges had led to the growth of the power and control of the federal government. The attempts to bring the nation through both the Depression and the war had utilized much experimentation. Franklin Roosevelt and his administration drew upon past experience and experimentation to bring the nation through crisis. Roosevelt's use of the radio to speak to the American people permitted him to rally the populace and persuade the public to consider new ideas and new approaches to the problems of the day. Essentially, Roosevelt convinced the nation that a more active role for the federal government both internationally and at home would prevent another Depression and another world war.

This transition was very important in American history and in the national ethos. Americans had traditionally distrusted a centralization of authority in the federal government. They had also traditionally repudiated international alliances and commitments. Yet both of these changes came about in the years following WWII.

In many ways, the period from 1945 to 1972 was a time of unprecedented prosperity for everyone in the nation. Wages increased, car and home ownership increased, and average educational levels increased when the veterans of the war took full advantage of the opportunity to receive a college education paid for by their G.I. benefits. People were willing to give the government this major role in perpetuating this prosperous society. Just as WWII had united the people in a common commitment to the purpose of supporting the troops and winning the war, they again rallied together to support the government in the Cold War.

Skill 16.5   Demonstrate knowledge of how to use historical concepts and themes to analyze events, patterns, and relationships in Illinois, the United States, and the world

One way to analyze historical events, patterns, and relationships is to focus on historical themes. There are many themes that run throughout human history, and they can be used to make comparisons between different historical times as well as between nations and peoples. While new themes are always being explored, a few of the widely recognized historical themes in the study of history are as follows:

Politics and political institutions can provide information of prevailing opinions and beliefs of a group of people and how they change over time. Historically, Illinois has produced several political reformers and is a traditional supporter of the Democratic Party. Looking at the political history of the state can reveal the popular social ideals that have developed in Illinois, and how they have changed over time.

Race and ethnicity is another historical theme that runs through the history of Illinois and the nation. For example, in 1919 a large riot broke out in Chicago among African-American residents. The causes of this riot, which lasted several days and left dozens dead, are still an area of historical research. The causes are probably related to a large migration of African-Americans from the South to northern cities in search of work, and to a lack of adequate employment and housing in Chicago. Racism and related factors certainly played a part. Researching the history of how peoples of different races treated one another reflects on many other social aspects of a society and can be a fruitful line of historical interpretation.

The study of **gender** issues is a theme that focuses on the relative places men and women hold in a society and is connected to many other themes, such as politics and economics. In the United States, for many years women were not allowed to vote, for example. In economic matters, married women were expected not to hold jobs. For women who did work, a limited number of types of work were available. Investigating the historical theme of gender can reveal changes in public attitudes, economic changes, and shifting political attitudes, among other things.

Economic factors drive many social activities, such as where people live and work and the relative wealth of nations. As a historical theme, economic history can connect events to their economic causes and explore the results. The Great Migration of African-Americans from the South to Illinois in the early decades of the 20th century can be interpreted along economic themes, for example, as many blacks were searching for better paying jobs in the North. One reason more jobs were available in the North was World War I, which took many northern men into the armed forces and away from the work force.

In this way, economic factors were related to political factors, and had repercussions in race relations. Historical themes are often connected in this way, and can provide a framework upon which to build a fuller interpretation of history.

Historical concepts are movements, belief systems, or other phenomena that can be identified and examined individually or as part of a historical theme. Capitalism, communism, democracy, racism, and globalization are all examples of historical concepts. Historical concepts can be interpreted as part of larger historical themes and provide insight into historical events by placing them in a larger historical context.

The historic concept of colonialism, for example, is one that is connected to the history of Illinois. Colonialism is the concept that a nation should seek to control areas outside of its borders for economic and political gain by establishing settlements and controlling the native inhabitants. Beginning in the 17th century, the nations of France and Britain were both actively colonizing North America, with the French initially controlling the area that is now Illinois. These colonial powers eventually clashed, and Illinois came under British control. Finally, following the Revolutionary War, Illinois was ceded to the new United States of America, which was of course made up of former British colonies.

This is an example of how following a historical concept can connect local history with larger national and worldwide movements.

Skill 16.6   Identify a wide range of instructional resources and technologies to support the learning of history

See Skill 15.6

COMPETENCY 17.0 UNDERSTAND MAJOR PRINCIPLES, CONCEPTS, AND PHENOMENA OF GEOGRAPHY AND THE INTERRELATIONSHIPS BETWEEN PEOPLE AND THEIR ENVIRONMENT

Skill 17.1   Demonstrate understanding of major geographic features of Illinois, the United States, and the world and their historical and contemporary significance

Illinois is bordered on the west by the Mississippi River and on the east by the Wabash and Ohio Rivers. The Illinois River drains a large portion of the state, and is a tributary to the Mississippi River. Lake Michigan forms the northeastern border of Illinois and is a major source of commerce, connecting Illinois trade partners to the north and east. Canals connect Lake Michigan to the Chicago River and Illinois River, and so to the Mississippi.

The land of Illinois can be divided into three regions:

The **Central Plains** cover nearly the entire state of Illinois from Lake Michigan to the west and south. The Central Plains were formed by glacial movement and consist of rolling, fertile hills. Charles Mound, at 1,235 feet elevation, is in this region at the northern border of Illinois.

In the southern portion of the state, south of the Central Plains, are the **Shawnee Hills.** This narrow strip of wooded hills runs across the entire state. The hills are sandstone, and contain several canyons and cliffs.

The **Gulf Coastal Plain** stretches up from the Gulf of Mexico, and covers the very southern tip of Illinois.

The Earth's surface is made up of 70 percent water and 30 percent land. Physical features of the land surface include mountains, hills, plateaus, valleys, and plains. Other minor landforms include deserts, deltas, canyons, mesas, basins, foothills, marshes, and swamps. Earth's water features include oceans, seas, lakes, rivers, and canals.

Mountains are landforms with rather steep slopes at least 2,000 feet or more above sea level. Mountains are found in groups called mountain chains or mountain ranges. At least one range can be found on six of the Earth's seven continents. North America has the Appalachian and Rocky Mountains; South America the Andes; Asia the Himalayas; Australia the Great Dividing Range; Europe the Alps; and Africa the Atlas, Ahaggar, and Drakensburg Mountains.

Hills are elevated landforms rising to an elevation of about 500 to 2000 feet. They are found everywhere on Earth, including Antarctica, where they are covered by ice.

Plateaus are elevated landforms, usually level on top. Depending on location, they range from being an area that is very cold to one that is cool and healthful. Some plateaus are dry because they are surrounded by mountains that keep out any moisture. An example is the Kenya Plateau in East Africa, which is very cool. The plateau extending north from the Himalayas is extremely dry, while those in Antarctica and Greenland are covered with ice and snow.

Plains are described as areas of flat or slightly rolling land, usually lower than the landforms next to them. Sometimes called lowlands (and sometimes located along **seacoasts**), they support the majority of the world's people. Some are found inland, and many have been formed by large rivers. This resulted in extremely fertile soil for successful cultivation of crops and numerous large settlements of people. In North America, the vast plains areas extend from the Gulf of Mexico north to the Arctic Ocean and between the Appalachian and Rocky Mountains. In Europe, rich plains extend east from Great Britain into central Europe on into the Siberian region of Russia. Plains in river valleys are found in China (the Yangtze River Valley), India (the Ganges River Valley), and Southeast Asia (the Mekong River Valley).

Valleys are land areas that are found between hills and mountains. Some have gentle slopes containing trees and plants; others have very steep walls and are referred to as canyons. One famous example is Arizona's Grand Canyon of the Colorado River.

Deserts are large dry areas of land receiving ten inches or less of rainfall each year. Among the better known deserts are Africa's large Sahara Desert, the Arabian Desert on the Arabian Peninsula, and the desert outback covering roughly one-third of Australia.

Deltas are areas of lowlands formed by soil and sediment deposited at the mouths of rivers. The soil is generally very fertile, and most fertile river deltas are important crop-growing areas. One well-known example is the delta of Egypt's Nile River, known for its production of cotton.

Mesas are the flat tops of hills or mountains usually with steep sides. Sometimes plateaus are also called mesas. Basins are considered to be low areas drained by rivers or low spots in mountains. Foothills are generally considered a low series of hills found between a plain and a mountain range. Marshes and swamps are wet lowlands providing growth of such plants as rushes and reeds.

Oceans are the largest bodies of water on the planet. The four oceans of the Earth are the **Atlantic Ocean,** one-half the size of the Pacific and separating North and South America from Africa and Europe; the **Pacific Ocean**, covering almost one-third of the entire surface of the Earth and separating North and South America from Asia and Australia; the **Indian Ocean,** touching Africa, Asia, and Australia; and the ice-filled **Arctic Ocean,** extending from North America and Europe to the North Pole. The waters of the Atlantic, Pacific, and Indian Oceans also touch the shores of Antarctica.

Seas are smaller than oceans and are surrounded by land. Some examples include the Mediterranean Sea found between Europe, Asia, and Africa; and the Caribbean Sea, touching the West Indies, South America, and Central America. A lake is a body of water surrounded by land. The Great Lakes in North America are a good example.

Rivers, considered a nation's lifeblood, usually begin as very small streams formed by melting snow and rainfall, flowing from higher to lower land, and emptying into a larger body of water, usually a sea or an ocean. Examples of important rivers for the people and countries affected by and/or dependent on them include the Nile, Niger, and Zaire Rivers of Africa; the Rhine, Danube, and Thames Rivers of Europe; the Yangtze, Ganges, Mekong, Hwang He, and Irrawaddy Rivers of Asia; the Murray-Darling in Australia; and the Orinoco in South America. River systems are made up of large rivers and numerous smaller rivers or tributaries flowing into them. Examples include the vast Amazon River system in South America and the Mississippi River system in the United States.

Canals are man-made water passages constructed to connect two larger bodies of water. Famous examples include the **Panama Canal** across Panama's isthmus connecting the Atlantic and Pacific Oceans and the **Suez Canal** in the Middle East between Africa and the Arabian Peninsula, connecting the Red and Mediterranean Seas.

Skill 17.2   Recognize how to use maps, globes, and other geographic tools to locate and derive information about people, places, and environments

We use **illustrations** of various sorts because it is often easier to demonstrate a given idea visually instead of orally. Sometimes it is even easier to do so with an illustration than a description. This is especially true in the areas of education and research because humans are visually stimulated. It is a fact that any idea presented visually in some manner is always easier to understand and to comprehend than simply getting an idea across verbally by hearing it or reading it. Among the more common illustrations used are various types of **maps, graphs, and charts**.

Photographs and globes are useful as well, but as they are limited in what kind of information they can show, they are rarely used, unless, as in the case of a photograph, it is of a particular political figure or a time that one wishes to visualize.

Although maps have advantages over globes and photographs, they do have a major disadvantage. This problem must be considered as well. The major problem of all maps comes about because most maps are flat, and the Earth is a sphere. It is impossible to reproduce exactly on a flat surface an object shaped like a sphere. In order to put the Earth's features onto a map, they must be stretched in some way. This stretching is called **distortion.**

Distortion does not mean that maps are wrong; it simply means that they are not perfect representations of the Earth or its parts. **Cartographers,** or mapmakers, understand the problems of distortion. They try to design maps so that there is as little distortion as possible.

The process of putting the features of the Earth onto a flat surface is called **projection.** All maps are really map projections. There are many different types. Each one deals in a different way with the problem of distortion. Map projections are made in a number of ways. Some are done using complicated mathematics. However, the basic ideas behind map projections can be understood by looking at the three most common types:

(1) <u>**Cylindrical Projections**</u> - These are done by taking a cylinder of paper and wrapping it around a globe. A light is used to project the globe's features onto the paper. Distortion is least where the paper touches the globe. For example, suppose that the paper was wrapped so that it touched the globe at the equator: the map from this projection would have just a little distortion near the equator. However, in moving north or south of the equator, the distortion would increase as you moved further away from the equator. The best known and most widely used cylindrical projection is the **Mercator Projection.** It was first developed in 1569 by Gerardus Mercator, a Flemish mapmaker.

(2) **Conical Projections** - The name for these maps comes from the fact that the projection is made onto a cone of paper. The cone is made so that it touches a globe at the base of the cone only. It can also be made so that it cuts through part of the globe in two different places. Again, there is the least distortion where the paper touches the globe. If the cone touches at two different points, there is some distortion at both of them. Conical projections are most often used to map areas in the **middle latitudes.** Maps of the United States are most often conical projections. This is because most of the country lies within these latitudes.

(3) **Flat-Plane Projections** - These are made with a flat piece of paper. It touches the globe at one point only. Areas near this point show little distortion. Flat-plane projections are often used to show the areas of the north and south poles. One such flat projection is called a **Gnomonic Projection.** On this kind of map all meridians appear as straight lines. Gnomonic projections are useful because any straight line drawn between points on it forms a **Great-Circle Route.**

Great-circle routes can best be described by thinking of a globe, where the shortest route between two points on it can be found by simply stretching a string from one point to the other. However, if the string were extended in reality, so that it took into account the globe's curvature, it would then make a great circle. A great circle is any circle that cuts a sphere, such as the globe, into two equal parts. Because of distortion, most maps do not show great-circle routes as straight lines; Gnomonic projections, however, do show the shortest distance between the two places as a straight line; because of this they are valuable for navigation. They are called great-circle sailing maps.

To properly analyze a given map one must be familiar with the various parts and symbols that most modern maps use. For the most part, this is standardized, with different maps using similar parts and symbols, which can include:

The Title - All maps should have a title, just like all books should. The title tells you what information is to be found on the map.

The Legend - Most maps have a legend. A legend tells the reader about the various symbols that are used on that particular map and what the symbols represent, (also called a *map key).*

The Grid - A grid is a series of lines that are used to find exact places and locations on the map. There are several different kinds of grid systems in use; however, most maps do use the longitude and latitude system, known as the **Geographic Grid System.**

Directions - Most maps have some directional system to show which way the map is being presented. Often on a map, a small compass will be present, with arrows showing the four basic directions: north, south, east, and west.

The Scale - This is used to show the relationship between a unit of measurement on the map versus the real world measure on the Earth. Maps are drawn to many different scales. Some maps show a lot of detail for a small area. Others show a greater span of distance; whichever is being used, one should always be aware of just what the scale is. For instance the scale might be something like 1 inch = 10 miles for a small area, or for a map showing the whole world it might have a scale in which 1 inch = 1,000 miles. The point is that one must look at the map key in order to see what units of measurements the map is using.

Maps have four main properties. They are (1) the size of the areas shown on the map, (2) The shapes of the areas, (3) consistent scales, and (4) straight-line directions. A map can be drawn so that it is correct in one or more of these properties. No map can be correct in all of them.

Equal areas - One property which maps can have is that of equal areas. In an equal area map, the meridians and parallels are drawn so that the areas shown have the same proportions as they do on the Earth. For example, Greenland is about $\frac{1}{8}^{th}$ the size of South America; thus it will be show as $\frac{1}{8}^{th}$ the size on an equal area map. The **Mercator projection** is an example of a map that does not have equal areas. In it, Greenland appears to be about the same size as South America. This is because the distortion is very bad at the poles, and Greenland lies near the North Pole.

Conformal - A second map property is conformal, or correct shapes. There are no maps which can show very large areas of the Earth in their exact shapes. Only globes can really do that; however, conformal maps are as close as possible to true shapes. The United States is often shown by a Lambert Conformal Conic Projection map.

Consistent Scales - Many maps attempt to use the same scale on all parts of the map. Generally, this is easier when maps show a relatively small part of the Earth's surface. For example, a map of Florida might be a consistent-scale map. Generally maps showing large areas are not consistent-scale maps. This is so because of distortion. Often such maps will have two scales noted in the key. One scale, for example, might be accurate to measure distances between points along the equator. Another might be then used to measure distances between the North Pole and the South Pole.

Maps showing physical features often try to show information about the elevation, or *relief,* of the land. *Elevation* is the distance above or below the sea level. The elevation is usually shown with colors; for instance, all areas on a map which are at a certain level will be shown in the same color.

Relief Maps – These show the shape of the land surface as flat, rugged, or steep. Relief maps usually give more detail than simply showing the overall elevation of the land's surface. Relief is also sometimes shown with colors, but another way to show relief is by using **contour lines.** These lines connect all points of a land surface which are the same height surrounding the particular area of land.

Thematic Maps - These are used to show more specific information, often on a single *theme,* or topic. Thematic maps show the distribution, or amount of something, over a certain given area. For example, topics such as population density, climate, economic information, cultural, political information, etc. would be visually comprehensive in a thematic map.

Information can be gained looking at a map that might take hundreds of words to explain otherwise. Maps reflect the great variety of knowledge covered by political science. To show such a variety of information, maps are made in many different ways. Because of this variety, maps must be understood in order to make the best sense of them.

Skill 17.3 Apply concepts of geography (i.e., location, movement, population, migration) to analyze contemporary and historical issues and trends

The six themes of geography are:

Location - *I*ncluding relative and absolute location. A relative location refers to the surrounding geography, e.g., "on the banks of the Mississippi River." Absolute location refers to a specific point, such as 41 degrees north latitude, 90 degrees west longitude, or 123 Main Street.

Spatial organization Is a description of how things are grouped in a given space. In geographical terms, this can describe people, places, and environments anywhere and everywhere on Earth. The most basic form of spatial organization for people is where they live. The vast majority of people live near other people, in villages and towns and cities and settlements. These people live near others in order to take advantage of the goods and services that naturally arise from cooperation. These villages, towns, cities, and settlements are, to varying degrees, near bodies of water. Water is a staple of survival for every person on the planet and is also a good source of energy for factories and other industries, as well as a form of transportation for people and goods. For example, in a city, where are the factories and heavy industry buildings? Are they near airports or train stations? Are they on the edge of town, near major roads? What about housing developments? Are they near these industries, or are they far away? Where are the other industry buildings? Where are the schools and hospitals and parks? What about the police and fire stations? How close are homes to each of these things? Towns and especially cities are routinely organized into neighborhoods, so that each house or home is near to most things that its residents might need on a regular basis. This means that large cities have multiple schools, hospitals, grocery stores, fire stations, etc.

Place - A place has both human and physical characteristics. Physical characteristics include features such as mountains, rivers, deserts, etc. Human characteristics are the features created by human interaction with their environment, such as canals and roads.

Human-Environmental Interaction - The theme of human-environmental interaction has three main concepts: humans adapt to the environment (wearing warm clothing in a cold climate, for instance), humans modify the environment (planting trees to block a prevailing wind, for example), and humans depend on the environment (for food, water, and raw materials).

Movement - The theme of movement covers how humans interact with one another through trade, communications, emigration, and other forms of interaction.

Regions - A region is an area that has some kind of unifying characteristic, such as a common language, a common government, etc. There are three main types of regions. Formal regions are areas defined by actual political boundaries, such as a city, county, or state. Functional regions are defined by a common function, such as the area covered by a telephone service. Vernacular regions are less formally defined areas that are formed by people's perception, e.g., "the Middle East," and "the South."

Geography involves studying location and how living things and Earth's features are distributed throughout the Earth. It includes where animals, people, and plants live and the effects of their relationship with Earth's physical features. Geographers also explore the locations of Earth's features, how they got there, and why it is so important. Another way to describe where people live is by the **geography** and **topography** around them. The vast majority of people on the planet live in areas that are very hospitable. Yes, people live in the Himalayas and in the Sahara, but the populations in those areas are small indeed when compared to the plains of China, India, Europe, and the United States. People naturally want to live where they won't have to work really hard just to survive, and world population patterns reflect this.

Two of the most important terms in the study of geography are *absolute* and *relative* location. Both technically describe the same thing, but both are also, in many respects, as different as day and night.

First, what is **location?** We want to know this in order to determine where something is and where we can find it. We want to point to a spot on a map and say, "That is where we are," or "That is where we want to be." In another way, we want to know where something is as compared to other things. It is very difficult for many people to describe something without referring to something else. Associative reasoning is a powerful way to think.

Absolute location is the exact whereabouts of a person, place, or thing, according to any kind of geographical indicators you want to name. You could be talking about **latitude** and **longitude** or **GPS** or any kind of indicators at all. For example, Paris is at 48 degrees north longitude and 2 degrees east latitude. You can't get much more exact than that. If you had a map that showed every degree of latitude and longitude, you could pinpoint exactly where Paris was and have absolutely no doubt that your geographical depiction was accurate.

Many geographers prefer to use absolute location because of its precision. If you have access to maps and compasses and GPS (Global Positioning System) indicators, why not describe the absolute location of something? It's much more accurate than other means of describing where something is. An absolute location can also be much simpler. Someone might ask you where the nearest post office is and you might say, "It's at the southeast corner of First Avenue and Main Street." That's about as absolute as you can get.

Relative location, on the other hand, is *always* a description that involves more than one thing. When you describe a relative location, you tell where something is by describing what is around it. The same description of where the nearest post office is in terms of absolute location might be this: "It's down the street from the supermarket, on the right side of the street, next to the dentist's office."

We use relative location to be not necessarily less precise, but to be more in tune with the real world. Very few people carry exact maps or GPS locators around with them. Nearly everyone, though, can find a location if they have it described to them in terms of what is nearby.

Absolute location can be a bit more map-like and direction-oriented as well. You might say that Chicago is east of Seattle or that St. Louis is north of New Orleans. This is not nearly as involved as the post office location description. In the same way, you might say that Chicago is on Lake Michigan.

Skill 17.4 **Recognize the connections among and common concerns of world societies (i.e., food production and distribution, human rights) and analyze the influence of these global connections and concerns on people, places, and events**

A **population** is a group of people living within a certain geographic area. Populations are usually measured on a regular basis by census, which also measures age, economic, ethnic, and other data. Populations change over time due to many factors, and these changes can have a significant impact on cultures.

When a population grows in size, it becomes necessary for it to either expand its geographic boundaries to make room for new people or to increase its density. Population density is simply the number of people in a population divided by the geographic area in which they live. Cultures with a high population density are likely to have different ways of interacting with one another than those with low density, as people live in closer to proximity to one another.

As a population grows, its economic needs change. More basic needs are required, and more workers are needed to produce them. If a population's production or purchasing power does not keep pace with its growth, its economy can be adversely affected. The age distribution of a population can impact the economy as well, if the number of young and old people who are not working is disproportionate to those who are. Parson Malthus was an economist whose theories led to economics being called "the dismal science." His theory can best be summed as saying that the population growth would exceed the growth of the food supply. This would result in the lower classes experiencing increasing poverty. Growth in some areas may spur migration to other parts of a population's geographic region that are less densely populated. This redistribution of population also places demands on the economy, as infrastructure is needed to connect these new areas to older population centers, and land is put to new use.

Populations can grow naturally when the rate of birth is higher than the rate of death or when new people from other populations are added through **immigration.** Immigration is often a source of societal change, as people from other cultures bring their institutions and language to a new area. Immigration also impacts a population's educational and economic institutions, as immigrants enter the workforce and place their children in schools.

Populations can also decline in number when the death rate exceeds the birth rate or when people migrate to another area. War, **famine,** disease and natural disasters can also dramatically reduce a population. The economic problems from population decline can be similar to those from overpopulation because economic demands may be higher than can be met. In extreme cases, a population may decline to the point where it can no longer perpetuate itself and its members, and their culture either disappears or is absorbed into another population.

Environmental and geographic factors have affected the pattern of **urban development** in the world. In turn, urban infrastructure and development patterns are interrelated factors, which affect one another.

The growth of urban areas is often linked to the advantages provided by its **geographic location.** Before the advent of efficient overland routes of commerce such as railroads and highways, water provided the primary means of transportation of commercial goods. Most large American cities are situated along bodies of water. New York's major cities include Buffalo, on Lake Erie; Albany, on the Hudson River; and of course New York City, situated on a large harbor where two major rivers meet the Atlantic Ocean. Where water traffic was not provided for naturally, New Yorkers built a series of canals, including the Erie Canal, which sparked the growth of inland cities.

As **transportation** technology advanced, the supporting infrastructure was built to connect cities with one another and to connect remote areas to larger communities. The railroad, for example, allowed for the quick transport of agricultural products from rural areas to urban centers. This newfound efficiency not only further fueled the growth of urban centers, but changed the economy of rural America. Where once farmers had practiced only subsistence farming—growing enough to support one's own family--the new infrastructure meant that one could convert agricultural products into cash by selling them at the market.

The cause of **human rights** has been advanced significantly since the 18t[h] century, both in theory and in fact. Several fundamental statements of human rights have extended and established human rights throughout the world.

The Declaration of the Rights of Man and of the Citizen is a document created by the French National Assembly and issued in 1789. It sets forth the "natural, inalienable, and sacred rights of man." It proclaims the following rights:

- Men are born and remain free and equal in rights. Social distinctions may only be founded upon the general good.
- The aim of all political association is the preservation of the natural and indisputable rights of man: liberty, property, security, and resistance to oppression.
- All sovereignty resides essentially in the nation. No body or individual may exercise any authority which does not proceed directly from the nation.
- Liberty is the freedom to do anything which injures no one else; hence the exercise of these rights has no limits except those which assure to the other members of the society the enjoyment of the same rights. These limits can only be determined by law.
- Law can only prohibit such actions as are hurtful to society.
- Law is the expression of the general will. Every citizen has a right to participate in the formation of law. It must be the same for all. All citizens, being equal in the eyes of the law, are equally eligible to all dignities and to all public positions and occupations according to their abilities.
- No person shall be accused, arrested, or imprisoned except in the cases and according to the forms prescribed by law.
- The law shall provide for such punishments only as are strictly and obviously necessary.
- All persons are held innocent until they have been declared guilty. If it is necessary to arrest a person, all harshness not essential to the securing of the prisoner's person shall be severely repressed by law.
- No one shall be disquieted on account of his opinions, including religious views, provided their manifestation does not disturb the peace.
- The free communication of ideas and opinions is one of the most precious of the rights of man.
- The security of the rights of man and of the citizen requires public military force. This force is, therefore, established for the good of all and not for the personal advantage of those to whom it shall be entrusted.
- A common contribution is essential for the maintenance of the public forces and for the cost of administration. This should be equitably distributed among all the citizens in proportion to their means.
- All the citizens have a right to decide, either personally or by their representatives, as to the necessity of the public contribution.
- Society has the right to require of every public agent an account of his administration.
- A society in which the observance of the law is not assured, nor the separation of powers defined, has no constitution at all.
- Since property is an inviolable and sacred right, no one shall be deprived thereof except where public necessity, legally determined, shall clearly demand it, and then only on condition that the owner shall have been previously and equitably indemnified.

The United Nations Declaration of Universal Human Rights (1948). The declaration opens with these words: "Whereas recognition of the inherent dignity and of the equal and inalienable rights of all members of the human family is the foundation of freedom, justice and peace in the world. Whereas disregard and contempt for human rights have resulted in barbarous acts which have outraged the conscience of mankind, and the advent of a world in which human beings shall enjoy freedom of speech and belief and freedom from fear and want has been proclaimed as the highest aspiration of the common people." The United Nations Declaration of Universal Human Rights includes the following ideals:

1. All human beings are born free and equal in dignity and rights. They are endowed with reason and conscience and should act towards one another in a spirit of brotherhood.
2. Everyone is entitled to all the rights and freedoms set forth in this Declaration, without distinction of any kind.
3. Everyone has the right to life, liberty, and security of person.
4. No one shall be held in slavery or servitude.
5. No one shall be subjected to torture or to cruel, inhuman, or degrading treatment or punishment.
6. Everyone has the right to recognition everywhere as a person before the law.
7. All are equal before the law and are entitled without any discrimination to equal protection of the law.
8. Everyone has the right to an effective remedy by the competent national tribunals for acts violating the fundamental rights granted him by the constitution or by law.
9. No one shall be subjected to arbitrary arrest, detention, or exile.
10. Everyone is entitled in full equality to a fair and public hearing by an independent and impartial tribunal, in the determination of his rights and obligations and of any criminal charge against him.
11. Everyone charged with a penal offence has the right to be presumed innocent until proven guilty according to law in a public trial at which he has had all the guarantees necessary for his defense. No one shall be held guilty of any penal offence on account of any act or omission which did not constitute a penal offence, under national or international law, at the time when it was committed
12. No one shall be subjected to arbitrary interference with his privacy, family, home, or correspondence, nor to attacks upon his honor and reputation.
13. Everyone has the right to freedom of movement and residence within the borders of each state. Everyone has the right to leave any country, including his own, and to return to his country.
14. Everyone has the right to seek and to enjoy in other countries asylum from persecution. This right may not be invoked in the case of prosecutions genuinely arising from nonpolitical crimes or from acts contrary to the purposes and principles of the United Nations.
15. Everyone has the right to a nationality. No one shall be arbitrarily deprived of his nationality nor denied the right to change his nationality.

16.16.   Men and women of full age have the right to marry and to found a family. They are entitled to equal rights as to marriage, during marriage, and at its dissolution. Marriage shall be entered into only with the free and full consent of the intending spouses. The family is the natural and fundamental group unit of society and is entitled to protection by society and the State.

17. Everyone has the right to own property alone or in association with others. No one shall be arbitrarily deprived of his property.

18. Everyone has the right to freedom of thought, conscience, and religion, including the right to change his religion or belief, and freedom to manifest his religion or belief in teaching, practice, worship and observance.

19. Everyone has the right to freedom of opinion and expression.

20. Everyone has the right to freedom of peaceful assembly and association. No one may be compelled to belong to an association.

21. Everyone has the right to take part in the government of his country, directly or through freely chosen representatives. Everyone has the right of equal access to public service in his country. The will of the people shall be the basis of the authority of the government.

22. Everyone has the right to social security and is entitled to realization of the economic, social, and cultural rights indispensable for his dignity and the free development of his personality.

23. Everyone has the right to work. Everyone, without any discrimination, has the right to equal pay for equal work. Everyone who works has the right to just and favorable remuneration. Everyone has the right to form and to join trade unions for the protection of his interests.

24. Everyone has the right to rest and leisure, including reasonable limitation of working hours and periodic holidays with pay.

25. Everyone has the right to a standard of living adequate for the health and well-being of himself and his family and the right to security in the event of unemployment, sickness, disability, widowhood, old age, or other lack of livelihood in circumstances beyond his control. Motherhood and childhood are entitled to special care and assistance. All children shall enjoy the same social protection.

26. Everyone has the right to education. Education shall be directed to the full development of the human personality and to the strengthening of respect for human rights and fundamental freedoms. Parents have a prior right to choose the kind of education that shall be given to their children.

27. Everyone has the right to participate freely in the cultural life of the community. Everyone has the right to the protection of the moral and materials interests resulting from any scientific, literary, or artistic production of which he is the author.

28. Everyone is entitled to a social and international order, in which the rights and freedoms set forth in this Declaration can be fully realized.

The United Nations Convention on the Rights of the Child brings together the rights of children as they are enumerated in other international documents. In this document, those rights are clearly and completely stated, along with the explanation of the guiding principals that define the way society views children. The goal of the document is to clarify the environment that is necessary to enable every human being to develop to his or her full potential. The Convention calls for resources and contributions to be made to ensure the full development and survival of all children. The document requires the establishment of appropriate means to protect children from neglect, exploitation, and abuse. The document also recognizes that parents have the most important role in raising children.

Nativism is the fear that certain new immigrants will introduce foreign political, economic, or cultural values and behaviors that threaten the prevailing norms and values of a nation or a society. It usually involves restrictions on immigrants and sometimes includes policies that favor the interests of established residents (i.e., "natives") over those of immigrants. During the reign of Louis XIV in France, the Huguenots, or French Protestants, were persecuted by the government, which was closely allied with the Roman Catholic Church. Louis was also attempting to limit the role of the Roman Catholic Church in France and determine its affairs. The Huguenots were severely oppressed, until they finally left the country.

| Skill 17.5 | Recognize basic concepts related to the structure and organization of human societies and processes of socialization and social interaction |

The traditions and behaviors of a culture are based on the prevailing beliefs and values of that culture. Beliefs and values are similar and interrelated systems.

Beliefs are those things that are thought to be true. Beliefs are often associated with religion, but beliefs can also be based on political or ideological philosophies. "All men are created equal," is an example of an ideological belief.

Values are what a society thinks is right and wrong, and are often based on and shaped by beliefs. The value that every member of the society has a right to participate in his government might be considered to be based on the belief that "All men are created equal," for instance.

A culture's beliefs and values are reflected in the cultural products it produces, such as literature, the arts, media, and architecture. These products become part of the culture and last from generation to generation, becoming one way that culture is transmitted through time. A common language among all members of a culture makes this transmission possible.

Sociologists have identified five different types of institutions around which societies are structured: family, education, government, religion, and economy. These institutions provide a framework for members of a society to learn about and participate in society, and allow for a society to perpetuate its beliefs and values to succeeding generations.

The **family** is the primary social unit in most societies. It is through the family that children learn the most essential skills for functioning in their society, such as language and appropriate forms of interaction. The family is connected to ethnicity, which is partly defined by a person's heritage.

Education is an important institution in a society, as it allows for the formal passing on of a culture's collected knowledge. The institution of education is connected to the family, as that is where a child's earliest education takes place. The United States has a public school system administered by the states that ensures a basic education and provides a common experience for most children.

A society's **governmental** institutions often embody its beliefs and values. Laws, for instance, reflect a society's values by enforcing its ideas of right and wrong. The structure of a society's government can reflect a society's ideals about the role of an individual in his society. The American form of democracy emphasizes the rights of the individual, but in return expects individuals to respect the rights of others, including those of ethnic or political minorities.

Religion is frequently the institution from which springs a society's primary beliefs and values, and can be closely related to other social institutions. Many religions have definite teachings on the structure and importance of the family, for instance. The U.S. Constitution guarantees the free practice of religion, which has led to a large number of denominations practicing in the U.S. today. Most Americans identify with Christian faiths.

A society's **economic** institutions define how an individual can contribute and receive economic reward from his society. The United States has a capitalist economy motivated by free enterprise. While this system allows for economic advancement for the individual, it can also produce areas of poverty and economic depression.

An example of an organization that promotes the rights of the individual is **The National Association for the Advancement of Colored People** (NAACP). This organization was founded in 1909 to assist African-Americans. In the early years, the work of the organization focused on working through the courts to overturn "Jim Crow" statutes, which legalized racial discrimination. The group organized voters to oppose Woodrow Wilson's efforts to weave racial segregation into federal government policy. Between WWI and WWII, much energy was devoted to stopping the lynching of blacks throughout the country.

Skill 17.6 **Analyze the nature and implications of various types of interactions between people and the environment and the effects of human activities (i.e., consumption of natural resources, pollution) on the environment**

Natural resources are naturally occurring substances that are considered valuable in their natural form. A commodity is generally considered a natural resource when the primary activities associated with it are extraction and purification, as opposed to creation. Thus, mining, petroleum extraction, fishing, and forestry are generally considered natural-resource industries, while agriculture is not.

Natural resources are often classified into **renewable** and **nonrenewable resources.** Renewable resources are generally living resources (fish, coffee, and forests, for example), which can restock (renew) themselves if they are not over-harvested. Renewable resources can restock themselves and be used indefinitely if they are sustained. Once renewable resources are consumed at a rate that exceeds their natural rate of replacement, the standing stock will diminish and eventually run out. The rate of sustainable use of a renewable resource is determined by the replacement rate and amount of standing stock of that particular resource. Nonliving renewable natural resources include soil as well as water, wind, tides, and solar radiation. Natural resources include soil, timber, oil, minerals, and other goods taken more or less as they are from the Earth.

In recent years, the depletion of natural capital and attempts to move to sustainable development has been a major focus of development agencies. **Deforestation,** or clear cutting, is of particular concern in rain forest regions, which hold most of the Earth's natural biodiversity--irreplaceable genetic natural capital. Conservation of natural resources is the major focus of Natural Capitalism, environmentalism, the ecology movement, and Green Parties. Some view this depletion as a major source of social unrest and conflicts in developing nations.

Environmental policy is concerned with the sustainability of the Earth, the region under the administration of the governing group or individual, or a local habitat. The concern of environmental policy is the preservation of the region, habitat, or ecosystem.

Because humans, both individually and in community, rely upon the environment to sustain human life, social and environmental policy must be mutually supportable. And because humans, both individually and in community, live upon the Earth, draw upon the natural resources of the Earth, and affect the environment in many ways, environmental and social policy must be mutually supportive.

If modern societies have no understanding of the limitations upon natural resources or how their actions affect the environment, and they act without regard for the sustainability of the Earth, it will become impossible for the Earth to sustain human existence. At the same time, the resources of the Earth are necessary to support human welfare. Environmental policies must recognize that the planet is the home of humans and other species.

In an age of **global warming,** unprecedented demand upon natural resources, and a shrinking planet, social and environmental policies must become increasingly interdependent if the planet is to continue to support life and human civilization.

For example, between 1870 and 1916, more than twenty-five million immigrants came into the United States, adding to the phenomenal **population growth** taking place. This tremendous growth aided business and industry in two ways: (1) The number of consumers increased, creating a greater demand for products and thus enlarging the markets for the products, and (2) With increased production and expanding business, more workers were available for newly created jobs. The completion of the nation's transcontinental railroad in 1869 contributed greatly to the nation's economic and industrial growth. Many wealthy industrialists and railroad owners saw tremendous profits steadily increasing due to this improved method of transportation. Yet, natural resources were required to support the growing population and its needs.

The world's environment is infinitely interconnected, so that a change in any part of it can have effects that are widely felt. The example of waste disposal can illustrate how local decisions are connected to global issues.

The issue of waste disposal of all kinds is primarily a local matter. For example, cities and towns usually supply water and sewer services to their residents. Sewage is treated to remove most of the contaminants and the water is released, usually into a local river or other water system. Cities situated downstream will be directly affected by the quality of water treatment by their upstream neighbors. This can have a cumulative effect, so that the quality of water treatment in one town can affect the water resources of another perhaps hundreds of miles away. Pollution recognizes no boundaries between cities, states, or countries. Just as polluted water can flow downstream, air polluted by industry can blow across national boundaries, affecting air quality for great distances.

Individual actions have a cumulative effect on global resources as well. Recycling is an example. An aluminum soda can made from smelted aluminum takes an equivalent of half a can of gasoline in energy to produce it. Aluminum cans made from recycled aluminum require about one-twentieth of the energy it takes to make them from smelted aluminum. One person recycling one soda can a day instead of throwing it into the trash saves the equivalent of over 16 gallons of gasoline a year. That reduction in energy usage is transmitted to the aluminum manufacturing plant and to the aluminum mining operation. Communities that provide recycling programs for materials such as aluminum, paper, steel, and other recyclable resources can increase the cumulative energy savings and reduce the usage of nonrenewable resources worldwide.

Tremendous progress in communication and transportation has tied all parts of the Earth and drawn them closer together. However, there are still vast areas of unproductive land, extreme poverty, food shortages, rampant diseases, violent friction between cultures, the ever-present nuclear threat, environmental pollution, rapid reduction of natural resources, urban overcrowding, acceleration in global terrorism and violent crimes, and a diminishing middle class.

Skill 17.7   Identify a wide range of instructional resources and technologies to support the learning of geography

See Skill 15.6.

COMPETENCY 18.0 UNDERSTAND CONCEPTS, SKILLS, AND PROCESSES OF INQUIRY IN THE SOCIAL SCIENCES (e.g., LOCATING, GATHERING, ORGANIZING, FORMULATING HYPOTHESES) AND HOW TO PROMOTE STUDENTS' DEVELOPMENT OF KNOWLEDGE AND SKILLS IN THIS AREA

Skill 18.1   Demonstrate knowledge of common themes and concepts in the social sciences (e.g., continuity, change, culture) and how to apply them in understanding people, places, and events

The study of social phenomena can draw on the methods and theories of several disciplines.

The field of **anthropology** is largely concerned with the institutions of a society and intercultural comparisons. Anthropologists observe people of a particular culture acting within their culture and interacting with people of other cultures and interpret social phenomena. Anthropology relies on **qualitative** research--such as researching the types of rituals a culture has—as well as **quantitative** research, such as measuring the relative sizes of ethnic groups.

Psychology is mainly centered on the study of the individual and his or her behavior. As humans are social animals, the methods of psychology can be used to study society and culture by asking questions about how individuals behave within these groups, what motivates them, and the ways they find to express themselves.

Sociology covers how humans act as a society and within a society, and examines the rules and mechanisms they follow as a society. Sociology also looks at groups within a society and how they interact. The field relies on research methods from several disciplines, including anthropology and psychology.

Other Social Science terms

Causality: The reason something happens, its cause, is a basic category of human thinking. We naturally want to know the cause of some major event in our lives. Within the study of history, causality is the analysis of the reasons for change. The question we are asking is why and how a particular society or event developed in the particular way it did given the context in which it occurred.

Conflict: Conflict within history is opposition of ideas, principles, values, or claims. Conflict may take the form of internal clashes of principles, ideas, or claims within a society or group or it may take the form of opposition between groups or societies.

Bias: A prejudice or a predisposition either toward or against something. In the study of history, bias can refer to the persons or groups studied, in terms of a society's bias toward a particular political system, or it can refer to the historian's predisposition to evaluate events in a particular way.

Interdependence: A condition in which two things or groups rely upon one another, as opposed to independence, in which each thing or group relies only upon itself.

Identity: The state or perception of being a particular thing or person. Identity can also refer to the understanding or self-understanding of groups, nations, etc.

Nation-state: A particular type of political entity that provides a sovereign territory for a specific nation, in which other factors also unite the citizens (e.g., language, race, ancestry, etc.).

Culture: The civilization, achievements, and customs of the people of a particular time and place.

Socialization is the process by which humans learn the expectations their society has for their behavior, in order that they might successfully function within that society.

Socialization takes place primarily in children as they learn and are taught the rules and norms of their culture. Children grow up eating the common foods of a culture and develop a "taste" for these foods, for example. By observing adults and older children, they learn about gender roles and appropriate ways to interact. The family is the primary influence in this kind of socialization, and contributes directly to a person's sense of self-importance and personal identity.

Through socialization, a person gains a sense of belonging to a group of people with common ideals and behaviors. When a person encounters people affiliated with other groups, his or her own group affiliation can be reinforced, contributing to a sense of personal identity.

Skill 18.2 Demonstrate understanding of the basic principles and procedures of inquiry in the social sciences (e.g., modes of inquiry, formulation of research questions and hypotheses, use of historical analysis to make informed decisions)

The world of social science research has never been so open to new possibilities. Where our predecessors were unable to tread for fear of exceeding the limits of the available data, data access and data transfer, analytic routines, or computing power, today's social scientists can advance with confidence. Where once social scientists of empirical bent struggled with punch cards, chattering computer terminals, and jobs disappearing into the black hole of remote mainframe processors, often never reappearing, we now enjoy massive arrays of data, powerful personal computers on our desks, online access to data, and suites of sophisticated analytical packages. Never before has the social scientist come so well armed. Advances in technology can free social scientists from the tyranny of simplification that has often hampered attempts to grasp the complexity of the world.

Refer to the content under Skill 18.3 for a thorough discussion of primary and secondary sources. Primary sources for a study in social sciences may be obtained directly: the children in the school where you are a teacher or via electronic means. For example, government sources contain much data for social sciences research such as census statistics, employment statistics, health statistics, etc., that can be readily accessed and manipulated.

Secondary sources may also be obtained in a hands-on fashion: interviews of people who had first-hand knowledge and books, journals, etc., that record primary statistics or analyses of primary statistics. However, the best source for obtaining that information is the Internet. An excellent resource for social science information is MOST (Management of Social Transformations) at http://portal. unesco.org/shs/en/ev.php-URL_ID=3511&URL_DO=DO_TOPIC&URL_ SECTION=201.html.

Skill 18.3 Apply principles and procedures for gathering, organizing, comparing, interpreting, analyzing, and summarizing social science information presented in various forms (e.g., tables, maps, graphs, narratives)

Geography can lend itself to many other disciplines. The versatility and breadth of geographical discussions contain many elements that can translate and have a bearing on problems and solutions in other fields of study.

One of the foremost examples of the influence of geography is its application to economics. People looking to locate manufacturing plants will naturally consider **geographic factors** when making their final decision. Will the plant depend on hydroelectric power? If so, should the plant be located near a natural water source, like a river or lake or dam? Will the plant be exporting or importing a large number of products? If so, where is the nearest airport and how far away are the nearest highways and residential areas? If the plant owners will depend heavily on land-based transportation, what is the surrounding terrain like? Can heavy trucks easily connect from plant to highway, and vice versa? Is privacy a concern? How will the company's actions affect the local community? Strip mining of local hills and mountains could be a source of much friction. If the plant is manufacturing secret products, then the owners will want to situate that plant as far away from the rest of civilization as possible, within the guidelines already mentioned.

Simpler decisions take place when a group of people is looking to open a new business or shopping mall. Practical considerations such as the locations of nearby homes and possible competitors factor into the decision of where to locate that new business or shopping mall. Is the city an urban hub, with shoppers already coming from nearby towns? If so, the new business can count on more than just the local population for business. If the business is a grocery store, can the owners count on a steady supply of varied foods and liquids to keep customers coming back? If the business is a niche market, then is the local population large enough to sustain such a niche?

Geography can extend to politics. The way an industry or set of industries or a large group of people treat the land around them can be the source of political debate. So can the treatment of nearby wildlife. Some of the most caustic debates nowadays are between **animal rights activists** and proponents of technological growth at all costs. On a more traditional note, the closer a city or town is to a major airport and the more population that city has, the more times political candidates will be visiting that city in search of support from voters who live there.

The resources used in the study of history can be divided into two major groups: **primary sources** and **secondary sources**. Primary sources are works, records, etc., that were created during the period being studied or immediately after it. Secondary sources are works written significantly after the period being studied and based upon primary sources. "Primary sources are the basic materials that provide the raw data and information for the historian. Secondary sources are the works that contain the explications of, and judgments on, this primary material" [Norman F. Cantor & Richard I. Schneider, *How to Study History,* Harlan Davidson, Inc., 1967, pp. 23-24].

Primary sources include the following kinds of materials:

- Documents that reflect the immediate, everyday concerns of people: memoranda, bills, deeds, charters, newspaper reports, pamphlets, graffiti, popular writings, journals or diaries, records of decision-making bodies, letters, receipts, snapshots, etc.
- Theoretical writings which reflect care and consideration in composition and an attempt to convince or persuade. The topic will generally show deeper and more pervasive values than is the case with "immediate" documents. These may include newspaper or magazine editorials, sermons, political speeches, philosophical writings, etc.
- Narrative accounts of events, ideas, trends, etc., written with intentionality by someone contemporary with the events described
- Statistical data, although statistics may be misleading
- Literature and nonverbal materials, novels, stories, poetry, and essays from the period, as well as coins, archaeological artifacts, and art produced during the period

Guidelines for the use of primary resources:

1. Be certain that you understand how language was used at the time of writing and that you understand the context in which it was produced.
2. Do not read history blindly, but be certain that you understand both explicit and implicit references in the material.
3. Read the entire text you are reviewing; do not simply extract a few sentences to read.
4. Although anthologies of materials may help you identify primary source materials, the full original text should be consulted.

Secondary sources include the following kinds of materials:

- Books written on the basis of primary materials about the period of time
- Books written on the basis of primary materials about persons who played a major role in the events under consideration
- Books and articles written on the basis of primary materials about the culture, the social norms, the language, and the values of the period
- Quotations from primary sources
- Statistical data on the period
- The conclusions and inferences of other historians
- Multiple interpretations of the ethos of the time

Guidelines for the use of secondary sources:

1. Do not rely upon only a single secondary source.
2. Check facts and interpretations against primary sources whenever possible.
3. Do not accept the conclusions of other historians uncritically.
4. Place greatest reliance on secondary sources created by the best and most respected scholars.
5. Do not use the inferences of other scholars as if they were facts.
6. Ensure that you recognize any bias the writer brings to his/her interpretation of history.
7. Understand the primary point of the book as a basis for evaluating the value of the material presented in relation to your questions.

Information can be gained looking at a map that might take hundreds of words to explain otherwise. Maps reflect the great variety of knowledge covered by social sciences. To show such a variety of information, maps are made in many different ways. Because of this variety, maps must be understood in order to make the best sense of them. Once they are understood, maps provide a solid foundation for social science studies.

To apply information obtained from **graphs** one must understand the two major reasons why graphs are used:

1. To present a <u>model or theory</u> visually in order to show how two or more variables interrelate
2. To present <u>real world</u> data visually in order to show how two or more variables interrelate

Most often used are those known as **bar graphs** and **line graphs.** (Charts are often used for similar reasons and are explained in the next section.)

Graphs are most useful when one wishes to demonstrate the sequential increase or decrease of a variable or to show specific correlations between two or more variables in a given circumstance. Most common is the **bar graph,** because it is easy to see and is an understandable way of visually showing the difference in a given set of variables. However, it is limited in that it cannot really show the actual proportional increase or decrease of each given variable in relation to other variables. (In order to show a decrease, a bar graph must show the "bar" under the starting line, thus removing the ability to really show how the various different variables would relate to each other.)

Thus in order to accomplish this, one must use a **line graph.** Line graphs can be of two types: a **linear** or **nonlinear** graph. A linear line graph uses a series of straight lines; a nonlinear line graph uses a curved line. Though the lines can be either straight or curved, all of the lines are called **curves.**

A line graph uses a number line, or **axis.** The numbers are generally placed in order, equal distances from one another. The number line is used to represent a number, degree, or some other variable at an appropriate point on the line. Two lines are used, intersecting at a specific point. They are referred to as the x-axis and the y-axis.

The y-axis is a vertical line and the x-axis is a horizontal line. Together they form a **coordinate system.** The difference between a point on the line of the x-axis and a point on the line of the y-axis is called the **slope** of the line, or the change in the value on the vertical axis divided by the change in the value on the horizontal axis. The y-axis number is called the **rise,** and the x-axis number is called the **run;** thus the equation for slope is:

SLOPE = $\underline{\text{RISE}}$ - (Change in value on the vertical axis)
$\quad\quad\quad\quad$ RUN - (Change in value on the horizontal axis)

The slope shows the amount of increase or decrease of a given **specific** variable. When using two or more variables, one can plot the amount of difference between them in any given situation. This makes presenting information on a line graph more involved. It also makes it more informative and accurate than a simple bar graph. Knowledge of the term slope, what it is, and how it is measured helps us to describe verbally the pictures we are seeing visually. For example, if a curve is said to have a slope of "zero," you should picture a flat line. If a curve has a slope of "one," you should picture a rising line that makes a 45 degree angle with the horizontal and vertical axis lines.

With **nonlinear** curves (the ones that really do curve) the slope of the curve is constantly changing, so as a result, we must then understand that the slope of the nonlinear curved line will be at a specific point. How is this done? The slope of a nonlinear curve is determined by the slope of a straight line that intersects the curve at that specific point.

In all graphs, an upward-sloping line represents a direct relationship between the two variables. A downward slope represents an inverse relationship between the two variables. In reading any graph, one must always be very careful to understand what is being measured, what can be deduced, and what cannot be deduced from the given graph.

To use **charts** correctly, one should remember the reasons one uses graphs. The general ideas are similar. It is usually a question as to which, a graph or chart, is more capable of adequately portraying the information one wants to illustrate. One can see the difference between them and realize that in many ways, graphs and charts are interrelated. One of the most common types-- because it is easiest to read and understand, even for the lay person--is the **pie chart.** You can see pie charts used often, especially when one is trying to illustrate the differences in percentages among various items or when one is demonstrating the divisions of a whole.

Skill 18.4   Recognize how to use children's and young adult literature to support learning in the social sciences

The foundation of American Indian writing is found in storytelling, oratory, and autobiographical and historical accounts of tribal village life; reverence for the environment; and the postulation that the Earth with all of its beauty was given in trust, to be cared for and passed on to future generations.

Early American Indian writings that would interest young adults are *Geronimo: His Own Story—Apache,* edited by S.M. Barrett; *Native American Myths and Legends,* by C.F. Taylor; and *When Legends Die* by Hal Barland.

Afro-American literature covers three distinct periods: pre--Civil War, post--Civil War and Reconstruction, and post--Civil War through the present. Some featured resources include Harriet Beecher Stowe's *Uncle Tom's Cabin,* Ernest Gaines' *The Autobiography of Miss Jane Pittman,* Maya Angelou's *I Know Why the Caged Bird Sings,* and Alex Haley's popular *Roots.*

Works that enlighten the colonial period include *The Mayflower Compact* and Thomas Paine's *Common Sense.* Benjamin Franklin's essays from *Poor Richard's Almanac* were popular during his day.

Folktales with characters such as Washington Irving's Ichabod Crane and Rip Van Winkle create a unique American folklore, with characters marked by their environment and the superstitions of the New Englander. The poetry of Fireside Poets such as James Russell Lowell, Oliver Wendell Holmes, Henry Wadsworth Longfellow, and John Greenleaf Whittier was recited by American families and read in the long New England winters.

Skill 18.5   Demonstrate knowledge of a wide range of instructional resources and technologies to support learning in the social sciences

See Skill 14.6

DOMAIN V.   **THE ARTS, HEALTH, AND PHYSICAL EDUCATION**

COMPETENCY 19.0 UNDERSTAND HISTORICAL, CULTURAL, AND SOCIETAL CONTEXTS FOR THE ARTS (VISUAL ARTS, MUSIC, DRAMA, DANCE) AND THE INTERRELATIONSHIPS AMONG THE ARTS

Skill 19.1 Demonstrate knowledge of characteristic features of various artistic traditions and the role of art in various contexts

It is important for teachers to understand and relate to students the significance of early art forms and how they have developed over time. Many early folk art tales were scarce in their art and media. However, now media and illustration is a tremendous part of any literature experience for young children.

There are many types of visual art that have grown in all areas. Teachers should incorporate themed units that easily relate cross-curriculum studies. Using themed units, such as a theme on vehicles, can show students early models of cars, trucks, motorcycles, and air planes, and how they have developed over time into the models we use today.

Performing art has also developed over time. A great experience for young students is to have a tribal performer demonstrate for students the dance and rituals performed by Native American dancers. These dances and ceremonies have evolved over hundreds of years. Students could then compare that performance to a ballet performance and discuss the similarities and differences and how each art has evolved over time.

Whether we express ourselves creatively from the theatrical stage, visually through fine art and dance, or musically, appreciating and recognizing the interrelationships of various art forms is essential to an understanding of ourselves and our diverse society.

By studying and experiencing works of fine art and literature and by understanding their place in cultural and intellectual history, we can develop an appreciation of the human significance of the arts and humanities through history and across cultures.

Through art projects, field trips, and theatrical productions, students can learn that all forms of art are a way for cultures to communicate with each other and the world at large. By understanding the concepts, techniques, and various materials used in the visual arts, music, dance, and the written word, students will begin to appreciate the concept of using art to express oneself. Perhaps they can begin by writing a short story which is then transformed into a play with costumes, music, and movement to experience the relationship between different art forms.

The arts have played a significant role throughout history. The communicative power of the arts is notable. Cultures use the arts for artistic expression to impart specific emotions and feeling, to tell stories, to imitate nature, and to persuade others. The arts bring meaning to ceremonies, rituals, celebrations, and recreation. By creating their own art and by examining art made by others, children can learn to make sense of and communicate ideas. This can be accomplished through dance, verbal communication, music, and other visual arts.

Through the arts and humanities, students will realize that although people are different, they share common experiences and attitudes. They will also learn that the use of nonverbal communication can be a strong adjunct to verbal communication.

Skill 19.2   Recognize the role and functions of the arts in various cultures and historical periods and ways in which the arts can be used to explore various cultures and historical periods

Art history is relatively new to academics. True art history relies on faithful reproductions of artworks as a springboard of discussion and study. Photography techniques after World War II made this possible; however, the appreciation and study of the visual arts has intrigued man for hundreds of years.. Art history features the study of biographies of individual artists. The most renowned of these was Michelangelo. In the 18th century, scholars began to argue that the real emphasis in the study of art belonged to the views of the learned beholder, not the unique viewpoint of the charismatic artist. By comparing visual arts to each other, one is able to make distinctions of style.

Art history has added to political history by using critical approaches to show how art interacts with power structures in society. The first critical approach was Marxism. Marxist art history attempted to show how art was tied to specific classes, how images contain information about the economy, and how images can make the status quo seem natural. In the book titled *The Social History of Art,* an attempt was made to show how class consciousness was reflected in major art periods. This book was very controversial when it was published during the 1950s because it makes gross generalizations about entire eras. However, it remains in print as a classic art historical text.

Cultural art predates history, as sculptures, cave paintings, and rock paintings have been found that are roughly 40,000 years old, but the precise meaning of such art is often disputed because we know so little about the cultures that produced them. Most art traditions have a foundation in the great ancient civilizations of Egypt, Persia, India, China, or Rome. Each of these early civilizations developed a unique and characteristic style of art. Because of their size and the duration of these civilizations, more art works have survived and more influence has been transmitted to other cultures and later times than any other era. The 18th century is referred to as the Age of Enlightenment, with artistic renderings of the physical universe as well as politically revolutionary visions. The late 19th century saw numerous artistic movements, such as Symbolism and Impressionism, which were torn down by the search for new standards and did not last much past the time of their invention. In the latter 20th century came Modernism, or the search for truth, which later led to the period of Contemporary Art.

Skill 19.3   Demonstrate understanding of how music, visual art, creative drama, and dance can be used as forms of communication, self-expression, and social expression (e.g., to express ideas and values, share life experiences, explore feelings)

In early years, students engage in many activities that help them develop their oral language skills and help them begin to read and write. Early childhood students take part in language activities that extend their vocabulary and conceptual knowledge. Students learn to follow directions and develop the language of schooling. They discuss the meanings of words from familiar and conceptually challenging selections read aloud. They also express themselves in complete thoughts.

In kindergarten, students listen to a wide variety of children's literature, including selections from classic and contemporary works. Students also listen to nonfiction and informational material. Students learn to listen attentively and ask and respond to questions and retell stories. Students know simple story structure and distinguish fiction from nonfiction. Kindergarten students identify and write the letters of the alphabet. Students learn that individual letters are different from printed words, words have spaces between them, and that print is read from left to right and from top to bottom. Through meaningful and organized activities, kindergarten students learn that spoken language is composed of sequences of sounds.

Students learn to segment and identify the sounds in spoken words. Students name each letter of the alphabet, begin to associate spoken sounds with the letter or letters that represent them, and begin to use this knowledge to read words and simple stories. In kindergarten, students write the letters of the alphabet, their names, and other words. Initially, students dictate messages and stories for others to write. Students begin to use their knowledge of sounds and letters to write by themselves.

- See also Skill 19.4

Skill 19.4   Recognize and evaluate strategies and activities intended to foster skills in creating, producing, viewing, responding to, analyzing, and appreciating music, visual art, drama, and dance

Teachers must be able to make judgments regarding the quality of art using their prior knowledge of the concepts and principles that are standards for effective art. Each teacher must develop a system that can be used for judging art and that will provide a framework for students to follow. Clearly explained expectations help guide students in their art lessons. Early childhood students often need very clear standards to follow.

Not only is it important for young students to make connections between the vocabulary of art, but the pictures or examples are always helpful too. For example when instructing a young pupil to use scissors and glue in a project, the words "glue" and "scissors" should be clearly defined, with a picture of each object next to the instructions. Once the tasks are clearly explained and labeled, it important to develop a testing system to evaluate how accurately each student meets the standards.

The most appropriate evaluation tool for young students is typically a rubric designed by the teacher. Evaluation using rubrics is very simple; the teacher just checks off each standard met by the students, with little or no effort. By monitoring each student while he or she is working, teachers are able to identify the skills mastered with ease.

Works of art should most often be interpreted through a wide variety of rich art and literature experience. Students will be able to react to art experiences by understanding the definitions of the basic principles of art, such as line, color, value, space, texture, shape, and form. Early childhood students are most greatly affected by these experiences. An excellent resource is the author Eric Carle. His books are age-appropriate for young children and include a wide variety of shape, color, line, and media for young students to explore.

Once students have been introduced to a wide range of materials, they are able to better relate and explain the elements they have observed through art work and generously illustrated literature. Literature is the most common form of exposure for young students, but video and other types of media also provide rich art experiences.

Theater

Students should be exposed to a wide variety of dramatic works to enhance the theater experience and provide endless opportunities for growth in the area of art and drama. Producers of plays need critics to enable them to better reach their audiences. Students need to judge the effectiveness of the plot, characters, and overall mood of the drama. Students have the opportunity to relate to the characters in the play and can express feelings such as empathy and compassion.

Drama is an expression that can be portrayed by the actors and can affect the audience in many ways. To determine the level of performance by actors, it is important to use technology to video the stage performance so that students can self-assess; it is also important to use a tool such as a rubric to make sure characters are meeting objectives during their performances, practices, and peer assessments.

Music

Students can explore creating moods with music, analyzing stories, and creating musical compositions that reflect or enhance moods. Their daily routines can include exploration, interpretation, and understanding of musical sound. Immersing them in musical conversations as we sing, speak rhythmically, and walk in step stimulates their awareness of the beauty and structure of musical sound.

As students acquire the skills and knowledge that music brings to their lives, they go through the similar to the development of language skills. Singing, chanting, and moving--exposing them in play to many different sound sources, including a variety of styles of music and reinforcing rhythm through patting, tapping, and moving--will enhance their awareness of musical sound. Involvement in music is thought to teach basic skills such as concentration, counting, listening, and promoting understanding of language.

Students can take music courses, which typically take the form of an overview course on the history of music or a music appreciation course that focuses on listening to music and learning about different musical styles.

A musical performance (a concert or a recital) may take place indoors in a hall or theater or outdoors in a field and may either require the audience to remain very quiet or encourage them to sing or dance along with the music. Although music cannot contain emotions in and of itself, it is sometimes designed to encourage the emotion of the listener/listeners. Music created for movies is a good example of its use to manipulate emotions.

Performance analysis works through and for the ear. The greatest analysts are those with the keenest ears; their insights reveal how a piece of music should be heard, which in turn implies how it should be played. Analysis consists of "putting oneself in the composer's shoes" and explaining what he was experiencing as he was writing.

An assessment based on performance of music would require students to create, produce, or do something in the music field. Proficiency would be demonstrated by a performance such as a musical recital.

Visual Art

Art criticism is one of the four foundational disciplines of Discipline-Based Art Education (DBAE), along with art production, art history, and aesthetics. Art criticism is responding to, interpreting meaning, and making critical judgments about specific works of art. Usually art criticism focuses on individual, contemporary works of art.

When initially introduced to art criticism, many people associate negative connotations with the word "criticism." This is understandable; the first definition given for criticism in *Webster's Ninth New Collegiate Dictionary* is "the act of criticizing, usually unfavorably." Yet Webster's second definition is more appropriate for art criticism: "the art of evaluating or analyzing works of art." Art criticism, in practice, generally is positive.

Any agreement on a simple definition of art criticism is difficult to obtain. In Practical Art Criticism, Edmund Feldman writes that art criticism is "spoken or written 'talk' about art" and that "the central task of criticism" is interpretation. Feldman developed a widely used sequential approach to art criticism based on description, analysis, interpretation, and judgment.

Stephen Dobbs, who wrote *The DBAE Handbook: An Overview of Discipline-Based Art Education,* states that through art criticism, people "look at art, analyze the forms, offer multiple interpretations of meaning, make critical judgments, and talk or write about what they see, think, and feel."

Terry Barrett, author of *Criticizing Art: Understanding the Contemporary,* bases his approach to art criticism on the four activities of describing, interpreting, judging, and theorizing about art. Barrett suggests that, although all four overlap, "Interpretation is the most important activity of criticism, and probably the most complex." Though interwoven with description, analysis, and judgment, interpretation of the meaning of individual works of art is of foremost concern in contemporary art criticism.

The Role of the Art Critic
In all four disciplines of DBAE the practice of each is based upon the roles of each discipline's practitioner or expert. For art criticism, the role model is the art critic. A professional art critic may be a newspaper reporter assigned to the art beat, a scholar writing for professional journals or texts, or an artist writing about other artists.

Journalistic criticism, written for the general public, includes reviews of art exhibitions in galleries and museums. Most people are familiar with journalistic art criticism because it appears in newspapers, popular magazines, and on radio and television. Feldman suggests that journalistic criticism deals with art mainly to the extent that it is newsworthy.

Scholarly art criticism is written for a more specialized art audience and appears in art journals, such as *Art in America, Art Papers,* and *Art News,* as well as in presentations at professional conferences or seminars. Scholar-critics may be college and university professors or museum curators, often with particular knowledge about a style, period, medium, or artist.

In both journalistic and scholarly art criticism, the viewer, according to Feldman, "confronts works of art and determines what they mean, whether they are any good, and, if so, why."

Art Criticism in the Classroom
Through art criticism activities in the classroom, students interpret and judge individual works of art. Interpretation is the most critical task of art criticism, but we recommend no prescribed order to follow. The work of art itself should guide the approach to inquiry. For example, a nonobjective painting initially may be approached through description, while a highly detailed, symbol-filled realistic painting probably would be best approached first through possible interpretations of meaning.

Critic's descriptions are lively. Critics write to be read, and they must capture their readers' attention and engage their readers' imaginations. Critics want to persuade their readers to see a work of art as they do. If they are enthused, they try to communicate their enthusiasm through their choice of descriptors and how they put them together in a sentence, a paragraph, and an article.

Terry Barrett states that written art criticism can be thought of as persuasive writing, with interpretations of meaning supported by reasoned judgments. Terry Barrett calls for "good, lively, interpretive writing about art" that may take many forms in the classroom. Similarly, Feldman states that words are virtually indispensable for communicating a critic's understanding and that "words enable us to build bridges between sensory impressions, prior experience, logical inferences, and the tasks of interpretation and explanation."

Dance

From the earliest days of civilization, drama and dance have been a part of human expression across many cultures and throughout the world, serving diverse cultural functions. Worship, the celebration of special events, ceremonies, and entertainment are just a few of these functions. Dance was a regular part of religious practices in most major religions and was considered an adjunct to praising God or other higher beings with music. Social events and the secular celebrations that were often linked to religious festivals were also marked by dancing, as were formal ceremonies, such as coronations.

Chinese Confucianism and Buddhism incorporate dance as part of religious practices. The trinity of Hindu gods (Brahma the Creator, Vishnu the Preserver, and Shiva the Destroyer) of India are closely associated with dance. Sculptures of Krishna, one of the physical forms or *avatars* of Vishnu, often show him with a flute posing in dance positions.

The Hebrews used dance as part of worship and general celebration, according to the many references to dance in the Bible's Old Testament.

Dance was and is part of praise, celebration, and everyday life among the varied peoples of Africa.

Puppet shows, known as <u>*wayang*</u>, were used to spread Hinduism and Islam among villagers in Java. Javanese and Balinese dances have stories about old Buddhist and Hindu kingdoms.

<u>*Randai*</u> is a folk theater tradition of the <u>Minangkabau</u> people of <u>West Sumatra</u>, usually performed for traditional ceremonies and festivals. It incorporates music, singing, dance, drama, and martial arts, with performances often based on semi-historical Minangkabau stories and legend.

Opera, a form of art that incorporates both music and drama, has been passed down through many generations and many cultures. The Italians, French, and Germans are but a few of the cultures to use opera as a way to entertain and teach moral lessons at the same time.

It is safe to say that drama and dance have been a rich and treasured part of cultural tradition and history in the past and will remain so in the future.

Skill 19.5 **Demonstrate knowledge of the interrelationships among the arts and the connections between the arts and other subject areas**

All of the arts, whether it's dance, music, theater, or fine art, fulfill a variety of purposes in society. They are used to present ideas, to teach or persuade, to entertain, and even to add beauty. The arts have significant value in daily life by providing fulfillment and nonverbal communication for the presentation of ideas and emotions. Studying the interrelationships among arts enables students to develop a complete appreciation of the arts as a mirror of society.

There are three separate processes involved in the arts. They are the creating of new work, the performing of the work, and responses to the work. Each of the processes is important and relies on the other. An artist creates a work to express ideas, emotions, or beliefs. Fine art may capture a moment in time, while the performing arts are performed for a live audience. The audiences for both art forms respond to the artistic expression based on the meaning of the work.

Each process is essential to the other, as each enhances the understanding and appreciation of the other two processes. To fully understand these processes it is important for the student to participate in each area. The students may be required to communicate an idea or emotion by using one of the arts and then respond to each other's work. The students may also be asked to communicate their idea or emotion using two different mediums to allow for the comparison of responses and the evaluation of each medium's effectiveness in presenting said idea. This provides an opportunity for the student to explore different art forms, techniques, and processes and to communicate ideas, experiences, and stories.

COMPETENCY 20.0   UNDERSTAND CONCEPTS, TECHNIQUES, AND MATERIALS RELATED TO VISUAL ART, MUSIC, AND DRAMATIC ACTIVITIES AND HOW TO PROVIDE STUDENTS WITH LEARNING OPPORTUNITIES THAT ENCOURAGE T HEM TO EXPRESS THEMSELVES THROUGH THE ARTS

Skill 20.1   Demonstrate knowledge of basic terms and concepts of visual art (e.g., elements of art and principles of design) and types and characteristics of materials, tools (including technology), techniques, and processes (e.g., drawing, painting, printmaking, desktop publishing) used to create and evaluate works of visual art

The components and strands of visual art encompass many areas. Students are expected to fine-tune observation skills and to be able to identify and recreate the experiences that teachers provide for them as learning tools. For example, students may walk as a group on a nature hike taking in the surrounding elements and then discuss the repetition found in the leaves of trees, or the bricks of the sidewalk, or the sizes and shapes of the buildings and how they may relate. They may also use such an experience to describe lines, colors, shapes, forms, and textures. Beginning elements of perspective are noticed at an early age. The questions of why buildings look smaller when they are at a far distance and bigger when they are closer are sure to spark the imagination of early childhood students. Students can then take their inquiry to a higher level of learning with some hands-on activities, such as building three dimensional buildings and construction using paper and geometric shapes. Eventually students should acquire higher-level thinking skills such as analysis, in which they begin to question artists and art work and analyze many different aspects of visual art.

Principles of Art
Students should have en early introduction to the principles of visual art and should become familiar with the basic level of the following terms:

abstract
  An image that reduces a subject to its essential visual elements, such as lines, shapes, and colors

background
  Those portions or areas of composition that are back of (behind) the primary, or dominant, subject matter or design areas

balance
  A principle of art and design concerned with the arrangement of one or more elements in a work of art so that they appear symmetrical or asymmetrical in design and proportion

contrast

A principle of art and design concerned with juxtaposing one or more elements in opposition, so as to show their differences

emphasis

A principle of art and design concerned with making one or more elements in a work of art stand out in such a way as to appear more important or significant

sketch

An image-development strategy; a preliminary drawing

texture

An element of art and design that pertains to the way something feels by representation of the tactile character of surfaces

unity

A principle of art and design concerned with the arrangement of one or more of the elements used to create a coherence of parts and a feeling of completeness or wholeness

Following the learning of generic ideas for the above terms and how they relate to the use of line, color, value, space, texture and shape, an excellent activity is to create with the students an "art sample book." Such books could include the different variety of material that would serve as examples for students to make connections to, such as sandpaper and cotton balls to represent texture elements. Samples of square pieces of construction paper can be designed into various shapes to represent shape. String samples can represent the element of lines, and other examples can be used to cover all areas. The sampling of art should also focus clearly on the colors necessary for the early childhood student. Color can be introduced more in-depth when discussing intensity or the strength and value of the color, which relates to the lightness or darkness of the colors. Another valuable tool regarding color is the use of a color wheel, which allows students to experiment with the mixing of colors to create their own art experience.

Visual Art Techniques

It is vital that students learn to identify characteristics of visual arts that include materials, techniques, and processes necessary to establish a connection between art and daily life. Early ages should begin to experience art in a variety of forms. It is important to reach many areas at an early age to establish a strong artistic foundation for young students. Students should be introduced to the recognition of simple patterns found in the art environment. They must also identify art materials such as clay, paint, and crayons. Each of these types of material should be introduced and explained for use in daily lessons with young children.

Young students may need to be introduced to items that are developmentally appropriate for their age and for their fine motor skills. Many pre-kindergarten and kindergarten students use oversized pencils and crayons for the first semester. Typically after this first semester, development occurs to enable children to gradually grow into using smaller-sized materials.

Students should begin to explore artistic expression at this age using colors and mixing. The color wheel is a vital lesson for young children and students to begin to learn the uses of primary and secondary colors. By the middle of the school year students should be able to explain this process. For example, a student needs orange paint but only has a few colors. Students should be able to determine that by mixing red and yellow, orange is created.

Teachers should begin to plan and use variation using line, shape, texture, and many different principles of design. By using common environmental figures such as people, animals, and buildings, teachers can base many art lessons on characteristics of readily available examples. Students should be introduced to as many techniques as possible to ensure that all strands of the visual arts and materials are experienced at a variety of levels.

By using original works of art students should be able to identify visual and actual textures of art and base their judgments on objects found in everyday scenes. Other examples that can be described as subjects could include landscapes, portraits, and still life.

The major areas that young students should experience include the following:

1. painting-using tempera or watercolors
2. sculpture-typically using clay or play-dough
3. architecture-building or structuring design using 3D materials such as cardboard and poster board to create a desired effect
4. ceramics- another term for pottery using a hollow clay sculpture and pots made from clay and fired in a kiln at a high temperature to strengthen the clay
5. metalworking-another term for engraving or cutting design or letters into metal with a sharp printmaking tool

Lithography is an example of planographics, where a design is drawn on a surface and then the print is lifted from the surface. There are different types of visual balance, and artists use these types to create art work that conveys a particular message or idea or view. Balance is a fundamental of design seen as a visual weight and counterweight. This is apparent in a single image or in the organization of images and objects in a composition. Examples of balance are:

- **Symmetrical Balance** - The same objects or arrangements are on both sides.
- **Asymmetrical Balance** - Objects or arrangements are on different sides.
- **Radial Balance** - The axis design, or pattern, appears to radiate from the center axis.
- **Horizontal Balance** - Works which utilise the picture plane from left to right.

Lines are the marks left by the painting tools which define the edges of objects in artwork. Their shape and thickness may express movement or tone. Texture in a painting is the "feel" of the canvas based on the paint used and its method of application. There are two forms of texture in painting: visual and tactile. Because texture uses two different senses, it is a unique element of art.

Color refers to the hue (e.g., red vs. orange) and intensity, or brightness (e.g., neon-green vs. yellow-green) of the colors used. Shapes are formed from the meeting of lines and the enclosing of areas in a two-dimensional space.

- See also Skill 19.4

Skill 20.2   Demonstrate knowledge of common musical terms and concepts (e.g., harmony, melody, rhythm); types and characteristics of instrumental and vocal music; and techniques, activities, technology, and materials for producing, listening to, analyzing, and responding to music

Music is a form of art that involves organized and audible sounds (notes) and silence (rests). It is normally expressed in terms of pitch, rhythm, and tone. Musical style is the basic musical language. A musical genre is a collection of music that shares a style.

Types of Music

Classical music is a class of music covering compositions and performances by professionally trained artists. Classical music is written traditionally. It is composed and written using music notation and as a rule is performed exactly as written. Classical music often refers to instrumental music in general, although opera is also considered classical.

Jazz is a form of music that grew out of a combination of folk music, ragtime, and band music. It has been called the first native art form to develop in the United States. The music has gone through a series of developments since its inception. In rough chronological order they are Dixieland, swing, big band, bebop, cool jazz, and smooth jazz.

Blues is a vocal and instrumental music form which came from West African spirituals, work songs, and chants. This musical form has been a major influence on later American popular music, finding expression in jazz, rock and roll, and country music. Due to its powerful influence that originated from America, blues can be regarded as the root of pop as well as American music. Elvis Presley and Eric Clapton feel they found their niche in the music industry from their predecessors in the blues industry.

Rock and roll, in its broadest sense, can refer to almost all pop music recorded since the early 1950s. Its main features include an emphasis on rhythm and the use of percussion and amplified instruments like the bass and guitar. Elvis Presley in the 1950s shocked the nation with his rhythm and gyrating hips in what was the early stages of rock and roll. Starting in the mid-1960s, a group of British bands, sometime referred to as the British Invasion, formed folk rock, as well as a variety of less-popular genres. The British Invasion evolved into psychedelic rock, which in turn gave birth to jam bands and progressive rock.

Rhythm and Music

In music, a "divisive" rhythm is when a larger period of time is divided into smaller units. "Additive" rhythms are when larger periods of time are made from smaller units of time added to a previous unit.

Any single strike or series of beats on a percussion instrument creates a rhythmic pattern, sometimes called a "drum beat." Percussion instruments are sometimes referred to as nonpitched, or untuned. This occurs when the sound of the percussion instrument has no pitch that can be heard by the ear. Examples of percussion instruments that are nonpitched are the snare drum, cymbals, and whistles.

The autoharp, or lyre, is a stringed instrument which has thirty to forty strings stretched across a flat soundboard and is usually plucked rather than strummed. In the acoustic version, the autoharp has no neck. Chord bars are attached to dampers, which mute all the other strings except the desired chord. An autoharp is sometimes called a zither. The zither is mainly used in folk music, most common in German-speaking Alpine Europe.

A keyboard instrument is any musical instrument played using a musical keyboard. The harpsichord and pipe organ were used in early European countries. The organ is the oldest instrument, appearing in the 3rd century BC, and until the 14th century was the only keyboard instrument. The harpsichord appeared at this time and was very common until the arrival of the piano in the 18th century.

The piano is popular because the player can vary the volume of the sound by varying the amount of intensity in which the keys are struck. Volume can also be adjusted with pedals, which act as dampers. Other widely used keyboard instruments include electronic instruments, which are largely referred to as keyboard-style synthesizers. Significant development of the synthesizer occurred in the 1960s, when digital synthesizers became more common.

Principles of Music

cantata- Developed in the baroque era, these compositions were written for solo and chorus voices, with orchestral accompaniment. With either secular or sacred lyrics, cantatas contain several movements.

concerto- A musical work written for one or more solo instruments with orchestral accompaniment; the concerto is usually comprised of three movements in a fast-slow-fast order.

mass- This choral type is usually associated with the Roman Catholic church service, thus following the form of that service and including six musical parts: the Kyrie Eleison, Gloria in Excelsis Deo, Credo in Unum Deum, Sanctus, Benedictus, and Agnus Dei. Specific masses for the dead are known as "requiem" masses. However, not all masses are written for church services. Since the medieval period, "concert masses" have been an accepted form of composition.

motet- From the French for "word," a motet is a choral work, utilizing a polyphonic approach. Motets from the 13t^h century were often written for three voices (triplum, motetus, and tenor) and combined texts from both sacred and secular sources. During the 15th and 16th centuries (Renaissance), the motet expanded to a contrapuntal work for four or five voices a cappella, utilizing a sacred text. The motet also appears in the Baroque and Romantic periods with both orchestral and a cappella variations.

opera- Originating from the Italian word for "work," opera is appropriately named! It is a musical work which, when produced, incorporates many of the other arts as well. Technically, it is a play in which all the dialogue (libretto) is sung, with orchestral accompaniment. The origins of opera were founded in Renaissance Florence by intellectuals reviving Greek and Roman drama. Since then, operatic forms have evolved through many stages. Major ones include "grand opera," or "opera seria," which consists of five acts and is serious in nature; "opera comique," which, regardless of emotional content, has spoken dialogue; "opera buffa," which is the comic opera usually based on farce; and "operetta," also with spoken dialogue and characterized by a light, romantic mood and popular theme.

oratorio- Developed during the Baroque era, an oratorio is a choral work of large scale, including parts for soloists, chorus, and orchestra alike. Themes are usually epic or religious in nature. Although the soloists may take the role of various characters and there may be a plot, an oratorio is usually presented in concert form, without action, costumes, or set design.

overture- Usually an overture is the introductory composition to an opera, written to capture the mood of the opera and even to showcase a musical motif from the opera. However, since in concerts overtures are often performed out of context, composers have now begun to write "concert overtures" meant to stand alone, without a larger body of music to follow.

sonata- A sonata is a succession of movements which have loosely related tonalities. The first of these movements usually is composed in a specific pattern, which is known as "sonata form." Sonata form, or sonata-allegro form, follows the pattern of development ABA or AABA, where A is the exposition, B is the development, and A (the final section) is the recapitulation.

suite- A musical suite is a group of dances, usually written for keyboards or an ensemble of stringed or wind instruments. The dances are usually unrelated except for a common key.

symphony- Fully refined by the 18th century, a symphony is a large scale work composed for a full orchestra. However, the various historic and stylistic periods, in addition to the development of instruments, have produced an evolution of this form. Because of this, "symphony" also refers to compositions for chamber orchestras and string quartets. Although some symphonies vary in the number of movements, in general, the four symphonic movements follow the tempo pattern of fast, slow, moderate, and fast, with a minuet included in the third movement.

Other Terms to Know

Accent - Stress of one tone over others, making it stand out; often it is the first beat of a measure.

Accompaniment - Music that goes along with a more important part--often harmony or rhythmic patterns accompanying a melody.

Adagio - Slow, leisurely.

Allegro - Lively, brisk, rapid.

Cadence - Closing of a phrase or section of music.

Chord - Three or more tones combined and sounded simultaneously.

Crescendo - Gradually growing louder.

Dissonance - A simultaneous sounding of tones that produce a feeling of tension or unrest and a feeling that further resolution is needed.

Harmony - The sound resulting from the simultaneous sounding of two or more tones consonant with each other.

Interval - The distance between two tones.

Melody - An arrangement of single tones in a meaningful sequence.

Phrase - A small section of a composition comprising a musical thought.

Rhythm - The regular occurrence of accented beats that shape the character of music or dance.

Scale - A graduated series of tones arranged in a specified order.

Staccato – Separate notes sounded in a short, detached manner.

Syncopation - The rhythmic result produced when a regularly accented beat is displaced onto an unaccented beat.

Tempo - The rate of speed at which a musical composition is performed.

Theme - A short, musical passage that states an idea. It often provides the basis for variations, development, etc.

Timbre - The quality of a musical tone that distinguishes voices and instruments.

Tone - A musical sound or the quality of a musical sound.

Culture and Music

The resources available to man to make music have varied throughout different ages and eras and have given the chance for a musical style or type to be created or invented due to diverse factors. Social changes, cultural features, and historical purpose have all shared a part in giving birth to a multitude of different musical forms in every part of the Earth.

Music can be traced to the people who created it by the instruments, melodies, rhythms, and records of performance (songs) that are composed in human communities. Starting from early musical developments as far back as nomadic cave dwellers playing the flute and beating on hand drums to the different electric instruments and recording technology of the modern music industry, the style and type of music produced has been closely related to the human beings who choose it for their particular lifestyle and way of existence.

Western music, rising chiefly from the fusion of classical and folkloric forms, has always been the pocket of a large variety of instruments and music generating new techniques to fit the change in expression provided by the expansion of its possibilities. Instruments such as the piano and the organ; stringed instruments like the violin, viola, cello, guitar, and bass; wind instruments like the flute, saxophone, trumpet, trombone, tuba, and saxophone; and electronic instruments like the synthesizer and electric guitar have all provided for the invention of new styles and types of music created and used by different people in different times and places.

The rites of Christianity during the early middle ages were the focus of social and cultural aspiration and became a natural meeting place for communities to come together consistently for the purpose of experiencing God, through preaching and music. Composers and performers fulfilled their roles with sacred music with Gregorian chants and oratorios. The art patron's court in the 15th and 14th centuries and the opera house of the 19th century satisfied the need of nascent, progressive society looking to experience grander and more satisfying music. New forms were generated such as the *concerto*, *symphony*, *sonata,* and *string quartet* that employed a zeal and zest for creation typical of the burgeoning intellect at the end of the middle ages and the beginning of modern society.

Traditional types and styles of music in America, India, China, and throughout the Middle East and Africa, using a variety of stringed instruments and percussion that differed from typical Western instruments, began a long and exciting process of merging with the Western musical world, around the beginning of widespread colonialism and the eventual integration it would achieve between disparate cultures. Western musical instruments were adopted to play the traditional musical styles of different cultures.

Blues music, arising from the southern black community in the United States, would morph into *Rock n' Roll* and *Hip Hop,* alongside the progression of the traditional folk music of European settlers.

Hispanic music would come about by Western musical instruments being imbued with African rhythms throughout the Caribbean in different forms like *Salsa*, *Merengue*, *Cumbia,* and *Son Cubano.*

Call-and-response songs are a form of verbal and nonverbal interaction between a speaker and a listener, in which statements by a speaker are responded to by a listener. In West African cultures, call-and-response songs were used in religious rituals, gatherings, and are now used in other forms such as gospel, blues, and jazz as a form of musical expression. In certain Native American tribes, call-and-response songs are used to preserve and protect the tribe's cultural heritage and can be seen and heard at modern-day "pow-wows." The men would begin the song in the role of speaker with singing and drumming, and the women would respond with singing and dancing.

A ballad is a song that contains a story. Instrumental music forms a part of folk music, especially dance traditions. Much folk music is vocal, since the instrument (the voice) that makes such music is usually handy. As such, most folk music has lyrics, and is descriptive about something. Any story form can be a ballad, such as fairy tales or historical accounts. It usually has simple repeating rhymes and often contains a refrain (or repeating sections) that are played or sung at regular intervals throughout. Ballads could be called hymns when they are based on religious themes. In the 20th century, "ballad" took on the meaning of a popular song "especially of a romantic or sentimental nature."

Folk music is music that has endured and been passed down by oral tradition and emerges spontaneously from ordinary people. In early societies, it arose in areas that were not yet affected by mass communication. It was normally shared by the entire community and was transmitted by word of mouth. A folk song is usually seen as an expression of a way of life now, past, or about to disappear. In the 1960s folk songs were sung as a way of protesting political themes.

The work song is typically a song sung a cappella by people working on a physical and often repetitive task. It was probably intended to reduce feelings of boredom. Rhythms of work songs also serve to synchronize physical movement in a chain gang or movement in marching. Frequently, the verses of work songs are improvised and sung differently each time. Examples of work songs could be heard from slaves working in the field, prisoners on chain gangs, and soldiers in the military.

- See also Skill 19.4

Skill 20.3   Demonstrate knowledge of basic types of dramatic activities (e.g., creative drama, puppet theater, pantomime, improvisation); of ways in which creative drama can be used across the curriculum; and of techniques, activities, technology, and materials for creating, producing, viewing, evaluating, and responding to drama

The framework and academic content in the area of theater requires that teachers are able to express the various venues of the arts. In theater students should learn to use all of their five senses to observe their environment and recreate experiences through drama and other theater skills.

Using role-play and prior knowledge of experiences, students should develop the ability to react to a feeling or a situation to expand their ability to develop character. Using sight, smell, taste, touch, hearing, and memory recall, students should become proficient with these skills so that they are able to retell stories, myths, and fables. Some experiences that the teacher should provide are costuming and props for performances.

Many students can relate to familiar jobs that are relevant to their everyday experiences. Some experiences that should be offered but not limited to include the following: firefighters, police officers, teachers, doctors, nurses, postal employees, clerks, and other service-related professions that students may have witnessed.

It is vital that teachers be trained in critical areas that focus on important principles of theater education. The basic course of study should include state-mandated topics in arts education, instructional materials, products in arts, both affective and cognitive processes of art, world and traditional cultures, and the most recent teaching tools, media and technology.

Concepts of Drama
Areas that should be included but not limited to are as follows:

Acting - Acting requires the student to demonstrate the ability to effectively communicate using skillful speaking, movement, rhythm, and sensory awareness.

Directing - Direction requires the management skills to produce and perform an onstage activity. This requires guiding and inspiring students as well as script and stage supervision.

Designing - Designing involves creating and initiating the onsite management of the art of acting.

Scriptwriting - Scriptwriting demands that a leader be able to produce original material and stage an entire production through the writing and designing of a story that has performance value.

Each of the above mentioned skills should be incorporated into daily activities with young children. It is important that children be exposed to character development through stories, role-play, and modeling through various teacher-guided experiences. Some of these experiences that are age-appropriate for early childhood level include puppet theater, paper dolls, character sketches, storytelling, and retelling of stories in a students' own words.

Theater in the Curriculum

Students must be able to create, perform, and actively participate in theater. Classes must be able to apply processes and skills involved in drama and theater. From acting, designing, and scriptwriting to creating formal and informal theater and media productions, there are a wide variety of skills that must encompass the theater expression. Literature in the classroom opens many doors for learning. Reading and rehearsing stories with children allows them to explore the area of imagination and creative play. Students can take simple stories such as "The Three Little Pigs" and act out such tales. Acting allows students to experience new-found dramatic skills and to enhance their creative abilities.

A school curriculum incorporating dramatic and theatrical forms should include the vocabulary for theater and the development of a criterion for evaluation of dramatic events. Students must understand and appreciate a dramatic work. A good drama curriculum should include the following:

- Acting - Acting involves the students' ability to skillfully communicate with an audience. It requires speaking, movement, sensory awareness, rhythm, and great oral communication skills.
- Improvisation- The actors must be able to respond to unexpected stimuli and be spontaneous, creative, and flexible to adapt to any scene that may be previously unscripted.
- Drama- A reenactment of life and life situations for entertainment purposes.
- Theater - Theater involves a more formal presentation in front of an audience. Typically it involves a script, set, direction, and production.
- Production - This often includes arranging for the entire theater performance and the production of the whole process.
- Direction - Coordinating and directing, or guiding, the onstage activities.
- Playmaking - This involves creating an original script and staging a performance without a set or formal audience.
- Pantomime - A form of communication by means of gesture and facial expressions. Telling a story without the use of words.

Various areas of art framework should be addressed, including but not limited to the following:

- Direction of theatrical productions, auditions, analysis of script, demonstration of vision for a project, knowledge of communication skills, social group skills, and creativity
- Understanding the principles of production
- Applying scheduling, budget, planning, promotion, roles and responsibilities of others, and knowledge of legal issues such as copyright
- Selection of appropriate works

Theatrical Materials

Students must realize the impact that technical aspects have regarding the overall message and impression of the performance. Students should be able to recognize the basic tools, media, and techniques involved in a theatrical production. Students must use professional resources for theater experiences. They should be able to accomplish the following tasks:

- Use of theatrical technology skills and facilities in creating the theater experience
- Use of school and community resources, including library and media centers, museums, and theater professionals as part of their production
- Visits to local theatrical institutions and attendance at theatrical performances as an individual and as a group.
- Understand the broad range of vocations/avocations in performing, producing, and promoting theater.

The mastery of skills above will be evident when students can engage in some of the following activities:
- Read and follow a lighting plot for a production; handle and focus lighting instruments properly
- Read a script for a production; then complete pictorial research on the costuming and accessories of the time period before designing costumes
- Write a short review of a local community performance for publication in the school newspaper
- Create a publicity campaign for the high school production
- Create props that engage the audience as well as draw in performers to the actual scenery of the stage

- See also Skill 19.4

Skill 20.4   Demonstrate knowledge of basic types of creative movement and dance; of ways in which creative movement and dance can be used across the curriculum; and of techniques, activities, technology, and materials for performing, viewing, evaluating, and responding to creative movement and dance

The various styles of dance are as follows:

- Creative dance
- Modern dance
- Social dance
- Dance of other cultures
- Structured dance
- Ritual Dance
- Ballet

Creative dance is the one that is most natural to a young child. Creative dance depicts feelings through movement. It is the initial reaction to sound and movement. The older elementary student will incorporate mood and expressiveness. Stories can be told to release the dancer into imagination. Isadora Duncan is credited with being the mother of modern dance. **Modern dance** today refers to a concept of dance where the expressions of opposites are developed, such as fast-slow, contract- release, variation of height and level, and fall and recover. Modern dance is based on four principles, which are substance, dynamism, metakinesis, and form.

Social dance requires a steadier capability than the previous levels, the social aspect of dance rather than the romantic aspect representing customs and pastimes. Adults laugh when they hear little ones go "eweeee" during a social dance. Changing partners frequently within the dance is something that is subtly important to maintain. Social dances refer to a cooperative form of dance with respect to one sharing the dance floor with others and having respect for one's partner. Social dance may be in the form of marches, waltzes, and the two-step.

The upper-level elementary student can learn dance in connection with historical **cultures** such as the minuet. The minuet was introduced to the court in Paris in 1650, and it dominated the ballroom until the end of the 18th century. The waltz was introduced around 1775 and was an occasion of fashion and courtship. The pomp and ceremony of it all makes for fun classroom experiences. Dance traditionally is central to many cultures, and the interrelatedness of teaching history, such as the Native American Indian dance, the Mexican hat dance, or Japanese theater (incorporating both theater of masks and dance) are all important exposures to dance and culture.

Structured dances are recognized by particular patterns such as the tango or the waltz and were made popular in dance studios and gym classes alike. Arthur Murray promoted dance lessons for adults.

Ritual dances are often of a religious nature that celebrate a significant life event such as a harvest season, the rain season, glorifying the gods, asking for favors in hunting, and birth and death dances. Many of these themes are carried out in movies and theaters today, but they have their roots in Africa, where circle dances and chants summoned the gods and sometimes produced trance-like states, in which periods of divine contact convey the spiritual cleansing of the experience.

Dancing at weddings today is a prime example of ritual dance. The father dances with the bride. Then the husband dances with the bride, and last, the two families dance with each other.

Ballet uses a barre to hold onto to practice the five basic positions used in ballet. Alignment is the way in which various parts of the dancer's body are in line with one another while the dancer is moving. It is very precise and executed with grace and form. The mood and expressions of the music are very important to ballet and form the canvas upon which the dance is performed.

- See also Skill 19.4

COMPETENCY 21.0 UNDERSTAND PRINCIPLES, CONCEPTS, AND PRACTICES RELATED TO MOVEMENT AND PHYSICAL FITNESS AND THE ROLE OF PHYSICAL ACTIVITY IN PROMOTING STUDENTS' PERSONAL AND SOCIAL DEVELOPMENT

Skill 21.1 Demonstrate understanding of fundamental motor, body control, and perceptual awareness skills and appropriate movement activities to promote the physical development of all students

Perceptual Awareness Skills

Perceptual motor development refers to one's ability to receive, interpret, and respond successfully to sensory signals coming from the environment. Because many of the skills acquired in school rely on the child's knowledge of his body and its relationship to the surroundings, good motor development leads directly to perceptual skill development. Development of gross motor skills leads to successful development of fine motor skills, which in turn helps with learning, reading, and writing. Adolescents with perceptual motor coordination problems are at risk for poor school performance, low self-esteem, and inadequate participation in physical activity. Without a successful intervention, these adolescents are likely to continue avoiding physical activity and experience frustration and teasing from their peers. Children with weak perceptual motor skills may be easily distracted or have difficulty with tasks requiring coordination. They spend much of their energy trying to control their bodies, exhausting them so much that they physically cannot concentrate on a teacher-led lesson. Unfortunately, perceptual motor coordination problems do not just go away, and they don't self-repair. Practice and maturity are necessary for children to develop greater coordination and spatial awareness. Physical education lessons should emphasize activities that children enjoy doing, are sequential, and require seeing, hearing, and/or touching. Discussing with students the actual steps involved in performing a fundamental skill is a great benefit. Activities and skills that can be broken down and taught in incremental steps include running, dribbling, catching or hitting a ball, making a basket in basketball, and setting a volleyball. Recommended strategies include introducing the skill, practicing in a variety of settings with an assortment of equipment, implementing lead-up games modified to ensure practice of the necessary skills, and incorporating students into an actual game situation.

Concepts of Body Awareness Applied to Physical Education Activities

Body awareness is a person's understanding of his or her own body parts and their capability of movement.

Instructors can assess body awareness by playing and watching a game of "Simon says" and asking the students to touch different body parts. You can also instruct students to make their bodies into various shapes, from straight to round to twisted, and varying sizes to fit into different-sized spaces.

In addition, you can instruct children to touch one part of their body to another and to use various body parts to stamp their feet, twist their neck, clap their hands, nod their heads, wiggle their noses, snap their fingers, open their mouths, shrug their shoulders, bend their knees, close their eyes, bend their elbows, or wiggle their toes.

Concept of Spatial Awareness Applied to Physical Education Activities

Spatial awareness is the ability to make decisions about an object's positional changes in space (i.e., awareness of three-dimensional space position changes). Developing spatial awareness requires two sequential phases: 1) identifying the location of objects in relation to one's own body in space, and 2) locating more than one object in relation to each object and independently of one's own body. Plan activities using different size balls, boxes, or hoops, and have children move towards and away; under and over; in front of and behind; and inside, outside, and beside the objects.

Concepts of Effort Qualities Applied to Physical Education

Effort qualities are the qualities of movement that apply the mechanical principles of balance, time, and force.

Balance - Activities for balance include having children move on their hands and feet, lean, move on lines, and balance and hold shapes while moving.

Time - Activities using the concept of time can include having children move as fast as they can and as slow as they can in specified, timed, movement patterns.

Force - Activities using the concept of force can include having students use their bodies to produce enough force to move them through space. They can also paddle balls against walls and jump over objects of various heights.

Skill 21.2 **Apply knowledge of basic principles and concepts of physical fitness (e.g., frequency, intensity, duration of training), the components of fitness (e.g., cardiovascular endurance, flexibility, muscular strength, body composition), and practices and activities that promote lifelong fitness and stress reduction**

Health Related Components of Physical Fitness

There are five health-related components of physical fitness: cardio-respiratory or cardiovascular endurance, muscle strength, muscle endurance, flexibility, and body composition.

Cardiovascular endurance – the ability of the body to sustain aerobic activities (activities requiring oxygen utilization) for extended periods.

Muscle strength – the ability of muscle groups to contract and support a given amount of weight.

Muscle endurance – the ability of muscle groups to contract continually over a period of time and support a given amount of weight.

Flexibility – the ability of muscle groups to stretch and bend.

Body composition – an essential measure of health and fitness. The most important aspects of body composition are body fat percentage and ratio of body fat to muscle.

Skill-Related Components of Physical Fitness

The skill-related components of physical fitness are agility, balance, coordination, power, reaction time, and speed. A student's natural ability in these areas greatly affects performance in fitness and athletic activities. While heredity plays a major role in each student's level of skill-related components, practice and coaching can improve performance.

Basic Training Principles

The **Overload Principle** is exercising at an above-normal level to improve physical or physiological capacity (a higher than normal workload).

The **Specificity Principle** is overloading a particular fitness component. In order to improve a component of fitness, you must isolate and specifically work on a single component. Metabolic and physiological adaptations depend on the type of overload; hence, specific exercise produces specific adaptations, creating specific training effects.

The **Progression Principle** states that once the body adapts to the original load/stress, no further improvement of a component of fitness will occur without the addition of an additional load.

There is also a **Reversibility-of-Training Principle,** in which all gains in fitness are lost with the discontinuance of a training program.

Modifications of Overload

We can modify overload by varying frequency, intensity, and time. Frequency is the number of times we implement a training program in a given period (e.g., three days per week). Intensity is the amount of effort put forth or the amount of stress placed on the body. Time is the duration of each training session.

Activities That Promote Fitness

The following is a list of physical activities that may reduce specific health risks, improve overall health, and develop skill-related components of physical activity.

1. **Aerobic Dance:**
Health-related components of fitness = *cardio-respiratory, body composition*
Skill-related components of fitness = *agility, coordination*

2. **Bicycling:**
Health-related components of fitness = *cardio-respiratory, muscle strength, muscle endurance, body composition*
Skill-related components of fitness = *balance*

3. **Calisthenics:**
Health-related components of fitness = *cardio-respiratory, muscle strength, muscle endurance, flexibility, body composition*
Skill-related components of fitness = *agility*

4. **Circuit Training:**
Health-related components of fitness = *cardio-respiratory, muscle strength, muscle endurance, body composition*
Skill-related components of fitness = *power*

5. **Cross Country Skiing:**
Health-related component of fitness = *cardio-respiratory, muscle strength, muscle endurance, body composition*
Skill-related components of fitness = *agility, coordination, power*

6. **Jogging/Running:**
Health-related components of fitness = *cardio-respiratory, body composition*

7. **Rope Jumping:**
Health-related components of fitness = *cardio-respiratory, body composition*
Skill-related components of fitness = *agility, coordination, reaction time, speed*

8. **Rowing:**
Health-related components of fitness = *cardio-respiratory, muscle strength, muscle endurance, body composition*
Skill-related components of fitness = *agility, coordination, power*

9. **Skating:**
Health-related components of fitness = *cardio-respiratory, body composition*
Skill-related components of fitness = *agility, balance, coordination, speed*

10. **Swimming/Water Exercises:**
Health-related components of fitness = *cardio-respiratory, muscle strength, muscle endurance, flexibility, body composition*
Skill-related components of fitness = *agility, coordination*

11. **Walking (brisk):**
Health-related components of fitness = *cardio-respiratory, body composition*

Skill 21.3   Recognize skill progressions, safety practices, equipment, strategies, rules, and appropriate behaviors for individual, group, and team activities and sports

The development of motor skills in children is a sequential process. We can classify motor skill competency into stages of development by observing children practicing physical skills. The sequence of development begins with simple reflexes and progresses to the learning of postural elements, locomotor skills, and, finally, fine motor skills. The stages of development consider both innate and learned behaviors.

STAGES OF MOTOR LEARNING

Stage 1 – Children progress from simple reflexes to basic movements such as sitting, crawling, creeping, standing, and walking.

Stage 2 – Children learn more complex motor patterns, including running, climbing, jumping, balancing, catching, and throwing.

Stage 3 – During late childhood, children learn more specific movement skills. In addition, the basic motor patterns learned in stage two become more fluid and automatic.

Stage 4 – During adolescence, children continue to develop general and specific motor skills and master specialized movements. At this point, factors including practice, motivation, and talent begin to affect the level of further development.

Sequential Development for Locomotor Skills Acquisition = crawl, creep, walk, run, jump, hop, gallop, slide, leap, skip, and step-hop.

Sequential Development for Nonlocomotor Skill Acquisition = stretch, bend, sit, shake, turn, rock and sway, swing, twist, dodge, and fall.

Sequential Development for Manipulative Skill Acquisition = striking, throwing, kicking, ball rolling, volleying, bouncing, catching, and trapping.

Rules for Individual and Dual Sports

ARCHERY:

- Arrows that bounce off the target or go through the target count as seven points.
- Arrows landing on lines between two rings receive the higher score of the two rings.
- Arrows hitting the petticoat receive no score.

BADMINTON:

- Intentionally balking an opponent or making preliminary feints results in a fault (side in = loss of serve; side out = point awarded to side in).
- When a shuttlecock falls on a line, it is in play (i.e., a fair play).
- If the striking team hits shuttlecock before it crosses the net, it is a fault.
- Touching the net when the shuttlecock is in play is a fault.
- The same player hitting the shuttlecock twice is a fault.
- The shuttlecock going through the net is a fault.

BOWLING:

- There is score for a pin knocked down by a pinsetter (human or mechanical).
- There is no score for the pins when any part of the foot, hand, or arm extends or crosses over the foul line (even after ball leaves the hand) or if any part of the body contacts division boards, walls, or uprights that are beyond the foul line.
- There is no count for pins displaced or knocked down by a ball leaving the lane before it reaches the pins.
- There is no count when balls rebound from the rear cushion.

RACQUETBALL/HANDBALL:

- A server steps outside the service area when serving faults.
- The server is out (relinquishes serve) if he/she steps outside of the serving zone twice in succession while serving.
- The server is out if he/she fails to hit the ball rebounding off the floor during the serve.
- The opponent must have a chance to take a position or the referee must call for play before the server can serve the ball.
- The server re-serves the ball if the receiver is not behind the short line at the time of the serve.
- A served ball that hits the front line and does not land back of the short line is "short;" therefore, it is a fault. The ball is also short when it hits the front wall and two sidewalls before it lands on the floor back of the short line.
- A serve is a fault when the ball touches the ceiling from rebounding off the front wall.
- A fault occurs when any part of the foot steps over the outer edges of the service or the short line while serving.
- A hinder (dead ball) is called when a returned ball hits an opponent on its way to the front wall—even if the ball continues to the front wall.
- A hinder is any intentional or unintentional interference of an opponent's opportunity to return the ball.

TENNIS:

A player loses a point when:

- The ball bounces twice on her side of the net.
- The player returns the ball to any place outside of designated areas.
- The player stops or touches the ball in the air before it lands out-of-bounds.
- The player intentionally strikes the ball twice with the racket.
- The ball strikes any part of a player or racket after an initial attempt to hit the ball.
- A player reaches over the net to hit the ball.
- A player throws his racket at the ball.
- The ball strikes any permanent fixture that is out-of-bounds (other than the net).
- A ball touching the net and landing inside the boundary lines is in play (except on the serve, where a ball contacting the net results in a "let"--a replay of the point).
- A player fails, on two consecutive attempts, to serve the ball into the designated area (i.e., double fault).

Rules for Team Sports

BASKETBALL:
- A player touching the floor on or outside the boundary line is out-of-bounds.
- The ball is out-of-bounds if it touches anything (a player, the floor, an object, or any person) that is on or outside the boundary line.
- An offensive player remaining in the three-second zone of the free-throw lane for more than three seconds is a violation.
- A ball firmly held by two opposing players results in a jump ball.
- A throw-in is awarded to the opposing team of the last player touching a ball that goes out-of-bounds.

SOCCER:
The following are direct free-kick offenses:
- Hand or arm contact with the ball
- Using hands to hold an opponent
- Pushing an opponent
- Striking/kicking/tripping or attempting to strike/kick/trip an opponent
- Goalie using the ball to strike an opponent
- Jumping at or charging an opponent
- Kneeing an opponent
- Any contact fouls

The following are indirect free-kick offenses:
- Same player playing the ball twice at the kickoff, on a throw-in, on a goal kick, on a free kick, or on a corner kick
- The goalie delaying the game by holding the ball or carrying the ball more than four steps
- Failure to notify the referee of substitutions/re-substitutions, and that player then handling the ball in the penalty area
- Any person who is not a player entering the playing field without a referee's permission
- Unsportsmanlike actions or words in reference to a referee's decision
- Dangerously lowering the head or raising the foot too high to make a play
- A player resuming play after being ordered off the field
- Being offsides: an offensive player must have two defenders between him and the goal when a teammate passes the ball to him or else he is offsides
- Attempting to kick the ball when the goalkeeper has possession or interference with the goalkeeper to hinder him/her from releasing the ball
- Illegal charging
- Leaving the playing field without referee's permission while the ball is in play

SOFTBALL:

- Each team plays nine players in the field (sometimes ten for slow pitch).
- Field positions are one pitcher, one catcher, four infielders, and three outfielders (four outfielders in ten-player formats).
- The four bases are sxity feet apart.
- Any ball hit outside of the first or third base line is a foul ball (i.e., runners cannot advance and the pitch counts as a strike against the batter).
- If a batter receives three strikes (i.e., failed attempts at hitting the ball) in a single at bat, he/she strikes out.
- The pitcher must start with both feet on the pitcher's rubber and can only take one step forward when delivering the underhand pitch.
- A base runner is out if:
    1. The opposition tags him with the ball before he reaches a base.
    2. The ball reaches first base before he does.
    3. He runs outside of the base path to avoid a tag.
    4. A batted ball strikes him in fair territory.
- A team must maintain the same batting order throughout the game.
- Runners cannot lead off and base stealing is illegal.
- Runners may overrun first base, but can be tagged out if off any other base.

VOLLEYBALL:

The following infractions by the receiving team result in a point awarded to the serving side, and the following infractions by the serving team result in side-out:

- Illegal serves or serving out of turn
- Illegal returns or catching or holding the ball
- Dribbling, or a player touching the ball twice in succession
- Contact with the net (two opposing players making contact with the net at the same time results in a replay of the point)
- Touching the ball after it has been played three times without passing over the net
- A player's foot completely touching the floor over the centerline
- Reaching under the net and touching a player or the ball while the ball is in play
- The players changing positions prior to the serve

Basketball Strategies:

Use a Zone Defense for these reasons and circumstances:

- To prevent drive-ins for easy lay-up shots
- When playing area is small
- When team is in foul trouble
- To keep an excellent rebounder near opponents' basket
- When opponents' outside shoot in weak
- When opponents have an advantage in height
- When opponents have an exceptional offensive player, or when the best defenders cannot handle one-on-one defense

Offensive Strategies Against Zone Defense:

- Using quick, sharp passing to penetrate a zone, forcing the opposing player out of his assigned position
- Overloading and mismatching

Offensive Strategies for One-On-One Defense:

- Using the "pick-and-roll" and the "give-and-go" to screen defensive players and to open up offensive players for shot attempts
- Teams may use free-lancing (spontaneous one-one-one offense), but more commonly they use "sets" of plays

Soccer Strategies:

- **Heading** – using the head to pass, to shoot, or to clear the ball.
- **Tackling** – objective is to take possession of the ball from an opponent. Successful play requires knowledgeable utilization of space.

Badminton Strategies:

Strategies for Return of Service:

- Returning serves with shots that are straight ahead
- Returning service so that opponent must move out of his/her starting position
- Returning long serves with an overhead clear or drop shot to the near corner
- Returning short serves with an underhand clear or a net drop to the near corner

Strategies for Serving:

- Serving long to the backcourt near the centerline
- Serving short when an opponent is standing too deep in his/her receiving court to return the serve or using a short serve to eliminate a smash return if an opponent has a powerful smash from the backcourt

Handball or Racquetball Strategies:

- Identifying the opponent's strengths and weaknesses
- Making opponent use less dominant hand, or backhand shots, if these shots are weaker
- Frequently alternating fastballs and lobs to change the pace (changing the pace is particularly effective for serving)
- Maintaining position near middle of court (the well) that is close enough to play low balls and corner shots
- Placing shots that keep the opponent's position at a disadvantage to return cross-court and angle shots
- Using high lob shots that go overhead but do not hit the back wall with enough force to rebound to drive an opponent out of position when he/she persistently plays close to the front wall

Tennis Strategies:

- Lobbing – using a high lob shot for defense, giving the player more time to get back into position
- Identifying opponent's weaknesses, attacking these weaknesses, and recognizing and protecting one's own weaknesses
- Outrunning and out-thinking an opponent
- Using change of pace, lobs, spins, approaching the net, and deception at the correct time
- Hitting cross-court (from corner to corner of the court) for maximum safety and opportunity to regain position
- Directing the ball where the opponent is not

Volleyball Strategies:

- Using forearm passes (bumps, digs, or passes) to play balls below the waist, to play hard-driven balls, to pass the serve, and to contact balls distant from a player.

General and Specific Safety Considerations for All Movement Activities

Aquatics

To promote water safety, physical education instructors should make students familiar with appropriate medical responses to life-threatening situations (e.g., recognizing signs that someone needs medical attention--not moving, not breathing, etc.; knowledge of the proper response--who to contact, and where to find them. With older children, instructors can introduce rudimentary first aid training. Finally, instructors must ensure that students are aware and observant of safety rules (e.g., no running near the water, no chewing gum while swimming, no swimming without a lifeguard, no roughhousing near or in the water, etc.).

Outdoor education

Related safety education should emphasize the importance of planning and research. Instructors should ask students to consider in advance what potential dangers of an activity might be and to prepare and plan accordingly. Of course, educator supervision is required. Outdoor education activities require first aid equipment and properly trained educators. Students should use proper safety gear when appropriate (e.g., helmets, harnesses, etc.). Instructors should generally obtain parental consent for outdoor education activities.

Combative activities

Related safety issues include stressing the potential harm that these activities can cause (stressing specific damage potential to musculoskeletal systems), emphasizing students' responsibility for the well-being of their training partners, maintaining discipline throughout the class (ensuring students remain focused on their training activities and alert to the instructor's instructions), and ensuring that students are aware and observant of the limits to force that they may apply (e.g., no-striking zones, like above the neck and below the belt; limits on striking force, like semi-contact or no-contact sparring; familiarity with the concept of a tap-out indicating submission). Students should perform warm up, cool down, and stretch, as with any physical training program.

Traditional sports

The main risk factors in traditional team and individual sports are equipment failure, accidental slips and falls, and physical contact leading to injuries. Instructors must ensure that all equipment is sound and safe to use. In addition, instructors should inspect the playing area for any dangerous conditions or obstacles. Finally, instructors must communicate and enforce the rules of the sport to minimize the danger caused by rough play.

Appropriate Behavior in Physical Education Activities

Appropriate Student Etiquette/Behaviors include following the rules and accepting the consequences of unfair action, good sportsmanship, respecting the rights of other students, reporting own accidents and mishaps, not engaging in inappropriate behavior under peer pressure, cooperation, paying attention to instructions and demonstrations, moving to assigned places and remaining in own space, complying with directions, practicing as instructed to do so, properly using equipment, and not interfering with the practice of others.

Appropriate Content Etiquette/Behaviors include the teacher describing the performance of tasks and students engaging in the task, the teacher assisting students with task performance, and the teacher modifying and developing tasks.

Appropriate Management Etiquette/Behaviors include the teacher directing the management of equipment, students, and space prior to practicing tasks; students getting equipment and partners; and the teacher requesting that students stop "fooling around."

Skill 21.4   Analyze how physical education activities can promote the development of personal, social, and workplace skills (e.g., responsibility, leadership, team building, perseverance, confidence, cooperation, fairness)

Personal and Social Skills

For most people, the development of social roles and appropriate social behaviors occurs during childhood. Physical play between parents and children, as well as between siblings and peers, serves as a strong regulator in the developmental process. Some examples of childhood play are chasing games, roughhousing, and wrestling or sport skills such as jumping, throwing, catching, and striking. These activities may be competitive or noncompetitive and are important for promoting social and moral development of both boys and girls. Unfortunately, fathers will often engage in this sort of activity more with their sons than their daughters. Regardless of the sex of the child, both boys and girls enjoy these types of activities.

Physical play during infancy and early childhood is central to the development of social and emotional competence. Research shows that children who engage in play that is more physical with their parents, particularly with parents who are sensitive and responsive to the child, exhibited greater enjoyment during the play sessions and were more popular with their peers. Likewise, these early interactions with parents, siblings, and peers are important in helping children become more aware of their emotions and in learning to monitor and regulate their own emotional responses. Children learn quickly through watching the responses of their parents which behaviors make their parents smile and laugh and which behaviors cause their parents to frown and disengage from the activity.

If children want the fun to continue, they engage in the behaviors that please others. As children near adolescence, they learn through rough-and-tumble play that there are limits to how far they can go before hurting someone (physically or emotionally), which results in termination of the activity or later rejection of the child by peers. These early interactions with parents and siblings are important in helping children learn appropriate behavior in the social situations of sport and physical activity.

Children learn to assess their social competence (i.e., ability to get along with others and acceptance by peers, family members, teachers, and coaches) in sport through the feedback received from parents and coaches. Initially, authority figures teach children, "You can't do that because I said so." As children approach school age, parents begin the process of explaining why a behavior is right or wrong because children continuously ask, "Why?"

Similarly, when children engage in sports, they learn about taking turns with their teammates, sharing playing time, and valuing rules. They understand that rules are important for everyone and that without these regulations, the game would become unfair. The learning of social competence is continuous as we expand our social arena and learn about different cultures. A constant in the learning process is the role of feedback as we assess the responses of others to our behaviors and comments.

In addition to the development of social competence, sport participation can help youth develop other forms of self-competence. Most important among these self-competencies is self-esteem. Self-esteem is how we judge our worth and indicates the extent to which an individual believes he is capable, significant, successful, and worthy. Educators have suggested that one of the biggest barriers to success in the classroom today is low self-esteem.

Children develop self-esteem by evaluating abilities and by evaluating the responses of others. Children actively observe parents' and coaches' responses to their performances, looking for signs of approval or disapproval of their behavior. Children often interpret feedback and criticism as either a negative or a positive response to the behavior. In sports, research shows that the coach is a critical source of information that influences the self-esteem of children.

Little League baseball players whose coaches use a "positive approach" to coaching (e.g., more frequent encouragement, positive reinforcement for effort, and corrective, instructional feedback) had significantly higher self-esteem ratings over the course of a season than children whose coaches used these techniques less frequently. The most compelling evidence supporting the importance of coaches' feedback was found for those children who started the season with the lowest self-esteem ratings and increased considerably in their self-assessment and self-worth. In addition to evaluating themselves more positively, low self-esteem children evaluated their coaches more positively than did children with higher self-esteem who played for coaches who used the "positive approach." Moreover, studies show that 95 percent of children who played for coaches trained to use the positive approach signed up to play baseball the next year, compared with 75 percent of the youth who played for untrained adult coaches.

We cannot overlook the importance of enhanced self-esteem on future participation. A major part of the development of high self-esteem is the pride and joy that children experience as their physical skills improve. Children will feel good about themselves as long as their skills are improving. If children feel that their performance during a game or practice is not as good as that of others, or as good as they think mom and dad would want, they often experience shame and disappointment.

Some children will view mistakes made during a game as a failure and will look for ways to avoid participating in the task if they receive no encouragement to continue. At this point, it is critical that adults (e.g., parents and coaches) intervene to help children to interpret the mistake or "failure." We must teach children that a mistake is not synonymous with failure. Rather, a mistake shows us that we need a new strategy, more practice, and/or greater effort to succeed at the task.

Workplace Skills

By participating in physical activities, students develop various aspects of the self that are easily applicable to other settings (e.g., the workplace). Communication is one skill that improves enormously through participation in sports and games. Students will come to understand that skillful communication can contribute to a better all-around outcome, whether it be winning the game or successfully completing a team project. They will see that effective communication helps to develop and maintain healthy personal relationships, organize and convey information, and reduce or avoid conflict.

Physical activities also teach students how to set personal goals. At first, one can set a physical goal such as running one mile in eight minutes. After accomplishing that specific feat, the student will feel capable and will be more willing to set greater goals in various fields within his life.

Finally, physical activities teach perseverance, the importance of following directions, leadership, and teamwork. Recovering from competitive loses and withstanding personal and team setbacks help develop perseverance. All games and sports have rules that participants must follow in order to participate. Leadership and teamwork are both integral parts of team sports. In the team sport setting, participants learn how to work together and lead others to achieve a common goal. These skills are invaluable in real life and the workplace.

Skill 21.5 **Demonstrate knowledge of the interactions between physical, emotional, and social well-being and the importance of movement and fitness experiences in establishing productive, lifelong habits and behaviors**

There is an important relationship to consider between physical activity and the development of personal identity and emotional and mental well-being, most notably, the impact of positive body image and self-concept. Instructors can help children develop positive body image and self-concept by creating opportunities for children to experience successes in physical activities and to develop a comfort level with their bodies. This is an important contributor to their personal and physical confidence. The following is a list of of the signs of stress and the psychological benefits of physical activity:

Emotional signs of stress include depression, lethargy, aggressiveness, irritability, anxiety, edginess, fearfulness, impulsiveness, chronic fatigue, hyper-excitability, inability to concentrate, frequent feelings of boredom, feeling overwhelmed, apathy, impatience, pessimism, sarcasm, humorlessness, confusion, helplessness, melancholy, alienation, isolation, numbness, purposelessness, isolation, self-consciousness, and inability to maintain an intimate relationship.

Behavioral signs of stress include elevated use of substances (alcohol, drugs; tobacco), crying, yelling, insomnia or excessive sleep, excessive TV watching, school/job burnout, panic attacks, poor problem-solving capability, avoidance of people, aberrant behavior, procrastination, accident proneness, restlessness, loss of memory, indecisiveness, aggressiveness, inflexibility, phobic responses, tardiness, disorganization, and sexual problems.

Physical signs of stress include pounding heart, stuttering, trembling/nervous tics, excessive perspiration, teeth grinding, gastrointestinal problems (constipation, indigestion, diarrhea, and queasy stomach), dry mouth, aching lower back, migraine/tension headaches, stiff neck, asthma attacks, allergy attacks, skin problems, frequent colds or low-grade fevers, muscle tension, hyperventilation, high blood pressure, amenorrhea, nightmares, and cold intolerance.

Positive coping strategies to cope with stress include using one's social support system, spiritual support, managing time, initiating direct action, re-examining priorities, active thinking, acceptance, meditation, imagery, biofeedback, progressive relaxation, deep breathing, massage, sauna, Jacuzzi, humor, recreation and diversions, and exercise. **Negative coping strategies** to cope with stress include using alcohol or other mind-altering substances, smoking, excessive caffeine intake, poor eating habits, negative "self-talk;" and expressing distress, anger, and other negative feelings in a destructive manner.

The **psychological benefits** of physical activity include the following: relief of stress, improved mental health via better physical health, reduction of mental tension (relieves depression, improves sleeping patterns, results in fewer stress symptoms), better resistance to fatigue, better quality of life, more enjoyment of leisure, better capability to handle some stressors, opportunity for successful experiences, better self-concept, better ability to recognize and accept limitations, improved appearance and sense of well-being, better ability to meet challenges, and better sense of accomplishments.

Lifelong Fitness

The trend in national standards for physical education is increasingly towards the development of an attitude among students that will promote the integration of movement activities into their routines over an entire lifespan. This requires a greater emphasis on the benefits of physical activities to health and well-being and a greater knowledge among students of the underlying mechanisms of human movement, so that they will be able to make informed choices about the movement activities that best compliment their changing set of skills, interests, and needs.

Skill 21.6   **Apply knowledge of considerations and procedures in selecting and using various activities, instructional resources, and technologies to promote students' physical development and wellness**

Physical education helps individuals attain a healthy level of fitness and provides significant experiences in movement. It offers an opportunity to refine and develop motor skills, stamina, strategies, and the pure pleasure of physical activity and participation. Children, infants, and the disabled are all entitled to benefit from physical education. Physical activities can be adapted by recognizing the individual's abilities, learning skills, and needs. This requires knowledge about the science of movement, the process of skill development, social and psychological components, physical fitness, assessment of the practices of physical activities, and development and implementation of proper and appropriate activities.

Children are at a developmental stage where their physical, emotional, motor, and social skills are not fully constructed. Children in different age groups have distinct and urgent developmental needs. A developmental need varies from child to child. Instructors should respect each child's developmental needs and pace of learning and deal with all students patiently. Instructors should put each child in an environment that stimulates him and offers challenges that are appropriate to his age, developmental needs, and ability. Instructors should not force a child to take up an activity. Coercion discourages the child and causes him to resist learning. However, incorporating motivation and stimulation into the activity can encourage the child without direct intervention of an adult. Self-motivation is the best tool for learning. Children need to challenge themselves through constant exploration and experimentation. The activity should suit the developmental age of the child so that he/she can perform it with minimal outside assistance. An adult should act as an assistant who provides help only when it is required.

The physical education program for children should be geared to suit their developmental needs (i.e., constructing their motor skills and developing their concept of movement). Physical activity should be fun, pleasurable, and aimed at developing and maintaining health. Motor skills are comprised of locomotor skills, nonlocomotor skills, and manipulative and coordination skills. Games like bean bag, parachute, hoola hoop, gymnastics, and ball activities, modified and adapted to suit the particular needs of children, are particularly helpful. Physical activity should have the scope to adapt itself to suit an individual child's needs and goals. Instructors can incorporate activities, such as wheelchair races or activities that require use of the hands, to accommodate handicapped students that cannot use their legs. For children in the grades 1to 3, instructors should incorporate concepts of movement and motor skills, allowing the child to perfect them. Concepts of movement like spatial consciousness regarding location, level, or height and direction; body awareness and recognition of how the body can be manipulated to perform an activity; effort required regarding time, flow, and force; and relationship to various objects and to others are developed through various activities.

With greater development of motor skills and concepts of movement, instructors can introduce more energetic and vigorous physical activities like volleyball, gymnastics, football, and hockey. Along with these skills, the curriculum should help develop group participation skills. It is essential to instill the values of physical education and its connection to general well-being and health. Apart from this, physical education for middle-grade children should help develop a good body image and enhance their social skills. Instructors can teach activities like advanced volleyball, dance, and gymnastics, which will help to develop these areas.

COMPETENCY 22.0 UNDERSTAND PRINCIPLES AND PRACTICES RELATED TO PERSONAL, FAMILY, AND COMMUNITY HEALTH AND SAFETY AND WAYS TO PROVIDE STUDENTS WITH KNOWLEDGE AND SKILLS THAT WILL HELP THEM MAKE SOUND HEALTH-RELATED DECISIONS

Skill 22.1   Apply knowledge of basic principles of nutrition, the effects of food choices on health, and the benefits of good hygiene, adequate sleep and rest, and regular physical activity

Exercise and diet maintain proper body weight by equalizing caloric intake to caloric output.

Nutrition and exercise are closely related concepts important to student health. An important responsibility of physical education instructors is to teach students about proper nutrition and exercise and how they relate to each other. The two key components of a healthy lifestyle are consumption of a balanced diet and regular physical activity. Nutrition can affect physical performance. Proper nutrition produces high energy levels and allows for peak performance. Inadequate or improper nutrition can impair physical performance and lead to short-term and long-term health problems (e.g., depressed immune system and heart disease, respectively). Regular exercise improves overall health. Benefits of regular exercise include a stronger immune system, stronger muscles, bones, and joints, reduced risk of premature death, reduced risk of heart disease, improved psychological well-being, and weight management.

The components of nutrition are **carbohydrates, proteins, fats, vitamins, minerals, and water.**

Carbohydrates – the main source of energy (glucose) in the human diet. The two types of carbohydrates are simple and complex. Complex carbohydrates have greater nutritional value because they take longer to digest, contain dietary fiber, and do not excessively elevate blood sugar levels. Common sources of carbohydrates are fruits, vegetables, grains, dairy products, and legumes.

Proteins – are necessary for growth, development, and cellular function. The body breaks down consumed protein into component amino acids for future use. Major sources of protein are meat, poultry, fish, legumes, eggs, dairy products, and grains.

Fats – a concentrated energy source and important component of the human body. The different types of fats are saturated, monounsaturated, and polyunsaturated. Polyunsaturated fats are the healthiest because they may lower cholesterol levels, while saturated fats increase cholesterol levels. Common sources of saturated fats include dairy products, meat, coconut oil, and palm oil. Common sources of unsaturated fats include nuts, most vegetable oils, and fish.

Vitamins and minerals – organic substances that the body requires in small quantities for proper functioning. People acquire vitamins and minerals in their diets and in supplements. Important vitamins include A, B, C, D, E, and K. Important minerals include calcium, phosphorus, magnesium, potassium, sodium, chlorine, and sulfur.

Water – makes up 55 to 75 percent of the human body. Essential for most bodily functions. Attained through foods and liquids.

Nutritional requirements *vary from person-to-person.* General guidelines for meeting adequate nutritional needs are *no more than 30 percent total caloric intake from fats* (preferably 10 percent from saturated fats, 10 percent from monounsaturated fats, and 10 percent from polyunsaturated fats), *no more than 15 percent total caloric intake from protein* (complete), *and at least 55 percent of caloric intake from carbohydrates* (mainly complex carbohydrates).

Exercise and diet help maintain proper body weight by equalizing caloric intake and caloric output. The benefits of exercise are:

Physiological benefits of physical activity include:
- improved cardio-respiratory fitness
- improved muscle strength
- improved muscle endurance
- improved flexibility
- more lean muscle mass and less body fat
- quicker rate of recovery
- improved ability of the body to utilize oxygen
- lower resting heart rate
- increased cardiac output
- improved venous return and peripheral circulation
- reduced risk of musculoskeletal injuries
- lower cholesterol levels
- increased bone mass
- cardiac hypertrophy and size and strength of blood vessels
- increased number of red cells
- improved blood-sugar regulation
- improved efficiency of thyroid gland
- improved energy regulation
- increased life expectancy

Psychological benefits of physical activity include:
- relief of stress
- improved mental health via better physical health
- reduced mental tension (relieves depression, improves sleeping patterns)
- better resistance to fatigue
- better quality of life
- more enjoyment of leisure
- better capability to handle some stressors
- opportunity for successful experiences
- better self-concept
- better ability to recognize and accept limitations
- improved appearance and sense of well-being
- better ability to meet challenges
- better sense of accomplishments

Sociological benefits of physical activity include:
- the opportunity to spend time with family and friends and make new friends
- the opportunity to be part of a team
- the opportunity to participate in competitive experiences
- the opportunity to experience the thrill of victory

Benefits of Sleep

Sleep gives the body a break from the normal tasks of daily living. During sleep the body performs many important cleansing and restoration tasks. The immune and excretory systems clear waste and repair cellular damage that accumulates in the body each day. Similarly, the body requires adequate rest and sleep to build and repair muscles. Without adequate rest, even the most strenuous exercise program will not produce muscular development. Finally, lack of rest and sleep leaves the body vulnerable to infection and disease.

Personal Hygiene

Personal hygiene describes routine grooming and cleaning practices. Personal hygiene is important for health, general wellness, and pleasurable social interaction. A basic personal hygiene program should include regular washing of the body and hair, more frequent washing of the hands and face, brushing the teeth twice a day, applying deodorant daily, and cleaning the clothes and place of residence.

Skill 22.2 Demonstrate knowledge of principles and techniques of conflict resolution and its relationship to health and well-being

Interpersonal conflict is a major source of stress and worry. Teaching students to successfully manage conflict will help them reduce stress levels throughout their lives, thereby limiting the adverse health effects of stress. The following is a list of conflict-resolution principles and techniques.

1. Think before reacting – In a conflict situation, it is important to resist the temptation to react immediately. You should step back, consider the situation, and plan an appropriate response. In addition, do not react to petty situations with anger.

2. Listen – Be sure to listen carefully to the opposing party. Try to understand the other person's point of view.

3. Find common ground – Try to find some common ground as soon as possible. Early compromise can help ease the tension.

4. Accept responsibility – In every conflict there is plenty of blame to go around. Admitting when you are wrong shows you are committed to resolving the conflict.

5. Attack the problem, not the person – Personal attacks are never beneficial and usually lead to greater conflict and hard feelings.

6. Focus on the future – Instead of trying to assign blame for past events, focus on what to do differently to avoid future conflict.

Skill 22.3 Apply knowledge of principles and strategies for accident prevention and risk reduction (e.g., making healthy choices by applying communication, self-monitoring, self-control, decision-making, and safety skills)

Participant screenings – evaluate injury history, anticipate and prevent potential injuries, watch for hidden injuries and reoccurrence of an injury, and maintain communication.

Standards and discipline – ensure that athletes obey rules of sportsmanship, supervision, and biomechanics.

Education and knowledge – stay current in knowledge of first aid, sports medicine, sport technique, and injury prevention through clinics, workshops, and communication with staff and trainers.

Conditioning – programs should be yearlong and participants should have access to conditioning facilities in and out of season to produce more fit and knowledgeable athletes that are less prone to injury.

Equipment – perform regular inspections; ensure proper fit and proper use.

Facilities – maintain standards and use safe equipment.

Field care – establish emergency procedures for serious injury.

Rehabilitation – use objective measures such as power output on an isokinetic dynamometer.

Prevention of Common Athletic Injuries

Foot – start with good footwear, foot exercises.

Ankle – use high-top shoes and tape support; strengthen plantar (calf), dorsiflexor (shin), and ankle eversion (ankle outward).

Shin splints – strengthen ankle dorsiflexors.

Achilles tendon – stretch dorsiflexion and strengthen plantar flexion (heel raises).

Knee – increase strength and flexibility of calf and thigh muscles.

Back – use proper body mechanics.

Tennis elbow – avoid lateral epicondylitis caused by bent elbow, hitting late, not stepping into the ball, heavy rackets, and rackets with strings that are too tight.

Head and neck injuries – avoid dangerous techniques (i.e., grabbing facemask) and carefully supervise dangerous activities like the trampoline.

School officials and instructors should base equipment selection on quality and safety; goals of physical education and athletics; participants' interests, age, sex, skills, and limitations; and trends in athletic equipment and uniforms. Knowledgeable personnel should select equipment; keeping in mind continuous service and replacement considerations (i.e., what's best in the year of selection may not be best the following year). One final consideration is the possibility of reconditioning versus the purchase new equipment.

Actions that Promote Safety and Injury Prevention

1. Having an instructor who is properly trained and qualified
2. Organizing the class by size, activity, and conditions of the class
3. Inspecting buildings and other facilities regularly and immediately giving notice of any hazards
4. Avoiding overcrowding
5. Using adequate lighting
6. Ensuring that students dress in appropriate clothing and shoes
7. Presenting organized activities
8. Inspecting all equipment regularly
9. Adhering to building codes and fire regulations
10. Using protective equipment
11. Using spotters
12. Eliminating hazards
13. Teaching students correct ways of performing skills and activities
14. Teaching students how to use the equipment properly and safely

Skill 22.4   Demonstrate understanding of factors that affect personal, interpersonal, family, and community health (e.g., pollution, cost of health care), and the implications and consequences of health risks for individuals and society

FAMILY HEALTH

The primary factors that affect family health include environmental conditions such as pollution and proximity to industrial areas, smoking and drinking habits of family members, economic conditions that affect nutritional factors, and general levels of education among family members as related to an understanding of healthy living habits.

The relative levels of pollution in the family's area can significantly contribute to family health. For example, proximity to industrial areas, which may be releasing carcinogenic emissions, can be dangerous. Similarly, a smoking habit within the home environment is highly detrimental, as it will negatively affect the respiratory and circulatory systems of all members of the household. A drinking habit can also pose a risk both to the individual and to those in proximity to him or her.

Economic conditions can affect family health, in that lower economic means can lead to neglect of some nutritional factors (which are critical to healthy living and proper physical and cognitive development). Similarly, families with two working parents may not have as much time to spend with children to monitor their eating habits. Education levels among family members as related to an understanding of healthy living habits are also significant. Even with all of the required financial means, parents/caregivers may not have the requisite knowledge to direct children to habits for healthy living.

Public Health

Factors that influence public health include availability of health care in the community, pollution levels, community resources to promote and facilitate healthy living habits, and awareness of healthy living habits among adults in the community.

Availability of health care in the community that is both accessible and affordable has a critical influence on public health. When health care is not readily available to the community, relatively minor problems will tend to go untreated and develop into bigger problems.

Pollution levels in the community can affect public health by exposing the community as a whole to toxic and carcinogenic chemicals that negatively affect systems including (but not limited to) the circulatory and respiratory systems.

Community resources are an important influence on public health. When financing is available to support health education and programs that encourage the development of healthy living habits, the health of the community will benefit. Conversely, if the community does not dedicate resources to this cause, the health of the community will suffer. Related to this is the issue of awareness of healthy living habits among adults in the community. A strong personal commitment among responsible community members sets an important example for others to follow.

Skill 22.5   **Recognize the roles of various health care providers, agencies, and organizations; sources of information about children's and family services; and techniques and criteria for evaluating the reliability and validity of health information and resources**

There are a variety of health care providers, agencies, and organizations involved with the maintenance of student health. On site, the school nurse assists ill or injured students, maintains health records, and performs health screenings. School nurses also assist students who have long-term illnesses such as diabetes, asthma, epilepsy, or heart conditions. Most schools maintain relationships with other outside health care agencies in order to offer more extensive health care services to students. These community partnerships offer students services such as vaccinations, physical examinations and screenings, eye care, treatment of minor injuries and ailments, dental treatment, and psychological therapy. These community partnerships may include relationships with the following types of health care professionals: physicians, psychiatrists, optometrists, dentists, nurses, audiologists, occupational therapists, physical therapists, dieticians, respiratory therapists, and speech pathologists.

Physicians are health care professionals licensed to practice medicine. A physician may choose to specialize in a specific area of medicine or to work in primary care. A psychiatrist is a physician who specializes in the care of psychological disorders. Optometrists are health care practitioners who conduct eye examinations and prescribe corrective lenses. Dentists are health care professionals who provide care of the teeth. They may either work in general practice or specialize in areas such as orthodontics (correction of abnormalities of the teeth). Nurses are allied health care professionals who provide medical care under the supervision of a medical doctor. Audiologists conduct screenings to detect hearing problems. Occupational therapists help people with disabilities to learn skills needed for activities of daily living. They also help people who have sustained injuries regain their fine motor skills. Physical therapists are allied health care professionals who help people with disabilities and injuries regain their gross motor skills. Dieticians provide counseling regarding nutrition and perform meal planning. Respiratory therapists specialize in identification and treatment of breathing disorders. Speech pathologists help people with speech problems.

There are also various agencies and organizations involved in maintaining the well-being of students. The state and local health departments provide a wide range of services such as services for children with disabilities, chronic disease control, communicable disease control, mental health programs, consumer safety, and health education. The state department of human services investigates reports of child abuse or neglect. The police department prevents crime and captures offenders. Police also work with schools to provide violence and substance abuse prevention programs. Firefighters extinguish fires, check for fire hazards, install smoke detectors, check fire alarms, and give presentations on fire safety. The National Health Information Center is a federal agency that provides references for trustworthy health information.

Health Information

We can find information relating to physical activity at local public and university libraries and online. Educators should regularly inform themselves about updates in the field and should periodically search for resources that they can use with their students. Instructors should encourage students to make use of free resources like libraries, and especially the Internet, to expand their own knowledge and understanding of the subject matter.

We can find products relating to physical activity at sporting goods stores, gym boutiques, nutritional supplement stores, and wholesalers. Local community centers may also sell or rent equipment, and prices may be more favorable.

We can find services for promoting consumer awareness skills in relation to physical activity, recreation, fitness, and wellness online and at local community centers. Many community centers have outreach programs to increase public participation in physical activities. Health food stores may also offer seminars on fitness and wellness. Physical education professionals can work to build ties between these publicly offered services and their own curriculums.

There is generally a wide array of information available related to health, fitness and recreational activities, products, facilities, and services. It can be difficult for the untrained consumer to sort through it all to find information that is pertinent and accurate.

When evaluating information relating to fitness and sports equipment, consumers (for example, parents of students who are seeking to equip their home with training facilities for themselves and their children) should ask the sales staff about the differences between their choices; not just in terms of prices, but also in terms of potential fitness benefits and especially safety (Is the equipment in question safe to use? Is it safe for all ages? Is a spotter required for its use?)

When evaluating weight-control products and programs, consumers should ask sales staff to explain the mechanism by which the program functions (e.g., does it limit caloric intake, maximize caloric expenditure, or function by means of some other process?) The word of the sales staff is not sufficient, however, and consumers should investigate further using the tools at their disposal, which include public and university libraries, the Internet, and physical education professionals at their children's schools.

When evaluating fitness-training facilities, consumers should consider several factors. These factors are quality and availability of training equipment, hygiene of the facility, and overall atmosphere. You can determine the general quality of the equipment by its age, and you can glean further information from a discussion with the training staff on-site. You can investigate the availability of the equipment by visiting the facility at peak training times (which vary depending on the demographics of the facility--again, you should ask the training staff for the appropriate times). If it takes too long for equipment to become available and lines seem to form, this may not be the best facility for your needs (unless you're not interested in visiting the facility during those hours). Most important, though, is the atmosphere at the facility. The best way to get a feel for this is to have some short conversations with some customers about their experiences there.

Exercise myths and gimmicks include:

- Drinking beer/alcoholic beverages is a good way to replenish loss of body fluids after exercising.
- Women should not exercise while menstruating or pregnant.
- Physically fit people will not die from heart disease.
- You cannot be too flexible.
- Spot reduction is effective.
- Children are naturally active and do not need to exercise.
- Muscle will turn into fat with the cessation of exercising.
- Fat can turn into muscle.
- Women will develop large muscles by weight training.
- You should exercise while sick, regardless how ill you are.
- Cardiac hypertrophy developed by exercising is harmful to health.
- Exercise increases the appetite.
- Exercise gets rid of sagging skin and wrinkles.
- Yoga is a good way to develop fitness.
- Losing cellulite requires special treatment; body wraps are a good way to lose weight.

Current trends in media advertising and marketing practices related to fitness, recreational, and sports products and programs will typically display happy and fit individuals participating in the activity or making use of the advertised product. This trend has positive and negative ramifications for the work of physical educators.

On the positive side, the media advertising and marketing trend paints physical activity in a very positive light (as it should). The exposure that students have to the media today makes this a very helpful reinforcement of the messages that physical education professionals work to promote in the classroom and school gymnasium. On the negative side, these trends ignore the reality that the current national level of fitness is poor, and obesity and heart disease are on the rise.

Skill 22.6 **Apply knowledge of how to select and use various activities, instructional resources, and technologies to promote students' development of skills that contribute to health and safety**

When selecting instructional methods, it is essential that the physical educator understands that the use of well-planned, sequential unit and lesson plans will maximize the value of the instruction. Additionally, the unit and lesson plans should not only build upon the students' prior physical education experience, but should also accommodate the various ability levels of the students and maximize the practice time for all students. When selecting an instructional format, the physical educator may choose to utilize more than one configuration in any given lesson. The physical educator can select from five basic instructional formats: cognitive structuring, large-group skill instruction, small-group skill instruction, individual skill instruction, and testing.

When utilizing <u>cognitive structuring</u>, the teacher addresses the whole class through lecture, demonstration, or questioning. This method is particularly effective for imparting basic knowledge in a short amount of time. <u>Large-group skill instruction</u> involves all of the students in the class in the related activities. In <u>small-group skill instruction</u> (also called stations), the instructor divides students into groups, each of which works on a different skill or activity. A significant advantage of this instructional format is the ability to maximize instruction in situations where equipment is limited. In addition, small-group activities increase the amount of practice time for each student. In the <u>individual skill instruction format</u>, the instructor asks each student to select a skill on which to work. The students independently decide when they are ready to progress to the next skill. When ready to progress, the students simply put away their equipment, gather equipment for the next selected skill, and work at their own pace on the next skill. This self-paced arrangement allows for the greatest chance of skill mastery. The final instructional format is <u>testing</u>. During testing, the instructor assesses the students utilizing a written or skills test.

Finally, the physical educator may choose to supplement his or her teaching with the use of instructional devices. Examples of instructional devices include basic physical education equipment such as cones or targets, but may also include other types of technology such as pedometers, DVDs, computer programs, or interactive white boards.

Teaching methods to facilitate psychomotor learning include:
1. **Task/Reciprocal** - The instructor integrates task learning into the learning setting by utilizing stations.
2. **Command/Direct** - Task instruction is teacher-centered. The teacher clearly explains the goals, explains and demonstrates the skills, allocates time for practice, and frequently monitors student progress.
3. **Contingency/Contract** - A task style of instruction that rewards completion of tasks.

Techniques that facilitate psychomotor learning include:
1. **Reflex movements** - Activities that create an automatic response to some stimuli. Responses include flexing, extending, stretching, and postural adjustment.
2. **Basic fundamental locomotor movements** - Activities that utilize instinctive patterns of movement established by combining reflex movements.
3. **Perceptual abilities** - Activities that involve interpreting auditory, visual, and tactile stimuli in order to coordinate adjustments.
4. **Physical abilities** - Activities to develop physical characteristics of fitness, providing students with the stamina necessary for highly advanced, skilled movement.
5. **Skilled movements** - Activities that involve instinctive, effective performance of complex movement including vertical and horizontal components.
6. **Nondiscursive communication** - Activities necessitating expression as part of the movement.

Teaching methods that facilitate cognitive learning include:
1. **Problem Solving** - The instructor presents the initial task and students come to an acceptable solution in unique and divergent ways.
2. **Conceptual Theory** - The instructor's focus is on acquisition of knowledge.
3. **Guided Inquiry** – Stages of instruction strategically guide students through a sequence of experiences.

Initially, performing skills will be variable, inconsistent, error-prone, "off-time," and awkward. Students' focus will be on remembering what to do. Instructors should emphasize clear information of the skill's biomechanics and correct errors in gross movement that affect significant parts of the skill. So students will not be overburdened with too much information, they should perform one or two elements at a time. Motivation results from supportive and encouraging comments.

Techniques to facilitate cognitive learning include:
1. **Transfer of learning** – Identifying similar movements of a previous learned skill present in a new skill.
2. **Planning for slightly longer instructions and demonstrations** as students memorize cues and skills.
3. **Using appropriate language** for the level of the students.
4. **Conceptual Thinking** - Giving more capable students more responsibility for their learning.

Aids to facilitate cognitive learning include:
1. Frequent assessments of student performance
2. Movement activities incorporating principles of biomechanics
3. Laser discs, computers, and software
4. Video recordings of student performance

Teaching methods and techniques that facilitate affective development include:
1. **Fostering a positive learning environment** – Instructors should create a comfortable, positive learning environment by encouraging and praising effort and emphasizing respect for others.
2. **Grouping students appropriately** – Instructors should carefully group students to best achieve equality in ability, age, and personality.
3. **Ensure all students achieve some level of success** – Instructors should design activities that allow students of all ability levels to achieve success and gain confidence.

Sample Test

Reading, Language, & Literature

1. To understand the origins of a word, one must study the:

   A. Synonyms

   B. Inflections

   C. Phonetics

   D. Etymology

2. Which of the following is not a characteristic of a fable?

   A. Animals that feel and talk like humans

   B. Happy solutions to human dilemmas

   C. Teaches a moral or standard for behavior

   D. Illustrates specific people or groups without directly naming them

3. All of the following are true about phonological awareness EXCEPT:

   A. It may involve print

   B. It is a prerequisite for spelling and phonics

   C. Activities can be done by the children with their eyes closed

   D. Starts before letter recognition is taught

4. If a student has a poor vocabulary the teacher should recommend that:

   A. The student read newspapers, magazines, and books on a regular basis

   B. The student enroll in a Latin class

   C. The student write the words repetitively after looking them up in the dictionary

   D. The student use a thesaurus to locate synonyms and incorporate them into his/her vocabulary

5. Which definition below is the best for defining diction?

A. The specific word choices of an author to create a particular mood or feeling in the reader

B. Writing which explains something thoroughly

C. The background, or exposition, for a short story or drama

D. Word choices which help teach a truth or moral

6. Which is an untrue statement about a theme in literature?

A. The theme is always stated directly somewhere in the text

B. The theme is the central idea in a literary work

C. All parts of the work (plot, setting, and mood should contribute to the theme in some way

D. By analyzing the various elements of the work, the reader should be able to arrive at an indirectly stated theme

7. Which is not a true statement concerning an author's literary tone?

A. Tone is partly revealed through the selection of details

B. Tone is the expression of the author's attitude toward his/her subject

C. Tone in literature is usually satiric or angry

D. Tone in literature corresponds to the tone of voice a speaker uses

8. The arrangement and relationship of words in sentences or sentence structure best describes:

A. Style

B. Discourse.

C. Thesis

D. Syntax

9. Which of the following is a complex sentence?

   A. Anna and Margaret read a total of fifty-four books during summer vacation

   B. The youngest boy on the team had the best earned-run average, which mystifies the coaching staff

   C. Earl decided to attend Princeton; his twin brother Roy, who aced the ASVAB test, will be going to Annapolis

   D. "Easy come, easy go," Marcia moaned

10. Followers of Piaget's learning theory believe that adolescents in the formal operations period:

   A. Behave properly from fear of punishment rather than from a conscious decision to take a certain action

   B. See the past more realistically and can relate to people from the past more than preadolescents

   C. Are less self-conscious and thus more willing to project their own identities into those of fictional characters

   D. Have not yet developed a symbolic imagination

11. Which of the following is a formal reading level assessment?

   A. A standardized reading test

   B. A teacher-made reading test

   C. An interview

   D. A reading diary

12. Middle and high school students are more receptive to studying grammar and syntax:

   A. Through worksheets and end -of-lesson practices in textbooks

   B. Through independent homework assignments

   C. Through analytical examination of the writings of famous authors

   D. Though application to their own writing

13. Which of the following is not a technique of prewriting?

   A. Clustering

   B. Listing

   C. Brainstorming

   D. Proofreading

14. **Which of the following is not an approach to keep students ever conscious of the need to write for audience appeal?**

    A. Pairing students during the writing process

    B. Reading all rough drafts before the students write the final copies

    C. Having students compose stories or articles for publication in school literary magazines or newspapers

    D. Writing letters to friends or relatives

15. **The children's literature genre came into its own in the:**

    A. Seventeenth century

    B. Eighteenth century

    C. Nineteenth century

    D. Twentieth century

16. **Which of the following should not be included in the opening paragraph of an informative essay?**

    A. Thesis sentence

    B. Details and examples supporting the main idea

    C. A broad general introduction to the topic

    D. A style and tone that grabs the reader's attention

17. **Which aspect of language is innate?**

    A. Biological capability to articulate sounds understood by other humans

    B. Cognitive ability to create syntactical structures

    C. Capacity for using semantics to convey meaning in a social environment

    D. Ability to vary inflections and accents

18. **Which of the following contains an error in possessive inflection?**

    A. Doris's shawl

    B. Mother's-in-law frown

    C. Children's lunches

    D. Ambassador's briefcase

19. To decode is to:

   A. Construct meaning

   B. Sound out a printed sequence of letters

   C. Use a special code to decipher a message

   D. None of the above

20. To encode means that you:

   A. Decode a second time

   B. Construct meaning from a code

   C. Tell someone a message

   D. None of the above

21. A teacher has taught his students several strategies to monitor their reading comprehension. These strategies include identifying where in the passage they are having difficulty, identifying what the difficulty is, and restating the difficult sentence or passage in their own words. These strategies are examples of:

   A. Graphic and semantic organizers

   B. Metacognition

   C. Recognizing story structure

   D. Summarizing

22. All of the following are examples of ongoing informal assessment techniques used to observe student progress EXCEPT:

   A. Analyses of student work product

   B. Collection of data from assessment tests

   C. Effective questioning

   D. Observation of students

23. A student has written a paper with the following characteristics: written in first person; characters, setting, and plot; some dialogue; and events organized in chronological sequence with some flashbacks. In what genre has the student written?

   A. Expository writing

   B. Narrative writing

   C. Persuasive writing

   D. Technical writing

24. Which of the following indicates that a student is a fluent reader?

A. Reads texts with expression or prosody

B. Reads word-to-word and haltingly

C. Must intentionally decode a majority of the words

D. In a writing assignment, sentences are poorly-organized structurally

25. Which of the following is an essential characteristic of effective assessment?

A. Students are the ones being tested; they are not involved in the assessment process

B. Testing activities are kept separate from teaching activities

C. Assessment should reflect the actual reading the classroom instruction has prepared the student for

D. Tests should use entirely different materials than those used in teaching so the result will be reliable

26. Which of the following is an essential characteristic of effective assessment?

A. When it comes to assessment, age and culture are irrelevant

B. Teaching should be aimed at a student's weaknesses

C. Assessment focuses only on the student's reading skills.

D. Assessment should be a natural part of the instruction and not intrusive

Read the passages and answer the questions that follow.

This writer has often been asked to tutor hospitalized children with cystic fibrosis. While undergoing all the precautionary measures to see these children (i.e., scrubbing thoroughly and donning sterilized protective gear (for the child's protection), she has often wondered why their parents subject these children to the pressures of schooling and trying to catch up on what they have missed because of hospitalization, which is a normal part of cystic fibrosis patients' lives. These children undergo so many tortuous treatments a day that it seems cruel to expect them to learn as normal children do, especially with their life expectancies being as short as they are.

27. What is meant by the word "precautionary" in the second sentence?

    A.   Careful

    B.   Protective

    C.   Medical

    D.   Sterilizing

28. What is the author's tone?

    A.   Sympathetic

    B.   Cruel

    C.   Disbelieving

    D.   Cheerful

29. What is the main idea of this passage?

    A.   There is a lot of preparation involved in visiting a patient of cystic fibrosis

    B.   Children with cystic fibrosis are incapable of living normal lives

    C.   Certain concessions should be made for children with cystic fibrosis

    D.   Children with cystic fibrosis die young

30. How is the author so familiar with the procedures used when visiting a child with cystic fibrosis?

    A.   She has read about it

    B.   She works in a hospital

    C.   She is the parent of one

    D.   She often tutors them

Math

31. $\left(\dfrac{-4}{9}\right)+\left(\dfrac{-7}{10}\right)=$

    A. $\dfrac{23}{90}$

    B. $\dfrac{-23}{90}$

    C. $\dfrac{103}{90}$

    D. $\dfrac{-103}{90}$

32. $(5.6) \times (^-0.11) =$

    A. $^-0.616$

    B.   0.616

    C. $^-6.110$

    D.   6.110

33. An item that sells for $375 is put on sale at $120. What is the percent of decrease?

    A.   25%

    B.   28%

    C.   68%

    D.   34%

34. Two mathematics classes have a total of 410 students. The 8:00 am class has 40 more than the 10:00 am class. How many students are in the 10:00 am class?

    A.   123.3

    B.   370

    C.   185

    D.   330

35. What measure could be used to report the distance traveled in walking around a track?

    A.   Degrees

    B.   Square meters

    C.   Kilometers

    D.   Cubic feet

36. What is the area of a square with a side of 13 feet?

    A.   169 feet

    B.   169 square feet

    C.   52 feet

    D.   52 square feet

37. What is the greatest common factor of 16, 28, and 36?

    A.   2

    B.   4

    C.   8

    D.   16

38. If $4x - (3 - x) = 7(x - 3) + 10$, then

    A. $x = 8$

    B. $x = -8$

    C. $x = 4$

    D. $x = -4$

39. Given the formula *d* =*rt*, (where *d* = distance, *r* =rate, and *t* =time), calculate the time required for a vehicle to travel 585 miles at a rate of 65 miles per hour.

    A.   8.5 hours

    B.   6.5 hours

    C.   9.5 hours

    (D.)   9 hours

40. The following chart shows the yearly average number of international tourists visiting Palm Beach from 1990-1994. How may more international tourists visited Palm Beach in 1994 than in 1991?

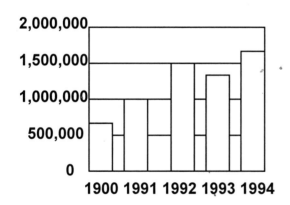

    1900 1991 1992 1993 1994

    A.   100,000

    (B.)   600,000

    C.   1,600,000

    D.   8,000,000

41. What is the probability of drawing two consecutive aces from a standard deck of cards?

    A. $\dfrac{3}{51}$

    (B.) $\dfrac{1}{221}$

    C. $\dfrac{2}{104}$

    D. $\dfrac{2}{52}$

42. A sofa sells for $520. If the retailer makes a 30% profit, what was the wholesale price?

    (A.) $400

    B. $676

    C. $490

    D. $364

Take 30% of each price & add.

400 × .30 = 120

400 + 120 = 520

43. Which of the following is an irrational number?

    (A.) .362626262...

    B. $4\frac{1}{3}$

    C. $\sqrt{5}$

    D. $-\sqrt{16}$

44. Corporate salaries are listed for several employees. Which would be the best measure of central tendency?

$24,000 $24,000 $26,000
$28,000 $30,000 $120,000

A. Mean

B. Median

C. Mode

D. No difference

45. Which statement is true about George's budget?

A. George spends the greatest portion of his income on food

B. George spends twice as much on utilities as he does on his mortgage

C. George spends twice as much on utilities as he does on food

D. George spends the same amount on food and utilities as he does on mortgage

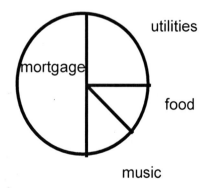

46. Given a drawer with 5 black socks, 3 blue socks, and 2 red socks, what is the probability that you will draw two black socks in two draws in a dark room?

A. 2/9
B. 1/4
C. 17/18
D. 1/18

47. Solve for x: $|2x + 3| > 4$

A. $-\frac{7}{2} > x > \frac{1}{2}$
B. $-\frac{1}{2} > x > \frac{7}{2}$
C. $x < \frac{7}{2}$ or $x < -\frac{1}{2}$
D. $x < -\frac{7}{2}$ or $x > \frac{1}{2}$

48. Graph the solution:
    $|x| + 7 < 13$

A.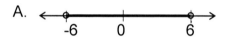

B.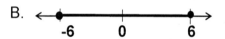

C.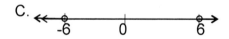

D.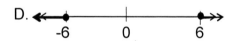

49. A boat travels 30 miles upstream in three hours. It makes the return trip in one and a half hours. What is the speed of the boat in still water?

A. 10 mph
B. 15 mph
C. 20 mph
D. 30 mph

50. Given segment AC with B as its midpoint, find the coordinates of C if A = (5,7) and B = (3, 6.5).

    A. (4, 6.5)
    B. (1, 6)
    C. (2, 0.5)
    D. (16, 1)

51. 3 km is equivalent to:

    A. 300 cm
    B. 300 m
    C. 3000 cm
    D. 3000 m

52. The mass of a cookie is closest to:

    A. 0.5 kg
    B. 0.5 grams
    C. 15 grams
    D. 1.5 grams

53. If the radius of a right circular cylinder is doubled, how does its volume change?

    A. No change
    B. Also is doubled
    C. Four times the original
    D. pi times the original

54. In similar polygons, if the perimeters are in a ratio of x:y, the sides are in a ratio of:

    A. $x : y$
    B. $x^2 : y^2$
    C. $2x : y$
    D. $1/2\, x : y$

55. Find the midpoint of (2,5) and (7,-4).

    A. (9,-1)
    B. (5,9)
    C. (9/2, -1/2)
    D. (9/2, 1/2)

56. $3x + 2y = 12$
    $12x + 8y = 15$

    A. All real numbers
    B. x = 4, y = 4
    C. x = 2, y = -1
    D. $\varnothing$

57. 303 is what percent of 600?

    A. 0.505%

    B. 5.05%

    C. 505%

    D. 50.5%

58. A car gets 25.36 miles per gallon. The car has been driven 83,310 miles. What is a reasonable estimate for the number of gallons of gas used?

    A. 2,087 gallons

    B. 3,000 gallons

    C. 1,800 gallons

    D. 164 gallons

59. The owner of a rectangular piece of land 40 yards in length and 30 yards in width wants to divide it into two parts. She plans to join two opposite corners with a fence as shown in the diagram below. The cost of the fence will be approximately $25 per linear foot. What is the estimated cost for the fence needed by the owner?

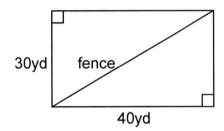

A. $1,250

B. $62,500

C. $5,250

D. $3,750

60. What measure could be used to report the distance traveled in walking around a track?

A. Degrees

B. Square meters

C. Kilometers

D. Cubic feet

Science

61. Carbon bonds with hydrogen by: _____

A. Ionic bonding
B. Non-polar covalent bonding
C. Polar covalent bonding
D. Strong nuclear force

62. Which of the following is not caused by a virus?

A. Influenza
B. AIDS
C. "The common cold"
D. Strep throat

63. Which skill refers to quantifying data, performing graphic analysis, making charts, and writing summaries?

A. Recording
B. Data gathering
C. Data processing
D. Evaluating

64. When several computers are connected together by a modem or telephone, it is a:

A. Processor
B. Network
C. Online
D. Hard drive

65. Computer simulations are most appropriate for:

A. Replicating dangerous experiments
B. Mastering basic facts
C. Emphasizing competition and entertainment
D. Providing motivational feedback

66. The Doppler Effect is associated most closely with which property of waves?

A. Amplitude
B. Wavelength
C. Frequency
D. Intensity

67. Accepted procedures for preparing solutions should be made with _____ .

A. Alcohol

B. Hydrochloric acid

C. Distilled water

D. Tap water

68. Enzymes speed up reactions by _____ .

A. Utilizing ATP
B. Lowering pH, allowing reaction speed to increase
C. Increasing volume of substrate
D. Lowering energy of activation

69. The transfer of heat by electromagnetic waves is called _____ .

A. Conduction
B. Convection
C. Phase change
D. Radiation

70. Which of the following is *not* considered ethical behavior for a scientist?

A. Using unpublished data and citing the source
B. Publishing data before other scientists have had a chance to replicate results
C. Collaborating with other scientists from different laboratories
D. Publishing work with an incomplete list of citations

71. Sound waves are produced by _____ .

A. Pitch
B. Noise
C. Vibrations
D. Sonar

72. Chemicals should be stored:

A. In the principal's office
B. In a dark room
C. According to their reactivity with other substances
D. In a double-locked room

73. In an experiment measuring the growth of bacteria at different temperatures, what is the independent variable?

    A. Number of bacteria
    B. Growth rate of bacteria
    C. Temperature
    D. Size of bacteria

74. Which is the correct order of methodology?

    1. **Collecting data**
    2. **Planning a controlled experiment**
    3. **Drawing a conclusion**
    4. **Hypothesizing a result**
    5. **Revisiting a hypothesis to answer a question**

    A. 1,2,3,4,5
    B. 4,2,1,3,5
    C. 4,5,1,3,2
    D. 1,3,4,5,2

75. What cell organelle contains the cell's stored food?

    A. Vacuoles
    B. Golgi Apparatus
    C. Ribosomes
    D. Lysosomes

76. Identify the correct sequence of the organization of living things from lower to higher order:

    A. Cell, Organelle, Organ, Tissue, System, Organism
    B. Cell, Tissue, Organ, Organelle, System, Organism
    C. Organelle, Cell, Tissue, Organ, System, Organism
    D. Organelle, Tissue, Cell, Organ, System, Organism

77. Which of the following is a correct explanation for scientific 'evolution'?

    A. Giraffes need to reach higher for leaves to eat, so their necks stretch. The giraffe babies are then born with longer necks. Eventually, there are more long-necked giraffes in the population

    B. Giraffes with longer necks are able to reach more leaves, so they eat more and have more babies than other giraffes. Eventually, there are more long-necked giraffes in the population

    C. Giraffes want to reach higher for leaves to eat, so they release enzymes into their bloodstream, which in turn causes fetal development of longer-necked giraffes. Eventually, there are more long-necked giraffes in the population

    D. Giraffes with long necks are more attractive to other giraffes, so they get the best mating partners and have more babies. Eventually, there are more long-necked giraffes in the population

78. Which of the following is the most accurate definition of a non-renewable resource?

    A. A nonrenewable resource is never replaced once used

    B. A nonrenewable resource is replaced on a timescale that is very long relative to human life spans

    C. A nonrenewable resource is a resource that can only be manufactured by humans

    D. A nonrenewable resource is a species that has already become extinct

79. Which kingdom is comprised of organisms made of one cell with no nuclear membrane?

    A. Monera
    B. Protista
    C. Fungi
    D. Algae

80. What are the most significant and prevalent elements in the biosphere?

    A. Carbon, Hydrogen, Oxygen, Nitrogen, Phosphorus

    B. Carbon, Hydrogen, Sodium, Iron, Calcium

    C. Carbon, Oxygen, Sulfur, Manganese, Iron

    D. Carbon, Hydrogen, Oxygen, Nickel, Sodium, Nitrogen

History & Social Science

81. Which two Native American nations or tribes inhabited the Mid-Atlantic and Northeastern regions at the time of the first European contact?

    A. Pueblo and Inuit

    B. Algonquian and Cherokee

    C. Seminoles and Sioux

    D. Algonquian and Iroquois

82. Which of the following were results of the Age of Exploration?

    A. More complete and accurate maps and charts

    B. New and more accurate navigational instruments

    C. Proof that the Earth is round

    D. All of the above

83. What was the long-term importance of the Mayflower Compact?

    A. It established the foundation of all later agreements with the native peoples

    B. It established freedom of religion in the original English colonies

    C. It ended the war in Europe between Spain, France, and England

    D. It established a model of small, town-based government that was adopted throughout the New England colonies

84. What was "triangular trade?"

A. It was regulated trade between the colonies, England and France

B. It was an approach to trade that transported finished goods from the mother country to the African colonies, slaves and goods from Africa to the North American Colonies, and raw materials and tobacco or rum back to the mother country

C. It was an approach to trade that resulted in colonists obtaining crops and goods from the Native tribes in exchange for finished goods from England

D. It was trade between the colonists of the three regions (Southern, mid Atlantic, and New England)

85. What intellectual movement during the period of North American colonization contributed to the development of public education and the founding of the first colleges and universities?

A. Enlightenment

B. Great Awakening

C. Libertarianism

D. The Scientific Revolution

86. Which of the following contributed to the severity of the Great Depression in California?

A. An influx of Chinese immigrants

B. The dust bowl drove people out of the cities

C. An influx of Mexican immigrants

D. An influx of Oakies

87. During the period of Spanish colonialism, which of the following was not a key to the goal of exploiting, transforming, and including the native people?

A. Missions

B. Ranchos

C. Presidios

D. Pueblos

88. The first European to see Florida and sail along its coast was:

A. Cabot

B. Columbus

C. Ponce de Leon

D. Narvaez

89. How did the United States gain Florida from Spain?

A. It was captured from Spain after the Spanish-American War

B. It was given to the British and became part of the original thirteen colonies

C. America bought it from Spain

D. America acquired it after the First World War

90. What is the form of local government that acts as an intermediary between the state and the city?

A. Metropolitan government

B. Limited government

C. Mayor-Council system

D. County Commission system

91. New York was initially inhabited by what two native peoples?

A. Sioux and Pawnee

B. Micmac and Wampanoag

C. Iroquois and Algonquin

D. Nez Perce and Cherokee

92. What was the name of the cultural revival after the Civil War that took place in New York?

A. The Revolutionary War

B. The Second Great Awakening

C. The Harlem Renaissance

D. The Gilded Age

93. Which one of the following is not a reason why Europeans came to the New World?

A. To find resources in order to increase wealth

B. To establish trade

C. To increase a ruler's power and importance

D. To spread Christianity

94. The year 1619 was memorable for the colony of Virginia. Three important events occurred, resulting in lasting effects on US history. Which one of the following is not one of the events?

    A. Twenty African slaves arrived

    B. The London Company granted the colony a charter, making it independent

    C. The colonists were given the right by the London Company to govern themselves through representative government in the Virginia House of Burgesses

    D. The London Company sent to the colony sixty women who were quickly married, establishing families and stability in the colony

95. The "divine right" of kings was the key political characteristic of:

    A. The Age of Absolutism

    B. The Age of Reason

    C. The Age of Feudalism

    D. The Age of Despotism

96. During the 1920s, the United States almost completely stopped all immigration. One of the reasons was:

    A. Plentiful cheap unskilled labor was no longer needed by industrialists

    B. War debts from World War I made it difficult to render financial assistance

    C. European nations were reluctant to allow people to leave, since there was a need to rebuild populations and economic stability

    D. The United States did not become a member of the League of Nations

97. Which one of the following would not be considered a result of World War II?

    A. Economic depressions and slow resumption of trade and financial aid

    B. Western Europe was no longer the center of world power

    C. The beginnings of new power struggles, not only in Europe but in Asia as well

    D. Territorial and boundary changes for many nations, especially in Europe

98. The belief that the United States should control all of North America was called:

A. Westward Expansion

B. Pan Americanism

C. Manifest Destiny

D. Nationalism

99. Capitalism and communism are alike in that they are both:

A. Organic systems

B. Political systems

C. Centrally planned systems

D. Economic systems

100. For the historian studying ancient Egypt, which of the following would be least useful?

A. The record of an ancient Greek historian on Greek-Egyptian interaction

B. Letters from an Egyptian ruler to his/her regional governors

C. Inscriptions on stele of the Fourteenth Egyptian Dynasty

D. Letters from a nineteenth century Egyptologist to his wife

Physical Education & Health

101. The physical education philosophy based on experience is:

A. Naturalism

B. Pragmatism

C. Idealism

D. Existentialism

102. The modern physical education philosophy that combines beliefs from different philosophies is:

A. Eclectic

B. Humanistic

C. Individualism

D. Realism

103. A physical education teacher emphasizes healthy attitudes and habits. She conducts her classes so that students acquire and interpret knowledge and learn to think/analyze, which is necessary for physical activities. The goals and values utilized and the philosophy applied by this instructor is:

A. Physical Development Goals and Realism Philosophy

B. Affective Development Goals and Existentialism

C. Motor Development Goals and Realism Philosophy

D. Cognitive Development Goals and Idealism Philosophy

104. Social skills and values developed by activity include all of the following except:

A. Winning at all costs

B. Making judgments in groups

C. Communicating and cooperating

D. Respecting rules and property

105. Activities that enhance team socialization include all of the following except:

A. Basketball

B. Soccer

C. Golf

D. Volleyball

106. Through physical activities, John has developed self-discipline, fairness, respect for others, and new friends. John has experienced which of the following?

A. Positive cooperation psycho-social influences

B. Positive group psycho-social influences

C. Positive individual psycho-social influences

D. Positive accomplishment psycho-social influences

107. Which of the following psycho-social influences is not negative?

A. Avoidance of problems

B. Adherence to exercise

C. Ego-centeredness

D. Role conflict

108. Which professional organization protects amateur sports from corruption?

    A. AIWA

    B. AAHPERD

    C. NCAA

    D. AAU

109. Which professional organization works with legislatures?

    A. AIWA

    B. AAHPERD

    C. ACSM

    D. AAU

110. Research in physical education is published in all of the following periodicals except the:

    A. School PE Update

    B. Research Quarterly

    C. Journal of Physical Education

    D. YMCA Magazine

111. The most effective way to promote the physical education curriculum is to:

    A. Relate physical education to higher thought processes

    B. Relate physical education to humanitarianism

    C. Relate physical education to the total educational process

    D. Relate physical education to skills necessary to preserve the natural environment

112. The affective domain of physical education contributes to all of the following except:

    A. Knowledge of exercise, health, and disease

    B. Self-actualization

    C. An appreciation of beauty

    D. Good sportsmanship

113. A physical education instructor anticipates and prevents potential injuries, watches for hidden injuries, and takes an injury evaluation of the entire class. Which of the following strategies to prevent injuries is the teacher demonstrating?

    A. Maintaining hiring standards

    B. Proper use of equipment

    C. Proper procedures for emergencies

    D. Participant screening

114. The ability for a muscle(s) to repeatedly contract over a period of time is:

    A. Cardiovascular endurance

    B. Muscle endurance

    C. Muscle strength

    D. Muscle force

115. Which of the following conditions is not associated with a lack of physical activity?

    A. Atherosclerosis

    B. Longer life expectancy

    C. Osteoporosis

    D. Certain cancers

Visual Art

116. Engravings and oil painting originated in this country.

    A. Italy
    B. Japan
    C. Germany
    D. Flanders

117. A combination of three or more tones sounded at the same time is called a

    A. Harmony
    B. Consonance
    C. Chord
    D. Dissonance

118. A series of single tones which add up to a recognizable sound is called a:

    A. Cadence
    B. Rhythm
    C. Melody
    D. Sequence

119. Which is a true statement about crafts?

    A. Students experiment with their own creativity
    B. Products are unique and different.
    C. Self-expression is encouraged
    D. Outcome is predetermined

120. The following is not a good activity to encourage fifth graders' artistic creativity:

A. Ask them to make a decorative card for a family member
B. Have them work as a team to decorate a large wall display
C. Ask them to copy a drawing from a book, with the higher grades being awarded to those students who come closest to the model
D. Have each student try to create an outdoor scene with crayons, providing a choice of scenery

121. An approach to musical instruction for young children that "combines learning music, movement, singing, and exploration" is:

A. Dalcroze Eurhythmics
B. The Kodaly Method
C. The Orff Approach
D. Education Through Music (ETM)

122. During the early childhood years (ages 3 to 5), drama and theater experiences are especially beneficial to children because they provide the opportunity for students to:

A. Apply the concept of turn-taking
B. Learn the importance of listening skills
C. Acquire the skills needed to become a proficient reader
D. Learn early drama skills using their five senses

123. In the area of performing arts, specifically dance, primary grades are expected to have a gross understanding of their motor movements. Which of the following movements would not be age-appropriate?

A. Basic rhythm
B. Early body awareness
C. Imagery
D. Listening skills

124. The history of theater is important at an early age to describe how theater has evolved over time. Which of the following is not a vital part of the many time periods of theater history?

A. Roman theater
B. American theater
C. Medieval drama
D. Renaissance theater

125. Creating movements in response to music helps students to connect music and dance in which of the following ways?

    A. Rhythm
    B. Costuming
    C. Speed
    D. Vocabulary skills

Answer Key

1.	D	26.	D	51.	D	76.	C	101.	B
2.	D	27.	B	52.	C	77.	B	102.	A
3.	A	28.	A	53.	C	78.	B	103.	D
4.	A	29.	C	54.	A	79.	A	104.	A
5.	A	30.	D	55.	D	80.	A	105.	C
6.	A	31.	D	56.	D	81.	D	106.	B
7.	C	32.	A	57.	D	82.	D	107.	B
8.	D	33.	C	58.	B	83.	D	108.	D
9.	B	34.	C	59.	D	84.	B	109.	B
10.	B	35.	C	60.	C	85.	A	110.	A
11.	A	36.	B	61.	C	86.	D	111.	C
12.	D	37.	B	62.	D	87.	B	112.	A
13.	D	38.	C	63.	C	88.	A	113.	D
14.	D	39.	D	64.	B	89.	C	114.	B
15.	A	40.	B	65.	A	90.	A	115.	C
16.	B	41.	B	66.	C	91.	C	116.	D
17.	A	42.	A	67.	C	92.	C	117.	C
18.	B	43.	A	68.	D	93.	B	118.	C
19.	B	44.	B	69.	D	94.	B	119.	D
20.	B	45.	C	70.	D	95.	A	120.	C
21.	B	46.	A	71.	C	96.	A	121.	D
22.	B	47.	D	72.	D	97.	A	122.	D
23.	B	48.	A	73.	C	98.	C	123.	C
24.	A	49.	B	74.	B	99.	D	124.	B
25.	C	50.	B	75.	A	100.	D	125.	A

Rationales for Sample Questions

1. D. Etymology

A synonym is an equivalent of another word and can substitute for it in certain contexts. Inflection is a modification of words according to their grammatical functions, usually by employing variant word endings to indicate such qualities as tense, gender, case, and number. Phonetics is the science devoted to the physical analysis of the sounds of human speech, including their production, transmission, and perception.

2. D. Illustrates specific people or groups without directly naming them

A fable is a short tale with animals, humans, gods, or even inanimate objects as characters. Fables often conclude with a moral, delivered in the form of an epigram (a short, witty, and ingenious statement in verse). Fables are among the oldest forms of writing in human history, appearing in Egyptian papyri of c1,500 BC. The most famous fables are those of Aesop, a Greek slave living in about 600 BC. In India, the Pantchatantra appeared in the third century. The most famous modern fables are those of seventeenth century French poet Jean de La Fontaine.

3. A. It may involve print

The key word here is EXCEPT, which will be highlighted in uppercase on the test as well. All of the options are correct aspects of phonological awareness except the first one, **A,** because phonological awareness DOES NOT involve print.

4. A. The student read newspapers, magazines, and books on a regular basis

It is up to the teacher to help the student choose reading material, but the student must be able to choose where s/he will search for the reading pleasure indispensable for enriching vocabulary.

5. A. The specific word choices of an author to create a particular mood or feeling in the reader

Diction refers to an author's choice of words, expressions, and style to convey his/her meaning.

6. A. The theme is always stated directly somewhere in the text

The theme may be stated directly, but it can also be implicit in various aspects of the work, such as the interaction between characters, symbolism, or description.

7. C. Tone in literature is usually satiric or angry

Tone in literature conveys a mood and can be as varied as the tone of voice of a speaker (see D., e.g., sad, nostalgic, whimsical, angry, formal, intimate, satirical, sentimental, etc.).

8. D. Syntax

Syntax is the grammatical structure of sentences.

9. B. The youngest boy on the team had the best earned-run average, which mystifies the coaching staff

Here, the use of the relative pronoun "which," whose antecedent is "the best run average," introduces a clause that is dependent on the independent clause, "The youngest boy on the team had the best earned-run average." The idea expressed in the subordinate clause is subordinate to the one expressed in the independent clause.

10. B. See the past more realistically and can relate to people from the past more than preadolescents

According to Piaget, adolescents 12 to 15 years old begin thinking beyond the immediate and obvious, and begin to theorize. Their assessment of events shifts from considering an action as "right" or "wrong" to considering the intent and behavior in which the action was performed. Fairy tale or other kinds of unreal characters have ceased to satisfy them, and they are able to recognize the difference between pure history and historical fiction.

11. A. A standardized reading test

If assessment is standardized, it has to be objective, whereas B, C, and D are all subjective assessments.

12. D. Through application to their own writing

At this age, students learn grammatical concepts best through practical application in their own writing

13. D. Proofreading

Proofreading cannot be a method of prewriting, since it is done on already written texts only.

14. D. Writing letters to friends or relatives

Reading all rough drafts will not encourage the students to take control of their text and might even inhibit their creativity. On the contrary, pairing students will foster their sense of responsibility, and having them compose stories for literary magazines will boost their self-esteem as well as their organization skills. As far as writing letters is concerned, the work of authors such as Madame de Sevigne in the seventeenth century is a good example of epistolary literary work.

15. A. seventeenth century

In the seventeenth century, authors such as Jean de La Fontaine and his *Fables*, Pierre Perreault's *Tales*, Mme d'Aulnoye's novels based on old folktales, and Mme de Beaumont's *Beauty and the Beast* all created a children's literature genre. In England, Perreault was translated, and a work allegedly written by Oliver Smith, *The Renowned History of Little Goody Two Shoes*, also helped to establish children's literature in England.

16. B. Details and examples supporting the main idea

The introductory paragraph should introduce the topic, capture the reader's interest, state the thesis, and prepare the reader for the main points in the essay. Details and examples, however, should be given in the second part of the essay, so as to help develop the thesis presented at the end of the introductory paragraph. This follows the inverted triangle method, consisting of a broad general statement followed by some information and then the thesis at the end of the paragraph.

17. A. Biological capability to articulate sounds understood by other humans

Language ability is innate, and the biological capability to produce sounds lets children learn semantics and syntactical structures through trial and error. Linguists agree that language is first a vocal system of word symbols that enables a human to communicate his/her feelings, thoughts, and desires to other human beings.

18. B. Mother's-in-law frown

Mother-in-law is a compound common noun, and the inflection should be at the end of the word, according to the rule.

19. B. Sound out a printed sequence of letters

The definition of this word in reading is what you have to know from your coursework.

20. B. Construct meaning from a code

You need to memorize these special definitions.

21. B. Metacognition

Metacognition may be defined as "thinking about thinking." Good readers use metacognitive strategies to think about and have control over their reading. Before reading, they might clarify their purpose for reading and preview the text. During reading, they might monitor their understanding, adjusting their reading speed to fit the difficulty of the text and fixing any comprehension problems they have. After reading, they check their understanding of what they read.

22. B. Collection of data from assessment tests

Assessment tests are formal progress-monitoring measures.

23. B. Narrative writing

These are all characteristics of narrative writing. Expository writing is intended to give information such as an explanation or directions, and the information is logically organized. Persuasive writing gives an opinion in an attempt to convince the reader that this point of view is valid or tries to persuade the reader to take a specific action. The goal of technical writing is to clearly communicate a select piece of information to a targeted reader or group of readers for a particular purpose in such a way that the subject can readily be understood. It is persuasive writing that anticipates a response from the reader.

24. A. Reads texts with expression or prosody

The teacher should listen to the children read aloud, but there are also clues to reading levels in their writing.

25. C. Assessment should reflect the actual reading the classroom instruction has prepared the student for

The only reliable measure of the success of a unit will be based on the reading the instruction has focused on.

26. D. Assessment should be a natural part of the instruction and not intrusive.

If assessment is to be effective, it must be ongoing and must not interfere with instruction and practice.

27. B. Protective

The writer uses expressions such as "protective gear" and "child's protection" to emphasize this.

28. A. Sympathetic

The author states that "it seems cruel to expect them to learn as normal children do," thereby indicating that she feels sorry for them.

29. C. Certain concessions should be made for children with cystic fibrosis

The author states that she wonders "why parents subject these children to the pressures of schooling" and states that "it seems cruel to expect them to learn as normal children do." In making these statements she appears to be expressing the belief that these children should not have to do what "normal" children do. They have enough to deal with--their illness itself.

30. D. She often tutors them

The writer states this fact in the opening sentence.

31. D. $\dfrac{^-103}{90}$

Find the LCD of $\dfrac{^-4}{9}$ and $\dfrac{^-7}{10}$. The LCD is 90, so you get $\dfrac{^-40}{90} + \dfrac{^-63}{90} = \dfrac{^-103}{90}$.

32. A. -0.616

Simple multiplication. The answer will be negative because a positive times a negative is a negative number. $5.6 \times {}^-0.11 = {}^-0.616$.

33. C. 68%

Use $(1 - x)$ as the discount. $375x = 120$.
$375(1 - x) = 120 \rightarrow 375 - 375x = 120 \rightarrow 375x = 255 \rightarrow x = 0.68 = 68\%$

34. C. 185

Let x = # of students in the 8 am class and $x - 40$ = # of student in the 10 am class. $x + (x - 40) = 410 \rightarrow 2x - 40 = 410 \rightarrow 2x = 450 \rightarrow x = 225$.
So there are 225 students in the 8 am class, and $225 - 40 = 185$ in the 10 am class.

35. C. Kilometers

Degrees measures angles, square meters measures area, cubic feet measures volume, and kilometers measures length. Kilometers is the only reasonable answer.

36. B. 169 square feet

Area = length times width (lw)
Length = 13 feet
Width = 13 feet (square, so length and width are the same)
Area = $13 \times 13 = 169$ square feet
Area is measured in square feet.

37. B. 4

The smallest number in this set is 16; its factors are 1, 2, 4, 8, and 16. Sixteen is the largest factor, but it does not divide into 28 or 36. Neither does 8. Four does factor into both 28 and 36.

38. C. x = 4

Solve for *x*.

$$4x - (3 - x) = 7(x - 3) + 10$$
$$4x - 3 + x = 7x - 21 + 10$$
$$5x - 3 = 7x - 11$$
$$5x = 7x - 11 + 3$$
$$5x - 7x = {}^{-}8$$
$${}^{-}2x = {}^{-}8$$
$$x = 4$$

39. D. 9 hours

We are given *d* = 585 miles and *r* = 65 miles per hour and *d* =*rt*. Solve for *t*. $585 = 65t \rightarrow t = 9$ hours.

40. B. 600,000

The number of tourists in 1991 was 1,000,000 and the number in 1994 was 1,600,000. Subtract to get a difference of 600,000.

41. B. $^{1/}_{221}$

There are 4 aces in the 52-card deck.

P(first ace) = $\dfrac{4}{52}$. P(second ace) = $\dfrac{3}{51}$.

P(first ace and second ace) = P(one ace) x P(second ace|first ace)

$= \dfrac{4}{52} \times \dfrac{3}{51} = \dfrac{1}{221}$.

42. A. $400

Let x be the wholesale price, then x + .30x = 520, 1.30x = 520. Divide both sides by 1.30.

43. C. $\sqrt{5}$

Irrational numbers are real numbers that cannot be written as the ratio of two integers. These are infinite non-repeating decimals. $\sqrt{5}$ fits this description.

44. B. Median

The median provides the best measure of central tendency in this case, where the mode is the lowest number and the mean would be disproportionately skewed by the outlier $120,000.

45. C. George spends twice as much on utilities as he does on food

The pie chart features a section titled utilities that is about twice the size of the section titled food. We can thus infer that George spends twice as much on utilities than he does on food.

46. A. 2/9

In this example of conditional probability, the probability of drawing a black sock on the first draw is 5/10. It is implied in the problem that there is no replacement; therefore the probability of obtaining a black sock in the second draw is 4/9. Multiply the two probabilities and reduce to the lowest terms.

47. D. $x<-\frac{7}{2}$ or $x>\frac{1}{2}$

The quantity within the absolute value symbols must be either > 4 or < -4. Solve the two inequalities 2x + 3 > 4 or 2x + 3 < -4.

48. A.

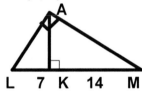

Solve by adding -7 to each side of the inequality. Since the absolute value of x is less than 6, x must be between -6 and 6. The end points are not included, so the circles on the graph are hollow.

49. B. 15 mph

Let x = the speed of the boat in still water and c = the speed of the current.

	rate	time	distance
upstream	x - c	3	30
downstream	x + c	1.5	30

Solve the system:
$$3x - 3c = 30$$
$$1.5x + 1.5c = 30$$

50. B. (1, 6)

51. D. 3000 m

To change kilometers to meters, move the decimal three places to the right.

52. C. 15 grams

A cookie is measured in grams.

53. C. Four times the original

If the radius of a right circular cylinder is doubled, the volume is multiplied by four because in the formula, the radius is squared; therefore the new volume is 2 x 2, or four times the original.

54. A. x : y

The sides are in the same ratio.

55. D. (9/2, 1/2)

Using the midpoint formula: x = (2 + 7)/2   y = (5 + -4)/2

56. D. $\varnothing$

Multiplying the top equation by -4 and adding results in the equation, 0 = -33. Since this is a false statement, the correct choice is the null set.

57. D. 50.5%

Use x for the percent. $600x = 303$. $\dfrac{600x}{600} = \dfrac{303}{600} \to x = 0.505 = 50.5\%$

58. B. 3,000 gallons

Divide the number of miles by the miles per gallon to determine the approximate number of gallons of gas used.

$$\frac{83310 \text{ miles}}{25.36 \text{ miles per gallon}} = 3285 \text{ gallons.} \quad \text{This is approximately 3,000 gallons.}$$

59. D. $3,750

Find the length of the diagonal by using the Pythagorean theorem. Let x be the length of the diagonal.

$$30^2 + 40^2 = x^2 \rightarrow 900 + 1600 = x^2$$
$$2500 = x^2 \rightarrow \sqrt{2500} = \sqrt{x^2}$$
$$x = 50 \text{ yards}$$

Convert to feet. $\quad \dfrac{50 \text{ yards}}{x \text{ feet}} = \dfrac{1 \text{ yard}}{3 \text{ feet}} \rightarrow 1500 \text{ feet}$

It cost $25 per linear foot, so the cost is (1500 ft)($25) = $3750.

60. C. Kilometers

Degrees measures angles, square meters measures area, cubic feet measures volume, and kilometers measures length. Kilometers is the only reasonable answer.

61. C. Polar covalent bonding

Each carbon atom contains four valence electrons, while each hydrogen atom contains one valence electron. A carbon atom can bond with one or more hydrogen atoms, such that two electrons are shared in each bond. This is covalent bonding, because the electrons are shared. (In ionic bonding, atoms must gain or lose electrons to form ions. The ions are then electrically attracted in oppositely charged pairs.) Covalent bonds are always polar when between two nonidentical atoms, so this bond must be polar. ("Polar" means that the electrons are shared unequally, forming a pair of partial charges, i.e., poles.) In any case, the strong nuclear force is not relevant to this problem.

62. D. Strep throat

Influenza, AIDS, and the "common cold" (rhinovirus infection), are all caused by viruses. (This is the reason that doctors should not be pressured to prescribe antibiotics for colds or the flu—i.e., they will not be effective since the infections are not bacterial.) Strep throat (properly called "streptococcal throat" and caused by streptococcus bacteria) is not a virus, but a bacterial infection.

63. C. Data processing

Data processing is any process that converts data into information.

64. B. Network

A collection of computers and related devices, connected in a way that allows them to share data, hardware, and software is a network. Thus, the **answer is (B)**.

65. A. Replicating dangerous experiments

A computer simulation is a computer program that attempts to simulate an abstract model of a particular system.

66. C. Frequency

The Doppler Effect accounts for an apparent increase in frequency when a wave source moves toward a wave receiver or apparent decrease in frequency when a wave source moves away from a wave receiver. (Note that the receiver could also be moving toward or away from the source.) As the wave fronts are released, motion toward the receiver mimics more frequent wave fronts, while motion away from the receiver mimics less frequent wave fronts. Meanwhile, the amplitude, wavelength, and intensity of the wave are not as relevant to this process (although moving closer to a wave source makes it seem more intense). The answer to this question is therefore (**C**).

67. C. Distilled water

Alcohol and hydrochloric acid should never be used to make solutions unless instructed to do so. All solutions should be made with distilled water, as tap water contains dissolved particles which may affect the results of an experiment. The correct **answer is C.**

68. D. Lowering energy of activation

Because enzymes are catalysts, they work the same way: they cause the formation of activated chemical complexes, which require a lower activation energy. Therefore, the **answer is D.** ATP is an energy source for cells, and pH or volume changes may or may not affect reaction rate, so these answers can be eliminated.

69. D. Radiation

Heat transfer via electromagnetic waves (which can occur even in a vacuum) is called radiation. (Heat can also be transferred by direct contact (conduction), by fluid current (convection), and by a matter-changing phase, but these are not relevant here.) The answer to this question is therefore **(D).**

70. D. Publishing work with an incomplete list of citations

One of the most important ethical principles for scientists is to cite all sources of data and analysis when publishing work. It is reasonable to use unpublished data (A), as long as the source is cited. Most science is published before other scientists replicate it (B), and frequently scientists collaborate with each other in the same or different laboratories (C). These are all ethical choices. However, publishing work without the appropriate citations is unethical. Therefore, the **answer is D.**

71. C. Vibrations

Sound waves are produced by a vibrating body. The vibrating object moves forward and compresses the air in front of it, then reverses direction so that pressure on the air is lessened and expansion of the air molecules occurs. The vibrating air molecules move back and forth parallel to the direction of motion of the wave as they pass the energy from adjacent air molecules closer to the source to air molecules farther away from the source. Therefore, the answer is (**C**).

72. D. In a double locked room

Chemicals should be stored with other chemicals of similar properties (e.g., acids with other acids) to reduce the potential for either hazardous reactions in the storeroom or mistakes in reagent use. Certainly, chemicals should not be stored in anyone's office, and the light intensity of the room is not very important because light-sensitive chemicals are usually stored in dark containers. In fact, good lighting is desirable in a storeroom, so that labels can be read easily. Chemicals may be stored off-site, but that makes their use inconvenient. Therefore, the best answer is (**D**).

73. C. Temperature

To answer this question, recall that the independent variable in an experiment is the entity that is changed by the scientist in order to observe the effects (the dependent variable or variables). In this experiment, temperature is changed in order to measure growth of bacteria, so **C is the answer.** Note that answer (A) is the dependent variable, and neither (B) nor (D) is directly relevant to the question.

74. B. 4, 2, 1, 3, 5

The correct methodology for the scientific method is first to make a meaningful hypothesis (educated guess), then plan and execute a controlled experiment to test that hypothesis. Using the data collected in that experiment, the scientist then draws conclusions and attempts to answer the original question related to the hypothesis. This is consistent only with answer (**B**).

75. A. Vacuoles

In a cell, the sub-parts are called organelles. Of these, the vacuoles hold stored food (and water and pigments). The Golgi Apparatus sorts molecules from other parts of the cell; the ribosomes are sites of protein synthesis; and the lysosomes contain digestive enzymes. This is consistent only with answer (**A**).

76. C. Organelle, Cell, Tissue, Organ, System, Organism

Organelles are parts of the cell; cells make up tissue, which makes up organs. Organs work together in systems (e.g., the respiratory system), and the organism is the living thing as a whole. Therefore, the answer must be (**C**).

77. B. Giraffes with longer necks are able to reach more leaves, so they eat more and have more babies than other giraffes. Eventually, there are more long-necked giraffes in the population.

Although evolution is often misunderstood, it occurs via natural selection. Organisms with a life/reproductive advantage will produce more offspring. Over many generations, this changes the proportions of the population. In any case, it is impossible for a stretched neck (A) or a fervent desire (C) to result in biologically mutated baby. Although there are traits that are naturally selected because of mate attractiveness and fitness (D), this is not the primary situation here, so answer (**B**) is the best choice.

78. B. A nonrenewable resource is replaced on a timescale that is very long relative to human life- spans.

Renewable resources are those that are renewed, or replaced, in time for humans to use more of them. Examples include fast-growing plants, animals, or oxygen gas. (Note that while sunlight is often considered a renewable resource, it is actually a nonrenewable but extremely abundant resource.) Nonrenewable resources are those that renew themselves only on very long timescales, usually geologic timescales. Examples include minerals, metals, or fossil fuels. Therefore, the correct answer is (B).

79. A. Monera

To answer this question, first note that algae are not a kingdom of their own. Some algae are in monera, the kingdom that consists of unicellular prokaryotes with no true nucleus. Protista and fungi are both eukaryotic, with true nuclei, and are sometimes multicellular. Therefore, the answer is (A).

80. A. Carbon, Hydrogen, Oxygen, Nitrogen, Phosphorus

Organic matter (and life as we know it) is based on carbon atoms, bonded to hydrogen and oxygen. Nitrogen and phosphorus are the next most significant elements, followed by sulfur and then trace nutrients such as iron, sodium, calcium, and others. Therefore, the answer is (A). If you know that the formula for any carbohydrate contains carbon, hydrogen, and oxygen, that will help you narrow the choices to (A) and (D) in any case.

81. D. Algonquian and Iroquois

The Algonquian and Iroquois nations inhabited the Mid-Atlantic and Northeastern regions of the U.S. These Native Americans are classified among the Woods Peoples. Some of the most famous of these nations are Squanto, Pocahontas, Chief Powhatan, Tecumseh, and Black Hawk. These two nations were frequently at odds over territory. The people of these nations taught early settlers about the land and survival in the new world. They introduced the settlers to maize and tobacco. The settlers and the Native Americans gradually developed respect and opened trade and cultural sharing.

82. D. All of the above

The importance of the Age of Exploration was not only the discovery and colonization of the New World, but also better maps and charts; new accurate navigational instruments; increased knowledge; great wealth; new and different foods and items not known in Europe; a new hemisphere as a refuge from poverty, persecution, and a place to start a new and better life; and proof that Asia could be reached by sea and that the Earth was round--ships and sailors would not sail off the edge of a flat Earth and disappear forever into nothingness.

83. D. It established a model of small, town-based government that was adopted throughout the New England colonies

Before setting foot on land in 1620, the **Pilgrims** aboard the Mayflower agreed to a form of self-government by signing the Mayflower Compact. The Compact served as the basis for governing the Plymouth colony for many years and set an example of small, town-based government that would proliferate throughout New England. The present day New England town meeting is an extension of this tradition. This republican ideal was later to clash with the policies of British colonial government

84. B. It was an approach to trade that transported finished goods from the mother country to the African colonies, slaves and goods from Africa to the North American colonies, and raw materials and tobacco or rum back to the mother country.

The New England and Middle Atlantic colonies at first felt threatened by these laws, as they had started producing many of the same products being produced in Britain. But they soon found new markets for their goods and began what was known as a **"triangular trade."** Colonial vessels started the first part of the triangle by sailing for Africa loaded with kegs of rum from colonial distilleries. On Africa's west coast, the rum was traded for either gold or slaves. The second part of the triangle was from Africa to the West Indies, where slaves were traded for molasses, sugar, or money. The third part of the triangle was home, bringing sugar or molasses (to make more rum), gold, and silver.

85. A. Enlightenment

Enlightenment thinking quickly made the voyage across the Atlantic Ocean. Enlightenment thinking valued human reason and the importance of education, knowledge, and scholarly research. Education in the middle colonies was influenced largely by the Enlightenment movement, which emphasized scholarly research and public service. Benjamin Franklin embodied these principles in Philadelphia, which became a center of learning and culture, owing largely to its economic success and ease of access to European books and tracts.

86. D. An influx of Oakies

The Dust Bowl of the Great Plains destroyed agriculture in the area. People living in the plains areas lost their livelihood, and many lost their homes and possessions in the great dust storms that resulted from a period of extended drought. People from all of the states affected by the Dust Bowl made their way to California in search of a better life. Because the majority of the people were from Oklahoma, they were all referred to as "Oakies." These migrants brought with them their distinctive plains culture. The great influx of people seeking jobs exacerbated the effects of the Great Depression in California.

87. B. Ranchos

The goal of Spanish colonialism was to exploit, transform, and include the native people of California. The Spanish empire sought to do this first by gathering the native people into communities where they could both be taught Spanish culture and be converted to Roman Catholicism and its value system. The social institution by which this was accomplished was the encouragement of the Mission System, which established a number of Catholic missions a day's journey apart. Once the native people were brought to the missions, they were incorporated into a mission society and indoctrinated in the teachings of Catholicism. The Presidios were fortresses that were constructed to protect Spanish interests and communities from invaders. The Pueblos were small civilian communities that attracted settlers with the gift of land, seed, and farming equipment. The function of the Pueblos was to produce food for the missions and for the presidios.

88. A. Cabot

John Cabot (1450-1498) was the English explorer who gave England claim to North America and the first European to see Florida and sail along its coast. (B) Columbus (1451-1506) was sent by the Spanish to the New World and has received false credit for "discovering America" in 1492, although he did open up the New World to European expansion, exploitation, and Christianity. (C) Ponce de Leon (1460-1521), the Spanish explorer, was the first European to actually land on Florida. (D) Panfilo de Narvaez (1470-1528) was also a Spanish conquistador, but he was sent to Mexico to force Cortes into submission. He failed and was captured.

89. C. America bought it from Spain

Spain received five million dollars for Florida, mostly to pay for damages incurred during the war. Following the War of 1812, Spain actually ceded Florida to the United States as part of the treaty. Florida, while under Spanish control, had been a difficult issue for the United States. Runaway slaves would often seek refuge there and the Seminole Indians of Florida would attack Georgia from the South. Therefore, in 1819, the Spanish agreed to put Florida into U.S. hands as part of a treaty to stop the fighting between the two nations. Andrew Jackson, the hero of the War of 1812, became the first governor of Florida.

90. A. Metropolitan Government

Metropolitan Government was the form of local government that acts as an intermediary between the state and the city and comes from the idea of municipal home rule first enacted by Missouri in 1875. As suburbs grew and cities declined slightly, it became more important to have an intermediary between the city and state governments.

91. C. Iroquois and Algonquin

The area now known as the State of New York was initially inhabited by several tribes that were part of one of two major Native American Nations. These were the Iroquois Nation and the Algonquian Nation. (A) Sioux and Pawnee tribal lands were found primarily in Minnesota and Nebraska respectively. (B) Micmac and Wampanoag were tribes primarily found in New England and Canada. (D) Nez Perce and Cherokee were found in the Pacific Northwest and the Eastern parts of the United States respectively.

92. C. The Harlem Renaissance

As African Americans left the rural South and migrated to the North in search of opportunity, many settled in Harlem in New York City. By the 1920s Harlem had become a center of life and activity for persons of color. The music, art, and literature of this community gave birth to a cultural movement known as the Harlem Renaissance. (A) The Revolutionary War (1776) occurred prior to the Civil War. (B) The Second Great Awakening occurred in the 1920s but like the (D) Gilded Age (1878 – 1889) affected the entire United States.

93. B. To establish trade

The Europeans came to the New World for a number of reasons; often they came to find new natural resources to extract for manufacturing. The Portuguese, Spanish, and English were sent over to increase the monarch's power and spread influences such as religion (Christianity) and culture. Therefore, the only reason given in this list that Europeans didn't come to the New World for was to establish trade.

94. B. The London Company granted the colony a charter, making it independent

In the year 1619, the Southern colony of Virginia had an eventful year, including the first arrival of twenty African slaves, the right to self-governance through representative government in the Virginia House of Burgesses (their own legislative body), and the arrival of sixty women sent to marry and establish families in the colony. The London Company did not, however, grant the colony a charter in 1619.

95. A. The Age of Absolutism

The "divine right" of kings was the key political characteristic of The Age of Absolutism and was most visible in the reign of King Louis XIV of France, as well as during the times of King James I and his son, Charles I. The divine right doctrine claims that kings and absolute leaders derive their right to rule by virtue of their birth alone. They see this both as a law of God and of nature.

96. A. Plentiful cheap, unskilled labor was no longer needed by industrialists

The primary reason that the United States almost completely stopped all immigration during the 1920s was because their once much-needed, cheap, unskilled-labor jobs, made available by the once booming industrial economy, were no longer needed. This has much to do with the increased use of machines to do the work once done by cheap, unskilled laborers.

97. A. Economic depressions and slow resumption of trade and financial aid

Following World War II, the economy was vibrant and flourished from the stimulant of war and an increased dependence of the world on the industries of the United States. Therefore, World War II didn't result in economic depressions and slow resumption of trade and financial aid. Western Europe was no longer the center of world power. New power struggles arose in Europe and Asia, and many European nations underwent changing territories and boundaries.

98. C. Manifest Destiny

The belief that the United States should control all of North America was called (B) Manifest Destiny. This idea fueled much of the violence and aggression towards those already occupying the lands, such as the Native Americans. Manifest Destiny was certainly driven by sentiments of (D) nationalism and gave rise to (A) westward expansion.

99. D. Economic Systems

While economic and (B) political systems are often closely connected, capitalism and communism are primarily (D) economic systems. Capitalism is a system of economics that allows the open market to determine the relative value of goods and services. Communism is an economic system where the market is planned by a central state. While communism is a (C) centrally planned system, this is not true of capitalism. (A) Organic systems are studied in biology, a natural science.

100. D. Letters from a nineteenth century Egyptologist to his wife

Historians use primary sources from the actual time they are studying whenever possible. (A) Ancient Greek records of interaction with Egypt, (B) letters from an Egyptian ruler to regional governors, and (C) inscriptions from the Fourteenth Egyptian Dynasty are all primary sources created at or near the actual time being studied. (D) Letters from a nineteenth century Egyptologist would not be considered primary sources, as they were created thousands of years after the fact and may not actually be about the subject being studied.

Physical Education

101. B. Pragmatism

As a school of philosophy, pragmatism is a collection of different ways of thinking. Given the diversity of thinkers and the variety of schools of thought that have adopted this term over the years, the term pragmatism has become almost meaningless in the absence of further qualification. Most of the thinkers who describe themselves as pragmatists indicate some connection with practical consequences or real effects as vital components of both meaning and truth.

102. A. Eclectic

Eclectics are so-called philosophers who attach themselves to no system in particular. Instead, they select what, in their judgment, is true of the other philosophers. In antiquity, the Eclectic philosophy is that which sought to unite into a coherent whole the doctrines of Pythagoras, Plato, and Aristotle. There is eclecticism in art as well as philosophy. The term was applied to an Italian school, which aimed at uniting the excellence of individual intellectual masters.

103. D. Cognitive Development Goals and Idealism Philosophy

Educators use cognitive development goals to describe the act of teaching children in a manner that will help them develop as personal and social beings. Concepts that fall under this term include social and emotional learning, moral reasoning/cognitive development, life-skills education, health education, violence prevention, critical thinking, ethical reasoning, and conflict resolution and mediation. This form of education involves teaching children and teenagers such values as honesty, stewardship, kindness, generosity, courage, freedom, justice, equality, and respect. Idealism is an approach to philosophical inquiry that asserts direct and immediate knowledge that can only be had as ideas or mental pictures. We can only know the objects that are the basis of these ideas indirectly.

104. A. Winning at all costs

Winning at all costs is not a desirable social skill. Instructors and coaches should emphasize fair play and effort over winning. Answers (B), (C), and (D) are all positive skills and values developed in physical activity settings.

105. C. Golf

Golf is mainly an individual sport. Though golf involves social interaction, it generally lacks the team element inherent in basketball, soccer, and volleyball.

106. B. Positive group psycho-social influences

Through physical activities, John developed his social interaction skills. Social interaction is the sequence of social actions between individuals (or groups) that modify their actions and reactions due to the actions of their interaction partner(s). In other words, they are events in which people attach meaning to a situation, interpret what others mean, and respond accordingly. Through socialization with other people, John feels the influence of the people around him.

107. B. Adherence to exercise

The ability of an individual to adhere to an exercise routine due to her/his excitement, accolades, etc. is not a negative psycho-social influence. Adherence to an exercise routine is healthy and positive.

108. D. AAU

The Amateur Athletic Union (AAU) is one of the largest nonprofit, volunteer sports organizations in the United States. A multisport organization, the AAU dedicates itself exclusively to the promotion and development of amateur sports and physical fitness programs. Answer (C) may be a tempting choice, but the NCAA deals only with college athletics.

109. B. AAHPERD

AAHPERD, or American Alliance for Health, Physical Education, Recreation, and Dance, is an alliance of six national associations. AAHPERD is the largest organization of professionals supporting and assisting those involved in physical education, leisure, fitness, dance, health promotion, and education, as well as all other specialties related to achieving a healthy lifestyle. AAHPERD is an alliance designed to provide members with a comprehensive and coordinated array of resources, support, and programs to help practitioners improve their skills and in turn, further the health and well-being of the American public.

110. A. School PE Update

Each school has a PE Update that publishes its own periodicals about physical activities. It aims at helping the students catch up on what is happening around them. The school produces this update to encourage their students to become more interested in all of the physical activities that they offer. School PE Updates, however, do not include research findings.

111. C. Relate physical education to humanitarianism

The government treats the physical education curriculum as one of the major subjects. Because of all of the games that we now participate in, many countries have focused their hearts and set their minds on competing with rival countries. Physical education is now one of the major, important subjects, and instructors should integrate physical education into the total educational process.

112. A. Knowledge of exercise, health, and disease

The affective domain encompasses emotions, thoughts, and feelings related to physical education. Knowledge of exercise, health, and disease is part of the cognitive domain.

113. D. Participant screening

In order for the instructor to know each student's physical status, she takes an injury evaluation. Such surveys are one way to know the physical status of an individual. It chronicles past injuries, tattoos, activities, and diseases the individual may have or had. It helps the instructor to know the limitations of each individual. Participant screening covers all forms of surveying and anticipation of injuries.

114. B. Muscle force

Muscle endurance gives the muscle the ability to contract over a period of time. Muscle strength is a prerequisite for the endurance of muscle. Cardiovascular endurance involves aerobic exercise.

115. C. Osteoporosis

General guidelines for nutritionally sound diets are 30 percent caloric intake from fats, no more than 15 percent caloric intake from proteins, and at least 55 percent caloric intake from carbohydrates.

Art

116. D. Flanders

This is based on the history and cultural aspects of artwork found in historical and cultural context.

117. C. Chord

Identifying tones, music, beats, etc. can be related to the artistic perception module

118. C. Melody

119. D Outcome is predetermined
Using crafting and artistic lessons can be related to Artistic Perception 1.2

119. D. Outcome is predetermined

Creativity and upper level thinking, reasoning, and creativity lessons can be related to Creative Expression threads

120. C. Ask them to copy a drawing from a book, with the higher grades being awarded to those students who come closest to the model

Encouraging artistic creativity can be located in the framework threads 2.2

121. D. Education Through Music (ETM)

Incorporating both musical and movement approaches related to the framework of dance and music.

122. D.

Students in Early Childhood ages are introduced to drama and theater using the five senses. Smell, feel, sound, touch, and taste are all senses that even the youngest children know and are able to relate to.

123. C. Imagery

Early Childhood students are expected to have a limited understanding of their bodies and general movement. However, early imagery is a tool that is only developed once a student begins to mature and doesn't typically happen until late elementary or early middle school.

124. B. American theater

American theater wasn't included as a type of theater in early age drama.

125. A. Rhythm

Students should be able to understand the connections made between movement and music is related by rhythm.

XAMonline, INC. 21 Orient Ave. Melrose, MA 02176

Toll Free number 800-509-4128

TO ORDER Fax 781-662-9268 OR www.XAMonline.com

ILLINOIS TEACHER CERTIFICATION SYSTEM - ICTS - 2006

PO#   Store/School:

Address 1:

Address 2 (Ship to other):

City, State Zip

Credit card number_____-_____-_____-_____   expiration_____

EMAIL _____

PHONE   **FAX**

13# ISBN 2007	TITLE	Qty	Retail	Total
978-1-58197-977-0	ICTS Assessment of Professional Teaching Tests 101-104			
978-1-58197-976-3	ICTS Basic Skills 096			
978-1-58197-996-1	ICTS Elementary-Middle Grades 110			
978-1-58197-997-8	ICTS Elementary-Middle Grades 110 Sample Questions			
978-1-58197-981-7	ICTS English Language Arts 111			
978-1-58197-991-6	ICTS Family and Consumer Sciences 172			
978-1-58197-987-9	ICTS Foreign Language- French Sample Test 127			
978-1-58197-988-6	ICTS Foreign Language- Spanish 135			
978-1-58197-992-3	ICTS Library Information Specialist 175			
978-1-58197-983-1	ICTS Mathematics 115			
978-1-58197-989-3	ICTS Physical Education 144			
978-1-58197-995-4	ICTS Principal 186			
978-1-58197-993-0	ICTS Reading Teacher 177			
978-1-58197-994-7	ICTS School Counselor 181			
978-1-58197-978-7	ICTS Science- Biology 105			
978-1-58197-979-4	ICTS Science- Chemistry 106			
978-1-58197-980-0	ICTS Science- Earth and Space Science 108			
978-1-58197-984-8	ICTS Science: Physics 116			
978-1-58197-982-4	ICTS Social Science- History 114			
978-1-58197-985-5	ICTS Social Science- Political Science 117			
978-1-58197-986-2	ICTS Social Science- Psychology 118			
978-1-58197-975-6	ICTS Special Education Learning Behavior Specialist I 155			
978-1-58197-990-9	ICTS Visual Arts Sample Test 145			

		SUBTOTAL	
FOR PRODUCT PRICES GO TO WWW.XAMONLINE.COM		Ship	$8.25
		TOTAL	